Towards Understanding the Qur'ān

Vol. VI

SŪRAHS 22–24

English version of

Tafhīm al-Qur'ān

SAYYID ABUL A'LĀ MAWDŪDĪ

Translated and edited by
Zafar Ishaq Ansari

assisted by
A.R. Kidwai

The Islamic Foundation

Towards Understanding the Qur'ān, Vol. VI, Sūrahs 22–24
English version of *Tafhīm al-Qur'ān*

Published by
THE ISLAMIC FOUNDATION,
Markfield Conference Centre,
Ratby Lane, Markfield,
Leicester LE67 9SY, United Kingdom
E-mail: publications@islamic-foundation.com
Website: www.islamic-foundation.com

Quran House, PO Box 30611, Nairobi, Kenya

PMB 3193, Kano, Nigeria

Distributed by
KUBE PUBLISHING LTD.
Tel: +44(0)1530 249230, Fax: +44(0)1530 249656
E-mail: info@kubepublishing.com

Translated and edited by: Zafar Ishaq Ansari

British Library Cataloguing in Publication Data

Mawdūdī, Sayyid Abul A'lā
Towards Understanding the Qur'ān
Vol. 6, Surahs 22–24
1. Islam, Koran – Critical Studies,
I. Title II. Anṣārī, Ẓafar Isḥāq
III. Islamic Foundation IV. Tafhīm
al-Qur'ān. *English*
297'.1226

ISBN 978–0–86037–293–6 *Casebound*
ISBN 978–0–86037–294–3 *Paperback*

Typeset by: N.A. Qaddoura

بسم الله الرحمن الرحيم

Contents

Transliteration Table

Arabic Consonants

Initial, unexpressed medial and final: ء ’

ا	ā	د	d	ض	ḍ	ك	k
ب	b	ذ	dh	ط	ṭ	ل	l
ت	t	ر	r	ظ	ẓ	م	m
ث	th	ز	z	ع	‘	ن	n
ج	j	س	s	غ	gh	هـ	h
ح	ḥ	ش	sh	ف	f	و	w
خ	kh	ص	ṣ	ق	q	ي	y

With a *shaddah*, both medial and final consonants are doubled.

Vowels, diphthongs, etc.

Short:	ـَ	a	ـِ	i	ـُ	u
Long:	ـَا	ā	ـِي	ī	ـُو	ū
Diphthongs:			ـَوْ	aw		
			ـَيْ	ay		

Editor's Preface

The sixth volume of *Towards Understanding the Qur'ān*, comprising *Sūrahs* 22–24, is being sent to the press after a considerable lapse of time. Readers from many parts of the world have had to wait for long to receive this volume. This delay is much regretted.

The present volume, as volumes III, IV and V, has been prepared with the assistance of Dr. A.R. Kidwai, who originally translated the notes of *Tafhīm* into English. That draft served as the base out of which the explanatory notes of the present volume have developed after a long, tedious, and thoroughgoing process of editing and re-editing. While the assistance provided by Dr. Kidwai is gratefully acknowledged, the responsibility for the present draft, whatever its inadequacies, rests with the present writer alone. The English rendering of the text of the *sūrahs* has, however, been done entirely by this writer.

In this volume, as in the previous ones, we have attempted to provide as adequate documentation as we could. In documenting the *Ḥadīth* we have followed the system of A.J. Wensinck in his *Concordance*. However, instead of referring to the number of the '*Bāb*', we have preferred to mention its title. It may also be noted that while referring to explanatory notes in the works of *Tafsīr*, instead of stating the volume and page number(s) of the *Tafsīr* works cited, we have generally referred to the *sūrahs* and verses of the notes. As for the Bible, all quotations are from its *Revised Standard Edition*. Furthermore, we have retained in this volume the other features that we followed in the previous volumes of this work, namely maps, Glossary of Terms, Biographical Notes, and Bibliography.

In finalizing the manuscript, I have greatly benefited from the editorial suggestions of Mrs. Susanne Thackray. Dr. A.R. Kidwai also kindly looked at the draft and favoured me with useful comments. In providing documentation I received valuable assistance from my colleague, Dr. A.R. Ashraf Baloch of the Islamic Research Institute who also helped me in providing a good deal of material on which the Glossary of Terms is based. In preparing the Biographical Notes, another colleague of mine of the Islamic Research Institute, Mr.

Iftikharul Hasan Mian, provided a help that was both valuable and timely. Mr. Amjad Mahmood and Mr. Gohar Zaman of the secretarial staff of the Islamic Research Institute assiduously typed the manuscript many a time before it assumed its final shape. Mr. E.R. Fox rendered valuable assistance in technical editing and proofreading and Mr. Naiem Qaddoura in setting the Arabic material. Dr. Kidwai oversaw, with an interest, zeal and meticulousness all his own, the typesetting of the work. Dr. M. Manazir Ahsan, thanks to his frequent reminders, did not permit this writer to remain indolent for long.

Last, but not least, I feel obligated to thank the members of my family and my close friends for the moral support they have provided me over the years. I have always valued their support and encouragement, but have been especially sustained by it during the last few years which have been among the most difficult and trying of my life. For during the years 1991–96 I have successively suffered the loss of some of those extremely near and dear to me. In 1991 I was deprived of my father to whom I owe much more than what anyone, even those closely acquainted with me and my father, can imagine. In 1996 I lost my friend, Khurram Murad, who meant to me much more than what is generally understood by the expression 'a very close friend'. Above all, in the same year the cruel hands of death snatched away from me my wife Shakeela, who was the main source of the many blessings that came my way since 1959 when we were joined together by our marriage in a relationship that has provided immense peace of mind and happiness throughout the thirty-seven years that we spent together. My main regret is that this volume is being published at a time when she is no more in the world to greet it with her characteristic expression of happiness and pride at whatever little I was ever able to do in service to the Qur'ān. My feeling of grief is all the more intense because she helped me a great deal more in my work on the present volume than on any previous ones. The present volume is, therefore, being dedicated to her memory in love, affection and gratitude, and with the earnest prayer that she may find a truly honourable place in Almighty God's eternal Gardens of Bliss.

To all those mentioned above, and to many others who assisted, encouraged and inspired me in various ways, I record my profound sense of gratitude. May Allah bless them all.

Islamabad
August 1998

Zafar Ishaq Ansari

N.B. ▶ *refers to the continuation of the paragraph adopted by Mawdūdī in the Urdu translation.*

Sūrah 22

al-Ḥajj

(The Pilgrimage)

(Madīnan Period)

Title

The title is derived from verse 27 of this *sūrah* in which the Prophet (peace be upon him) was directed to proclaim *Ḥajj*.

Period of Revelation

In this *sūrah* we find an amalgam of the characteristics of both the Makkan and Madīnan *sūrahs*. Commentators on the Qur'ān differ for this reason about whether the *sūrah* is Makkan or Madīnan. In our view, however, the contents and style of the *sūrah* bear witness to the fact that a part of it was revealed in the last phase of the Makkan period of the Prophet's life, while the other part was revealed at the beginning of the Madīnan period.

It is natural, therefore, that the *sūrah* should combine the characteristics of *sūrahs* of both the Makkan and Madīnan periods. The content and style of the early part, however, clearly indicate that the *sūrah* was revealed in Makka, and most probably, during the last phase of the Makkan period, just a little before the *Hijrah*. This part concludes with verse 24.

From verse 25 onwards the tenor of the content suddenly changes and one has the distinct feeling that the portion commencing from this verse till the end of the *sūrah* was revealed during the Madīnan period. It is not improbable that this portion might have been revealed in the month of Dhū al-Ḥijjah in the very first year after the *Hijrah*. This seems to be corroborated by the contents of verses 25 through 41 and the context of the revelation of verses 39–40. The migrants had then arrived in Madina only shortly after saying goodbye to their hearth and home. During the *Ḥajj* period they must have experienced some nostalgia for Makka, their home town, and found themselves reminiscing about the throngs of people bustling in and around Makka during the *Ḥajj*. They would also have been tormented by the fact that the Quraysh, who were immersed in polytheism, had prevented them even from visiting Makka. They would also have been waiting, expectantly, to receive God's permission to fight against those who had driven them out of their homes, had denied them the right to visit the Holy Mosque, and had forced them to live a life of misery and suffering for no other reason than that they wanted to follow the way prescribed for them by God.

This, then, was the right psychological background against which verses 25–41 were revealed. In these verses, it was clearly stated that the sole purpose of the construction of the Holy Mosque and of instituting the ritual of *Ḥajj* was that people may serve the One True God. The fact was, however, that blatant polytheism was rampant both in and around the Holy Mosque, whereas the followers of the One True God were barred from entering it. Thereafter, the Muslims were granted permission to fight against those oppressors, to dismantle their power, and to establish that righteous order of life under which goodness flourishes and evils are suppressed. According to 'Abd Allāh ibn 'Abbās, Mujāhid, 'Urwah ibn al-Zubayr, Zayd ibn Aslam, Muqātil ibn Ḥayyān, Qatādah and other major commentators of the Qur'ān, this is the first Qur'ānic verse which grants the Muslims permission to wage war. (See Ibn Kathīr's comments on verse 39 – Ed.) This is corroborated by traditions in *Ḥadīth* and *Sīrah* works, which indicate that soon after this sanction was granted, practical steps were also taken against the Quraysh. It was in Ṣafar 2 A.H. that the first expedition was dispatched towards the coastal region of the Red Sea. This expedition is variously known as the expedition of Dawwān or Abwā'. (See Ibn Hishām, vol. 1, p. 591 – Ed.)

Subject Matter and Themes

Essentially, this *sūrah* addresses three groups of people: the polytheists of Makka, wavering Muslims, and true men of faith.

The polytheists were first addressed during the Makkan period, and this naturally concluded in the Madīnan period. It was emphatically impressed upon them that they were following the unfounded ideas of *Jāhilīyah*. Rather than placing their trust in the One True God, they had mistakenly turned to false gods who were, of themselves, totally powerless. Not only that, but they also denied God's Messenger (peace be upon him). In view of their blatant wickedness, they were doomed to the same fate which had befallen iniquitous nations of the past. By giving the lie to the Prophet and subjecting the most righteous elements of their nation to heartless persecution, they had courted their own ruin. Their iniquity was, thus, bound to expose them to a severe punishment from God – a punishment against which their false deities would be unable to provide any protection. Alongside this severe note of warning, the basic teachings of Islam are explained so that they may be fully comprehended. The notes of counsel and advice are interspersed throughout the *sūrah*. Moreover, persuasive arguments are also put forward against associating others with God in His Divinity as well as in support of God's Unity and of the Hereafter.

In addition to the polytheists, there were also some wavering elements in the Muslim community. These were they who had apparently made the commitment to serve God, but who were not prepared to take any risk on that behalf. This *sūrah*, then, also addresses them, severely reproaching them for their weakness. They are virtually told that their faith lacks sincerity. For whenever they enjoy comfort, happiness, and affluence, they show their loyalty to God but then altogether distance themselves from Him as soon as they face any adversity in God's cause. Thus, they deprive themselves of God's support. To adopt such an attitude is preposterous, for it cannot avert any loss, calamity or suffering which God wills for them.

As for the believers, the discourse addressed to them can be divided into two categories. In the first instance, they are addressed along with the generality of Arabs, but in the second, the address is exclusively directed at them, the true believers. The first situation consists of a severe censure of the Makkan polytheists for having barred the Muslims from entering the Holy Mosque. This was declared to be wrong since the Holy Mosque was in no way their private property, and they had no right to prevent anyone from performing Pilgrimage.

This critical observation was not only intrinsically correct, but it also undermined the position of the Quraysh politically. Basically, it raised serious questions in the minds of all the Arab tribes about the status of the Quraysh in relation to the Ka'bah: were they its custodians or were they its owners? If the Quraysh could prevent some people from performing *Ḥajj* or *'Umrah* simply because they were hostile to them, and could get away with it, then they could do the same with anyone whom they disliked. They would, thus, have the authority to prevent whomsoever they wished from entering the sacred precincts of Makka. While recounting the history of the Holy Mosque, it is pointed out that when Abraham (peace be upon him) constructed the Ka'bah in compliance with God's command, he made a proclamation granting permission of *Ḥajj* to all and sundry; he granted the same rights to the Makkans and the outsiders as far as the right of Pilgrimage is concerned. At the same time, it was made clear that the house erected in Makka was meant for worship of the One True God rather than as a backdrop against which to perform polytheistic rituals. How outrageously ironic it was then that while the worship of the One True God was prohibited in the Holy Mosque there was complete licence to worship idols.

In another section of the discourse, the believers are granted permission to have recourse to force if they are subjected to repressive measures by the Quraysh. At the same time, they are told how to conduct themselves and which objectives to pursue should they attain political power. This theme occurs both in the middle and the concluding parts of the *sūrah*. In the very last verse, verse 78, the appellation of 'Muslims' is formally conferred upon the believers. They are also appraised that they are the true heirs to Abraham (peace be upon him) and that they have been chosen to bear witness to the truth of God's Message before all mankind. In this capacity, it was made incumbent upon them to turn themselves into excellent examples of humanity by establishing Prayers, dispensing *Zakāh*, doing good, and engaging – with full trust in their Lord – in the struggle to uphold the Word of God.

For a better understanding of the contents of the present *sūrah*, readers should see our introductory remarks to *Sūrahs al-Baqarah* and *al-Anfāl*. (*Towards Understanding the Qur'ān*, vol. I, pp. 39 ff. and vol. III, pp. 119 ff. – Ed.)

In the name of Allah, the Most Merciful, the Most Compassionate.

بِسْمِ ٱللَّهِ ٱلرَّحْمَٰنِ ٱلرَّحِيمِ

(1) O mankind, fear the (wrath of) your Lord! Indeed, the earthquake of the Hour (of Judgement) will be an awesome thing.[1] (2) On the Day when you witness it, the suckling woman shall utterly neglect the infant she suckles, and every pregnant woman shall cast her burden, ▶

يَٰٓأَيُّهَا ٱلنَّاسُ ٱتَّقُواْ رَبَّكُمْۚ إِنَّ
زَلْزَلَةَ ٱلسَّاعَةِ شَيْءٌ عَظِيمٌ ١ يَوْمَ تَرَوْنَهَا
تَذْهَلُ كُلُّ مُرْضِعَةٍ عَمَّآ أَرْضَعَتْ
وَتَضَعُ كُلُّ ذَاتِ حَمْلٍ حَمْلَهَا

---

1. The earthquake mentioned here will be one of the preliminary signs of the Last Day. Most probably it will take place at a time when the earth will suddenly start whirling rapidly in a direction opposite to its erstwhile direction, and when the sun will rise from the west rather than from the east. This view is held by some of the early Qur'ānic commentators such as 'Alqamah and Sha'bī. (See Ālūsī, *Rūḥ al-Ma'ānī*, comments on the verse – Ed.) The same point is borne out by the lengthy *ḥadīth* cited on the authority of Abū Hurayrah by Ibn Jarīr al-Ṭabarī and Ibn Abī Ḥātim. According to this *ḥadīth*, the Prophet (peace be upon him) said that the Trumpet would be blown three times. When blown for the first time, it would cause extreme fright and consternation; the second blowing of the Trumpet would cause everyone to die; and at the third sounding, everyone would be resurrected and stand before God for His judgement. While giving a graphic account of the first Trumpet blow, the Prophet (peace be upon him) said that the earth would then resemble a boat that is tossed about by tempestuous waves, or it would resemble a suspended lamp that is violently shaken by strong gusts of wind. (See Ibn Kathīr's comments on the verse – Ed.) The state of the inhabitants of the earth at that moment is portrayed at several places in the Qur'ān:

> So, when the Trumpet is blown with a single blast, and when the earth and the mountains are borne away and crushed with one stroke, on that Day shall the Great Event come to pass (*al-Ḥāqqah* 69: 13–15).
>
> When the earth will be shaken to its utmost convulsion, and the earth will throw up its burdens, and man will cry out: 'What is the matter with it?' (*al-Zalzalah* 99: 1–3).
>
> On the Day when the first commotion of the quake shall shake everything, followed by a repetition of the quake. On that Day

and you will see people as though they are drunk, when they are not drunk;[2] but dreadful shall be Allah's chastisement.[3]	وَتَرَى ٱلنَّاسَ سُكَـٰرَىٰ وَمَا هُم بِسُكَـٰرَىٰ وَلَـٰكِنَّ عَذَابَ ٱللَّهِ شَدِيدٌ ۝٢

people's hearts shall shiver and their eyes shall stare with awe (*al-Nāzi'āt* 79: 6–9).

When the earth shall be shaken to its depths, and the mountains shall be crumbled to pieces, becoming scattered dust (*al-Wāqi'ah* 56: 4–6).

Then how shall you, if you reject [the Message of the Prophet], guard yourselves against the affliction of the Day that will make children grey-headed, and to whose severity will cause the heaven to be cleft asunder? (*al-Muzzammil* 73: 17–18).

True, a few Qur'ānic commentators believe that this earthquake will coincide with the resurrection of the dead. Several traditions are also cited in support of this view. (See Ibn Kathīr's comments on the verse – Ed.) However, the explicit statement of the Qur'ān does not allow one to accept this. For, according to the Qur'ān, when this quaking takes place mothers will flee from the babies they are suckling and pregnant women will abort their foetuses. Obviously, such incidents cannot take place in the Next Life. In the Next Life, no woman will suckle her baby, nor will there be any occasion for pregnant women to abort their foetuses. This is obvious because, according to the clear statements of the Qur'ān, all worldly ties will then have ended, and everyone will stand before God in his individual capacity to render an account of his deeds. For these reasons, the tradition that we have cited (see p. 5) is to be preferred over the views of the commentators just mentioned.

Even though the chain of narration of this tradition has a formal defect, this is offset by the fact that it conforms to the Qur'ānic statements on the subject. As for the traditions on this subject in opposition to this tradition, even if they appear to be more in conformity with the formal criteria of authentification, they are weakened by the fact that they do not conform to the categorical statements of the Qur'ān.

2. In the above verse, the word that is used is *murḍi'ah* rather than *murḍi'*. In Arabic usage, *murḍi'* denotes the woman who suckles. As for *murḍi'ah*, it is used with reference to a woman in the actual state of suckling a child from her breast. However, when the earthquake of Doomsday strikes, mothers will flee in fright, abandoning the babies they are suckling, too panic-stricken even to be able to think of what will happen to their babies.

3. The purpose of the above verse is not to portray the events of the Last Day. Rather, it aims at instilling fear of God's chastizement in the hearts of

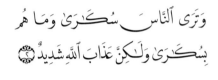

(3) Among people there are some who wrangle about Allah[4] without knowledge and follow every rebellious devil, (4) although it is decreed about him that he shall lead into error whosoever takes him for a friend, and will direct him to the torment of the Fire. (5) O mankind! If you have any doubt concerning Resurrection then know that it is surely We Who created you from dust, then from a drop of sperm,[5] then from a clot of blood, then from a little lump of flesh, some of it shapely ▶

وَمِنَ ٱلنَّاسِ مَن يُجَٰدِلُ فِى ٱللَّهِ
بِغَيْرِ عِلْمٍ وَيَتَّبِعُ كُلَّ شَيْطَٰنٍ مَّرِيدٍ ۝٣
كُتِبَ عَلَيْهِ أَنَّهُۥ مَن تَوَلَّاهُ فَأَنَّهُۥ يُضِلُّهُۥ
وَيَهْدِيهِ إِلَىٰ عَذَابِ ٱلسَّعِيرِ ۝٤ يَٰٓأَيُّهَا
ٱلنَّاسُ إِن كُنتُمْ فِى رَيْبٍ مِّنَ
ٱلْبَعْثِ فَإِنَّا خَلَقْنَٰكُم مِّن تُرَابٍ ثُمَّ مِن
نُّطْفَةٍ ثُمَّ مِنْ عَلَقَةٍ ثُمَّ مِن مُّضْغَةٍ مُّخَلَّقَةٍ

people so that they may shun whatever incurs God's displeasure. Hence, this brief description of the Last Day is followed by a discourse that addresses the main theme.

4. When one considers the discourse that follows, it is clear that the issue under debate was not whether God actually existed or not. The real issue of contention was: what are the rights of God against His creatures, what is the extent of God's authority, and what is the attitude that one should adopt to His directives and commands? The Prophet Muḥammad (peace be upon him) sought to persuade people to accept that there is no God except the One True God, and that the Hereafter is bound to come to pass. It was on these matters that people questioned the Prophet (peace be upon him). The debate ultimately led to the question of what lies in God's power and what lies beyond it? Is the universe governed by the One True God or do any other beings share His Divinity with Him?

5. This verse means either that each man was created from materials all of which are derived from the earth and that the actual process starts with creating the sperm. Or else it means that the human species began its existence with the Prophet Adam (peace be upon him), who was directly created from clay, whereafter all generations were created from sperm, as stated elsewhere in the Qur'ān: 'He began the creation of man with clay, and made his progeny from the quintessence of a despised fluid' (*al-Sajdah* 32: 7–8).

وَغَيْرِ مُخَلَّقَةٍ لِّنُبَيِّنَ لَكُمْ ۚ وَنُقِرُّ فِي
الْأَرْحَامِ مَا نَشَاءُ إِلَىٰ أَجَلٍ مُّسَمًّى ثُمَّ
نُخْرِجُكُمْ طِفْلًا ثُمَّ لِتَبْلُغُوا أَشُدَّكُمْ ۖ
وَمِنكُم مَّن يُتَوَفَّىٰ وَمِنكُم مَّن يُرَدُّ إِلَىٰ
أَرْذَلِ الْعُمُرِ لِكَيْلَا يَعْلَمَ مِن بَعْدِ عِلْمٍ شَيْئًا ۚ
وَتَرَى الْأَرْضَ هَامِدَةً فَإِذَا أَنزَلْنَا عَلَيْهَا
الْمَاءَ اهْتَزَّتْ وَرَبَتْ وَأَنبَتَتْ مِن كُلِّ
زَوْجٍ بَهِيجٍ ﴿٥﴾

and other shapeless.[6] (We are rehearsing this) that We may make the reality clear to you. We cause (the drop of sperm) that We please to remain in the wombs till an appointed time. We bring you forth as infants (and nurture you) that you may come of age. Among you is he that dies (at a young age) and he who is kept back to the most abject age so that after once having known, he reaches a stage when he knows nothing.[7] You see the earth dry and barren and then no sooner than We send down water upon it, it begins to quiver and swell and brings forth every kind of beauteous vegetation.▶

---

6. This refers to the different stages of gestation through which the foetus passes in the mother's womb. The stages of gestation known today with the help of powerful microscopes, and through them alone, are not mentioned in the Qur'ān. Instead, only those major changes are mentioned with which even the illiterate bedouin of that time were familiar. What is said here is that once the sperm settles down and fertilizes, it turns into congealed blood, then into a lump of flesh which is initially devoid of any definite shape, and then it develops into a human baby whose features gradually crystallize. Since those stages of human gestation were common knowledge because of abortion, reference is specifically made only to those stages. Thus, no detailed knowledge of embryology was required then, nor it is required now, for grasping the main stages through which the human embryo passes before its birth.

7. This refers to that state of senility when man loses awareness of the state he is in. Someone who may once have been known for his mental sharpness and for imparting wisdom to others, degenerates into a decrepit old man; his mental state reverting to almost that of a small child. All that he once took pride in – his knowledge, experience, and wisdom – depart from him and he becomes altogether empty-headed and senseless, and the laughing-stock of even children.

(6) All this is because Allah, He is the Truth,[8] and because He resurrects the dead, and because He has power over everything, (7) (all of which shows that) the Hour shall surely come to pass – in this there is no doubt – and Allah shall surely resurrect those that are in graves.[9]

ذَٰلِكَ بِأَنَّ ٱللَّهَ هُوَ ٱلْحَقُّ وَأَنَّهُۥ يُحْىِ
ٱلْمَوْتَىٰ وَأَنَّهُۥ عَلَىٰ كُلِّ شَىْءٍ قَدِيرٌ ﴿٦﴾ وَأَنَّ
ٱلسَّاعَةَ ءَاتِيَةٌ لَّا رَيْبَ فِيهَا وَأَنَّ ٱللَّهَ
يَبْعَثُ مَن فِى ٱلْقُبُورِ ﴿٧﴾

---

8. In the context of the present discourse, this Qur'ānic verse carries three meanings: first, that God alone is truthful, and that the fanciful opinion that Life after Death is beyond the range of the possible is absolutely baseless. Second, that God is not a phantom, a being invented merely to obviate the intellectual difficulties people face in comprehending the riddle of existence. He is also not a figment of the philosopher's imagination, nor just a necessary being, nor simply the first cause. He is, instead, the True, All-Powerful Master Who acts according to His own Will. He unceasingly rules over the whole universe, of every little part of it, and does so by dint of His Infinite Power, His Will, His Knowledge and His Wisdom. Third, since God is the Truth, all His acts are animated with purposefulness and wisdom. He is far from being One Who acts in sport and play, Who contrives a plaything merely to entertain Himself with for a while and then capriciously shatters it to pieces.

9. The above verse mentions the various stages of man's birth, the effects of rain on the earth, and the growth of vegetation as arguments in support of the following truths: (1) that God is the Truth; (2) that God restores the dead to life; (3) that God has power over everything; (4) that the Hour of Judgement is bound to come; and (5) that God will most surely raise the dead to life.

Now let us see how the above-mentioned phenomena serve as supporting evidence in favour of the five truths mentioned above. Even if one were to close one's eyes to the working of the universe and consider merely one's own creation, still one would be able to appreciate how God's Will is actively involved in the life of every single individual, and that the different stages in the birth and growth of every single individual is determined by His Will. Some people are of the opinion that all this is part of a set of laws which are regulated by a nature that is blind and mute, and devoid of both knowledge and will. However, if one sees things with open eyes and a perceptive mind, one then knows how the wilful decision of an All-Powerful and Wise Being is tied up with the manner in which every single human being comes into existence, as well as the manner in which he passes through different stages of growth and development. All that man partakes is bereft of even an atom of sperm. Nor does his food contain anything which has the power to generate the properties which characterize man. When this food is digested, it is transformed into such things as hair, flesh and bones, which in themselves lack reproductive qualities. And yet, it is these lifeless ingredients that give birth to sperm in men and ovaries in women, the combination of which leads to the constant birth of living beings.

Now let us move away from this and cast a glance around us. We see that there are almost limitless seeds of a variety of things that are scattered all around by the birds and wind. There are also roots of a very large number of plants and trees which lie hidden in the earth. In this arid terrain there is no trace of any plant life. The barren tracts of land seem altogether dead, as if they were a large graveyard. But as soon as a few drops of rain fall on a piece of land, verdant life begins to pulsate all over. Every dead root is resurrected; every lifeless seed becomes a living plant. This process of the resurrection of the dead takes place every year before our very own eyes.

The third thing which is established by human observation is that God has power over everything. Man may disregard other parts of this vast universe, and simply consider the earth on which he lives; in fact, he may simply reflect over the life of plants and human beings to the exclusion of all other aspects relating to the earth. Would such a reflection lead him to the conclusion that God has the power to do only what we see Him doing and that His power does not extend beyond that; and that if He decides to do something more than what He has done up until now, it will be beyond the range of His capacity to do so? Such conclusions about God's capacity and power are patently unjustified. In fact this would be evident were we to consider the extent of man's capacity up until the recent past. We know well that until the previous century, it was thought that man was capable of manufacturing only those vehicles that could operate on the earth. It was considered absolutely beyond man's power to manufacture vessels that would fly in the air. But aeroplanes made by man have shown how grossly conservative people's estimates of man's capacity were. Now if anyone were to estimate the extent of God's power only on the basis of what He has done uptil now, he would only provide evidence of the smallness of his own mind, for God's power in any case, is not bound by man's conservative estimates.

The fourth and fifth propositions are that the Day of Judgement is inevitable and that God is bound to raise all those who have suffered death. These are logical corollaries of the three premises mentioned above. If one looks at God's acts as reflections of God's power, one is bound to be convinced that He has the power to bring about the Doomsday whenever He wills. Additionally, He can also resurrect all those that are dead, i.e. the same people whom He once brought into existence from nothing.

Now, if one considers God's acts from the vantage-point of God's wisdom, human reason bears witness that God is bound to do both. This is so because without these two acts of God, the requirements of wisdom are not fulfilled

(8) And among people are those that wrangle about Allah without knowledge,[10] without any true guidance,[11] and without any scripture to enlighten them.[12] ▶	وَمِنَ ٱلنَّاسِ مَن يُجَـٰدِلُ فِى ٱللَّهِ بِغَيْرِ عِلْمٍ وَلَا هُدًى وَلَا كِتَـٰبٍ مُّنِيرٍ ۝٨

and it is inconceivable that any wise person, let alone God, would disregard that. Man is possessed of only a limited amount of wisdom. But even this limited wisdom enables him to appreciate that when a person entrusts his wealth or property or business to anyone, sooner or later he calls him to account for the same.

In other words, there is a logical nexus between the bestowal of trust and calling the trustee to account, a nexus that even man, despite the limited nature of his wisdom, can never ignore. Again, it is because of this very wisdom that man distinguishes between voluntary and involuntary acts. He associates moral responsibility with acts of a voluntary character, and declares some of those acts to be good and others bad. He praises and likes to reward those who do good, whereas he likes to see those engaged in evil acts punished, so much so that he establishes a fully-fledged institution – the judiciary – to this end. Now, can one believe that He who created wisdom and which He bestowed on man, will Himself be devoid of it? Can one seriously entertain the proposition that God, Who created man and charged him with this huge world with its immense resources and endowed him with enormous powers, would forget about man after all this and never call him to account? Can any sound-minded person be persuaded to believe that criminals, who have managed to escape the punishment they deserve or those who have not been punished in proportion to their crimes, will never be brought to book? Furthermore, can one seriously believe that those who have not been rewarded in this world for the good they have done, remain deprived of their reward ever after? If this is not the case, then there can be no escaping the conclusion that Life after Death is an inevitable concomitant of God's wisdom. Indeed it is not Life after Death that should be a matter of surprise; it would be surprising if it were not.

10. This refers to the knowledge that one gains through direct observation and first-hand experience.

11. That is, knowledge gained indirectly from some evidence or as a result of the guidance of a knowledgeable person.

12. This refers to the knowledge gained from the Scriptures.

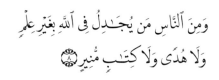

(9) They wrangle arrogantly,[13] intent on leading people astray from the Way of Allah.[14] Such shall suffer disgrace in this world and We shall cause them to taste the chastisement of burning (in the Next). (10) That is the outcome of what your own hands have wrought, for Allah never wrongs His creatures.

(11) And among people is he who worships Allah on the borderline;[15] if any good befalls him, he is satisfied; but if a trial afflicts him, he utterly turns away.[16] ▶

ثَانِيَ عِطْفِهِۦ لِيُضِلَّ عَن سَبِيلِ ٱللَّهِۖ لَهُۥ فِى
ٱلدُّنْيَا خِزْىٌۖ وَنُذِيقُهُۥ يَوْمَ ٱلْقِيَٰمَةِ عَذَابَ
ٱلْحَرِيقِ ﴿٩﴾ ذَٰلِكَ بِمَا قَدَّمَتْ يَدَاكَ وَأَنَّ
ٱللَّهَ لَيْسَ بِظَلَّٰمٍ لِّلْعَبِيدِ ﴿١٠﴾ وَمِنَ ٱلنَّاسِ مَن
يَعْبُدُ ٱللَّهَ عَلَىٰ حَرْفٍۖ فَإِنْ أَصَابَهُۥ خَيْرٌ ٱطْمَأَنَّ
بِهِۦۖ وَإِنْ أَصَابَتْهُ فِتْنَةٌ ٱنقَلَبَ عَلَىٰ وَجْهِهِۦ

13. This consists of three things: (1) adamance and intransigence arising out of ignorance and folly, (2) arrogance and egotistic presumptuousness, and (3) indifference to the sincere counsel of others.

14. Previously mention was made of those who are themselves misguided. Here, reference is being made to those who are not simply misguided, but who are also bent upon misleading others.

15. This alludes to those whose allegiance to the true faith is peripheral; to those who, rather than be at the centre, prefer to sit on the fence. These are like reluctant soldiers who, being on the periphery, are ready to throw in their lot with the winning party, be it their own side or the enemy's.

16. This alludes to those immature, self-serving and vacillating people who embrace faith only to promote their own self-interest. Their allegiance to Islam rests on the condition that they will have the opportunity for the unfettered pursuit of self-interest, of their being able to enjoy every possible ease and comfort. Allegiance to Islam, in their view, should not mean their being asked to make any sacrifice in its cause. Nor should this allegiance lead to denial of anything in the world which they cherish. If all these interests are guaranteed, they are happy with their God and satisfied with their faith.

He will incur the loss of this world and the Hereafter. That indeed is a clear loss.[17]
(12) He invokes, instead of Allah, those who can neither harm nor benefit him.[18] That indeed is straying far away. ▶

خَسِرَ ٱلدُّنْيَا وَٱلْـَٔاخِرَةَ ۚ ذَٰلِكَ هُوَ ٱلْخُسْرَانُ
ٱلْمُبِينُ ﴿١١﴾ يَدْعُوا۟ مِن دُونِ ٱللَّهِ مَا لَا يَضُرُّهُۥ
وَمَا لَا يَنفَعُهُۥ ۚ ذَٰلِكَ هُوَ ٱلضَّلَـٰلُ ٱلْبَعِيدُ ﴿١٢﴾

However, if they are faced with misfortune or suffer loss or hardship in the cause of God, or if any of their desires remain unfulfilled, they are prone to scepticism about everything – about God's Godhead, about the truth of prophethood, and about religion itself. In this state of mind, they are naturally prepared to bow in reverence before every doorstep.

17. This is a vital truth which is succinctly stated here. The verse portrays an ambivalent, wavering Muslim, one whose state is the worst. So far as an unbeliever is concerned, because of his convictions he is neither bothered by the idea of God nor of the Next Life, nor is he concerned with the idea of observing God's Laws. Hence, he concentrates, single-mindedly, on pursuing material objectives. As a result, even if he deprives himself of the good of the Hereafter, he is at least able to achieve some success in the present world. On the other hand, when the true believer firmly and resolutely follows the teachings of the religion of God, he ultimately achieves worldly success as well. Furthermore, even if he remains deprived of worldly success, at least felicity and success in the Next Life are fully assured.

A wavering believer, however, is likely to have no success either in this world or the Next. For, when he rushes to achieve worldly gains, the vestiges of belief in God and the Hereafter and his concern for morality, whatever its extent, all prevent him from riding rough-shod. The result is that he does not have the single-mindedness needed for the kind of unbridled pursuit of worldly interests which is the hallmark of rank unbelievers. Conversely, when he thinks of working for his success in the Hereafter, he is impeded from proceeding in that direction because of his excessive greed for worldly benefits, his fear of worldly losses, and his disinclination to observe the restrictions placed by religion on seeking to satisfy his carnal desires. In fact, worldliness impairs his belief and corrupts his conduct to such an extent that he can hardly escape punishment in the Hereafter. Thus, he courts failure both in this world and in the World to Come.

18. The preceding verse categorically refutes the notion that deities other than the One True God can either benefit or harm anyone insofar as they are devoid of the power to do so. The present verse goes a step further, asserting

(13) He invokes those that are more likely to cause him harm than benefit. Such is surely an evil patron, and an evil associate.[19] (14) (In contrast) Allah will assuredly cause those who believe and act righteously[20] to enter Gardens beneath which rivers flow. For, most certainly, Allah does whatever He pleases.[21] ▶

يَدْعُوا۟ لَمَن ضَرُّهُۥٓ أَقْرَبُ مِن نَّفْعِهِۦ ۚ لَبِئْسَ
ٱلْمَوْلَىٰ وَلَبِئْسَ ٱلْعَشِيرُ ﴿١٣﴾ إِنَّ ٱللَّهَ يُدْخِلُ
ٱلَّذِينَ ءَامَنُوا۟ وَعَمِلُوا۟ ٱلصَّٰلِحَٰتِ
جَنَّٰتٍ تَجْرِى مِن تَحْتِهَا ٱلْأَنْهَٰرُ ۚ إِنَّ
ٱللَّهَ يَفْعَلُ مَا يُرِيدُ ﴿١٤﴾

---

that those deities are more likely to be a source of harm. This is so because when a man prays to them and turns to them for aid, he instantly suffers a significant loss, the loss of his faith. As to the benefit for the sake of which he invoked those false gods, even an unbeliever acknowledges that – regardless of the intrinsic truth or otherwise of the matter – there is apparently no surety or even likelihood that he will be able to obtain that benefit. It is possible, however, that in order to put him to further test God may make some of his wishes fulfilled by his approach to these false gods. It is possible though that even if he suffers the loss of his faith, the wish that had prompted him to sacrifice his faith might nevertheless also remain unfulfilled.

19. Whoever puts a person on an erroneous course, be he a human being or Satan, is an evil patron and an evil companion.

20. In contrast to the opportunist, self-seeking, and wavering believers are those sincere believers, the true men of faith. They are the ones who, after due reflection, have firmly made up their mind to believe in God, in the Prophet (peace be upon him), and in the Hereafter. Once they reach this stage of firm conviction, they resolutely and steadfastly pursue the way of the truth they opted for. They continue to follow this course regardless of whether they are confronted with adversity or prosperity, whether mountains of affliction impede their onward march or favours are lavished upon them.

21. God's power is simply unlimited, both in this world and the Next. He grants a person whatever He Wills and withholds from him whatever He Wills. If He decides to reward someone, no one can prevent Him. Likewise, if He decides to withhold something from a person, no one has the power to force God to bestow it upon him.

(15) Anyone who fancies that Allah will not support him in this world and in the Hereafter, let him reach out to heaven through a rope, and then make a hole in the sky and see whether his device can avert that which enrages him.[22]

مَن كَانَ يَظُنُّ أَن لَّن يَنصُرَهُ ٱللَّهُ
فِى ٱلدُّنْيَا وَٱلْءَاخِرَةِ فَلْيَمْدُدْ بِسَبَبٍ
إِلَى ٱلسَّمَآءِ ثُمَّ لْيَقْطَعْ فَلْيَنظُرْ هَلْ يُذْهِبَنَّ
كَيْدُهُۥ مَا يَغِيظُ ﴿١٥﴾

---

22. There is much disagreement among commentators of the Qur'ān concerning the import of this verse. What follows is a summary of their various views. (1) Whoever believes that God will not help the Prophet Muḥammad (peace be upon him), let him commit suicide by fastening a rope from the roof and hanging himself with it. (2) Whoever believes that God will not help the Prophet Muḥammad (peace be upon him) should climb up to the heavens with the help of a rope, and then try to prevent all help reaching the Prophet from God. (3) Whoever believes that God will not help the Prophet Muḥammad (peace be upon him) let him try to reach the heavens in order to prevent revelations from being made. (4) He who believes that God will not help the Prophet Muḥammad (peace be upon him) should try to reach the heavens to ensure that the Prophet (peace be upon him) is deprived of his livelihood. (5) Whoever believes that God will not help those who hold such an opinion let him commit suicide by fastening a rope from his roof and hanging himself with it. (6) Whoever believes that God will not help those who hold such an opinion, let him somehow reach the heavens and try his luck in securing help from above. (See Ibn Kathīr's comments on the verse – Ed.)

It is obvious that the first four opinions are altogether out of context. As for the last two, although they have some relevance, they nonetheless fail to do full justice to the import of the discourse. If one remembers the context of the discourse, it is quite clear that reference is being made to those who, as believers, are content with sitting on the fence. As long as things go well, they are happy. But as soon as they encounter any adversity, or are faced with a situation that is not to their liking, they turn away from the One True God and start prostrating themselves at the temple of one false deity after another.

What explains this behaviour? Simple: such people are not satisfied with what God decrees for them. Ultimately, this stems from their fancy that there are others beside God who decide regarding man's fate. Hence, when they despair of God, they place all their expectations in others than the One True God. Accordingly, such people are being told that they may do whatever they can. They can even climb up to the heavens in order to find out whether

(16) Even so We have revealed the Qur'ān with Clear Signs. Verily Allah guides whomsoever He wills.

(17) On the Day of Resurrection Allah will most certainly judge among those who believe,[23] and those who became Jews,[24] and Sabaeans,[25] and ▶

وَكَذَٰلِكَ أَنزَلْنَٰهُ ءَايَٰتٍۭ بَيِّنَٰتٍ
وَأَنَّ ٱللَّهَ يَهْدِى مَن يُرِيدُ ﴿١٦﴾ إِنَّ
ٱلَّذِينَ ءَامَنُوا۟ وَٱلَّذِينَ هَادُوا۟ وَٱلصَّٰبِـِٔينَ

---

anything can change God's decrees. Climbing up to or making a hole in the heavens signifies the utmost effort that man can imagine. Most obviously, then, it is not meant to be taken literally.

23. This refers to all Muslims: that is, to those Muslims before the advent of the Prophet (peace be upon him) who believed in the Messengers and Scriptures of their respective times, as well as to those who, in the days of the Prophet Muḥammad (peace be upon him), believed in him in addition to believing in the earlier Messengers. These believers include those who are sincere in their faith, as well as those on the periphery who waver between belief and unbelief.

24. For further details see *Towards Understanding the Qur'ān*, vol. II, *al-Nisā'* 4, n. 72, p. 44.

25. In the olden days, two communities were known as Sabaeans – the followers of the Prophet John (peace be upon him) who inhabited, in large numbers, the upper region of Iraq called al-Jazīrah. They practised baptism according to the way of the Prophet John. The other community bearing this name consisted of star-worshippers who claimed to follow the religion of the Prophets Shīth and Idrīs (peace be upon them). They believed that the planets held ascendancy over the elements, and that the angels had ascendancy over the planets. Based in Ḥarrān, they were scattered over different parts of Iraq. This second group is also known for its mastery of philosophy, science and medicine. It is, however, more likely that the Qur'ān here refers to the former group, i.e. to the followers of the Prophet John. This seems so because the other group was probably not known at the time the Qur'ān was revealed.

Christians,[26] and Magians,[27] and those who associate others with Allah in His Divinity.[28] Surely Allah watches over everything.[29]

(18) Have you not seen that all those who are in the heavens and all those who are in the earth[30] ▶

وَٱلنَّصَـٰرَىٰ وَٱلْمَجُوسَ وَٱلَّذِينَ أَشْرَكُوٓا۟ إِنَّ
ٱللَّهَ يَفْصِلُ بَيْنَهُمْ يَوْمَ ٱلْقِيَـٰمَةِ ۚ إِنَّ ٱللَّهَ عَلَىٰ
كُلِّ شَىْءٍ شَهِيدٌ ﴿١٧﴾ أَلَمْ تَرَ أَنَّ ٱللَّهَ يَسْجُدُ لَهُۥ
مَن فِى ٱلسَّمَـٰوَٰتِ وَمَن فِى ٱلْأَرْضِ

26. For an explanation see *Towards Understanding the Qur'ān*, vol. II, *al-Mā'idah* 5, n. 36, pp. 146–8.

27. The term 'Magians' refers to the fire-worshippers of Persia who believed in the two gods of light and darkness and claimed to be the followers of Zoroaster. Their faith and morality became greatly corrupted as a result of the erroneous doctrines and practices of Mazdak, so much so that they had no qualms about marrying their sisters, a practice which actually was in vogue with them.

28. This refers to those polytheists of Arabia who did not have any specific name to identify themselves with. In order to distinguish them from other religious entities, the Qur'ān refers to them as *mushrikūn* (those engaged in *shirk*) and *al-ladhīna ashrakū* (those who committed *shirk*). The Qur'ān does so despite the fact that polytheistic beliefs and practices had also made their inroads among other religious communities, the only ones remaining immune from polytheism being the Muslims.

29. The differences of opinion among the various communities concerning God will not be definitively resolved in the present world. It can only be settled for good on the Day of Judgement. It is then that it will be decided beyond all doubt as to who is in error and who is in the right. In a sense, the Scriptures have already decided this question even in the present world. However, the Qur'ānic usage in the above verse – signifying final judgement and resolution of the dispute between the different contending parties – clearly identifies that a judgement will uphold, once and for all, the claim of one party and so reject the claims made by all other parties.

30. For an explanation see *Towards Understanding the Qur'ān*, vol. IV, *al-Ra'd* 13, nn. 24–5, p. 230, and *al-Naḥl* 16, nn. 41–2, pp. 334–5.

prostrate themselves before Allah;[31] and so do the sun and the moon, and the stars and the mountains, and the trees, and the beasts, and so do many human beings,[32] and even many of those who are condemned to chastisement?[33] ▶

وَٱلشَّمۡسُ وَٱلۡقَمَرُ وَٱلنُّجُومُ وَٱلۡجِبَالُ
وَٱلشَّجَرُ وَٱلدَّوَآبُّ وَكَثِيرٞ مِّنَ
ٱلنَّاسِۖ وَكَثِيرٌ حَقَّ عَلَيۡهِ ٱلۡعَذَابُۗ

31. These include angels, heavenly bodies and all the creatures that might exist in worlds other than the earth. These might include beings possessed of reason and free-will like human beings, or animals, plants, or solid matter, air and light that are devoid of reason and free-will.

32. This specifically refers to those who deliberately and wilfully, rather than involuntarily, prostrate themselves before God. Mention follows immediately thereafter of those who, in contrast wilfully refuse to prostrate themselves before God. This is so in spite of the fact that they are in the firm grip of natural laws and are among those who involuntarily prostrate themselves before God's Will. The reason why the latter group deserves punishment is that they act rebelliously in a domain where they have been endowed with free-will.

33. True, the dispute among these different groups will finally be resolved on the Day of Judgement. A sensible person, however, can see for himself even in the present life who is in the right, whose contention will eventually be upheld. The working of the entire universe bears out that it is only the One True God Whose Godhead, fully and most pervasively, embraces the whole universe. Everything, from the particle of dust to the massive planet is bound by the same law, a law from which no one can deviate even so much as a hair's breadth. A believer, out of his genuine belief in God, willingly submits to Him. But even atheists who deny the existence of God and polytheists who associate other helpless beings with God in His Divinity, find themselves forced to obey Him in certain matters in the manner of air and water. None – neither angel, *jinn*, Messenger, saint, nor any of the so-called gods and goddesses – has as much as a shred of the power that makes them deserve to be set up as God, as an object of worship. Nor can anyone be considered God's peer, or as someone who resembles God. Nor is it conceivable that a law without a Law-Giver, or a nature without its Creator, a system without anyone to set it up, is able to bring such an immense universe into existence, regulate its working with such absolute perfection, or exhibit those wonderful

And he whom Allah humiliates, none can give him honour.[34] Allah does whatever He wills.[35]

(19) These two groups (– the believers and unbelievers –) are in dispute[36] about their Lord. As for those that ▶

وَمَن يُهِنِ ٱللَّهُ فَمَا لَهُۥ مِن مُّكْرِمٍ ۚ إِنَّ
ٱللَّهَ يَفْعَلُ مَا يَشَآءُ ۩ ﴿١٨﴾ ۞ هَٰذَانِ
خَصْمَانِ ٱخْتَصَمُوا۟ فِى رَبِّهِمْ ۖ فَٱلَّذِينَ

---

feats of power and wisdom which are evident in every nook and cranny of the universe. Now, it is possible that some people fail to pay heed to the Prophets despite the existence of the universe – this awesome, open book – and dispute with them about God because they accepted man-made beliefs in preference to the teachings of the Prophets. The rank error of such people is as evident in this world as it will be on the Day of Judgement.

34. The expressions 'to humiliate', or 'confer honour upon someone', signify, respectively, the attitudes of rejecting the truth or following it. The former is bound to lead one to humiliation and the latter to achieving a position of honour. Anyone who does not perceive with open eyes the truths that are clear and radiant, and fails to give heed to those who, out of sincerity and good-will, try to explain things to him and try to help him with good counsel is simply inviting humiliation and disgrace upon himself. It is God's Will that a man shall have whatever he has himself asked for. Thus, if God does not confer upon someone the honour of following the truth, who, then, can confer that honour upon him?

35. It is incumbent upon everyone who recites this verse to perform *sajdah* (prostration). In fact, there is unanimity in the obligatoriness of all those who recite this verse to make *sajdah*. For the rationale of and injunctions with regard to the *sajdah* of Qur'ān-recitation see *Towards Understanding the Qur'ān*, vol. III, *al-A'rāf* 7, n. 157, pp. 117–18.

36. The groups that contend about God are very many. Nevertheless, the present verse divides them into two broad categories. One consists of those who accept the teachings of the Prophets and adopt the right attitude in serving God. The other consists of those who do not accept the teachings of the Prophets, reject the truth, and embrace unbelief. The essence of this latter attitude remains one and the same no matter how numerous the disagreements among the exponents of such an attitude are, or the extent to which the different versions of unbelief vary from one to another.

disbelieve, garments of fire have been cut out for them;[37] boiling water shall be poured down over their heads, (20) causing (not only) their skins but all that is in their bellies as well to melt away. (21) There shall be maces of iron to lash them.

(22) Whenever they try, in their anguish, to escape from Hell, they will be driven back into it, (and shall be told): "Now taste the torment of burning." (23) (On the other hand), Allah will cause those who believed and acted righteously to enter the Gardens beneath which rivers flow. They shall be decked in them with bracelets of gold and pearls[38] and their raiment shall be of silk. ▶

كَفَرُواْ قُطِّعَتْ لَهُمْ ثِيَابٌ مِّن نَّارٍ يُصَبُّ
مِن فَوْقِ رُءُوسِهِمُ ٱلْحَمِيمُ ﴿١٩﴾ يُصْهَرُ بِهِۦ
مَا فِى بُطُونِهِمْ وَٱلْجُلُودُ ﴿٢٠﴾ وَلَهُم مَّقَٰمِعُ
مِنْ حَدِيدٍ ﴿٢١﴾ كُلَّمَآ أَرَادُوٓاْ أَن يَخْرُجُواْ
مِنْهَا مِنْ غَمٍّ أُعِيدُواْ فِيهَا وَذُوقُواْ عَذَابَ
ٱلْحَرِيقِ ﴿٢٢﴾ إِنَّ ٱللَّهَ يُدْخِلُ ٱلَّذِينَ ءَامَنُواْ
وَعَمِلُواْ ٱلصَّٰلِحَٰتِ جَنَّٰتٍ تَجْرِى
مِن تَحْتِهَا ٱلْأَنْهَٰرُ يُحَلَّوْنَ فِيهَا مِنْ أَسَاوِرَ
مِن ذَهَبٍ وَلُؤْلُؤًا ۖ وَلِبَاسُهُمْ فِيهَا حَرِيرٌ ﴿٢٣﴾

---

37. Here, something which is inevitably bound to happen in the future has been described in the past tense. This in order to emphasize its inevitability; to give the impression as if it is something that has already taken place. As for the expression 'garments made out of fire', this seems possibly to refer to the same thing mentioned in *Sūrah Ibrāhīm* 14: 49–50. (The verse mentions that the guilty ones shall be 'secured in chains', and 'their garments shall be black as if made out of pitch, and the flames of the fire shall cover their faces ...' – Ed.) For further explanation see *Towards Understanding the Qur'ān*, vol. IV, *Ibrāhīm* 14, n. 58, p. 277.

38. What is meant by this is that the believers will be made to don royal dress. At the time the Qur'ān was revealed, kings and nobles wore jewellery of gold and precious stones. Such custom is in vogue even in our own time among the petty rulers, the *nawābs* and *rājahs*, of India.

(24) They were guided (to accept) the pure word;[39] they were guided to the Way of the Praiseworthy (Lord).[40]

(25) Indeed those who disbelieve[41] and who (now) hinder[42] people from the ▶

وَهُدُوٓاْ إِلَى ٱلطَّيِّبِ مِنَ ٱلۡقَوۡلِ وَهُدُوٓاْ
إِلَىٰ صِرَٰطِ ٱلۡحَمِيدِ ﴿٢٤﴾ إِنَّ ٱلَّذِينَ
كَفَرُواْ وَيَصُدُّونَ عَن

39. Although the expression used here connotes a general significance, it refers, in fact, to that true statement and sound creed whose acceptance made them believers. (This consisted of affirming that there is no God other than Allah and that Muḥammad is His Messenger – Ed.)

40. As we have stated in the introduction to this *sūrah*, in our opinion this verse concludes that part of the *sūrah* which was revealed during the Makkan period. The content and style of the verses up until the present one are those of the Makkan *sūrahs*. To put it differently, there is nothing in these verses to suggest that this part of the *sūrah* was revealed either wholly or partially in Madina.

Some commentators, however, believe that verse 19 of this *sūrah* belongs to the Madīnan period. (See Ibn Kathīr's comments on the verse – Ed.) This view is based on the assumption that the two disputing parties mentioned refer to those who fought against each other in the Battle of Badr. This assumption, however, does not hold much water. The context does not indicate that the particular battle referred to is the Battle of Badr. Instead, the statement is couched in quite general terms. Commentators also seem to indicate that a reference is made here to the perennial dispute between belief and unbelief from the very beginning of time, a dispute which will last till the Day of Judgement. However, had there been any connection between this verse and the Battle of Badr it would have been located in *Sūrah al-Anfāl* rather than in the present *sūrah* or in this particular context. If one accepts such a line of argument, it implies that the verses revealed subsequently were placed quite arbitrarily according to the whims of people and without any regard for textual coherence. On the contrary, we find a highly cohesive order in the Qur'ān, something which is in itself, emphatic refutation of such an argument.

41. This refers to those who rejected outright the Message of the Prophet Muḥammad (peace be upon him). What follows makes it evident that the reference here is to the unbelievers of Makka.

42. That is, they prevent the Prophet Muḥammad (peace be upon him) and his Companions from performing *Ḥajj* and *'Umrah*.

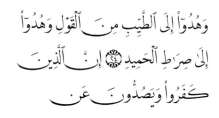

Way of Allah and hinder them from the Holy Mosque which We have set up (as a place of worship) for all people, equally for those who dwell therein and for those who come from outside, (they surely deserve punishment).[43] ▶	سَبِيلِ ٱللَّهِ وَٱلْمَسْجِدِ ٱلْحَرَامِ ٱلَّذِى جَعَلْنَٰهُ لِلنَّاسِ سَوَآءً ٱلْعَٰكِفُ فِيهِ وَٱلْبَادِ ۚ

43. The Holy Mosque is not the property of any individual, family or tribe. It is meant instead for everyone and, hence, no one can bar others from visiting it. This gave rise to two legal questions regarding which Muslim jurists have disagreed. First, whether the expression 'Holy Mosque' stands for the Mosque itself, or for the sacred precincts of Makka? Second, what is meant by the statement that 'those who dwell therein', and 'those who come from outside' enjoy equal rights over it?

Some scholars are of the opinion that the verse refers only to the Mosque and not to the entire area covered by the term *Ḥaram*. (See Ibn Kathīr's comments on the verse – Ed.) This seems to be indicated by the apparent meaning of the words used here. As for equality of rights, what is meant is equality in the right of worship. In this respect, the Prophet Muḥammad (peace be upon him) said: 'Decendants of 'Abd Manāf! Those of you who are placed in authority over the affairs of men shall not prohibit anyone from performing *ṭawāf* or praying for a while [in it] whenever he likes, be it in day or night.' (For this command of the Prophet (peace be upon him), see Tirmidhī, *K. al-Ḥajj*, 'Bāb mā jā' fī al-Ṣalāh ba'd al-'Aṣr wa ba'd al-Ṣubḥ'. The words of the *ḥadīth* are:

يابني عبد مناف من ولى منكم من أمور الناس شيئا فلا يمنعن أحدا طاف بهذا البيت
أو صلى أيــَّة ساعة شاء من ليل أو نهار

See also Aḥmad ibn Ḥanbal, *Musnad*, vol. 4, p. 8:

يابني عبد مناف لاتمنعوا أحدا طاف بهذا البيت أو صلى أيّة ساعة من ليل أو نهار – Ed.)

Hence, exponents of this opinion contend that it is wrong to think that the Qur'ān speaks here of the whole area of Makka. Nor is it legitimate to think that this verse declares that Makkans and outsiders are entitled to the same rights in all respects. They point out, by way of evidence, that from pre-Islamic times the land in Makka was considered to be the property of its inhabitants which they could inherit, buy, sell or lease, and these rights continued to be recognized even after the advent of Islam. This is evident, for instance, from the purchase of Ṣafwān ibn Umayyah's house for four thousand dirhams during 'Umar ibn al-Khaṭṭāb's caliphate so as to transform it into a prison-house. (See Ibn Kathīr's comments on the verse – Ed.) Hence, what equality means is simply equality in the right to worship. This, then, is the opinion of Imām Shāfi'ī, as also of some other scholars.

Another group, however, is of the opinion that the expression 'Holy Mosque' here stands for the whole sacred area of Makka. The first argument advanced in support of this opinion is that the specific act of the Makkan polytheists, for which they are here reproached, is in barring the Muslims from *Ḥajj*. It is also significant that this act is denounced on the grounds that all have equal rights there. Now, it is quite evident that the performance of *Ḥajj* rites is not confined to the Holy Mosque. Instead, its rituals are performed at several places, such as Ṣafā, Marwah, Muzdalifah and 'Arafāt. Moreover, the Qur'ān frequently employs the expression 'Holy Mosque' to denote the sacred precincts of Makka rather than in the narrow sense of the 'Holy Mosque of Makka'. There are several examples of this in the Qur'ān:

> . . . Barring people from the way of Allah and denying entry into the Holy Mosque and expelling its inmates from it are more awesome acts in the sight of Allah . . . (*al-Baqarah* 2: 217).
>
> This privilege is for those whose families do not live near the Holy Mosque (*al-Baqarah* 2: 196).

In these verses, the expression 'Holy Mosque' quite evidently denotes the sacred precincts of Makka rather than the Mosque itself. Hence, the equality mentioned in the above verse cannot be limited to the Mosque itself; rather, it embraces the entire precincts. Furthermore, this group of scholars does not limit equality to matters pertaining to worship or to acts relating to sanctity and reverence. They rather contend that within the area of the *Ḥaram* there should be equality in other respects as well. They are also of the opinion that the land of Makka falls into the category of common *waqf*, i.e. endowment on behalf of God. Hence, none has any property rights over its land or its buildings. Anyone can stay wherever he likes. No one has the right to stop anyone from staying wherever he wants nor can anyone be evicted from the place where he is staying.

These scholars marshal a number of traditions in support of this view. For instance, they adduce a *ḥadīth* narrated by 'Abd Allāh ibn 'Umar to the effect that the Prophet (peace be upon him) said: 'Makka is a site [for pilgrims]; its land may not be sold nor its buildings rented.' (See the comments of Qurṭubī and Jaṣṣās on the verse. The former attributes the transmission of the *ḥadīth* to 'Abd Allāh ibn 'Amr ibn al-'Āṣ rather than to 'Abd Allāh ibn 'Umar – Ed.) Ibrāhīm al-Nakha'ī also narrates a *mursal* tradition from the Prophet:

'Allah has made Makka a sacred territory: it is unlawful to sell its land or to receive rent on its houses.' (See Ālūsī, *Rūḥ al-Ma'ānī*, vol. 17, p. 138 – Ed.) It may be pertinent to point out that the *mursal*[1] traditions of Ibrāhīm al-Nakha'ī are rated as *marfū'*.[2] This in view of his well-known practice of narrating a *mursal* tradition which was in fact a tradition transmitted by 'Abd Allāh ibn Mas'ūd. 'Alqamah ibn Naḍlah also reported that in the time of the Prophet (peace be upon him) and of Abū Bakr and 'Umar ibn al-Khaṭṭāb the land of Makka was treated as *sawā'ib*, that is, land on which a person might live as long as he needed to, and pass it on to others when he did not. (See the comments of Ibn Kathīr on the verse; and Ālūsī, *Rūḥ al-Ma'ānī*, vol. 17, p. 138 – Ed.) 'Abd Allāh ibn 'Umar reports that 'Umar even issued the order that no Makkan may close his door during the days of *Ḥajj*. In fact Mujāhid reports that 'Umar directed the residents of Makka to keep the courtyards to their houses open; he asked them to have no door to their courtyards so that a pilgrim might stay wherever he wished. (See the comments of Ibn Kathīr on the verse, vol. 3, p. 215 – Ed.) The same tradition is reported by 'Aṭā' who adds that the only exception that was made was in respect of Suhayl ibn 'Amr who, because of his trading requirements, needed to keep his camels in an enclosure. He was, therefore, allowed to have a door to his courtyard. 'Abd Allāh ibn 'Umar says that he who receives rent on his houses in Makka fills his belly with fire. (See the comments of Ibn Kathīr, vol. 3, p. 215; and Ālūsī, *Rūḥ al-Ma'ānī*, vol. 17, p. 138, 'Bay' Arāḍī Makkah wa Ijārat Buyūtihā'. Ibn Kathīr has attributed this statement to 'Abd Allāh ibn 'Amr ibn al-'Āṣ, whereas Ālūsī and Jaṣṣās have attributed it to 'Abd Allāh ibn 'Umar – Ed.) The same opinion is held by 'Abd Allāh ibn 'Abbās who says that Allah sanctified the precincts of Makka into a mosque where all have equal rights. He was of the opinion that the people of Makka had no right to receive any rent from outsiders. In the same vein, 'Umar ibn 'Abd al-'Azīz issued the directive to the governor of Makka that no one may receive rent on houses in Makka.

In view of these traditions, the majority of Successors subscribed to the above-mentioned opinion. Among the leading jurists of that age, Mālik, Abū Ḥanīfah, Sufyān al-Thawrī, Aḥmad ibn Ḥanbal and Isḥāq ibn Rāhawayh are of the opinion that the sale of Makkan land and the renting out of houses there, at least during the *Ḥajj* season, are not lawful. Most jurists concede, however, the right to property on the houses of Makka and, accordingly,

---

1. A *mursal* tradition from the Prophet (peace be upon him) narrated by a Successor, or anyone belonging to the generation(s) following the Successors, stating that the Prophet (peace be upon him) said or did or tacitly approved something, even though the narrator, not being a Companion, did not have any direct contact with the Prophet. (See al-Sayyid al-Sharīf al-Jurjānī, *al-Ta'rīfāt*, Beirut, Dār al-Surūr, n.d., q.v. *'mursal'* – Ed.)

2. A *marfu'* tradition is a tradition from the Prophet (peace be upon him) which has been narrated by a Companion (*ibid.*, q.v. *'marfū''* – Ed.)

Whosoever deviates therein from the Right Way and acts with iniquity,[44] We shall cause him to taste a painful chastisement.	وَمَن يُرِدْ فِيهِ بِإِلْحَادٍ بِظُلْمٍ نُّذِقْهُ مِنْ عَذَابٍ أَلِيمٍ ٢٥

consider it permissible to rent out houses even though they may not rent out land.

This viewpoint seems closer to the spirit of the Qur'ān, the *Sunnah* and the practice of the Rightly-Guided Caliphs. For God did not prescribe *Ḥajj* as an obligatory duty on Muslims around the world in order to provide a source of income to the residents of Makka; nor in order to provide them with an opportunity to fleece pilgrims by charging exorbitant rents. Makka is to be treated as a common endowment for the benefit of all believers. No one has proprietary rights over it. Every pilgrim has the right to stay on any spot that he finds available. (For a detailed discussion of the question and for the traditions mentioned here see the comments of Ibn Kathīr and Ālūsī on the verse. See also Qurṭubī who, however, does not go into details – Ed.)

44. *Ẓulm* does not signify a specific act, but rather embraces all acts that do not conform with righteousness and share the attribute of 'wrong-doing'. Such acts are sinful regardless of the place where they are committed. However, to commit them within the sacred precincts of the *Ḥaram* is all the more iniquitous. Commentators, for example, are of the opinion that if someone swears without there being any legitimate reason for this in the precincts of the *Ḥaram*, then it amounts to blaspheming the *Ḥaram*, and so the present verse applies to such a person.

Apart from ordinary sins, there are certain acts which violate the sanctity of the *Ḥaram* quite directly and blatantly on the grounds of this verse. The following represent some instances of violating the sanctity of the *Ḥaram*.

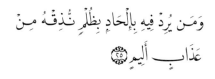

If someone who commits a homicide outside the sacred precincts or commits any other crime which entails a *ḥadd*-punishment and seeks refuge in the sacred precincts, no action will be taken against him as long as he stays there. The *Ḥaram* is considered to have enjoyed this immunity since the time of the Prophet Abraham. The only exception being made, quite temporarily, was on the day of the conquest of Makka after which the age-old inviolability of Makka was restored. The Qur'ān says that: 'Whoever enters it becomes secure' (*Āl 'Imrān* 3: 97). Statements from each of the following Companions, 'Umar ibn al-Khaṭṭāb, 'Abd Allāh ibn 'Umar and 'Abd Allāh ibn Abbās, have authentically been reported to the effect that even if offspring were to get hold of those who had killed their father, they still could not touch them as long as they remained in the precincts of Makka. (See Ālūsī's comments on *Āl 'Imrān* 3: 97 – Ed.) Accordingly, a majority of Successors and Ḥanafī, Ḥanbalī and *Ahl al-Ḥadīth* scholars are of the opinion that *qiṣāṣ* cannot be meted out in the *Ḥaram* area for crimes committed outside it. (See the comments of Ibn Kathīr on *Āl 'Imrān* 3: 97 and Tirmidhī, *K. al-Ḥajj*, 'Bāb mā jā' bi Jarḥat Makkah' – Ed.)

Fighting and bloodshed have also been forbidden within the sacred precincts. The Prophet (peace be upon him) prohibited it in his address on the day following the conquest of Makka, declaring: 'O People! God has sanctified Makka from the very beginning and it will remain so till the Last Day. It is forbidden for anyone who believes in God and the Last Day to shed blood within its precincts.' Then he added: 'If someone were to cite this fighting of mine to legitimize the shedding of blood within the sacred precincts, let him know that God has made it especially lawful for His Messenger, and even so for a certain hour on a certain day, after which its sanctity is restored as it was ever in the past.'

Such is the sanctity of Makka that its self-grown trees may not be felled and its self-grown grass may not be uprooted; nor may any birds and animals be hunted in Makka. Nor may any animals be driven away from Makka for the purposes of game outside its precincts. The only exception in this regard are snakes, scorpions and other harmful animals which may be killed even in the sacred precincts. Exception has also been made with regard to wild grass, there being explicit injunctions on all these matters in the collections of *Ḥadīth*. (See Abū Dā'ūd, *K. al-Manāsik*, 'Bāb Taḥrīm Ḥaram Makkah' – Ed.)

It is a part of the inviolability of the *Ḥaram* that one may not pick up in the *Ḥaram* articles that have been dropped by others. According to a tradition of Abū Dā'ūd: 'The Prophet (peace be upon him) forbade people to pick up the articles dropped by pilgrims.' (See Abū Dā'ūd, *K. al-Luqṭah* – Ed.)

Likewise, whoever visits the sacred area for the purpose of *Ḥajj* or *'Umrah* may not enter without *iḥrām*. There is, however, some difference of opinion among jurists about whether it is obligatory for all persons who enter the sacred area to observe *iḥrām* even if their purposes be for other than Pilgrimage. 'Abd Allāh ibn 'Abbās believes that no one may enter the sacred area without *iḥrām*, regardless of the purpose of his visit. A statement to this effect is attributed to both Aḥmad ibn Ḥanbal and Shāfi'ī. There is, however, an opinion regarding those who frequent the *Ḥaram* in connection with their occupation to the effect that such people are exempt from the requirements of *iḥrām*. This is the opinion of Aḥmad ibn Ḥanbal and Shāfi'ī. There is another opinion, however, that anyone who lives within the *mīqāt* may enter Makka without *iḥrām*. However, those living outside the *mīqāt* may not do so. This position is held by Abū Ḥanīfah.

THE KA'BAH AND THE ROUTE FOR SA'Ī BETWEEN AṢ-ṢAFĀ AND AL-MARWAH

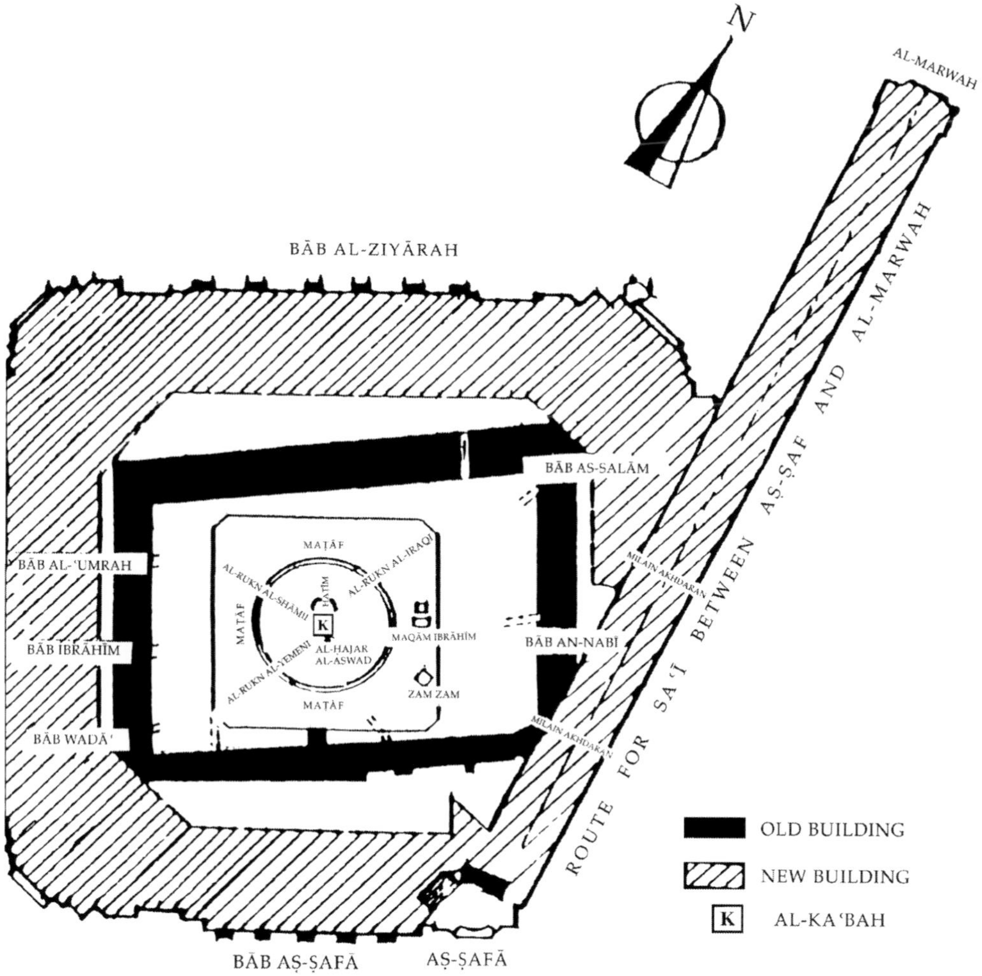

(26) Call to mind when We assigned to Abraham the site of the House (Ka'bah), directing him: "Do not associate aught with Me" and "Keep My House pure for those who walk around it,[45] and for those who stand and who bow down and who prostrate themselves (in worship), (27) and publicly proclaim Pilgrimage for all mankind so that they come to you on foot and mounted on[46] lean camels[47] from every distant point ▶

وَإِذْ بَوَّأْنَا لِإِبْرَٰهِيمَ مَكَانَ ٱلْبَيْتِ أَن
لَّا تُشْرِكْ بِى شَيْـًٔا وَطَهِّرْ بَيْتِىَ لِلطَّآئِفِينَ
وَٱلْقَآئِمِينَ وَٱلرُّكَّعِ ٱلسُّجُودِ ﴿٢٦﴾ وَأَذِّن فِى
ٱلنَّاسِ بِٱلْحَجِّ يَأْتُوكَ رِجَالًا وَعَلَىٰ كُلِّ
ضَامِرٍ يَأْتِينَ مِن كُلِّ فَجٍّ عَمِيقٍ ﴿٢٧﴾

---

45. According to some commentators, this marks the end of the commandment addressed to the Prophet Abraham (peace be upon him). They consider the commandment concerning the proclamation of *Ḥajj* (verse 26) to be part of God's command addressed to the Prophet Muḥammad (peace be upon him). (See Ālūsī's comments on the verse – Ed.) It appears from the context, however, that this last verse is also addressed to the Prophet Abraham (peace be upon him), constituting as it does, a part of the command directed to him at the time of the construction of the Ka'bah. Moreover, it is evident from the thrust of the above discourse that the Ka'bah was constructed, from the very beginning, for the sole purpose of worshipping the One True God, and, hence, a general summons was made to all devotees of God to perform *Ḥajj*.

46. *Ḍāmir*, the word used in the verse, denotes a lean and thin camel. (See *Lisān al-'Arab*, q.v. *ḍ-m-r* – Ed.) The purpose of using such an expression is to portray pilgrims who journey to the Holy Mosque from far-off lands. The result is that their camels become frail because of the long and strenuous journey during which they are deprived of both food and water.

47. This marks the end of the command which was originally given to the Prophet Abraham (peace be upon him). A new directive was, however, added in order to elaborate the original command. Our view that this addition was made is based on the fact that the earlier discourse concludes

(28) to witness the benefits in store for them,[48] and pronounce the name of Allah during the appointed days over the cattle that He has provided them.[49] ▶	لِّيَشْهَدُوا۟ مَنَـٰفِعَ لَهُمْ وَيَذْكُرُوا۟ ٱسْمَ ٱللَّهِ فِىٓ أَيَّامٍ مَّعْلُومَـٰتٍ عَلَىٰ مَا رَزَقَهُم مِّنۢ بَهِيمَةِ ٱلْأَنْعَـٰمِ ۖ

with the directive to circumambulate the ancient House of God. It is obvious that this could not have been enjoined at the time of the construction of the Ka'bah. For further details regarding the construction of the Ka'bah by the Prophet Abraham (peace be upon him) see *Towards Understanding the Qur'ān*, vol. I, *al-Baqarah* 2: 125–9; *Āl 'Imrān* 3: 96–7 and vol. IV, *Ibrāhīm* 14: 35–41.

48. This signifies both religious and worldly benefits. It was precisely because of the blessings of Ka'bah and *Ḥajj* that ever since the days of the Prophet Abraham (peace be upon him), for a period spanning two and a half thousand years, the people of Arabia have had a powerful focal point for their unity, one which preserved their wider Arab identity and prevented it from dissipation under the impact of tribal particularisms. By keeping themselves attached with this centre, and thanks to *Ḥajj* which brought people from all parts of the Arabian peninsula to Makka, their language and culture remained much the same, and they were also able to retain their Arab consciousness. Moreover, they also had the opportunity to exchange views and transmit information and cultural mores. Again, this was due to the great blessing of *Ḥajj*, in that the Arabs enjoyed at least four months of absolute peace in their land in an age of rampant lawlessness. Ultimately, this ensured security of travel for individuals and trade caravans. *Ḥajj* was also a great blessing for the economic life of the Arabs. For further details see *Towards Understanding the Qur'ān*, vol. I, *Āl 'Imrān* 3, nn. 80–1, p. 274 and vol. II, *al-Nisā'* 4, nn. 90–6, pp. 46–7 and *al-Mā'idah* 5, n. 113, pp. 195–6.

After the advent of Islam, the advantages of *Ḥajj* became manifold. Initially, it was a blessing for the Arabs alone. But now Muslims the world over became the recipients of its blessings.

49. The expression *bahīmat al-an'ām* denotes cattle such as camels, oxen, sheep and goats as is clearly stated in *al-An'ām* 6: 142–4.

That the name of God should be pronounced over those animals means that the name of God should be pronounced while slaughtering them. This is mentioned in the phrase that follows.

The allegorical expression 'to pronounce the name of Allah over the cattle Allah has provided them' has been employed throughout the Qur'ān

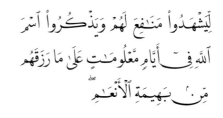

So eat of it and feed the distressed and the needy.[50] ▶	فَكُلُوا۟ مِنْهَا وَأَطْعِمُوا۟ ٱلْبَآئِسَ ٱلْفَقِيرَ ﴿٢٨﴾

in connection with sacrificial animals. On all such occasions when this expression has been used, people are told that slaughtering these animals without pronouncing the name of God over them, or slaughtering them in the name of anyone other than God, is a characteristic practice of unbelievers and polytheists. On the contrary, a Muslim can only slaughter an animal after pronouncing the name of God. Similarly, whenever he makes a sacrificial offering, he is required to consecrate it to God.

There is disagreement as to which days are meant by the 'appointed days' mentioned in this verse. According to one view, the expression signifies the first ten days of the month of Dhū al-Ḥijjah. This view was held by 'Abd Allāh ibn 'Abbās, Ḥasan al-Baṣrī, Ibrāhīm al-Nakha'ī, Qatādah and several other Companions and Successors. Abū Ḥanīfah too subscribes to this view. We also find a statement from Shāfi'ī and Aḥmad ibn Ḥanbal in support of it. According to another statement by Shāfi'ī and Aḥmad ibn Ḥanbal the expression refers to the 10th of Dhū al-Ḥijjah and the three days following. This variation is also supported by 'Abd Allāh ibn 'Abbās, 'Abd Allāh ibn 'Umar, Ibrāhīm al-Nakha'ī, Ḥasan al-Baṣrī, and 'Aṭā'.

According to the third view, the expression signifies three days, from the 10th to the 12th of Dhū al-Ḥijjah. Reports on the authority of 'Umar ibn al-Khaṭṭāb, 'Alī ibn Abī Ṭālib, 'Abd Allāh ibn 'Umar, 'Abd Allāh ibn 'Abbās, Anas ibn Mālik, Abū Hurayrah, Sa'īd ibn al-Musayyab and Sa'īd ibn Jubayr are cited in this respect. Among jurists, Sufyān al-Thawrī, Mālik, Abū Yūsuf and Muḥammad ibn al-Ḥasan al-Shaybānī also hold this view. This is also accepted by the Ḥanafī and Mālikī schools.

There are, however, some isolated opinions on the subject. For instance, the 'appointed days', according to some, end with the 10th of Dhū al-Ḥijjah. According to others, the 'appointed days' include the subsequent day (i.e. the 11th of Dhū al-Ḥijjah) that is, one may sacrifice animals up until that day. These statements, however, are considered tenuous insofar as they are not supported by strong evidence. (See the comments of Ibn Kathīr, Ālūsī and Qurṭubī on the verse – Ed.)

50. Some scholars have interpreted the statement '. . . eat of it and feed the distressed and the needy . . .' to mean that both eating and feeding are obligatory since the directive is couched in the imperative. According to others, this statement means that while it is desirable that he who makes the sacrifice should also eat of the sacrificial animal, what is obligatory is to feed others. This view is held by Shāfi'ī and Mālik.

In the opinion of some other scholars, it is *mustaḥab* (recommended; desirable) that one should both eat of the sacrificed animal and feed others. The reason for this desirability being that in the time of *Jāhilīyah* people considered it unlawful to partake of the meat of sacrificial animals.

As for feeding others, this is desirable because it helps and supports the poor. This is the opinion of Abū Ḥanīfah. Ibn Jarīr al-Ṭabarī, however, cites the statements of Ḥasan al-Baṣrī, 'Aṭā', Mujāhid and Ibrāhīm al-Nakha'ī to the effect that the imperative mode of the verse does not make it obligatory to partake of the animal. According to them, this command belongs to the category of the following commands in the Qur'ān (which simply indicate the permissibility of the acts in question even though they are couched in the imperative form – Ed.):

> But once you are free from Pilgrimage restrictions, then hunt (*al-Mā'idah* 5: 2).
>
> And when the Prayer is finished, disperse through the land and seek of Allāh's bounty (*al-Jumu'ah* 62: 10).

As is evident from verse 5: 2 the imperative to 'hunt' does not make it obligatory for everyone to hunt after being released from the restrictions of *iḥrām*. It is also evident from verse 62: 10 that the imperative to 'disperse through the land' after the Friday Prayer is over is not of an obligatory character. What is meant by the imperative is that there is no harm in doing so. Since some people considered it unlawful to partake of sacrificial meat, they are in effect being told that there is no such prohibition. (See Jaṣṣās, 'Bāb fī Akl luḥūm al-Hadāyā', vol. 3, p. 235 – Ed.) Additionally, the injunction that the distressed and needy should be fed does not mean that the rich and the prosperous may not be offered anything of the sacrificial animals. It is perfectly lawful to distribute sacrificial meat among one's friends, neighbours, and relatives, regardless of whether they are needy or not. This view is supported by the practice of the Companions. According to 'Alqamah, 'Abd Allāh ibn Mas'ūd sent his sacrificial animals through him and directed him to slaughter them on the Day of Sacrifice, partake of them, distribute them among the needy, and also send of them to his brother's house (i.e. the house of 'Abd Allāh ibn Mas'ūd's brother – Ed.). A statement has come down on the authority of 'Abd Allāh ibn 'Umar that one-third of this meat should be consumed, one-third distributed among neighbours, and one-third given to the needy.

(29) Thereafter, let them tidy up[51] and fulfil their vows[52] and circumambulate the Ancient House."[53]

ثُمَّ لْيَقْضُواْ تَفَثَهُمْ وَلْيُوفُواْ نُذُورَهُمْ وَلْيَطَّوَّفُواْ
بِٱلْبَيْتِ ٱلْعَتِيقِ ﴿٢٩﴾ ذَٰلِكَ وَمَن يُعَظِّمْ
حُرُمَٰتِ ٱللَّهِ فَهُوَ خَيْرٌ لَّهُۥ عِندَ رَبِّهِۦ

(30) Such (was the purpose of building the Kaʿbah). Whosoever, then, venerates Allah's sanctities will find it to be good for him in the sight of his Lord.[54] ▶

51. On the 10th of Dhū al-Ḥijjah, the Day of Sacrifice, after the pilgrims are finished offering their sacrifices, they may remove their *iḥrām*, have their hair cut, and take a bath; in sum, the offering of the sacrifice marks the end of the restrictions which are binding upon pilgrims while they are in a state of *iḥrām*. The word *tafath* literally means the dirt and filth caused by travelling. However, in the context of *Ḥajj* the usage carries a special meaning which is alluded to above. For, as long as a pilgrim does not complete certain rituals of *Ḥajj* and sacrifice, he may neither cut his hair, clip his nails, nor clean his body in certain other ways (such as removing the hair from his armpits, etc. – Ed.). It may be noted in this regard that even after a pilgrim has offered sacrifice and become free of the restrictions imposed on him, one restriction nonetheless still remains: he may not have sexual intercourse with his spouse until the completion of *ṭawāf al-ifāḍah.*

52. This refers to the vow which a person might have made on this occasion.

53. The expression 'ancient house' for the Ka'bah is significant. To say that some place is *'atīq* (ancient) conveys the following meanings in Arabic: (1) that it is hallowed by time; (2) that it is independent and does not form anyone's property; and (3) that it is an object of reverence and veneration. All these apply to the place for which the word *'atīq* is used in the verse. The word *ṭawāf* here signifies *ṭawāf al-ifāḍah* or *ṭawāf al-ziyārah* which is performed after one has made the sacrificial offering on the Day of Sacrifice, and after one has removed the pilgrim's garb. This Qur'ānic statement further underlines that this particular *ṭawāf* should be performed after one has offered the sacrifice, removed the *iḥrām* and taken a bath.

54. Apparently this is a general exhortation: that everyone should honour the restrictions laid down by God. In the present context, however,

Cattle have been made lawful for you[55] except those mentioned to you (as unlawful).[56] So shun the abomination of idols[57] and shun all words of falsehood.[58] ▶

وَأُحِلَّتْ لَكُمُ ٱلْأَنْعَٰمُ إِلَّا مَا يُتْلَىٰ عَلَيْكُمْ ۖ فَٱجْتَنِبُوا۟ ٱلرِّجْسَ مِنَ ٱلْأَوْثَٰنِ وَٱجْتَنِبُوا۟ قَوْلَ ٱلزُّورِ ﴿٣٠﴾

the restrictions meant are those enjoined in connection with the Holy Mosque of Makka, *Ḥajj*, *'Umrah*, the *Ḥaram* and the *Ḥaram* of Makka. Moreover, this verse also subtly reproaches the Quraysh who were guilty of driving the Muslims away from the Holy Mosque, of barring them from performing *Ḥajj* and of overlaying *Ḥajj* with polytheistic practices. Likewise, they are reproached for polluting the House of God with polytheism and the desecration of many of those sanctities which were laid down in the time of Abraham (peace be upon him).

55. The statement that 'Cattle have been made lawful to you except those mentioned to you as unlawful' is made for two purposes. One, that the Quraysh and the polytheists of Arabia considered *baḥīrah*, *sā'ibah*, *waṣīlah* and *ḥām* among the animals that were inviolable. It was, therefore, made clear that no sanctity was attached to them; that it was lawful to slaughter all cattle, including these. Second, since the hunting of animals is forbidden in the state of *iḥrām*, it is necessary to clarify that slaughtering cattle and eating them is not forbidden. The main purpose of this above verse, then, is to make these clarifications.

56. This refers to the injunctions about prohibiting the eating of carcasses, blood, the flesh of swine, and animals slaughtered in the name of anything other than God. See *al-An'ām* 6: 145 and *al-Naḥl* 16: 115.

57. One ought to shun worship of idols in the manner a man of sound instinct is repelled by, and tries to flee from, filth. The implicit suggestion being that idols are an abomination and no sooner a person approaches them, than he is contaminated with that filth.

58. The words here seem to have a general import and signify that every kind of falsehood, slander and false testimony is forbidden. However, in the present context, these words are specifically aimed at denouncing the false beliefs, norms, practices and superstitions which are rooted in unbelief and polytheism. To associate others with God in His Divinity and to hold any of God's creatures as His partners in His essence, attributes, rights and authority is the greatest conceivable falsehood and this is denounced here.

(31) Become exclusively devoted to Allah, ascribing Divinity to none other than Him. Whoso ascribes Divinity to aught beside Allah, it is as though he fell down from the sky whereafter either the birds will snatch him away, or the wind will sweep him to a distant place (causing him to be shattered to pieces).[59]	حُنَفَآءَ لِلَّهِ غَيْرَ مُشْرِكِينَ بِهِۦ ۚ وَمَن يُشْرِكْ بِٱللَّهِ فَكَأَنَّمَا خَرَّ مِنَ ٱلسَّمَآءِ فَتَخْطَفُهُ ٱلطَّيْرُ أَوْ تَهْوِى بِهِ ٱلرِّيحُ فِى مَكَانٍ سَحِيقٍ ﴿٣١﴾

This denunciation also embraces the falsehood that had misled the polytheists of Arabia into believing that it was unlawful to kill *baḥīrah*, *ḥām*, etc., for human beings have no right to declare, of their own accord, anything to be lawful or unlawful, as the Qur'ān says: 'And do not utter falsehoods by letting your tongues declare: "This is lawful" and "that is unlawful", thus fabricating lies against Allah' (*al-Naḥl* 16: 116).

Likewise, the interdiction contained in this verse also covers false oaths and false testimonies. This point is further elaborated in the following *ḥadīth:* 'False testimony amounts to associating others with God in His Divinity.' The Prophet (peace be upon him) said so and supported it by reference to the above verse. According to Islamic Law, false testimony is a cognizable offence. Abū Yūsuf and Muḥammad ibn al-Ḥasan al-Shaybānī are of the opinion that if anyone is convicted of false testimony by a court, this should be made public and the person so convicted should be sentenced to a long term of imprisonment. 'Umar ibn al-Khaṭṭāb also held this opinion and applied it. According to Makḥūl, 'Umar ibn al-Khaṭṭāb said: 'He [i.e. the culprit] should be flogged, his head should be shaved, his face should be blackened, and he should be subjected to long-term imprisonment.' (See Jaṣṣās, 'Bāb Shahādat al-Zūr', vol. 3, p. 241, Ibn Kathīr, vol. 3, p. 220, and Aḥmad ibn Ḥanbal, *Musnad*, vol. 4, p. 178 – Ed.) 'Abd Allāh ibn 'Āmir narrates from his father that once a person was convicted by 'Umar ibn al-Khaṭṭāb of false testimony whereupon he got him to stand in a public place and had it proclaimed that the person concerned, the son of so and so, was guilty of false testimony, and that he should be known as such. Thereafter, he imprisoned him. (See Jaṣṣās, 'Bāb Shahādat al-Zūr', vol. 3, p. 242 – Ed.) In our time, this purpose can be served by publicizing the same in newspapers (and via electronic media – Ed.).

59. The word 'sky' in this parable stands for the natural state of man wherein he is the servant of none except God and his nature recognizes no

(32) Such is the fact. And whoso venerates the sanctity of all that have been ordained as symbols of Allah[60] surely does so because it is part of the true piety of the hearts.[61]

ذَٰلِكَ وَمَن يُعَظِّمْ شَعَٰٓئِرَ ٱللَّهِ فَإِنَّهَا مِن تَقْوَى ٱلْقُلُوبِ ﴿٣٢﴾

---

other doctrine than this, i.e. the doctrine of pure monotheism. When a man embraces the guidance brought by the Prophets, it helps him adhere to monotheism on the grounds of knowledge and sound insight and this carries him to even greater heights. On the other hand, when someone embraces polytheism or atheism, he falls away from this natural state and is then confronted with either of the following two situations. First, that Satan and those who are out to misguide others, those who are metaphorically called 'birds' in the above account, pounce upon him, each trying to snatch him away. Second, that he is carried to and fro by his lusts, emotions and fancies, all of which are likened in the above verse to the wind, with the result that he is ultimately hurled into some abysmal ditch.

The word *saḥīq* used here is derived from the root *s-ḥ-q* which signifies 'to grind' (see *s-ḥ-q* in *Lisān al-'Arab* – Ed.). A place can be termed as *saḥīq*, if it is so deep that anything that falls into it is reduced to particles. Here, a depraved state of thought and action is likened to a ditch, where he who falls in is blown to pieces.

60. Reflective of the manifestations of God-consciousness are deeds such as Prayer, fasting and *Ḥajj*, or such objects as mosques and sacrificial animals. For further details see *Towards Understanding the Qur'ān*, vol. II, *al-Mā'idah* 5, n. 5, pp. 128–9.

61. That someone 'venerates' the symbols of God is indicative of his inner piety. It shows that he is possessed of some degree of God-consciousness which prompts him to revere God's symbols. In other words, if someone deliberately desecrates God's symbols, this shows a lack of God-consciousness in him. It indicates either that he lacks belief in God; or if there is in him any vestige of belief in God, he is bent upon adopting a rebellious posture towards Him.[1]

---

1. The sequence of notes in the text here deviates from the original translation of the Qur'ānic text of Sayyid Mawdūdī in *Tafhīm al-Qur'ān*. We have indicated number 61 before 60 in the English translation of the Qur'ānic text in order that those readers who wish to compare the notes in English with those of the original Urdu are not confused – Ed.

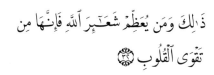

(33) You may derive benefit (from sacrificial animals) until an appointed time.[62] ▶	لَكُمْ فِيهَا مَنَٰفِعُ إِلَىٰٓ أَجَلٍ مُّسَمًّى

62. The preceding verse sets out a general directive: that the symbols of God should be revered, characterizing such reverence as a manifestation of inner piety. The present statement, which follows the previous one, seeks to rectify a common misunderstanding. Sacrificial animals are, as we know, one of God's symbols, a fact that was recognized by the pre-Islamic Arabs, and has been affirmed in this very *sūrah* of the Qur'ān: 'We have appointed sacrificial camels among the symbols of [devotion to] Allah' (22: 36).

It was, however, not quite clear as to what were the practical implications of recognizing sacrificial animals as the symbols of devotion to God. Several questions arise in this respect: when sacrificial animals are being taken to the Ka'bah, is it unlawful to derive any benefit from them? Is it sacrilegious to use them for riding or to employ them to transport goods, to milk them, and consume their milk? The Arabs of the time had misperceptions. The result being that they would take great care of sacrificial animals while leading them to the place of sacrifice. They considered it sinful to make any use of them whatsoever *en route*. The present verse, removing those misperceptions, affirms that one may benefit from the animals consecrated for sacrifice *en route* to the place of sacrifice; that to do so is not at all a derogation of God's symbols. This point is also corroborated by the traditions which have been transmitted by Abū Hurayrah and Anas ibn Mālik. According to them, the Prophet (peace be upon him) once saw someone walking, holding the rein of the camel in his hand, and that he asked him to ride the camel. The man replied that the camel was meant for sacrifice. The Prophet (peace be upon him) nevertheless told him to use it for riding. (See Jaṣṣās, 'Bāb Rukūb al-Badnah', vol. 3, p. 242 – Ed.)

As for the expression 'until an appointed time', this means 'up until the time when an animal is consecrated for sacrifice'. This is the opinion of such commentators as 'Abd Allāh ibn 'Abbās, Qatādah, Mujāhid, Ḍaḥḥāk and 'Aṭā'. According to this interpretation, a person may benefit from these animals as long as he does not set them apart for sacrifice. But once he has designated them as sacrificial animals with the intention of taking them to the Ka'bah, he forfeits the right to benefit from them. (See Jaṣṣās, 'Bāb Rukūb al-Badnah', vol. 3, p. 242 and Ibn Kathīr, vol. 3, p. 221 – Ed.) Such an interpretation, however, does not seem correct. Had this been the case, the Qur'ānic permission above to benefit from them would be pointless. After all, there was never any confusion about benefitting from animals other than those consecrated for sacrifice, and quite evidently, the Qur'ānic permission relates specifically to such animals. Moreover, the verse pointedly deals with animals to whom the appellation 'the symbols of God' might apply, and this applies only to those animals that

Thereafter their place (of sacrifice) is near the Ancient House.[63]

ثُمَّ مَحِلُّهَآ إِلَى ٱلْبَيْتِ ٱلْعَتِيقِ ﴿٣٣﴾ وَلِكُلِّ أُمَّةٍ جَعَلْنَا مَنسَكًا لِّيَذْكُرُوا۟ ٱسْمَ ٱللَّهِ عَلَىٰ مَا رَزَقَهُم مِّنۢ بَهِيمَةِ ٱلْأَنْعَٰمِ ۗ فَإِلَٰهُكُمْ إِلَٰهٌ وَٰحِدٌ فَلَهُۥٓ أَسْلِمُوا۟ ۗ

(34) For every people We have laid down a ritual of sacrifice (– although the purpose of the ritual is the same –) that they pronounce the name of Allah over the cattle He has provided them.[64] Your Lord is One God; so submit yourselves to Him alone. ▶

had already been consecrated for sacrifice. Some other commentators such as 'Urwah ibn al-Zubayr and 'Aṭā' ibn Abī Rabāḥ are of the opinion that the 'appointed time' refers to the time of sacrifice. Before the actual sacrifice one may use sacrificial animals for transport, partake of their milk, take their young ones, shear their wool or hair. Shāfi'ī also upholds this view. Though Abū Ḥanīfah is inclined to the former view, he also grants permission to benefit from sacrificial animals in case of need.

63. It refers elsewhere in the Qur'ān to sacrificial animals as those that are 'brought to the Ka'bah' (*al-Mā'idah* 5: 95). This does not mean that the sacrifice should be performed inside the Ka'bah, or in the Holy Mosque. It rather means that it is meant for sacrifice within the sacred precincts of the *Ḥaram*. This is corroborated by the fact that often when the Qur'ān uses the words 'Ka'bah, the House of Allah', or the 'Holy Mosque', it means the sacred precincts of Makka rather than the building known as the Ka'bah.

64. This verse brings out two fundamental truths. First, that sacrifice has always been an integral part of the system of worship in all versions of Divine Law. The essential requirements for consecrating worship for the One True God is that all forms in which men have ever worshipped other deities be consecrated exclusively for God. For instance, men have bowed down and prostrated themselves before false gods; God's Law, as revealed to the Prophets, however, consecrated these rites exclusively to God. In the past, men made pecuniary offerings to others than the One True God. The Law of God forbade the making of offerings to others than God, and laid down *Zakāh* and *Ṣadaqah* as the acceptable, indeed obligatory forms of pecuniary

And give, (O Prophet), glad tidings to those that humble themselves[65] (before Allah), (35) whose hearts shiver whenever Allah is mentioned, who patiently bear whatever affliction comes to them, who establish Prayer, and who spend (for good purposes) out of what We have provided them.[66]

وَبَشِّرِ ٱلْمُخْبِتِينَ ﴿٣٤﴾ ٱلَّذِينَ إِذَا ذُكِرَ ٱللَّهُ وَجِلَتْ قُلُوبُهُمْ وَٱلصَّٰبِرِينَ عَلَىٰ مَآ أَصَابَهُمْ وَٱلْمُقِيمِى ٱلصَّلَوٰةِ وَمِمَّا رَزَقْنَٰهُمْ يُنفِقُونَ ﴿٣٥﴾

offerings to God. In the past people visited the shrines of false gods; the Law declared certain sites to be sacred or the House of God, and directed believers to make Pilgrimage to and circumambulate around them. Men had fasted for the sake of others than God; the Law of God laid down that men shall fast, but only for the sake of the One True God. Likewise, men had offered sacrificial animals at the altars of deities: the Law prohibited all sacrificial offerings to anyone other than the One True God, and made it obligatory that such sacrifices be offered to Him.

The other point emphasized in this verse is that what really matters is that sacrifice be truly made for the sake of God rather than for the legal minutiae of the act. Whilst details of sacrifice have varied in different times, lands, and communities, the common denominator, however, has always been the spirit and purpose of sacrifice.

65. It is hard to find a one-word equivalent for *mukhbitīn*. Essentially, it embraces the following three meanings: (1) to eschew arrogance and vanity and humble oneself before God; (2) to feel gratified at serving God; and (3) to feel satisfied with whatever God has decreed. (See Ālūsī, *Rūḥ al-Ma'ānī*, vol. 4, p. 154 – Ed.)

66. As we have pointed out earlier, God never calls the things that are unlawfully earned or are inherently impure as His sustenance (*rizq*). The meaning of this verse, therefore, is that believers spend out of the lawful and wholesome sustenance bestowed on them by God. Again, this spending is not to be understood in its absolute sense. For the spending which is approved by Islam consists of spending to meet the legitimate needs of oneself and one's family, spending to assist one's relatives, neighbours and the needy, spending to support acts of public welfare, and spending in order to generously contribute to efforts aimed at upholding the Word of God. The Qur'ān does not sanction extravagant expenditure, nor spending on luxury, nor excessive ostentatious

(36) We have appointed sacrificial camels[67] among the symbols of (devotion to) Allah. There is much good[68] in them for you. ▶	وَٱلْبُدْنَ جَعَلْنَـٰهَا لَكُم مِّن شَعَـٰٓئِرِ ٱللَّهِ لَكُمْ فِيهَا خَيْرٌ

spending to display one's piety. Such spending is not *infāq*, because it is not sufficiently meritorious. Such forms of expenditure are in fact condemned as extravagant and wasteful. At the same time, the Qur'ān does not approve of a person being stingy and niggardly in his spending, of spending so sparingly that one's dependants live in unduly straitened circumstances, spending on oneself much less than is warranted by one's financial position, or an aversion to providing assistance to God's creatures. Whatever a person spends in this way is not deemed, in Islamic parlance, as *infāq*. It is rather considered as *bukhl* (miserliness; niggardliness) or *shuḥḥ al-nafs* (covetousness; avarice).

67. In Arabic usage, the word *budn* which is used in this verse denotes camels only.[1] However, the Prophet (peace be upon him) clarified that it is permissible to sacrifice oxen as well as camels. As with camels, seven people may have a share in the sacrifice of an oxen. Jābir ibn 'Abd Allāh reported that 'the Prophet (peace be upon him) commanded us that we may share in sacrifice: a camel on behalf of seven persons and also a cow on behalf of seven persons'. (See Muslim, *K. al-Ḥajj*, 'Bāb Bayān Wujūb al-Iḥrām wa annahū yajūz Ifrād al-Ḥajj wa al-Tamattu' wa al-Qirān'.) In Muslim the words of the tradition narrated by Jabīr are as follows:

أمرنا رسول الله صلى الله عليه وسلم أن نشترك في الأضاحي البدنة عن سبعة والبقرة عن سبعة

68. To say that 'there is much good for you in them' implies that people derive much benefit from them. This is suggestive of why people should sacrifice animals: in other words, man is required to make sacrifices in the name of God for the innumerable benefits that have been bestowed upon him by God. Sacrifice, however, should not only be offered to thank God, but also to acknowledge His Supremacy and Lordship. It is required that man should fully appreciate all that he has is an endowment from God.

As far as sacrifice is concerned, such an appreciation should fill man's heart and should be manifest from his actions. Sacrifice indeed is quite pervasive. *Īmān* and *islām* constitute the sacrifice of one's inner self. Prayer and fasting represent bodily sacrifice. *Zakāh* represents sacrifice of the wealth which God

1. This seems questionable.The word *budn* seems to signify both camels and oxen. See *b-d-n* in *Lisān al-'Arab*, root *b-d-n*. See also Ālūsī, *Rūḥ al-Ma'ānī*, vol. 17, p. 155 – Ed.)

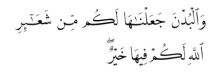

So make them stand (at the time of sacrifice)[69] and pronounce the name of Allah over them,[70] and when they ▶	فَٱذۡكُرُواْ ٱسۡمَ ٱللَّهِ عَلَيۡهَا صَوَآفَّۖ فَإِذَا

has granted us in a variety of forms. *Jihād* represents the sacrifice of time, and of mental and physical capacities. Fighting in the way of God represents the sacrifice of life. Each of these amount to thanking God for the different kinds of bounties and endowments we have received from Him. Likewise, the sacrifice of animals has also been enjoined in order that we may thank God and acknowledge the great favour He has conferred upon us by His subduing on our behalf a great many of the animals He created. As a result, we benefit from them: we ride them, we employ them in cultivation, in transporting goods, and we partake of their meat and milk. In fact, we also use their hair, blood and bones in countless ways.

69. It needs to be pointed out that a camel is slaughtered in a standing position. One of its feet is tied, and a sharp knife slits through its throat, causing an abundance of blood to gush out. After a considerable amount of blood is drained out, the camel falls to the ground. This is what is meant by the word *ṣawāff*. 'Abd Allāh ibn 'Abbās, Mujāhid and Ḍaḥḥāk have also explained the verse in this sense. (See Ibn Kathīr, vol. 2, p. 223 – Ed.) In fact this mode of slaughter is also reported on the authority of the Prophet (peace be upon him). According to a tradition in both *Ṣaḥīḥ al-Bukhārī* and *Ṣaḥīḥ Muslim*, 'Abd Allāh ibn 'Umar once observed someone slaughtering a camel while it was in the sitting position. To which he said: 'Slaughter it while it is in a standing position, and is tied, as was the practice of Abū al-Qāsim [i.e. the Prophet Muḥammad] (peace be upon him).' (See Bukhārī, *K. al-Ḥajj*, 'Bāb Naḥr al-Ibl Muqayyadah' and Muslim, *K. al-Ḥajj*, 'Bāb Naḥr al-Budun' – Ed.) It is also narrated by Jābir ibn 'Abd Allāh that the Prophet (peace be upon him) and his Companions used to tie one leg of the camel such that it was standing on its remaining three legs and then they would slaughter it. (See Abū Dā'ūd, *K. al-Manāsik*, 'Bāb Kayfa Tunḥar al-Budun' – Ed.) This mode of slaughtering is also implicit in the present Qur'ānic verse which says: '. . . and when they fall down on their sides' (*al-Ḥajj* 22: 36). For a camel can only fall down if it is slaughtered in a standing position; had it been lying on the ground at the time of slaughter the above account would not be applicable.

70. These words once again reinforce the point that an animal does not become lawful unless it is slaughtered in the name of God. Hence, God does not direct us to slaughter an animal, but simply to pronounce His name on it. The fact that this expression signifies the slaughtering of animals establishes

fall down on their sides[71] (after they are slaughtered), eat and also feed them who do not ask and those who ask. ▶	وَجَبَتْ جُنُوبُهَا فَكُلُوا۟ مِنْهَا وَأَطْعِمُوا۟ ٱلْقَانِعَ وَٱلْمُعْتَرَّ ۚ

that in Islamic Law there is no concept of slaughtering an animal without pronouncing God's name on it.

It is pertinent to point out that the practice of saying: بسم الله، الله اكبر while slaughtering an animal is derived from the present verse. For it lays down the directive to pronounce God's name while slaughtering animals, whereas verse 37 identifies that God should be magnified in recognition of His bestowal of true Guidance. In the traditions, we find mention of several sets of expressions to be pronounced at the time of slaughtering an animal.

Some of the formulas recited on this occasion are:

(1) بسم الله والله اكبر، اللهم منك ولك

'In the name of Allah; Allah is Great. O Allah! This is from You and this is for You.' (See the comments of Ālūsī, *Rūḥ al-Ma'ānī*, vol. 17, p. 155 on verse 36 – Ed.)

(2) بسم الله، لاإلـه إلا الله، اللهم منك ولك

'Allah is Great. There is no god other than Allah. Allah! This is from You and is offered to You.' (See the comments of Ālūsī, *Rūḥ al-Ma'ānī*, *ibid.*, on verse 36 – Ed.)

(3) إنّي وجهت وجهي للذي فطر السماوات والأرض حنيفا وما أنا من المشركين،
إن صلاتي ونسكي ومحياي ومماتي لله رب العالمين لاشريك لـه وبذلك أمرت
وأنا أول الـمسلمين، اللّهم منك ولك

'I have exclusively directed myself to Him Who created the heavens and the earth and I am not of those who associate others with Allah in His Divinity. My Prayers and my [ritual] sacrifice and my living and my dying are all for Allah, the Lord of the Worlds. O my Allah, this is from You and is offered to You.' (See Abū Dā'ūd, *K. al-Aḍāḥī*, 'Bāb mā yustaḥabbu min al-Ḍaḥāyā' – Ed.)

71. 'Falling down on their sides' does not simply mean that the sacrificial animal's body touches the ground when it falls down after slaughter. It also means that its body becomes still when its wreathing ceases and it completely dies. (Thus it is required that until the animal is fully dead, no part of its flesh be cut off – Ed.) The Prophet (peace be upon him) said: 'Whatever is cut

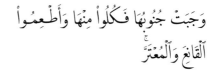

Thus have We subjected these animals that you may give thanks.[72] (37) Neither their flesh reaches Allah nor their blood; it is your piety that reaches Him.[73] He has subjected these animals (to you) that you may magnify Allah[74] for the guidance He has bestowed upon you. ▶

كَذَٰلِكَ سَخَّرْنَٰهَا لَكُمْ لَعَلَّكُمْ
تَشْكُرُونَ ﴿٣٦﴾ لَن يَنَالَ ٱللَّهَ لُحُومُهَا
وَلَا دِمَآؤُهَا وَلَٰكِن يَنَالُهُ ٱلتَّقْوَىٰ مِنكُمْ
كَذَٰلِكَ سَخَّرَهَا لَكُمْ لِتُكَبِّرُوا۟
ٱللَّهَ عَلَىٰ مَا هَدَىٰكُمْ

off from an animal that is alive, is like a carcass.' (See Abū Dā'ūd, Tirmidhī and Aḥmad ibn Ḥanbal's *Musnad*.) (See Abū Dā'ūd, *K. al-Ṣayd*, 'Bāb fī Ṣayd Quṭi'a minhu Qiṭ'ah', Tirmidhī, *K. al-Aḍāḥī*, 'Bāb mā quṭi'a min al-Ḥayy fa huwa Mayyit' and Aḥmad ibn Ḥanbal, *Musnad*, vol. 5, p. 218 – Ed.)

72. This again alludes to the reason for instituting the ritual of sacrificing animals: the purpose is to offer thanks to God for His great favour in making the cattle subservient to man.

73. In pre-Islamic times, the Arabs used to offer the flesh of the animals they sacrificed at the altars of idols. In like manner, they brought the flesh of animals so sacrificed to the Ka'bah, smearing the walls of the Ka'bah with their blood. Exposing the underlying folly of this practice, the Qur'ān points out that what reaches God is not the blood or the flesh of the sacrificed animal, but rather piety. If a man sacrifices an animal out of genuine feelings of gratitude to God, and does so with purity of intention and for the sake of God alone, then the purity of his spirit and intention is bound to reach God. Devoid of that purity of spirit, however, the mere offering of blood and flesh are meaningless. The same point is made in the following *ḥadīth* which states that the Prophet (peace be upon him) said: 'God does not look at your faces or complexions; He rather looks at your intentions and your deeds.' (See Ibn Mājah, *K. al-Zuhd*, 'Bāb al-Qanā'h' and Aḥmad ibn Ḥanbal, *Musnad*, vol. 2, p. 285. In both these works there occurs the word أموالكم instead of آلوانكم – Ed.)

74. That is, one should sincerely acknowledge God's greatness and paramountcy, and this should be reflected in one's deeds. Here, once again, we find reference to the objective of sacrifice. Sacrifice has been made obligatory not only to express man's gratitude to God for making the cattle subservient to him, it has also been instituted in order that man may fully remember, both in thought and deed, the Lordship of God Who subjected the cattle, His creatures, to man's control. This enables man to avoid falling prey

to the illusion that he is the true master of whatever he happens to possess. The formula recited at the time of slaughtering an animal (see n. 70 above), emphatically states that God is the true Master of everything including the animals that men sacrifice: 'O my Allah, this is from You and is offered to You.' (See Ibn Mājah, *K. al-Aḍāḥī*, 'Bāb Aḍāḥī Rasūl Allāh' – Ed.)

It must also be pointed out here that the Qur'ānic injunction with regard to sacrifice is not just meant for pilgrims. Nor is it meant to be performed only in Makka at the time of *Ḥajj*. Sacrifice is obligatory on all Muslims who can afford it, regardless of where they might be. For, by offering this sacrifice, they can thank God for making the cattle subservient to them and, thereby, extol the greatness of God. Indeed, Muslims who are unable to perform Pilgrimage, often sacrifice animals at the time of *Ḥajj*, and in this way at least they are able to do one thing that all pilgrims do in the neighbourhood of the Ka'bah.

The obligatory nature of sacrificing animals is amply borne out by a number of sayings of the Prophet (peace be upon him). Many authentic traditions establish that the Prophet (peace be upon him) used to sacrifice animals on the occasion of *'Īd al-Aḍḥā* during the Madīnan period of his life, and that sacrifice came into vogue among Muslims for that reason. Abū Hurayrah narrates that the Prophet (peace be upon him) said: 'He who has the means and yet does not offer sacrifice shall not approach our Prayer-place.' (See Ibn Mājah, *K. al-Aḍāḥī*, 'Bāb al-Aḍāḥī Wājibah am lā' – Ed.) Whilst all narrators of this tradition are reliable, the only disagreement there is relates to whether the tradition goes back to the Prophet himself or stops at the Companions. According to another tradition narrated by 'Abd Allāh ibn 'Umar: 'The Prophet (peace be upon him) stayed in Madina for ten years and every year he made a sacrifice.' (See Tirmidhī, *K. al-Aḍāḥī*, 'Bāb al-Dalīl 'alā ann al-Uḍḥiyyah Sunnah' – Ed.) According to still another tradition, Anas ibn Mālik narrates that on the day of *'Īd al-Aḍḥā* the Prophet (peace be upon him) said: 'He who has slaughtered before the Prayer should repeat his sacrifice. As for him who sacrifices after the Prayer, his sacrificial duty is completed, and he [will be deemed] to have correctly followed the way of Muslims.' (See Bukhārī, *K. al-Aḍāḥī*, 'Bāb Sunnat al-Uḍḥiyyah wa qāla Ibn 'Umar hiya Sunnah wa Ma'rūf'. The words of the *ḥadīth* from Anas ibn Mālik in Bukhārī are as follows:

من ذبح قبل الصلاة فإنما ذبح لنفسه ومن ذبح بعد الصلاة فقد تم نسكه وأصاب سنة المسلمين – Ed.)

Now, it is known that on the Day of Sacrifice [that is, on the 10th of Dhū al-Ḥijjah] no Prayer is held in Makka. Hence the whole question of sacrificing animals before or after the *'Īd* Prayer in Makka is totally irrelevant. Hence, it is certain that the Prophet's above statement was not made on the occasion of *Ḥajj* in Makka, it could only have been made in Madina. According to a tradition narrated by Jābir ibn 'Abd Allāh, on one occasion when the Prophet (peace be upon him) led the *'Īd al-Aḍḥā* Prayer in Madina, some people thought

Give glad tidings, (O Prophet), to those who do good. (38) Surely[75] Allah defends those who believe. ▶	وَبَشِّرِ ٱلْمُحْسِنِينَ ﴿٣٧﴾ ۞ إِنَّ ٱللَّهَ يُدَٰفِعُ عَنِ ٱلَّذِينَ ءَامَنُوٓا۟

that he had offered the sacrifice before the Prayer. So thinking, they offered their own. When the Prophet (peace be upon him) came to know of this he directed those people to repeat their sacrifice. (See Muslim, *K. al-Aḍāḥī*, 'Bāb Sunan al-Uḍḥiyyah' – Ed.)

Thus, it is beyond all doubt that the sacrifice made by Muslims all over the world on the occasion of *'Īd al-Aḍḥā* is a *sunnah* introduced by the Prophet (peace be upon him). If there is any disagreement on the subject it is whether offering the sacrifice is a *wājib* (obligatory) or simply a *sunnah* (i.e. a recommended) act. Ibrāhīm al-Nakha'ī, Abū Ḥanīfah, Mālik, Muḥammad ibn al-Ḥasan al-Shaybānī and, according to one report, Abū Yūsuf regard it as *wājib* whereas Shāfi'ī and Aḥmad ibn Ḥanbal consider it a *sunnah*. Sufyān al-Thawrī is also of the opinion that he who does not offer the sacrifice is not guilty of a sin. Nonetheless, no Muslim scholar subscribes to the opinion that if Muslims abandoned it altogether it would not be a sin. The preposterous view that the institution of sacrifice can be altogether abolished is an innovation of our own times and has been put forward by people who are guided by nothing else but their own desires.

75. This marks the beginning of a new discourse. In order to better understand it, one should recall that this part was revealed on the occasion of the first *Ḥajj* after the Muslims had migrated to Madina. Obviously, both the *Muhājirūn* and *Anṣār* were quite annoyed over the fact that they had been denied the opportunity to perform *Ḥajj* and were forcibly restrained from visiting Makka. Moreover, the persecution perpetrated on the Muslims in Makka was still fresh in people's minds. Additionally, they were incensed at the fact that even after *Hijrah*, the Makkan Quraysh were not prepared to leave them in peace in Madina.

The first part of the discourse revealed on this occasion consists of a detailed discussion of the true purpose of building the Ka'bah, of establishing the institution of *Ḥajj* and laying down the rites pertaining to sacrifice. It was, thereby, shown how the true purpose of all these institutions had been grossly distorted by *Jāhilīyah*. Thus, the Muslims were infused with a sincere zeal to change the current state of affairs, and to do so with a reformist spirit rather than with vengeance. At the same time, by instituting the ritual of sacrifice in Madina, the Muslims were able to share a privilege they had been denied by their enemies. That is to perform a rite which was performed by all pilgrims during the *Ḥajj* season, and to do so while staying in their homes without even making the Pilgrimage. All this because the ritual of

Certainly[76] Allah has no love for the perfidious, the thankless.[77] (39) Permission (to fight) has been granted to those for they have been wronged.[78] ▶	إِنَّ ٱللَّهَ لَا يُحِبُّ كُلَّ خَوَّانٍ كَفُورٍ ﴿٣٨﴾ أُذِنَ لِلَّذِينَ يُقَٰتَلُونَ بِأَنَّهُمْ ظُلِمُوا۟

sacrifice was instituted as a religious rite independent of Pilgrimage so that even those who did not perform *Ḥajj* could still give thanks to God for His blessings and so glorify Him.

In the second part of the discourse, the Muslims are permitted to unsheathe their swords against the injustice to which they had been subjected in the past, and from which they still suffered.

76. The verb *yudāfi'u* is derived from the root *d-f-'* which literally means to ward off, to repel an attack, to defend. When the word *df'* is used as a verb in the present tense, however, it also suggests the following two connotations: first, that there is an enemy which is on the offensive and that the defending party is engaged in repelling it. Second, that this encounter is not a one-time affair. Rather, whenever there is any such offence, it should be met with an operation aimed at resisting it.

If one bears both these meanings in mind, the statement that 'Allah defends those who believe' acquires special significance. It means that the believers are not alone; that God, Himself, is a party with them. He helps and supports them, counters the stratagems of their enemies, and wards off the harm that their enemies try to inflict upon them. The verse, therefore, is in the nature of a tiding from God to the believers. Undoubtedly, nothing else could have inspired them with greater assurance or be a source of greater comfort than this bounty from God.

77. This explains why God becomes a party with the votaries of the truth in the conflict between faith and unbelief. The reason being that those who fight against the truth engage in treachery and are guilty of ingratitude to God for all the bounties bestowed on them by Him. They are guilty of breaching every trust, of responding to each of God's innumerable bounties with ingratitude. Hence, God does not like them and, instead, supports those devotees to the truth who strive against them.

78. We have already mentioned in the introduction to this *sūrah* that it contains the very first verse in which leave was granted to the Muslims to engage in fighting (*qitāl*) in the way of God. The present verse, however, simply grants Muslims the *permission* to fight. It was only later that they were

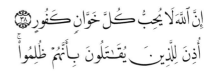

Verily Allah has the power to help them:[79] (40) those who were unjustly expelled from their homes[80] for no other reason than their saying: "Allah is Our Lord."[81] ▶

وَإِنَّ ٱللَّهَ عَلَىٰ نَصْرِهِمْ لَقَدِيرٌ ﴿٣٩﴾
ٱلَّذِينَ أُخْرِجُوا۟ مِن دِيَـٰرِهِم بِغَيْرِ حَقٍّ
إِلَّآ أَن يَقُولُوا۟ رَبُّنَا ٱللَّهُ ۗ

---

commanded to fight. The verses embodying this command are as follows: (1) 'Fight in the cause of Allah those who fight you' (*al-Baqarah* 2: 190); (2) 'And slay them wherever you catch them, and turn them out from where they have turned you out' (*al-Baqarah* 2: 191); (3) 'And fight them until there is no more oppression and the way prescribed by Allah prevails' (*al-Baqarah* 2: 193); (4) 'Fighting is prescribed upon you and you dislike it' (*al-Baqarah* 2: 216); (5) 'Then fight in the cause of Allah and know that Allah hears and knows all things' (*al-Baqarah* 2: 244).

There was only a short lapse of time between the granting of permission to fight and the command to do so. To the best of our knowledge, such permission was granted in Dhū al-Ḥijjah 1 A.H., while the command was given a little before the Battle of Badr, either in Rajab or Sha'bān 2 A.H.

79. Although the Muslims were few in number, God could still make them prevail against the polytheists of Arabia. It might be noted that at the time when the Muslims were granted permission to take up arms against their tormentors, their power was limited to the confines of a small town and the total number of *Muhājirūn* and *Anṣār* did not reach even the figure of one thousand. It was in this situation that the challenge was thrown down to the Quraysh, the latter enjoying the support of many polytheistic tribes of Arabia, and who, a little later on, also gained the support of the Jews.

In this context, it was appropriate that the Muslims be assured that Allah, being 'Immensely Strong, overwhelmingly Mighty' was fully capable of supporting them. This assurance gave them encouragement to take on the whole of Arabia. Moreover, this was also a warning to the unbelievers that they were not pitted against only a handful of Muslims, but were in fact engaged in an encounter with the Almighty God. If they, indeed, had the power to confront Him, they were welcome to try.

80. This phrase makes it quite clear that this part of *Sūrah al-Ḥajj* was definitely revealed after the *Hijrah*.

81. One can possibly gauge the extent of the persecution suffered by the Muslims in Makka, forcing them to migrate to Madina, by the following incidents:

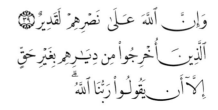

If Allah were not to repel some through others, monasteries and churches and synagogues[82] ▶	وَلَوْلَا دَفْعُ ٱللَّهِ ٱلنَّاسَ بَعْضَهُم بِبَعْضٍ لَّهُدِّمَتْ صَوَٰمِعُ وَبِيَعٌ وَصَلَوَٰتٌ

When Ṣuhayb al-Rūmī was about to migrate, the unbelieving Quraysh told him that since he had arrived in Makka empty-handed and had become rich during his stay there, he could leave only if he left all his belongings behind. Quite obviously, all that Ṣuhayb had earned was by dint of hard work. Yet he was forced to leave everything behind so that when he reached Madina he was once again empty-handed.

Umm Salamah and her husband, Abū Salamah, set out to migrate along with their suckling baby. They were stopped on the way by Banū Mughīrah, the tribe to which Umm Salamah belonged. The relatives of Umm Salamah told her husband that he was free to go wherever he wanted but could not take along any female member of their tribe. He was, thus, forced to leave his wife behind. Then Banū 'Abd al-Asad, the tribe to which Abū Salamah belonged, approached him and told him that since the baby belonged to the tribe, he should also leave that behind. He was, thus, separated from both his wife and child, and remained so for almost a year. Likewise, Umm Salamah had to live alone, and it was only after much difficulty that she managed to retrieve her baby and leave for Madina. She travelled all this distance on a camel with the baby in her lap, using routes dreaded by even armed caravans. (See Ibn Hishām, vol. 1, p. 469 – Ed.)

'Ayyāsh ibn Rabī'ah, a cousin of Abū Jahl, reached Madina along with 'Umar ibn al-Khaṭṭāb. While on his way, Abū Jahl sent someone to 'Ayyāsh with a false report that his mother had vowed that if he did not return to her, she would not move out of the scorching sun into the shade, nor comb her hair. Moved by love for his mother, 'Ayyāsh decided to return to Makka. On his return journey, he was captured by his brothers and brought to Makka tied with ropes. As he entered Makka, one of his brothers announced: 'O people of Makka! Here is an example for you to retrieve the members of your families.' 'Ayyāsh was interned for a long time, but eventually he was rescued by a courageous Muslim who helped him migrate to Madina.

Almost everyone who dared to migrate to Madina was subjected to similar persecution. The Makkan unbelievers were callous and did not even allow these oppressed Muslims to depart in a decent manner. (See Ibn Hishām, vol. 1, p. 474 f. – Ed.)

82. The Qur'ān uses the following expressions: *ṣawāmi'*, *biya'* and *ṣalawāt*. While the word *ṣawāmi'* signifies a place inhabited by monks and ascetics, *biya'* and *ṣalawāt* stand respectively for Christian and Jewish places of worship. *Ṣalawāt* is a derivative of *ṣalawta*, originally an Aramaic word.

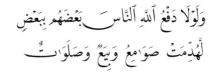

and mosques wherein the name of Allah is much mentioned, would certainly have been pulled down.[83] Allah will most certainly help those who will help Him.[84] Verily Allah is Immensely Strong, Overwhelmingly Mighty.[85] ▶

وَمَسَٰجِدُ يُذْكَرُ فِيهَا ٱسْمُ ٱللَّهِ كَثِيرًا ۗ وَلَيَنصُرَنَّ ٱللَّهُ مَن يَنصُرُهُۥٓ ۗ إِنَّ ٱللَّهَ لَقَوِىٌّ عَزِيزٌ ﴿٤٠﴾

It is not unlikely that the words 'salute' and 'salutation', derive from the word *ṣalawta*, finding their way first into Latin and, thereafter, into English. (For these words see Ālūsī, *Rūḥ al-Ma'ānī*, vol. 17, p. 163 – Ed.)

83. It is indeed one of God's great favours that He has not bestowed perpetual power and authority on any particular group of people. On the contrary, He keeps removing one group of people from its position of power through another. Had a particular group been granted that privilege on a permanent basis, they would have destroyed virtually everything, forts, castles, palaces, and centres of political, industrial and commercial activity as also places of worship. The same point is made elsewhere in the Qur'ān: 'And were it not that Allah repelled men with one another, the earth would surely be overlaid with mischief; but Allah is Bounteous to the people of the world' (*al-Baqarah* 2: 251).

84. That those who summon mankind to monotheism, strive to establish the true faith, and seek to promote righteousness in place of evil are helpers of God is a recurrent theme in the Qur'ān. This is so because the above-mentioned tasks are God's, and those who exert themselves in the performance of these tasks, thereby, become His helpers. For further elaboration see *Towards Understanding the Qur'ān*, vol. I, *Āl 'Imrān* 3, n. 50, p. 257.

85. These are the characteristics of those who help God and who are deserving of God's aid and support. When power is bestowed on them, rather than on those who engage in evil deeds and who strut about arrogantly exulting in their power, such people concern themselves with such noble tasks like establishing Prayer. Likewise, rather than squandering their wealth on luxury and self-indulgence, they use it in the way of *Zakāh*. Again, they use their power to promote goodness and to extirpate evil.

This verse succinctly states the basic objective of the Islamic state. It also clearly expresses the main characteristics of its functionaries and rulers. Anyone who wants to comprehend the nature of the Islamic state will be able to do so with the help of this single verse.

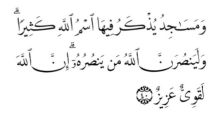

(41) (Allah will certainly help) those who, were We to bestow authority on them in the land, will establish Prayers, render *Zakāh*, enjoin good, and forbid evil. The end of all matters rests with Allah.[86]

(42) (O Prophet), if they give the lie to you,[87] then before them the people of Noah ʿĀd and Thamūd, also gave the lie (to the Prophets), (43) and so too did the people of Abraham and the people of Lot; (44) and so did the dwellers of Midian, and Moses too was branded a liar. Initially I granted respite to the unbelievers for a while and then seized them.[88] ▶

ٱلَّذِينَ إِن مَّكَّنَّٰهُمۡ فِي ٱلۡأَرۡضِ أَقَامُواْ ٱلصَّلَوٰةَ
وَءَاتَوُاْ ٱلزَّكَوٰةَ وَأَمَرُواْ بِٱلۡمَعۡرُوفِ وَنَهَوۡاْ عَنِ
ٱلۡمُنكَرِۗ وَلِلَّهِ عَٰقِبَةُ ٱلۡأُمُورِ ﴿٤١﴾ وَإِن
يُكَذِّبُوكَ فَقَدۡ كَذَّبَتۡ قَبۡلَهُمۡ قَوۡمُ نُوحٖ
وَعَادٞ وَثَمُودُ ﴿٤٢﴾ وَقَوۡمُ إِبۡرَٰهِيمَ وَقَوۡمُ لُوطٖ
﴿٤٣﴾ وَأَصۡحَٰبُ مَدۡيَنَۖ وَكُذِّبَ مُوسَىٰ
فَأَمۡلَيۡتُ لِلۡكَٰفِرِينَ ثُمَّ أَخَذۡتُهُمۡۖ

86. It is, in fact, God Who decides to whom governance of a territory should be entrusted. People who are intoxicated with power are prone to misunderstand that it is they who decide the fate of people. But God, Who has the power to transform a tiny seed into a huge tree, and Who conversely, can turn a huge tree into a pile of ashes, also has the power to strike a fatal blow and make an example of those who, by their acts of repression, struck terror into the hearts of people making themselves appear too well entrenched to be removed from power. On the other hand, He can also raise the drown-trodden to heights of power that none can dream of.

87. This alludes to the unbelievers of Makka.

88. No people in the past were visited with God's scourge immediately after they rejected the Prophet sent to them, calling him a liar. On the contrary, each people was granted respite several times in order that they might understand and mend their ways. Yet each of them was eventually punished after all the dictates of justice had been fully met. The unbelievers of Makka should, therefore, not misperceive the fact that they have not as

How dreadful was My punishment![89] (45) How many towns have We destroyed because their people were steeped in iniquity: so they lie fallen down upon their turrets! How many wells[90] lie deserted; and how many towering palaces lie in ruins! (46) Have they not journeyed in the land that their hearts might understand and their ears might listen? For indeed it is not the eyes that are blinded; it is rather the hearts in the breasts that are rendered blind.[91]

فَكَيْفَ كَانَ نَكِيرِ ﴿٤٤﴾ فَكَأَيِّن مِّن قَرْيَةٍ
أَهْلَكْنَـٰهَا وَهِىَ ظَالِمَةٌ فَهِىَ خَاوِيَةٌ عَلَىٰ
عُرُوشِهَا وَبِئْرٍ مُّعَطَّلَةٍ وَقَصْرٍ مَّشِيدٍ ﴿٤٥﴾ أَفَلَمْ
يَسِيرُوا۟ فِى ٱلْأَرْضِ فَتَكُونَ لَهُمْ قُلُوبٌ
يَعْقِلُونَ بِهَآ أَوْ ءَاذَانٌ يَسْمَعُونَ بِهَا ۖ فَإِنَّهَا
لَا تَعْمَى ٱلْأَبْصَـٰرُ وَلَـٰكِن تَعْمَى ٱلْقُلُوبُ
ٱلَّتِى فِى ٱلصُّدُورِ ﴿٤٦﴾

---

yet been punished and they should not, therefore, look upon the warnings of the Prophet (peace be upon him) as hollow and baseless. They should instead realize that the respite which they are enjoying has been granted to them in keeping with God's way of dealing with nations to whom He sends Prophets. If they do not make proper use of the respite granted to them they are bound to meet the same fate as that of their predecessors and be dealt an awesome punishment.

89. The word *nakīr* used in the verse is far too rich to be adequately expressed by a one-word equivalent such as punishment. The word rather signifies two things: (1) strong disapproval of someone's evil ways; (2) the infliction of a severe punishment on him, a punishment that reduces him to a miserable thing, so miserable he does not even remain recognizable. In view of the above, the Qur'ānic statement means that by incurring God's Wrath for their misdeeds, a woeful fate has befallen them.

90. In Arabic usage, the word *bi'r* connotes 'well' in addition to 'habitat'. When a town is inhabited by a particular tribe it is also mentioned by reference to its well. Likewise, if an Arab is told that all the wells are dried up, he readily understands that this alludes to the desertion and abandonment of that habitat.

91. One should not lose sight of the fact that the Qur'ānic discourse is couched in literary rather than scientific phraseology. One should not, therefore, get stuck with the question of how can anyone say that the organ,

(47) They ask you to hasten the punishment.[92] Allah shall most certainly not fail His promise; but a Day with your Lord is as a thousand years of your reckoning.[93] (48) How many towns did I respite at first though they were steeped in iniquity, and then I seized them! To Me are all destined to return.

(49) Say (O Muḥammad): "O people! I have been sent to you only as a plain warner[94] (before the Doom strikes you)." ▶

وَيَسْتَعْجِلُونَكَ بِٱلْعَذَابِ وَلَن يُخْلِفَ ٱللَّهُ
وَعْدَهُۥ ۚ وَإِنَّ يَوْمًا عِندَ رَبِّكَ كَأَلْفِ سَنَةٍ
مِّمَّا تَعُدُّونَ ﴿٤٧﴾ وَكَأَيِّن مِّن قَرْيَةٍ أَمْلَيْتُ
لَهَا وَهِىَ ظَالِمَةٌ ثُمَّ أَخَذْتُهَا وَإِلَىَّ ٱلْمَصِيرُ
﴿٤٨﴾ قُلْ يَٰٓأَيُّهَا ٱلنَّاسُ إِنَّمَآ أَنَا۠ لَكُمْ
نَذِيرٌ مُّبِينٌ ﴿٤٩﴾

---

the heart, which is located in man's bosom, think? In literary usage, emotions, feelings, thoughts, in fact all actions of the brain are ascribed to the heart. When a person says that he remembers something, he expresses the idea by saying that such and such a thing is preserved or stored in his heart.

92. This refers to the ludicrous statement repeatedly made by the Makkan unbelievers to the effect that if Muḥammad (peace be upon him) was indeed a Prophet sent by God, then why had his detractors not been visited by the scourge that ought to afflict those who deny a true Prophet? Why did such a scourge not specifically visit them even though they had repeatedly been warned by their Prophet that were they to deny him they would be seized by a calamity?

93. It is preposterous to think that the consequences of obeying or disobeying God's injunctions can be observed instantly. If a nation is warned that a certain pattern of behaviour it follows will prove catastrophic, it is absurd for them to retort that they have taken that course for the last ten, twenty, or fifty years, and still no calamity has befallen them. For it often takes not days, months or years, but centuries for the consequences of a people's behaviour to become fully evident.

94. It is clarified here that the decision about the fate of a people does not rest with the Prophet (peace be upon him). His job is merely to warn them before God's punishment actually overtakes them. As for the ultimate decision,

(50) So those who believe and act righteously shall be granted forgiveness and an honourable sustenance,[95] (51) whereas those who strive against Our Signs, seeking to profane them, they are the friends of the Fire!

(52) Never did We send a Messenger or a Prophet before you[96] (O Muḥammad), but that whenever he had a desire,[97] Satan interfered with that desire.[98] ▶

فَالَّذِينَ ءَامَنُوا۟ وَعَمِلُوا۟ ٱلصَّـٰلِحَـٰتِ لَهُم
مَّغْفِرَةٌ وَرِزْقٌ كَرِيمٌ ﴿٥٠﴾ وَٱلَّذِينَ
سَعَوْا۟ فِىٓ ءَايَـٰتِنَا مُعَـٰجِزِينَ أُو۟لَـٰٓئِكَ
أَصْحَـٰبُ ٱلْجَحِيمِ ﴿٥١﴾ وَمَآ أَرْسَلْنَا مِن
قَبْلِكَ مِن رَّسُولٍ وَلَا نَبِىٍّ إِلَّآ إِذَا
تَمَنَّىٰٓ أَلْقَى ٱلشَّيْطَـٰنُ فِىٓ أُمْنِيَّتِهِۦ

---

it rests with God alone. He alone decides who is to be granted respite and till when, and who is to be punished and in what manner.

95. The word *maghfirah* signifies overlooking one's faults, weaknesses and being indulgent. The other expression used here, *rizq karīm*, signifies the sustenance which is both instrinsically good and which is provided in an honourable manner.

96. For further clarification on the distinction between the terms *rasūl* and *nabī* see *Towards Understanding the Qur'ān*, vol. V, *Maryam* 19, n. 30, pp. 161–3.

97. The word *tamannā* is employed in Arabic to denote two things (see *m-n-y* in *Lisān al-'Arab* – Ed.): (1) to wish and yearn for something, and (2) to recite.

98. Were the word *tamannā* to be taken in the first sense, the verse would mean that Satan obstructs the fulfilment of the wishes of all Prophets and Messengers, but God fulfils them despite Satan's efforts. Taken in the second sense, (namely, that of recitation), the verse would mean that whenever the Prophet (peace be upon him) recited the Word of God to people, Satan sowed doubts in their hearts, dressed it up with weird meanings, and prompted people to misconstrue the Qur'ān in every possible sense other than the right one.

Allah eradicates the interference of Satan and strengthens His Signs.[99] Allah is All-Knowing, All-Wise.[100] (53) (He does this) in order that He may make the evil caused by Satan a trial for those in whose hearts there is sickness (of hypocrisy), whose hearts are hard (and vitiated). Surely these wrong-doers have gone too far in their dissension. (54) (He does this) in order that those endowed with knowledge may know that it is the Truth from your Lord and that they may have faith in it and their hearts may humble themselves before Him. ▶

فَيَنسَخُ ٱللَّهُ مَا يُلْقِى ٱلشَّيْطَٰنُ ثُمَّ يُحْكِمُ
ٱللَّهُ ءَايَٰتِهِۦ ۗ وَٱللَّهُ عَلِيمٌ حَكِيمٌ ﴿٥٢﴾ لِّيَجْعَلَ
مَا يُلْقِى ٱلشَّيْطَٰنُ فِتْنَةً لِّلَّذِينَ فِى قُلُوبِهِم
مَّرَضٌ وَٱلْقَاسِيَةِ قُلُوبُهُمْ ۗ وَإِنَّ
ٱلظَّٰلِمِينَ لَفِى شِقَاقٍۭ بَعِيدٍ ﴿٥٣﴾ وَلِيَعْلَمَ
ٱلَّذِينَ أُوتُوا۟ ٱلْعِلْمَ أَنَّهُ ٱلْحَقُّ مِن
رَّبِّكَ فَيُؤْمِنُوا۟ بِهِۦ فَتُخْبِتَ لَهُۥ قُلُوبُهُمْ ۗ

---

99. According to the first meaning, the import of the statement is that notwithstanding Satan's obstructions, God will see to it that the Prophet's wish is fulfilled. And, quite obviously, what can a Prophet (peace be upon him) wish for other than the successful accomplishment of his mission? God subsequently confirmed the truth of His promise made to the Prophet (peace be upon him) when his mission was indeed fully accomplished.

If, however, the word is understood in the latter sense, the statement would suggest that God removes all the doubts Satan planted in peoples' minds and that He repels all the incriminations made about the teachings of the Prophets. Additionally, whatever misconceptions people might entertain regarding a particular verse are clarified by God in His revealing another verse with clearer import.

100. God knows full well the tricks to which Satan resorted and what their impact was. God's wisdom counters all Satan's evil designs, and frustrates them.

Verily Allah always directs those that believe to the Right Way.[101]	وَإِنَّ ٱللَّهَ لَهَادِ ٱلَّذِينَ ءَامَنُوٓا۟ إِلَىٰ صِرَٰطٍ مُّسْتَقِيمٍ ﴿٥٤﴾

101. That is, God made Satan's evil designs a means of testing people so that those who are righteous may be distinguished from those who are evil. In the nature of things, those whose minds have been corrupted derive wrong conclusions from such things and this in turn becomes a means of misleading them. As for those whose minds are straight, those very things lead them to confirm the truthfulness of God's Prophets and His Books. The result is that these people are led to believe that all these are no more than Satan's mischiefs. They know that the Prophet's call is essentially to nothing other than truth and righteousness. Had this not been so, Satan would not have carried on so desperately.

If one bears in mind the context of the present discourse, one can easily grasp the import of the present verse. The specific stage through which the mission of the Prophet (peace be upon him) was then passing misled many of those who were concerned only with appearances. Such people, therefore, behaved as though the Prophet had failed in his mission. For what people could observe was simply that the person who wished his people to believe in him, virtually found no other way after thirteen years of striving than to bid farewell to his homeland and this with only a handful of followers. When people considered the Prophet's claim that he was God's Messenger and that he enjoyed God's support in this context, or when they considered the proclamation of the Qur'ān that unbelievers who reject a true Prophet are seized with God's scourge, they were inclined to doubt the veracity of both the Prophet and the Qur'ān. In this way the detractors of the Prophet (peace be upon him) were encouraged to let their tongues loose, so much so that they started mocking him, saying: 'Where is God's support that you so much talk about? What has happened to God's scourge against which you have been warning us?'

The preceding verses contain a response to these questions, as indeed do the present ones. There is, however, a difference: while the preceding verses were addressed to the unbelievers, the current ones are addressed to those believers who are somewhat influenced by the unbelievers' propaganda. The main thrust of the present discourse is as follows:

> There is nothing new about a people's rejection of the Messenger sent to them, nor about their calling him a liar. History is replete with such instances. At the same time, the tragic fate which these rejecters suffered is also well known; a fate which they could see with their

own eyes in the ruins of the nations of Arabia that were obliterated by God's scourge. Those who wished to draw any lesson from all that could do so.

As for the query as to why God's punishment did not overtake the Makkans following their rejection of the Messenger (peace be upon him), and their branding him a liar, it is pointed out that the Qur'ān nowhere says that God's punishment will strike down wrong-doers the very moment that they deny the Prophet (peace be upon him). Furthermore, the Prophet (peace be upon him) never claimed that it would be he who would strike them down with a scourge. It is God alone Who decides such punishment, and He does not punish a whole nation in a hurry. Instead, before punishing a people He grants them sufficient respite. He has done so in the past and is doing so even now. Periods of respite sometimes extend to several centuries. Hence, if a nation that denies a Prophet has not been punished so far, this does not mean that the warnings in the Qur'ān amount to no more than empty words.

Also, there is nothing new in the fact that obstructions were set in motion so as to prevent the desires and aspirations of a Prophet from materializing. Nor was there anything new in the false allegations or the storm of doubts and objections against the teachings of a Prophet. All this had been witnessed by previous Messengers. What is important to note, however, is that eventually God smothers all such Satanic mischiefs. Despite all obstructions, the call to truth flourishes and any doubts and misgivings that are created are obviated by the revelation of clear and unambiguous verses. Satan and his disciples employ a variety of designs to bring disgrace to God's Signs. God, however, thwarts these designs and turns them instead into a means of distinguishing between good and bad people. Thus, good people are attracted to the truth, and evil ones are separated, and become distinct from it.

This, then, is the thrust of these verses, as understood in the context against which this discourse was revealed. Regrettably, however, one particular report of this incident has given rise to a serious misunderstanding. This is of such a serious nature that not only the meaning of the verses in question is distorted, but the very foundation of Islam seems to be jeopardized. We are taking note of this, here, such that the students of the Qur'ān are aware of the manner in which they can distinguish between adequate and inadequate methods in the use of historical reports for a proper understanding of the Qur'ān. Basically, we are treating this question at some length so that one may become aware of the unwholesome consequences of accepting, uncritically, all historical reports, and become conscious of the pitfalls in excessive traditionalism, and that one, thus, may come to know the right ways of critically examining the reports that have come down to us. For, if one makes any mistakes in examining these reports, one is bound to end up with faulty interpretations of the Qur'ān. The incident in question is reported as follows:

> The Prophet (peace be upon him) once felt the desire that God reveal something in the Qur'ān that might remove the hatred of the unbelieving Quraysh for Islam so that they might come close to it; or at least that the Qur'ān should not say anything so blatantly critical about their faith that might antagonize them further. It was whilst the Prophet (peace be upon him) had this wish in mind, and he was sitting in a large gathering of the Quraysh that *Sūrah al-Najm* was revealed to him. He, thus, began to recite it, but when he reached the verses: افرأيتم اللات والعزّى ومناة الثالثة الأخرى (Have you seen al-Lāt and al-'Uzzā, and another, the third, al-Manāt, *al-Najm* 53: 19–20), suddenly he involuntarily uttered the following words:
>
> تلك الغرانقة العلى وإن شفاعتهن لترجى
>
> (These are exalted deities whose intercession should surely be looked forward to.)

He then proceeded further, reciting the remaining verses of the *sūrah*. At the conclusion of the *sūrah* when the Prophet (peace be upon him) prostrated himself, all those present in the gathering, both believers and unbelievers, followed suit. The unbelieving Quraysh said that there no longer remained any disagreement between them and Muḥammad (peace be upon him). They contended that their belief was also the same: that while God was the Creator and Sustainer, that did not detract from the fact that other gods and goddesses would still intercede with Him.

The angel Gabriel visited the Prophet (peace be upon him) that same evening and expressed his disapproval of what he had done; his having added to the revelation the sentences which he [i.e. Gabriel] had not brought to him. This grieved the Prophet (peace be upon him) intensely, whereupon God revealed the following verses which occur in *Banī Isrā'īl*:

> They had all but tempted you away from what We have revealed to you that you may invent something else in Our Name. Had you done so, they would have taken you as their trusted friend. Indeed, had We not strengthened you, you might have inclined to them a little, whereupon We would have made you taste double [the chastisement] in the world and double the chastisement after death, and then you would have found none to help you against Us (*Banī Isrā'īl* 17: 73–5).
>
> This incident, however, continued to torment the Prophet (peace be upon him) until this above verse of the present *sūrah* was revealed. This aimed at consoling him, identifying as it did that something similar had happened to the earlier Messengers as well.

At the same time, the Muslims who had migrated to Abyssinia also came to learn that the Quraysh had prostrated themselves along with the Prophet (peace be upon him) when the latter had recited this verse. Understandably, this led them to assume that a reconciliation had been brought about between the Prophet (peace be upon him) and the unbelievers. Many migrants, therefore, returned to Makka, only to learn that the report was false and that the hostility between Islam and unbelief persisted as before. (See the comments of Ibn Kathīr and Qurṭubī on verse 52 – Ed.)

This incident is mentioned by Ṭabarī in his *Tafsīr* as well as by several other commentators in their exegeses of the Qur'ān. It is also found in Ibn Sa'd's *Ṭabaqāt*, in al-Wāḥidī's *Asbāb al-Nuzūl*, in the *Maghāzī* of Mūsā ibn 'Uqbah, and in the *Ḥadīth* collections of Ibn Abī Ḥātim, Ibn al-Mundhir, Ibn Marduwayh and al-Ṭabarānī. The report has also been transmitted on the authority of the following narrators: Muḥammad ibn Qays, Muḥammad ibn Ka'b al-Quraẓī, 'Urwah ibn al-Zubayr, Abū Ṣāliḥ, Abū al-'Āliyah, Sa'īd ibn Jubayr, Ḍaḥḥāk, and Abū Bakr ibn 'Abd al-Raḥmān ibn 'Abbās, the only one among the Companions said to do so.

Leaving aside several minor discrepancies in the details of these various accounts, there are two serious areas of disagreement. First, the utterance ascribed to the Prophet (peace be upon him) in praise of the deities differs in almost every single report. We have attempted to examine all these reports and have found at least fifteen different versions of what the Prophet (peace be upon him) is supposed to have said.

The other major discrepancy is that according to some reports this utterance was instigated by Satan and the Prophet (peace be upon him) mistook this Satanic inspiration for genuine revelation. In other reports, it is claimed that the sentences uttered by the Prophet (peace be upon him) reflected his own desire. According to still others, the Prophet (peace be upon him) had dozed off for a short while and these sentences were uttered in that state, or that he deliberately uttered them, meaning to couch them in the form of a question so as to negate the power of the deities concerned to intercede with God, or that Satan pronounced these words, joining his voice with the Prophet's, the assumption being that that statement was made by the Prophet (peace be upon him), or in other reports that the words were uttered by one of the idolaters.

Ibn Kathīr, Bayhaqī, Qāḍī 'Iyāḍ, Ibn Khuzaymah, Abū Bakr ibn al-'Arabī, Rāzī, Qurṭubī, Badr al-Dīn al-'Aynī, Shawkānī and Ālūsī are among the scholars who reject this report lock, stock and barrel. Ibn Kathīr, for instance, says: 'All the chains of transmission of this report that have been narrated are *mursal* and *munqata'* (interrupted).' Bayhaqī, rejects it, saying that it is not established according to the canons of transmission. When Ibn Khuzaymah was asked about it he said: 'It is an invention of Zanādiqah (heretics).' Qāḍī 'Iyāḍ states: 'That this report is weak is established by the fact that none of the compilers of the six authentic collections of *Ḥadīth* have narrated it, nor does it occur in any sound, uninterrupted, fault-free chain of narration; nor is it narrated by trustworthy narrators.' Rāzī, Abū Bakr ibn al-'Arabī and Ālūsī all examined this report in detail and forcefully rejected it. On the other hand, however, such a leading scholar of *Ḥadīth* as Ibn Ḥajar, a distinguished jurist such as Abū Bakr al-Jaṣṣāṣ, and the rationalistically inclined commentator of the Qur'ān al-Zamakhsharī, and a no less distinguished authority on *Tafsīr*, history and *Fiqh* than Ṭabarī are of the opinion that this report is genuine and regard it as the right explanation of the verse in question. Here is the argument advanced by Ibn Ḥajar:

> The chains of narrators of this report, except the one by Sa'īd ibn Jubayr, are either weak (*ḍa'īf*) or interrupted (*munqaṭa'*). However, the sheer numerousness of the chains of narration of the report suggests that there is some basis to the report. Moreover, it has also been reported through a chain of narration as an uninterrupted tradition backed up by a chain of reliable narrators which has been recorded by al-Bazzār. (This refers to the following chain of narrators: Yūsuf ibn Ḥammād, Umayyah ibn Khālid, Shu'bah, Abū Bishr, Sa'īd ibn Jubayr, 'Abd Allāh ibn 'Abbās.) Although two chains of narration of this tradition are *mursal*, its narrators fulfil the conditions as laid down in the standard works of *Ḥadīth*. Both these chains of narration have been recorded by Ṭabarī; the one through Yūnus ibn Yazīd, is Ibn Shihāb al-Zuhrī's and the other through Mu'ammar ibn Sulaymān and Ḥammād ibn Salamah is from Dā'ūd ibn Abū Hind from Abū al-'Āliyah.

So far as the supporters of this report are concerned, they consider it completely sound. Even its detractors have failed to subject it to critical scrutiny. One group of scholars rejects it simply on the ground that its chains of narrators are not sound. In other words, had this been so, i.e. the chain sound, they would have confirmed the truth of the narration. Another group reject it out of hand on the premise that if the story is accepted as true, everything pertaining to Islam becomes doubtful. To accept the report means there is no strong basis for belief in any of the teachings of Islam. This because there is no way of knowing which elements of Islam have retained their original, pristine form, and which have been corrupted under the influence of Satan, or as a result of human desires.

Obviously, to reject this tradition may appeal to those who are determined to remain loyal to their faith. But surely it is not persuasive for those who are either already in a state of reluctance or who are inclined to scepticism about Islam. Nor does this argument satisfy those who have not made up their minds about whether they should believe or not, and would like to do so only after making further inquiry. Surely, such people cannot accept the proposition that whatever renders Islam doubtful should be rejected *ipso facto*. The contention being that as long as this tradition is endorsed by as much as at least one well-known Companion, several Successors, and a number of reliable narrators of *Ḥadīth*, why should it be dismissed simply on the basis that it renders doubtful the basic tenets of Islam? Why should Islam not be considered doubtful when this story proves it so?

Let us now turn to the right method of criticism to be followed in evaluating the soundness of the tradition in question. If this method is followed, it is evident that regardless of the soundness of the chain of narration, this story is altogether incredible.

The first and foremost factor which establishes the falsity of the report is the internal evidence of the story itself. In this respect, the incident took place at a time when the Muslims had already migrated to Abyssinia and when these migrants heard about it all a number of them returned to Makka. Let us take a look, then, at the chronological sequence of events. (See Ibn Sa'd, *Ṭabaqāt*, vol. 1, pp. 213 f. – Ed.)

According to authentic, historical reports, the migration to Abyssinia took place in the month of Rajab in the fifth year of Prophethood. On learning about this incident and the resultant reconciliation between the Prophet (peace be upon him) and the Makkan unbelievers, a group of migrants returned to Makka after three months, i.e. in the month of Shawwāl during the fifth year of Prophethood. This, unmistakably, establishes that the incident took place in the fifth year after the conferment of Prophethood on Muḥammad (peace be upon him).

It is claimed that the verse of *Banī Isrā'īl* under discussion was revealed as a means of reproaching the Prophet (peace be upon him). The fact is, however, that these verses were revealed after the Prophet's Ascension (*Mi'rāj*). Furthermore, according to the most reliable historical reports, *Mi'rāj* took place in the eleventh or twelfth year of Prophethood. This means, then, that God took the Prophet (peace be upon him) to task for what he had done some five or six years previously!

Moreover, as is clearly indicated by the context, the verse was revealed in 1 A.H. In other words, two and a half years after the Prophet (peace be upon him) was reproached in *Sūrah Banī Isrā'īl*, it is pointed out that the unjustified addition to God's revelation was made by him at the prompting of Satan, and that the addition now stood abrogated.

Can any sensible person believe that the Prophet (peace be upon him) would be reproached for one of his acts six years after it occurred, and that almost nine years after the Prophet's utterance which had brought about God's reproach it would be declared abrogated?

Moreover, according to this report, the incident in question was alluded to in *Sūrah al-Najm*. When the Prophet (peace be upon him) reached the words مناة الثالثة الأخرى (see *al-Najm* 53: 19–20), he added a statement either of his own volition or under Satan's influence. However, after he had added those few words, he resumed the recitation of subsequent verses of the *sūrah*. The tradition in question mentions that on hearing the Prophet's praise for their deities, the Makkan unbelievers felt intensely happy and declared that the difference between them and the Prophet (peace be upon him) had ended.

Now let us attempt to read the relevant verses of *Sūrah al-Najm*, adding the words the Prophet (peace be upon him) is supposed to have interjected, and see how it reads:

> Have you then considered al-Lāt and al-'Uzzā? And al-Manāt, the other one, the third? *These are exalted deities whose intercession should surely be looked forward to*. Shall sons be yours and for Him (i.e. Allah) there should be daughters? This is an unfair division! Nay, these are but names that you have named and Allah has sent down no authority for it. They are merely following conjectures and fancies of their liking without receiving any guidance from Allah (*al-Najm* 53: 19–23).

Just consider the location of the italicized words and you are bound to be struck by its incongruity, by its being totally discordant with the main thrust of the discourse. For, if these words are there, the relevant verses would assert in one breath that the deities of the Makkan unbelievers are exalted and have the power to intercede with God, and in the very next, emphasize the stupidity of the doctrine by identifying the unfairness of the division, i.e. daughters for God, and sons for themselves. This is not only mischievously unfair, but also something for which God has not given any sanction.

Let us disregard for the moment that this statement is too preposterous to have been made by an intelligent person. Let us assume instead that for a moment Satan temporarily had such influence over the Prophet (peace be upon him) that he indeed uttered these words in praise of other deities. But what happened to the audience, the Quraysh? Had they gone altogether insane that notwithstanding a devastating refutation of their beliefs in subsequent verses, they took these two sentences, supposedly uttered by the Prophet, at face value and assumed that their deities had indeed been extolled? It will be seen that the whole thrust of *Sūrah al-Najm*, right from its opening verse to the one that concludes it, is in blatant opposition to the statement that allegedly occurs in between – a statement which affirms an exalted position for the deities of the Quraysh. Does it stand to reason that the Quraysh would listen to the whole of *Sūrah al-Najm*, and still remain convinced that they had ceased to have any differences with the Prophet (peace be upon him)?

This is the internal testimony of the account which establishes its utter baselessness and absurdity. The next point to be considered is whether the circumstantial context mentioned for the revelation of these three verses is in consonance with the sequence of revelation of the Qur'ānic text.

According to accounts of the incident, the verses in question were made a part of *Sūrah al-Najm*, revealed in the fifth year of Prophethood. However, the verses which are supposed to contain the Prophet's reproach occur in *Sūrah Banī Isrā'īl* (verses 73–5). Thereafter, the verses concerned were abrogated and the whole incident explained in *Sūrah al-Ḥajj* (see verses 52–4 – Ed.).

Quite naturally, either of the two things must have happened. The first possibility is that the verses containing the Prophet's reproach and the abrogation of the verses were revealed, one following the other, shortly after the incident took place. In this case, the verses of reproach should have been revealed along with *Sūrah Banī Isrā'īl* and the verse of abrogation along with *Sūrah al-Ḥajj*. If so, it seems very strange, indeed inexplicable, that these interrelated verses did not form part of *Sūrah al-Najm*. Instead, the verses which supposedly censure the Prophet (peace be upon him) were deferred for a full six years, and were then made part of *Sūrah Banī Isrā'īl*. Likewise, it seems strange that the verse clarifying the whole incident was held in abeyance for a further two and a half years, and then not made part of any *sūrah* until the revealing of *Sūrah al-Ḥajj*. This runs counter to the process of the collection of the Qur'ān. For it would suggest that the verses revealed on different occasions were left lying dispersed, separated from one another, and only placed in different *sūrahs* after a lapse of several years.

If the first alternative is not tenable, let us consider the second: that the verses of reproach were revealed six years after the incident, and the verse of abrogation eight or nine years later. This of course lends itself to the criticism we have made above, namely, that this is extremely odd. Moreover, it raises the question of what the events were which occasioned the revelation of these verses of *Sūrah Banī Isrā'īl* and *Sūrah al-Ḥajj*.

This brings us to the third canon of criticism, namely, that the adequacy or otherwise of the interpretation of a Qur'ānic verse should be determined on the basis of whether it fits into the context of the Qur'ānic text. Let us now look at verses 73–5 of *Sūrah Banī Isrā'īl*. Taking note of those verses that precede and follow the ones in question, do we find in them anything that calls for the reproach of the Prophet (peace be upon him), and that too with regard to an incident that had taken place six years previously? One may well consider whether the words employed here إن كادوا ليفتنونك ('They had all but tempted you away . . .' *Banī Isrā'īl* 17: 73) indicate that the Prophet (peace be upon him) was reproached; and also whether the verse can be considered to endorse or refute the Prophet's having fallen prey to the unbelievers' mischievous designs. Likewise, let us look at *Sūrah al-Ḥajj* which is before us, and specifically at the verses that precede and follow the one in question (i.e. verse 52). Is there any reasonable ground to believe how, in this context, the Prophet (peace be upon him) would be abruptly reassured and told not to be too concerned at his act of having mixed with the Qur'ān something extraneous to it? He need not worry because Satan had caused the Prophets of the past to do similar acts, and whenever a Prophet makes such a mistake, God abrogates those verses which have been mixed with true revelation under Satanic influence, and subsequently strengthens His own signs.

We have emphatically stated earlier and would like to reiterate here that no matter how well-supported a tradition might be in respect of its chain of narration, it can never be accepted if it testifies to its own falsity, or if the words of the Qur'ānic text or their context and sequence are in discordance with that tradition. In fact, arguments based on these considerations are so unassailable that they should convince both those who are overly sceptical and those who are unbiased seekers after the truth that the account in question is altogether false.

As for a believer, it is obvious that he can never accept the account in question because it conflicts sharply with a large number of Qur'ānic verses and, hence, can in no way be considered authentic. It is easier for a believer to accept that it was the narrators of the report who were misled by Satan rather than to believe that the Prophet (peace be upon him) was so misguided that he added anything, however insignificant, to the text of the Qur'ān. Nor can a believer entertain the view that the Prophet (peace be upon him) would have toyed with the idea, even for a moment, of adulterating the pure Message of monotheism with elements of polytheism so as to win over unbelievers. Nor is it conceivable that the Prophet (peace be upon him) would have desired that God not reveal to him something that would offend the unbelievers. Nor can it be imagined that revelation was communicated to the Prophet (peace be upon him) in a manner that was not absolutely safe and beyond all doubt. For it is only in such circumstances that it is possible for both Gabriel and Satan to communicate messages to the Prophet (peace be upon him), causing uncertainty in his mind and mistaking the words of Satan for those of Gabriel. Each of these assumptions is opposed to explicit statements of the Qur'ān and is antithetical to our well-established beliefs regarding the Qur'ān and the Prophet (peace be upon him). May God save us from that exaggerated traditionalism which prompts us to accept monstrosities about the Qur'ān and the Prophet (peace be upon him) simply on such technical grounds as the uninterrupted transmission of a tradition, or the trustworthiness of the narrators of that tradition, or the sheer numerousness of the channels through which it has been transmitted.

It seems pertinent at this point to remove a misunderstanding which might agitate some minds because of the story being told by a large number of narrators of *Ḥadīth*. For one might ask: if there is no truth in this story, how could a calumny, which calls into question the integrity of the Qur'ān and the Prophet (peace be upon him), gain currency among the Muslims? How did it come about that such a large number of narrators, including some very prominent and trustworthy ones, took part in transmitting it?

The problem can be well appreciated by turning to the *Ḥadīth* literature itself. The incident, as reported in the works of Bukhārī, Muslim, Abū Dā'ūd, Nasā'ī and Aḥmad ibn Ḥanbal is as follows: the Prophet (peace be upon him) recited *Sūrah al-Najm* and when at its conclusion he prostrated himself, all those present followed suit. This is what took place and there is nothing for us to question about why it did. First, people fell into prostration because of the unusual force of the Qur'ānic verses, made all the more effective by the moving manner in which the Prophet (peace be upon him) recited them. We know that the unbelievers of Makka, despite their lack of belief

(55) The unbelievers will not cease to be in doubt about it until the Hour suddenly comes upon them, or the chastisement of an ominous day[102] overtakes them. ▶

وَلَا يَزَالُ ٱلَّذِينَ كَفَرُوا۟ فِى مِرْيَةٍ مِّنْهُ حَتَّىٰ تَأْتِيَهُمُ ٱلسَّاعَةُ بَغْتَةً أَوْ يَأْتِيَهُمْ عَذَابُ يَوْمٍ عَقِيمٍ ﴿٥٥﴾

in the Qur'ān, were nonetheless well aware of its attractiveness. In fact, it was precisely for this reason that they branded the Prophet (peace be upon him) a sorcerer. However, it appears that some of the Quraysh subsequently regretted their being involuntarily carried away, even if temporarily, by the spell of these verses. It is likely, therefore, that in order to justify their actions they fabricated the story that they had actually joined the Prophet (peace be upon him) in prostration following his recitation of certain verses of the Qur'ān which extolled their deities.

Let us, now, consider the other part of the story, that is that the news about the incident reached the Muslim migrants to Abyssinia in such a way that they were given the impression that reconciliation had come about between the Prophet (peace be upon him) and the Quraysh. The basis for this notion being that many people had actually seen both believers and unbelievers together in a state of prostration. The rumour that the two groups had become reconciled spread far and wide, with the result that 33 migrants returned to Makka.

These three components of the story, the Quraysh falling into prostration, their reason for their so doing, and the return of Muslim migrants from Abyssinia, became so mixed up over the course of a century that a fanciful story emerged to the point at which people who were otherwise trustworthy began to narrate it. Human beings are, after all human beings. Hence we occasionally come across lapses even by those who are otherwise extremely righteous and blessed with mature understanding. Understandably, their lapses cause much greater harm than those of ordinary people.

Those who go to excess in the veneration of our esteemed forbears are at times inclined to uncritically accept their mistaken notions along with the sound opinions that have come down from them. Indeed, they even go a step further and reckon those mistakes as among the good deeds which characterize their overall behaviour. On the other hand, there are those who, actuated by evil intent, deliberately collect and parade the lapses of good people, arguing that the entire heritage of Islam passed on to us by such people should be dumped and set on fire.

102. Literally the word *'aqīm* means 'barren'. Here the word has been employed to characterize a particular day. The implication being that it would be an ominous day when no effort would succeed, when every endeavour on

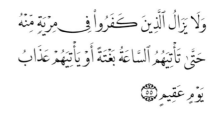

(56) On that Day all sovereignty shall be Allah's and He will judge among them. Then those who believed and acted righteously shall be in Gardens of Bliss. (57) A humiliating chastisement awaits those who disbelieved and denied Our Signs. (58) As for those who migrated in the way of Allah, whereafter they were slain, or died, Allah will certainly grant them a goodly provision. Indeed, Allah is the Best of all those who provide. (59) He will surely admit them to a resort which will please them. Most certainly Allah is All-Knowing, Most Forbearing.[103] ▶

ٱلْمُلْكُ يَوْمَئِذٍ لِّلَّهِ يَحْكُمُ بَيْنَهُمْ ۚ فَٱلَّذِينَ ءَامَنُوا۟
وَعَمِلُوا۟ ٱلصَّٰلِحَٰتِ فِى جَنَّٰتِ ٱلنَّعِيمِ
﴿٥٦﴾ وَٱلَّذِينَ كَفَرُوا۟ وَكَذَّبُوا۟ بِـَٔايَٰتِنَا
فَأُو۟لَٰٓئِكَ لَهُمْ عَذَابٌ مُّهِينٌ ﴿٥٧﴾ وَٱلَّذِينَ
هَاجَرُوا۟ فِى سَبِيلِ ٱللَّهِ ثُمَّ قُتِلُوٓا۟ أَوْ مَاتُوا۟
لَيَرْزُقَنَّهُمُ ٱللَّهُ رِزْقًا حَسَنًا ۚ وَإِنَّ ٱللَّهَ لَهُوَ خَيْرُ
ٱلرَّٰزِقِينَ ﴿٥٨﴾ لَيُدْخِلَنَّهُم مُّدْخَلًا يَرْضَوْنَهُۥ ۗ
وَإِنَّ ٱللَّهَ لَعَلِيمٌ حَلِيمٌ ﴿٥٩﴾

---

man's part would end in failure, when every hope would turn into despair. The other meaning of the expression 'barren day' is that it is a day destined not to turn into night.

In both senses, the expression signifies that the day on which a nation's destruction takes place will be a barren one for that nation. For instance, the day the people of Noah witnessed the great flood was a barren day for them. In like manner, the people of 'Ād, Thamūd and Lūṭ, the people of Midian, and several other nations were totally annihilated by God's scourge. Each of these days was a barren day for the people in question. This because they were unable to witness its morrow. Nor had they any effective device whereby they could avert the disaster.

103. God is All-Knowing, that is, He knows full well who sincerely migrated in His cause, and He also knows the reward that each of them deserves for his good deeds.

The statement that Allah is Most Forbearing suggests that because of this attribute, He will not bring to aught a person's major acts of goodness and services if minor lapses and weaknesses are found in his life-record. He will rather overlook these and forgive such people their sins.

(60) That indeed is so, as for him who retaliates in proportion to the excess committed against him, and is thereafter again subjected to transgression, Allah will surely aid him.[104] Verily Allah is All-Pardoning, All-Forgiving.[105]

(61) So shall it be[106] because it is Allah Who causes the night to emerge out of the day ▶

۞ ذَٰلِكَ وَمَنْ عَاقَبَ بِمِثْلِ مَا عُوقِبَ بِهِۦ ثُمَّ بُغِىَ عَلَيْهِ لَيَنصُرَنَّهُ ٱللَّهُ ۗ إِنَّ ٱللَّهَ لَعَفُوٌّ غَفُورٌ ﴿٦٠﴾ ذَٰلِكَ بِأَنَّ ٱللَّهَ يُولِجُ ٱلَّيْلَ فِى ٱلنَّهَارِ

104. Previously, reference was made to those who were subjected to wrongs and injustices but who failed to act in response to these (see verse 58 above – Ed.). The present verse, however, identifies those who had recourse to force in response to the persecution perpetrated by wrong-doers.

Shāfi'ī infers from this verse that retribution is to be inflicted exactly in the form in which the wrong itself was inflicted. For instance, if someone kills a person by drowning him, he will also be drowned. Likewise, if someone burns another person to death, he will be punished in like manner. However, the Ḥanafīs are of the opinion that irrespective of the mode in which a person is killed, the murderer will be subjected to retribution in one and the same established manner, i.e. regardless of how he had committed his treachery.

105. This verse may be interpreted in two ways, and presumably both are valid. First, that even though killing and bloodshed are not good *per se*, killing and shedding the blood of wrong-doers will nevertheless be pardoned by God. Second, that since man is a creature of God, Who is Oft-Pardoning, man should also be inclined to pardon others. Men of faith should be characteristically forbearing, magnanimous and tolerant. They are perfectly entitled to retaliate, but it does not befit them to take revenge and act vindictively.

106. The present paragraph relates to the previous one in its entirety. The upshot of this verse is that those who follow the course of unbelief and injustice will be punished and those who believe and act righteously will be rewarded; that the standard-bearers of truth who have been wronged, will see their own wrongs redressed; and those who seek to forcefully confront injustice will be aided by God. So, what is the reason underlying all these

and causes the day to emerge out of the night[107] and Allah is All-Hearing, All-Seeing.[108] (62) So shall it be because Allah, He is the Truth, and all whom they invoke instead of Him are false.[109] Allah is Most High, All-Great. (63) Do you not see that Allah sends down water from the sky whereby the earth turns green?[110] ▶

وَيُولِجُ ٱلنَّهَارَ فِى ٱلَّيْلِ وَأَنَّ ٱللَّهَ سَمِيعٌۢ بَصِيرٌ
﴿٦١﴾ ذَٰلِكَ بِأَنَّ ٱللَّهَ هُوَ ٱلْحَقُّ وَأَنَّ مَا يَدْعُونَ
مِن دُونِهِۦ هُوَ ٱلْبَٰطِلُ وَأَنَّ ٱللَّهَ هُوَ ٱلْعَلِىُّ
ٱلْكَبِيرُ ﴿٦٢﴾ أَلَمْ تَرَ أَنَّ ٱللَّهَ أَنزَلَ مِنَ
ٱلسَّمَآءِ مَآءً فَتُصْبِحُ ٱلْأَرْضُ مُخْضَرَّةً

assurances? The verse suggests that this will happen because of certain of God's attributes, i.e. those mentioned here.

107. God rules over the whole universe, and it is because of His Will that day and night follow in succession. In addition to this apparent meaning, the verse also subtly points to the fact that God, Who brings about the brightness of the day after the darkness of night, and Who subsequently overwhelms the brightness of the day with the darkness of night, is equally capable of bringing about the decline and fall of those who are presently at the zenith of their power and glory. In like manner, the darkness of ignorance and unbelief which is presently struggling to prevent the break of the morn of the truth will soon give way, by God's command, to the brightness of truth and knowledge that will illuminate the whole world.

108. God is All-Hearing and All-Seeing; He is neither blind nor deaf to what happens in the world.

109. God wields all power and is Lord in every sense of the term. Those who serve Him, therefore, cannot suffer and lose. Conversely, all other deities are no more than illusions; the attributes and authority ascribed to them have no basis in fact. Hence, all those who turn away from the One True God and depend instead on false deities can never achieve success and felicity.

110. Here again a subtle message underlies the apparent meaning of the verse. For, taken literally, the verse affirms God's Power. What is, however, hinted at is that in the same way as the sprinkling of even a light shower makes barren land blossom into verdure, so the blessed downpour of revelation in the time of the Prophet (peace be upon him) will soon show its blessed results. The barren desert of Arabia will be quickened to life and turn

Verily Allah is Subtle, All-Aware.[111] (64) To Him belongs all that is in the heavens and all that is in the earth. Surely Allah – He alone is Self-Sufficient, Praiseworthy.[112] (65) Have you not seen how Allah has subjected to you all that is in the earth, and the vessels that sail in the sea by His command, and it is He Who holds back the sky that it may not fall on earth ▶

إِنَّ ٱللَّهَ لَطِيفٌ خَبِيرٌ ۝٦٣ لَّهُۥ مَا فِى
ٱلسَّمَٰوَٰتِ وَمَا فِى ٱلْأَرْضِ ۗ وَإِنَّ ٱللَّهَ لَهُوَ
ٱلْغَنِىُّ ٱلْحَمِيدُ ۝٦٤ أَلَمْ تَرَ أَنَّ ٱللَّهَ سَخَّرَ لَكُم
مَّا فِى ٱلْأَرْضِ وَٱلْفُلْكَ تَجْرِى فِى ٱلْبَحْرِ
بِأَمْرِهِۦ وَيُمْسِكُ ٱلسَّمَآءَ أَن تَقَعَ عَلَى ٱلْأَرْضِ

---

into a flourishing centre of knowledge, of good morals and of a righteous and benevolent civilization never before witnessed.

111. To say that Allah is 'subtle' means that He accomplishes what He Wills by ways that are not quite tangible. When He Wills to bring about a change, He designs that it comes about in a manner which cannot even be imagined. One sees, for instance, the system of procreation in the world with the result that hundreds of thousands of babies are born every day. But who knows whether one of these will be an Abraham providing spiritual leadership to the greater part of the world, or a Chenghis Khan bringing about large-scale devastation and destruction in his wake. When the microscope was first invented who could have imagined that it would ultimately contribute to the manufacture of atomic and hydrogen bombs? In short, God's plans are fulfilled in such fine and imperceptible ways that people are hardly aware of them before their actual fulfilment.

God has also been characterized as 'All-Aware'. This underlines that God fully knows the circumstances and needs of all. God also knows full well the true interests of each of us. He is also well aware as to how He should manage the affairs of His realm.

112. God alone is self-sufficient. He and He alone is in need of no one, while everyone else is in perpetual need of Him. Likewise, He alone is truly praiseworthy. All praise is essentially due to Him and He alone deserves to be gratefully extolled for everything that is good. Moreover, He is intrinsically praiseworthy, independent of whether people actually utter words of praise for Him or not.

except by His leave?[113] Surely Allah is Most Gentle, Ever Compassionate to people. (66) And it is He Who has endowed you with life and it is He who causes you to die, and it is He Who will then resurrect you. Man is indeed extremely prone to denying the Truth.[114]

(67) For every people[115] We have prescribed a way of worship[116] which they follow. So, (O Muḥammad), let them not dispute with you concerning this, ▸

إِلَّا بِإِذْنِهِۦٓ ۗ إِنَّ ٱللَّهَ بِٱلنَّاسِ لَرَءُوفٌ رَّحِيمٌ
٦٥ وَهُوَ ٱلَّذِىٓ أَحْيَاكُمْ ثُمَّ يُمِيتُكُمْ ثُمَّ
يُحْيِيكُمْ ۗ إِنَّ ٱلْإِنسَٰنَ لَكَفُورٌ
٦٦ لِّكُلِّ أُمَّةٍ جَعَلْنَا مَنسَكًا هُمْ نَاسِكُوهُ ۖ
فَلَا يُنَٰزِعُنَّكَ فِى ٱلْأَمْرِ ۚ

113. The word 'heaven' signifies the whole celestial sphere every part of which is held in its proper place solely by the Will and Power of God.

114. This refers to deliberate denials of the truth expounded by the Prophets.

115. That is, the community of each Prophet.

116. The word *mansak* is not used here in the limited sense of ritual sacrifice. It rather signifies the whole system of worship. In an earlier instance, we translated the same word as 'the ritual of sacrifice' because in that context what was indicated was the ritual of sacrifice and nothing else. The use of the word on that occasion was followed by the Qur'ānic statement: 'that they pronounce the name of Allah over the cattle He has provided them'. (See verse 34 of the present *sūrah* – Ed.)

However, in the present verse there is no basis for taking this word in its limited sense of just the 'ritual of sacrifice'. Likewise, in translating the word *mansak* we have used the expression 'way of worship and service' since here both situations are meant. In other words, it refers to the mode of worship and service which is synonymous with the word *Sharī'ah* in the Qur'ān as: 'For each of you We have appointed a Law and a way of Life' (*al-Mā'idah* 5: 48).

and call them to Your Lord.[117] You are certainly on the Straight Way.[118] (68) And if they dispute with you, say: "Allah knows well what you do. (69) Allah will judge among you on the Day of Resurrection concerning matters about which you disagreed." (70) Are you not aware that Allah knows all that is in the heaven and the earth? Surely it is all preserved in a Book. Indeed that is easy with Allah.[119]

(71) Instead of Allah they worship those concerning whom He has revealed no sanction and concerning whom they have no true knowledge.[120] ▶

وَٱدۡعُ إِلَىٰ رَبِّكَۖ إِنَّكَ لَعَلَىٰ هُدٗى مُّسۡتَقِيمٖ
٦٧ وَإِن جَٰدَلُوكَ فَقُلِ ٱللَّهُ أَعۡلَمُ
بِمَا تَعۡمَلُونَ ٦٨ ٱللَّهُ يَحۡكُمُ بَيۡنَكُمۡ يَوۡمَ
ٱلۡقِيَٰمَةِ فِيمَا كُنتُمۡ فِيهِ تَخۡتَلِفُونَ ٦٩ أَلَمۡ
تَعۡلَمۡ أَنَّ ٱللَّهَ يَعۡلَمُ مَا فِي ٱلسَّمَآءِ وَٱلۡأَرۡضِۚ
إِنَّ ذَٰلِكَ فِي كِتَٰبٍۚ إِنَّ ذَٰلِكَ عَلَى ٱللَّهِ
يَسِيرٞ ٧٠ وَيَعۡبُدُونَ مِن دُونِ ٱللَّهِ مَا لَمۡ
يُنَزِّلۡ بِهِۦ سُلۡطَٰنٗا وَمَا لَيۡسَ لَهُم بِهِۦ عِلۡمٞۗ

---

117. The earlier Prophets prescribed a particular way (*mansak*) for their communities. In like manner, the Prophet Muḥammad (peace be upon him) also prescribed a particular way for his community. No one is entitled to dispute this because this is the only way that is suitable for the present age. This point is put forward in the Qur'ān as follows: 'Then We put you on the right way of religion: so follow that and do not follow the desires of those who do not know' (*al-Jāthiyah* 45: 18). For further details see *Tafhīm al-Qur'ān*, vol. IV, *al-Shūrā* 42, n. 20.

118. This statement further elaborates the point we identified in n. 117 above in explaining the preceding verse.

119. For a better understanding of the nexus between the contents of the present paragraph and the present discourse, one should recall verses 55–7 of the present *sūrah*.

120. None of the Scriptures specifically state that God associated others with Him in His Godhead, and that consequently such others should also

None shall be able to help such evil-doers.[121] (72) When Our Signs are plainly recited to them, you will perceive utter repugnance on their faces and it all but seems as if they will soon pounce upon those who recite Our Signs to them. Say: "Shall I tell you what is worse than that?[122] The Fire with which Allah has threatened those who disbelieve. That is truly an evil end."

(73) O people, a parable is set forth: pay heed to it. Those who call upon aught other than Allah shall never be able to create even a fly, ▶

وَمَا لِلظَّـٰلِمِينَ مِن نَّصِيرٍ ٧١ وَإِذَا تُتْلَىٰ
عَلَيْهِمْ ءَايَـٰتُنَا بَيِّنَـٰتٍ تَعْرِفُ فِى وُجُوهِ
ٱلَّذِينَ كَفَرُوا۟ ٱلْمُنكَرَ ۖ يَكَادُونَ يَسْطُونَ
بِٱلَّذِينَ يَتْلُونَ عَلَيْهِمْ ءَايَـٰتِنَا ۗ قُلْ أَفَأُنَبِّئُكُم
بِشَرٍّ مِّن ذَٰلِكُمُ ۗ ٱلنَّارُ وَعَدَهَا ٱللَّهُ ٱلَّذِينَ
كَفَرُوا۟ ۖ وَبِئْسَ ٱلْمَصِيرُ ٧٢ يَـٰٓأَيُّهَا ٱلنَّاسُ
ضُرِبَ مَثَلٌ فَٱسْتَمِعُوا۟ لَهُۥٓ ۚ إِنَّ ٱلَّذِينَ
تَدْعُونَ مِن دُونِ ٱللَّهِ لَن يَخْلُقُوا۟ ذُبَابًا

---

be worshipped beside God. Nor have any of those who are considered to be God's partners been able to know from any truly authentic source that they are indeed God's partners. Hence, the whole pantheon of false deities, the myriad of different notions and inventions about their attributes and powers, the diverse forms of worship, acts of devotion and various Prayers that are addressed to them, the offerings and Pilgrimages performed in order to please them, none has any sanction. Those who engage in such things do no more than follow the baseless fancies of the ignorant.

121. These foolish people think that their false deities will help them in this world and in the Next. In point of fact, they have none to help them. So far as the false deities are concerned, they will be unable to assist for they are absolutely helpless. Nor will God help them for they have rebelled against Him. Hence, they are harming only themselves by engaging in this folly.

122. The unbelievers fly into a bitter rage when they hear God's Messages. The unbelievers also subject those who rehearse God's Message to the worst kind of maltreatment. Such people are here told that they should look forward to a retribution for their deeds that is much more severe than the treatment

even if all of them were to come together to do that. And if the fly were to snatch away anything from them, they would not be able to recover that from it. Powerless is the supplicant; and powerless is he to whom he supplicates.[123] (74) They have not formed a true estimate of Allah. Indeed, Allah is All-Powerful, All-Mighty.

(75) Allah chooses Messengers from among angels and from among human beings (to convey His command).[124] Allah is All-Hearing, All-Seeing. (76) He knows all that is before them and that which is hidden from them.[125] ▶

وَلَوِ ٱجْتَمَعُوا۟ لَهُۥ ۖ وَإِن يَسْلُبْهُمُ ٱلذُّبَابُ شَيْـًٔا
لَّا يَسْتَنقِذُوهُ مِنْهُ ۚ ضَعُفَ ٱلطَّالِبُ وَٱلْمَطْلُوبُ
٧٣ مَا قَدَرُوا۟ ٱللَّهَ حَقَّ قَدْرِهِۦٓ ۗ إِنَّ ٱللَّهَ
لَقَوِىٌّ عَزِيزٌ ٧٤ ٱللَّهُ يَصْطَفِى مِنَ ٱلْمَلَٰٓئِكَةِ
رُسُلًا وَمِنَ ٱلنَّاسِ ۚ إِنَّ ٱللَّهَ سَمِيعٌۢ
بَصِيرٌ ٧٥ يَعْلَمُ مَا بَيْنَ أَيْدِيهِمْ وَمَا خَلْفَهُمْ ۗ

---

they have meted out to those who are righteous. Essentially, they should look forward to God's awesome punishment.

123. One who turns to a powerful being for help does so because of a realization of his own weakness. But the false gods whose help people are invoking are themselves absolutely weak, so much so that at times they are weaker than flies. Those who invoke other than God for help are themselves utterly weak and helpless. Furthermore, they pin all their hopes and reliance on those who are devoid of even a morsel of power.

124. The most superior among those creatures whom the polytheists recognized as deities, were either angels or Prophets. But even those are no more than a means to communicate God's commands, i.e. those whom He chooses for that task. The function which they perform neither elevates them to the position of God, nor makes them His partners.

125. This expression is frequently used in the Qur'ān to refute the polytheistic version of intercession. Viewed in this context, it implies that

And it is to Allah that all affairs are returned.[126]

(77) Believers, bow down and prostrate yourselves before Your Lord and serve Your Lord and do good that you may prosper.[127] ▶

وَإِلَى ٱللَّهِ تُرْجَعُ ٱلْأُمُورُ ﴿٧٦﴾ يَـٰٓأَيُّهَا ٱلَّذِينَ
ءَامَنُوا۟ ٱرْكَعُوا۟ وَٱسْجُدُوا۟ وَٱعْبُدُوا۟ رَبَّكُمْ
وَٱفْعَلُوا۟ ٱلْخَيْرَ لَعَلَّكُمْ تُفْلِحُونَ ۩ ﴿٧٧﴾

the worship of angels, Prophets and saints is wrong regardless of whether it is performed under the impression that they are independently capable of relieving the people's distress or of fulfilling their needs, or because of belief that those false gods will effectively intercede with God. All this is wrong because it is God alone Who both sees and hears everything, Who knows all the aspects of every person's life, both public and private, Whose wisdom embraces all the wisdom that there is, be it explicit or hidden. No creature knows, not even angels and Prophets, which actions are propitious and which are not. Hence God has not bestowed upon any of His creatures, not even upon those closest to Him, the absolute right of intercession with Him, let alone the assurance that He will accept every intercession of theirs.

126. All matters pertaining to the universe are disposed of by God. It is He alone to Whom all such matters, large or small, are referred for decision. Hence, there is none else than Him to whom people should turn for help. It is pointless to invoke beings who themselves are devoid of the power to fulfil their own needs, let alone those of others.

127. This is the way, the only way through which one may expect to achieve true success. However, even those who follow this way should be wary of arrogance, complacency and belief that because of their religious devotion and righteous conduct they are bound to attain true success. Instead, they should seek God's bounty and focus all their hopes on His Grace and Mercy. No person can achieve true success unless God bestows it upon him, for no one has the power to achieve success by dint of his own power.

The expression used in this verse لعلكم تفلحون literally means 'perhaps you will prosper'. The statement made here though does not mean that the attainment of prosperity and success is subject to any doubt. This expression can be better appreciated if we regard it as being part of a royal, majestic discourse. Suppose a king were to say to any of his servants: 'Do this and you might be given a good position.' This seemingly non-committal statement suffices to fill that person with utmost joy and makes him celebrate the event. This because the statement hints at a favour, even if that favour is not couched in categorical terms. For it cannot even be conceived that a benevolent and gracious master would raise certain expectations in his servants and then disappoint them.

Shāfi'ī, Aḥmad ibn Ḥanbal, 'Abd Allāh ibn Mubārak and Isḥāq ibn Rāhawayh consider this to be one of those verses of recitation whereby it is obligatory for the person to prostrate. That it is obligatory both for him who recites it as for him who listens to it. Abū Ḥanīfah, Mālik, Ḥasan al-Baṣrī, Sa'īd ibn al-Musayyab, Sa'īd ibn Jubayr, Ibrāhīm al-Nakha'ī and Sufyān al-Thawrī, however, do not accept this opinion. What follows is a summary of the arguments advanced by the two groups.

The first group bases its opinion on the apparent command to prostrate. Another piece of evidence from which they derive support for their views is the following tradition narrated by 'Uqbah ibn 'Āmir as recorded in the *Musnad* of Aḥmad ibn Ḥanbal and in the *Ḥadīth* collections of Abū Dā'ūd, Tirmidhī, Ibn Marduwayh and Bayhaqī: 'I asked, "O Messenger of God! Has *Sūrah al-Ḥajj* been made superior to all other *sūrahs* by virtue of having two verses of prostration in it?" The Prophet (peace be upon him) replied: "Yes; he who does not prostrate himself after reciting those verses should better not recite it." ' (See Abū Dā'ūd, *K. al-Ṣalāh*, 'Bāb Tafrī'Abwāb al-Sujūd' and Tirmidhī, 'Abwāb al-Jumu'ah, 'Bāb mā jā' fī al-Sajdah wa fī al-Ḥajj' – Ed.) The third argument advanced in support of this view is the tradition found in the works of Abū Dā'ūd and Ibn Mājah on the authority of 'Amr ibn al-'Āṣ that the Prophet (peace be upon him) directed him to prostrate himself twice while reciting *Sūrah al-Ḥajj*. (See Abū Dā'ūd, *K. al-Ṣalāh*, 'Bāb Tafrī'Abwāb al-Sujūd' – Ed.) The fourth argument consists of the tradition from 'Umar ibn al-Khaṭṭāb, 'Alī ibn Abī Ṭālib, 'Uthmān ibn 'Affān, 'Abd Allāh ibn 'Umar, 'Abd Allāh ibn 'Abbās, Abū al-Dardā', Abū Mūsā al-Ash'arī and 'Ammār ibn Yāsir in which it has been claimed that there are two places in this *sūrah* which require prostration.

The second group, on the other hand, contends that the verse under discussion does not specifically lay down the command to prostrate. Instead, the verse simply mentions *rukū'* and prostration together, and whenever such an expression is used in the Qur'ān, it signifies Prayer as such. Moreover, the combination of *rukū'* and prostration is specifically restricted to Prayer. These scholars also call into question 'Uqbah ibn 'Āmir's tradition on the grounds of its weak chain of narrators. This tradition was narrated by Ibn Lahī'ah on the authority of Abū al-Muṣ'ab who was among those who mounted an attack by catapult on the Ka'bah along with Ḥajjāj ibn Yūsuf al-Thaqafī. They also reject the tradition from 'Amr ibn al-'Āṣ as untrustworthy, arguing that it was narrated by Sa'īd al-'Itqī from 'Abd Allāh ibn Munayn al-Kilābī. Both are considered *majhūl* for it is not known who they are nor what level of trustworthiness they command. As for the traditions of the Companions cited in support of this view, it is contended that 'Abd Allāh ibn 'Abbās explained the statement concerning the two prostrations as follows: 'The first

(78) Strive in the cause of Allah in a manner worthy of that striving.[128] He has chosen you (for His task),[129] ▶	وَجَٰهِدُواْ فِى ٱللَّهِ حَقَّ جِهَادِهِۦۚ هُوَ ٱجْتَبَىٰكُمْ

is for obligatory; the second is for the purpose of instruction.' (See Jaṣṣāṣ, vol. 3, p. 225 – Ed.)

128. *Jihād* does not simply mean fighting and war. The word denotes: 'to strive, to exert to the utmost'. The words *jihād* and *mujāhid* imply the existence of forces of resistance against whom it is necessary to wage a struggle. Moreover, the stipulation that *jihād* should be *fī sabīl Allāh* (in the way of God) makes it clear that there are forces of resistance which obstruct people from serving God and pursuing His good pleasure, and that it is necessary to engage in strife and struggle to overcome them.

As for the purpose of *jihād* it is to remove the forces obstructing man from following the Way of God so that one may be able to serve God in an adequate manner, exalt His Word, and subdue unbelief and rebellion against Him. The first and foremost target of this struggle should be one's own self which always prompts one to rebel against God's commands and distracts one from belief and obedience. Unless one conquers one's own self within, one cannot fight against the forces without. It is against this background that once the Prophet (peace be upon him) told those who were returning home after waging a *jihād*: 'You have now come from a smaller *jihād* to a larger *jihād*.' Asked what was meant by larger *jihād*, the Prophet (peace be upon him) said: 'A man's striving against his own self.' After one has waged this *jihād*, one finds oneself in a battlefield spread the world over. One finds the world full of those who have rebelled against God and who incite others to rebellion. To strive against these forces and to devote all the power of one's mind, heart and body in this connection is what is required of man. The present verse embodies this requirement.

129. Of all mankind, the believers were chosen for the task mentioned in the present verse. The same point is also made at other places in the Qur'ān: 'We appointed you to be the community of the middle way . . . ' (*al-Baqarah* 2: 143). 'You are now the best of people brought forth for mankind' (*Āl 'Imrān* 3: 110).

It is perhaps pertinent to point out here that this is one of several verses which establish the excellence of the Prophet's Companions. The verse also shows how wrong are those who are prone to launch attacks on the Companions. For it is quite obvious this verse directly identifies the Companions as those chosen by God, and further that it extols other members of the *Ummah* indirectly.

and He has not laid upon you any hardship in religion.[130] Keep to the faith of your father Abraham.[131] ▶	وَمَا جَعَلَ عَلَيْكُمْ فِي ٱلدِّينِ مِنْ حَرَجٍ مِّلَّةَ أَبِيكُمْ إِبْرَٰهِيمَ

130. This proclaims that the believers are free from all the unjust shackles forged by the theologians, priests, and lawyers of previous religious communities. It is declared here that no longer are there any restrictions that obstruct intellectual progress, nor any restraints in the practical affairs of man's life which impede the growth of culture and civilization. This because they have been provided with a set of simple, straightforward beliefs and a body of practicable laws. While adhering to this one may make as much progress as one wants. The point mentioned here in a positive manner has elsewhere been couched in negative terms, as follows: 'He [the Prophet] enjoins upon them what is good and forbids them what is evil. He makes the clean things lawful to them and prohibits all corrupt things, and removes from them their burdens and the shackles that were upon them' (*al-A'rāf* 7: 157).

131. Although Islam can be described as the faith of Noah, Moses and Jesus (peace be upon them), it can also be described as the faith of Abraham. The Qur'ān repeatedly calls it 'the faith of Abraham'. It also calls upon others to follow it. There are three main reasons for this. First, because the immediate addressees of the Qur'ān were Arabs and they were more familiar with Abraham than with any other Prophet. The towering figure of Abraham dominated their history, traditions and religious life. Second, the Jews and Christians, the polytheists of Arabia and the Sabaeans of the Middle East were all agreed on recognizing Abraham as their patriarch. No Prophet enjoyed this position. Third, Abraham came before the emergence of Judaism, Christianity and Sabaeanism. Insofar as Arab polytheists are concerned, they conceded that idolatry was introduced among them by 'Amr ibn Luḥayy, a chief of Banū Khuzā'ah who brought the idol of Hubal from Moab. 'Amr ibn Luḥayy lived in the fifth or sixth century B.C. In other words, polytheism had gained currency several centuries after Abraham. It is also implied that if Abraham was in the right and did not profess any of their distorted beliefs and practices, then it is his faith that should be embraced. Now the Message of the Prophet Muḥammad (peace be upon him) was clear and simple: 'Follow the faith of Abraham.' For further details see *Towards Understanding the Qur'ān*, vol. I, *al-Baqarah* 2, nn. 134–5, pp. 115–17 and *Āl 'Imrān* 3, nn. 58 and 79, pp. 263 and 273–4 and vol. IV, *al-Naḥl* 16, n. 120, p. 374.

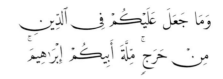

Allah named you Muslims earlier and even in this (Book),[132] that the Messenger may be a witness over you, and that you may be witnesses over all mankind.[133] So establish Prayer, and pay *Zakāh*, and hold fast to Allah.[134] He is your Protector. What an excellent Protector; what an excellent Helper!

هُوَ سَمَّىٰكُمُ ٱلْمُسْلِمِينَ مِن قَبْلُ وَفِى
هَـٰذَا لِيَكُونَ ٱلرَّسُولُ شَهِيدًا عَلَيْكُمْ
وَتَكُونُوا۟ شُهَدَآءَ عَلَى ٱلنَّاسِ ۚ فَأَقِيمُوا۟
ٱلصَّلَوٰةَ وَءَاتُوا۟ ٱلزَّكَوٰةَ وَٱعْتَصِمُوا۟ بِٱللَّهِ
هُوَ مَوْلَىٰكُمْ ۖ فَنِعْمَ ٱلْمَوْلَىٰ وَنِعْمَ ٱلنَّصِيرُ ﴿٧٨﴾

---

132. The word 'you' in the statement '. . . and named you Muslims' does not only refer to the believers at the time of revelation of this verse, nor only to those who subsequently joined the fold of Islam. It rather refers to all those who, since the beginning of human history, have believed in monotheism, in the After-Life, in the institution of Prophethood and in the Scriptures. The thrust of the statement is that the believers of the past were not named after the Prophets they followed, i.e. they were not called Noahites, Abrahamites, or Mosites, etc. Rather, they were simply called 'Muslims' since their basic characteristic of life was their submission to God. In like manner, believers of today are known as Muslims, rather than Muhammadans. This has presented something of a puzzle to those who wondered which Scripture before the advent of the Prophet Muḥammad (peace be upon him) mentions his followers as Muslims.

133. For a detailed discussion see *Towards Understanding the Qur'ān*, vol. I, *al-Baqarah* 2, n. 44, p. 62. This point is discussed in greater detail in the present author's monograph *Shahādat-i Ḥaqq*. (This is now available in English translation as *Witnesses Unto Mankind*, Leicester: The Islamic Foundation, 1985 – Ed.)

134. The believers are being told to firmly hold on to God. They are required to derive from Him both general guidance and practical laws for their everyday lives. They are also directed to obey Him, to hold Him alone in awe, to centre all their hopes in Him, to seek help from none other than Him, and to place all their reliance and trust in Him alone.

Sūrah 23

Al-Mu'minūn

(The Believers)

(Makkan Period)

Title

The title is derived from verse 1 of this *sūrah* which characterizes the believers as those who attain true success.

Period of Revelation

The style and content of the *sūrah* indicate that it was revealed in the mid phase of the Makkan period of the Prophet's life. The text indicates the background against which it was revealed, one characterized by the fierce confrontation raging between the Prophet (peace be upon him) and the unbelievers. The persecution perpetrated by the Makkan unbelievers had, however, not yet reached its climax. Verses 75–6 of the *sūrah* also indicate that these were revealed at a time when Makka was in the grip of a severe famine, an event which, according to reliable traditions, occurred in this mid phase of the Makkan period of the Prophet's life. We learn from a tradition by 'Urwah ibn al-Zubayr that this *sūrah* was revealed when 'Umar had already embraced Islam. In particular, he mentions 'Umar's statement, on the authority of 'Abd al-Raḥmān ibn 'Abd al-Qārī, that the *sūrah* was revealed in his presence. In fact, 'Umar directly observed the effects of the revelation on the Prophet (peace be upon him). After the revelation ended, the Prophet (peace be upon him) said to him: 'Ten such verses have just been revealed to me that if anyone were to follow them, he would certainly enter Paradise.' Then he recited the first few verses of this *sūrah*. (Tirmidhī, *K. Tafsīr al-Qur'ān*, 'Bāb min Sūrah al-Mu'minūn.' See also Aḥmad ibn Ḥanbal, *Musnad*, Nasā'ī, and Ḥākim – Ed.)

Themes and Subject Matter

Obedience to the Prophet (peace be upon him) forms the central theme of this *sūrah*, and the whole discourse revolves around it. The *sūrah* opens by stating that those who have accepted the Message of the Prophet (peace be upon him) have begun to manifest certain moral characteristics which indicate that they will achieve true success, both in this world and in the Next.

Attention is then drawn to the creation of man, of the heavens and the earth, of plants and animals, and also of other phenomena in the universe. All this aims at inculcating belief in monotheism and the Hereafter to which the Prophet (peace be upon him) invited everyone. Emphasis is placed on the fact that these truths are corroborated by man's own being and by the entire system of the universe.

This is followed by accounts of several Prophets and the nations to which they were sent. These appear, at first sight, to be mere stories of the past. They do, however, impress upon the minds of the audience the following basic points.

First, that there was nothing unusual about the doubts and objections raised by the unbelievers against the Prophet's Message. Prophets of yore, even those whom the Quraysh recognized as such, had also been subjected to much the same kind of opposition at the hands of ignorant people of their times. It was now for people to see what the lessons of history were: who was right, the Prophets or their detractors?

Second, that the teachings pertaining to monotheism and the Hereafter which were being expounded by Muḥammad (peace be upon him) were the same as those expounded by the earlier Prophets at different periods in history. Thus, what the Prophet Muḥammad (peace be upon him) was preaching was not novel, but rather a teaching which mankind was well acquainted with from the past.

Third, that the communities which did not give ear to the Prophets and persisted in opposing them were eventually destroyed.

Fourth, that God had sent the same religion in all previous epochs and that all the Prophets belonged to one and the same religious community. All religions other than the One True Religion of God, as expounded by the Prophets, are man-made concoctions; none is from God.

After stories about the Prophets, emphasis is then placed on showing people that worldly prosperity, wealth and riches, the numerousness of one's offspring, pomp and glory, and power and authority do not prove that the individual or group enjoying them is on the Right Path. Nor does any of it prove that God holds that particular individual or group in special favour; or that the attitude which it has adopted is to God's liking. Conversely, someone's poverty or resourcelessness does not prove with certitude that God is displeased with him. What earns God's pleasure or displeasure depends on whether one truly believes and fears God and whether one is truthful or not.

These points are especially stressed because opposition to the Prophet (peace be upon him) was spearheaded by the Makkan aristocracy, by the chiefs of different clans, by those in authority in Makka. Both these leaders and their followers suffered from the delusion that their ever-increasing worldly attainments indicated that they enjoyed the special favour of God and other deities. As for the Prophet Muḥammad (peace be upon him) and his Companions, they were utterly resourceless and destitute which, in their view, clearly showed that they were not favoured by God, and that other deities were, of course, also hostile to them.

This is followed by the marshalling of an array of arguments to persuade the Makkans to affirm the truth of the Prophet's call. They are told that the famine signifies God's warning and, therefore, they should mend their ways and follow the Right Path. If they fail to take heed, they will be subjected to a much more severe chastisement, one which will simply crush them to pieces.

Thereafter, the attention of the people is once again drawn to the numerous signs that lie scattered all over the universe and in their own beings. In short, they are asked to look around with open eyes to see if the doctrines of monotheism and the Hereafter as preached by the Prophet (peace be upon him) are not corroborated by the numerous signs dispersed all around. Do their intellect and natural instincts not bear witness to the truth of the Prophet's Message? Following this the Prophet Muḥammad (peace be upon him) was directed to adhere to fair means alone in defending himself against the evil ways of his enemies lest he is provoked by Satan to return evil for evil.

The *sūrah* concludes with issuing a warning to the unbelievers that they will face a severe reckoning in the Hereafter. They are also warned that they will be seriously taken to task for their unjustified hostility to the Prophet's Message as well as to his followers (peace be upon them).

In the name of Allah, the Most Merciful, the Most Compassionate.	بِسْمِ ٱللَّهِ ٱلرَّحْمَٰنِ ٱلرَّحِيمِ
(1) The believers have indeed attained true success:[1] ▶	قَدْ أَفْلَحَ ٱلْمُؤْمِنُونَ ۝١

1. The word 'believers' referred to in this verse stands for those who embraced the Prophet's call, accepted him as their guide and leader, and willingly consented to follow the way of life expounded by him.

The Arabic word *falāḥ* means success and prosperity. It is used as an antonym of *khusrān* which signifies loss and failure. To say that someone has acquired *falāḥ* therefore, amounts to saying that he has achieved his objective; that he has attained prosperity and well-being, that his efforts have borne fruit, and that his condition has ameliorated.

The opening statement of this *sūrah*, namely that 'the believers have indeed attained true success', can only be appreciated with reference to the circumstantial background against which this discourse was revealed. At the time of its revelation, the chief opponents of the Message of Islam consisted, on the one hand, of the wealthy notables of Makka whose trade was flourishing, who enjoyed all the appurtenances of worldly prosperity. On the other hand, there were the followers of Islam. In sharp contrast to the former, most of them were in a poor and wretched condition when they embraced Islam. Only a few Muslims belonged to well-to-do families or had achieved some success in business. Even they, however, were reduced to severe adversity because of the persecution and pressures to which they were subjected by their own people.

Given this background, the opening verse which proclaims the success and prosperity of the believers suggests that man-made standards of success and failure are false; that the assumptions entertained by men in this regard are ill-founded; that they lack the correct vision that enables them to have a long-range view of things. No wonder, for what they conceive of as success and prosperity is nothing but sheer loss and failure. Likewise, contrary to the claim of their contemporaries who thought of the believers as those who had failed and had incurred utter loss, the followers of the Prophet (peace be upon him) were indeed those who had attained true success. By responding to the call to embrace the truth they had not struck a bad bargain; rather they had been fortunate in obtaining what would confer on them lasting success in both this life and the Next. By their refusal to embrace the call to the truth, the unbelievers, in contrast, had incurred a serious loss, the dire consequences of which would afflict them in this world and in the Hereafter.

This idea forms the central theme of the *sūrah* and the whole discourse from the beginning to the end is focused on driving home this point.

(2) those who, in their Prayers,[2] humble themselves;[3] ▶

ٱلَّذِينَ هُمْ فِى صَلَاتِهِمْ خَٰشِعُونَ ﴿٢﴾

2. Verses 1–9 set forth the qualities of the believers. Veritably, these qualities serve as evidence in support of the claim that it is the act of believing that led the believers to success. In other words: how can those who have developed such wholesome qualities in their lives owing to their faith not attain true success? If they cannot be successful, then who can?

3. The true meaning of *khushū'* is to lower oneself before someone, to be submissive, to display humility. The state called *khushū'* is related both to the heart and to the outward condition of one's bodily organs. The *khushū'* of the heart consists in man's feeling of being overwhelmed by someone's awe, grandeur and majesty. As for *khushū'* of the bodily organs, it manifests itself in a number of ways: one's head is lowered in the presence of him whom one holds in awe; the organs of the body are loosened; one's gaze is downcast; one speaks in a subdued voice. In short, outward *khushū'* covers all the physical manifestations which naturally appear when one comes face to face with someone exceedingly mighty and awesome. In the context of Prayer, *khushū'* signifies both the state of the heart and its outward manifestations. In fact, *khushū'* is the essential spirit of Prayer. It is reported in a *ḥadīth* that once the Prophet (peace be upon him) observed someone playing with his beard during Prayer. On this he observed: 'Had his heart been in a state of humility [before God] the organs of his body would also have been in a state of humility.' (Cited by Ālūsī in his *Rūḥ al-Ma'ānī*, vol. 18, p. 3 – Ed.)

Although *khushū'* is essentially a condition of the heart which also manifests itself outwardly, the *Sharī'ah* does additionally prescribe certain rules which are required to be observed in Prayer. These serve two purposes. First, they help create the state of mind that is conducive to *khushū'*. Second, while the state of *khushū'* naturally vacillates, these rules ensure that at least a certain minimum of *khushū'* is observed at the outward level. For instance, one of these rules is that during Prayer one should neither move one's head left or right, nor should one look upward. At most, one can cast glances out of the corner of one's eyes. According to the Ḥanafī and Shāfi'ī schools, even one's gaze should not go beyond the spot on which one prostrates. However, the Mālikī school is of the opinion that all one is required to do is to look straight ahead [i.e. one's gaze may go beyond the spot on which one prostrates]. It is also forbidden to move about or bend in different directions while one is praying. Likewise, it is also forbidden to fold one's clothes over and over again, or to brush them or play with them. People have also been directed not to clean the place on which they sit or perform prostration while they are bending to prostrate. It is also inconsistent with the etiquette of Prayer to stand in an overly erect position, or to recite the Qur'ān too loudly, or to recite it in a sing-song style. Similarly, to yawn or belch loudly during Prayer is not

(3) who avoid whatever is vain and frivolous;[4] ▶	وَٱلَّذِينَ هُمْ عَنِ ٱللَّغْوِ مُعْرِضُونَ ۝٣

consistent with the good manners of praying. To perform the Prayer too hastily is also highly disapproved of. It is rather required that each part of the Prayer should be performed with deliberation and care, with peace and tranquillity. Not until one has completed one part of the Prayer, such as prostration, rising or sitting down, can one proceed to the next part. If one is put to inconvenience by something, it can be driven away with one hand. What is, however, disallowed is that one should violently move or engage both hands in anything other than the rituals of Prayer.

Apart from observing these outward rules, it is exceedingly important that while praying one should avoid thinking deliberately about irrelevant matters. Should some such ideas involuntarily come to one's mind, once or even constantly, there is nothing to worry about for that is man's natural weakness. Yet one should try one's level best that one's heart remain oriented to God, and that the statements made by one's tongue accord with what one's heart also feels. During Prayers if some unrelated ideas involuntarily come to mind all one is required to do is turn one's attention away from them and direct it instead towards Prayer. This should be done as soon as one realizes, i.e. becomes aware, of this interference.

4. The word *laghw* signifies all that is useless, irrelevant and fruitless. All things, be they words of the mouth or actions of the body, which have no utility, which lead to no beneficial results, which are neither genuinely needed nor serve any useful purpose, fall under the purview of *laghw*.

We have translated *mu'riḍūn* (معرضون) as those 'who avoid whatever is vain and frivolous . . .' We are conscious, however, that this expression fails to do full justice to what the Qur'ān says here. The thrust of the verse is that the believers do not concern themselves with things that are vain and frivolous; they rather pay no attention to them at all. They even abstain from approaching places where people are engaged in frivolous things let alone directly participate in them. If they come face to face with frivolities, they simply move away and scrupulously pass them by; and if they are confronted with them, they remain detached and withdrawn. This is what has been said elsewhere in the Qur'ān: 'The believers do not bear witness to falsehood and, if they pass by a vain thing, they pass by it with honourable avoidance' (*al-Furqān* 25: 72).

What has been pithily stated here in just a few words in fact constitutes one of the most vital characteristics of a believer. A true believer is he who is always conscious of his duties. He looks at his being placed in the world as though he were in an examination hall where he is taking a test. Life to him amounts to being put in a position in which it is required of him to complete his examination. Such realization makes him behave in the manner of a serious-minded student who, while seated in the hall,

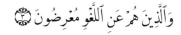

(4) who observe *Zakāh*;[5] ▶	وَٱلَّذِينَ هُمْ لِلزَّكَوٰةِ فَٰعِلُونَ ۝٤

fully concentrates on the examination, knowing that the time allocated to him to complete the test is very short. Like the student he is also conscious that the few hours granted to him for so doing is extremely crucial for his future career. He, therefore, utilizes each and every second so that he might give his best possible performance. Without wasting a single moment, a believer spends all the time available to him on pursuits which produce beneficial results. Even in selecting his leisure activities, he chooses those that eventually produce better results. Rather than being inclined to 'kill time', he regards time as a precious and invaluable commodity which he naturally tries to utilize in the best possible way.

Moreover, a believer is blessed with good taste, chaste temperament and fine sensibility. He is not attracted to things that are obscene or vulgar. He engages in useful conversation, but certainly not silly gossip. He enjoys humour, wit and refined jokes, but he refrains from vulgarity, obscene jokes and clownishness. He is not someone who is habituated to silly chatting. He is tormented if he is placed in bad company or a society rife with abuse, back-biting, evil insinuations, lying, dirty songs and obscene talk. It may be remembered that one of the numerous bounties of Paradise that the Qur'ān mentions is that in it one will not come across any word that is vain: 'In it [i.e. Paradise] they shall hear no vanity' (*al-Ghāshiyah* 88: 11).

5. The significance of 'observing *Zakāh*' is entirely different from paying *Zakāh*, and it is a mistake to overlook the difference between the two meanings. It would appear important that in this verse whilst describing the attributes of believers, the Qur'ān departs from the usual usage *yu'tūn al-zakāh*, 'they pay *zakāh*', and employs instead the unusual expression *li al-zakāt fā'ilūn*, 'they observe *zakāh*'. In Arabic, *zakāh* signifies two things: (1) purity, and (2) growth.

To remove all that obstructs the growth of a thing and to enable its essence to grow are the two concepts that bring out the full meaning of *zakāh*. When this word is employed in the Islamic context, it applies to (1) the amount of wealth that is given away in order to achieve purification; and (2) the striving to purify oneself. Had the expression been *yu'tūn al-zakāh*, they pay *zakāh*, it would simply have meant that believers give away a part of their wealth so as to purify themselves. This would have restricted the act simply to giving away wealth. The actual expression used here, however, is *li al-zakāt fā'ilūn* which signifies that the believers are actively engaged in purification. In such a case, the matter does not end with their giving away part of their wealth, rather it embraces a whole range of acts including purification of one's self, purification of one's morality, purification of one's wealth; in sum, the purification of virtually everything.

Moreover, this is a wide-ranging concept according to which the process of purification is not confined to the life of an individual, but extends to the

(5) who strictly guard their private parts[6] (6) save from their wives, or those whom their right hands possess; for with regard to them they are free from blame – (7) As for those who seek beyond that, they are transgressors[7] –►

وَٱلَّذِينَ هُمْ لِفُرُوجِهِمْ حَـٰفِظُونَ ﴿٥﴾
إِلَّا عَلَىٰٓ أَزْوَٰجِهِمْ أَوْ مَا مَلَكَتْ
أَيْمَـٰنُهُمْ فَإِنَّهُمْ غَيْرُ مَلُومِينَ ﴿٦﴾ فَمَنِ ٱبْتَغَىٰ
وَرَآءَ ذَٰلِكَ فَأُو۟لَـٰٓئِكَ هُمُ ٱلْعَادُونَ ﴿٧﴾

---

lives of all those amidst whom we live. It is better, therefore, to understand the present verse as meaning that the believers are those who are constantly engaged in the task of purification. In other words, they seek to purify themselves as well as others. They not only try to purify themselves but also to bring about purification in the world outside themselves. The Qur'ān also refers to this aspect of the believers' concern in other places: 'Those who purify themselves, and remember the name of their Lord and perform Prayer will prosper' (*al-A'lā* 87: 14–15). 'Truly he who caused it to grow it [to wit his self] succeeds; and he who corrupts it, fails' (*al-Shams* 91: 9–10).

The present verse, however, has a wider connotation than the two mentioned above. For, whereas the other verses emphasize the task of self-purification, the present verse concentrates on the act of purification itself; one that embraces both the individual and society.

6. This means two things. First, that the believers cover the private parts of their body; that is, they shun nudity. Second, that they guard their chastity and modesty; that they are not unfettered in the exercise of their sexual urges. (For further elaboration see *al-Nūr* 24, nn. 30–2 below.)

7. This parenthetical statement is made in order to dispel any misconception which might arise from the above statement about strictly guarding one's private parts. Some people have believed in the past as some people also believe now that the sexual urge is, in itself, an evil. Such people are of the opinion that it is unbecoming of those who are righteous, of those who are truly devoted to God to fulfil their sexual desires even in a perfectly legitimate way. It is possible that such a misconception might have been strengthened if the statement had ended on the note that believers who guard their private parts are those who succeed. This could, however, have given the wrong message that piety demands that people practise absolute abstinence, lead an hermatic and reclusive life, and stay away from all the botherations of conjugal life. The Qur'ān, therefore, makes the additional remark in parenthesis that there is nothing inherently bad in fulfilling one's sexual desires providing it is done in a legitimate manner. Sin only entails that one exceeds the legitimate limits and seeks to gratify one's sexual urges beyond what is appropriate and lawful.

Several rules can be derived from the above Qur'ānic statement, rules that we will attempt below to state succinctly:

(1) It is made clear that one need not guard one's private parts from two kinds of women – one's wives and slave-girls. The first category consists, according to Arabic usage and several Qur'ānic statements, of those women whom one has duly married. The second category are termed as *mā malakat aymānuhum*. Use of this expression in both the Arabic language as well as the instances of its use in the Qur'ān make it quite evident that it signifies slave-girls, i.e. women whom one has come to possess.

Thus, this verse makes it clear that it is perfectly lawful for a person to have sexual relations both with one's wives and the slave-girls in one's possession. Likewise, it is clear from this verse that with regard to the latter it is not marriage, but ownership which provides the legitimizing basis for sexual relations with them. Had marriage alone been the legitimate ground for sexual relations, there would have been no need to mention a separate category because any woman whom a person marries would fall in the category of *azwāj* (wives).

Some Qur'ānic commentators of our own time who deny the legitimacy of sexual relations with slave-girls, refer to the following verse in support of the doctrine that one is only allowed to have such relations with one's wives: 'And those of you who cannot afford to marry free believing women (*muḥṣanāt*), then marry such believing women whom your right hands possess' (*al-Nisā'* 4: 25).

They argue on the basis of this verse that sexual relations with slave-girls can be established only after marrying them. For, this verse of *Sūrah al-Nisā'* states, that if one does not have the means to marry free believing women, then one may marry a slave-girl, or so they contend. It is, however, strange that these scholars cite only that particular part of the Qur'ānic verse which suits their purpose and leave aside the remaining element which goes against their position. The verse in question actually lays down the following code for marrying slave-girls: 'Marry them, then, with the leave of their guardians, and give them their bridal-due in a fair manner' (*al-Nisā'* 4: 25). Now quite obviously this verse is not addressed to the owners of slave-girls, but to those who intend to marry a slave-girl who is in someone else's possession. Such a person, if he does not have the resources to marry a free woman, is being directed to marry a slave-girl with the permission of her owner. Had the verse related to the owners themselves, the statement about obtaining the owner's leave would be quite redundant. Nonetheless, those who are bent on distorting the meaning and message of the Qur'ān highlight only that part which pertains to marrying slave-girls, and suppress the statement made about the leave of their guardians.

Moreover, this incorrect inference runs counter to the directive laid down in other places in the Qur'ān. Anyone who is interested in making an honest and objective study of this question with the intention so as to find the true Qur'ānic position should read the above verse in conjunction with the following verses: *al-Nisā'* 4: 3 and 25, *al-Aḥzāb* 33: 50–2, and *al-Ma'ārij* 70: 30. Taken together, these clearly spell out the Qur'ānic position on the issue. (For further details see *Towards Understanding the Qur'ān*, vol. II, *al-Nisā'* 4, n. 44, pp. 26–8 and the author's *Tafhīmāt*, vol. 2, pp. 290–324, and *Rasā'il wa Masā'il*, vol. 1, pp. 324–33).

(2) The use of the proposition *'alā* in making an exception of those with whom one is not required to guard one's private parts (*illā 'alā azwājihim aw mā malakat aymānuhum*), makes it all the more clear that the law that is being laid down here is specifically meant for men. However, what has been stated in verses 1 to 11 of the *sūrah,* is equally applicable to both men and women despite the fact that the pronoun *hum* (in verse 2) is masculine. This is so because in Arabic the masculine pronoun is used to denote a group of people consisting of genders. However, in the command relating to the guarding of private parts an indication is given that the meaning applies only to males, this by use of the preposition *'alā*. Had the preposition *li* been used instead of *'alā*, it would have covered both males and females. Unable to grasp this subtle nuance, a woman in the time of Caliph 'Umar ibn al-Khaṭṭāb had sexual relations with her male slave. When the matter was reported in a gathering of the Prophet's Companions, they unanimously expressed the opinion that she had interpreted the Book of God incorrectly.

This should not, however, give rise to the misunderstanding that since this exception applies to males alone, it is not lawful for wives to have sexual relations with their husbands. Such a misconception is pointless since husbands have not been asked to guard their private parts from their wives. Thus, the same command applies to wives in relation to their husbands. Quite obviously, no further clarification or elaboration on this count was needed.

In sum, the above exception is practically confined to relations between males and their slave-girls. As a corollary of this rule, it is unlawful for women to have sexual relations with their male slaves. This prohibition for women is accounted for by virtue of the fact that while a male slave would be able to fulfil the woman's sexual desires, he would not be able, because of his slavery, to become the head (*qawwām*) of the family. As a consequence of such a relationship, the foundations of family life would be weakened.

(3) The words of the verse: 'But those who seek beyond that – such are the transgressors', prohibit all forms of sexual relations, except the two specified in the verse. These words not only prohibit sexual relations with all those women who do not fall into the above two categories, but also prohibit such relations with other males as also with all animals. The only form of sexual gratification about which there is some disagreement among jurists is masturbation. Aḥmad ibn Ḥanbal regarded it as lawful while Mālik and Shāfi'ī considered it totally forbidden. The Ḥanafī school whilst looking upon it as an unlawful act, is of the view that if someone is overpowered by sexual passion to commit such an act occasionally rather than habitually, God might pardon him.

(4) Some commentators on the Qur'ān cite this verse to prove the prohibition of *mut'ah* (temporary marriage). They argue that a woman in temporary marriage is neither a wife nor a slave-girl. So far as her

not being a slave-girl is concerned, this is quite obvious. Now as far as her being a wife is concerned, we find that none of the laws with regard to marriage apply to her. She neither inherits her male partner nor does the latter inherit her. Nor is the waiting period (*'iddah*) applicable in her case, nor divorce or maintenance, nor the other rules in respect to matters pertaining to marriage such as *īlā', ẓihār* and *li'ān*. A temporary wife is also not counted as one of the four wives, the maximum one may have at any time. As she does not belong to the category of either wife or slave-girl, those who have sexual relations with temporary wives fall into the category of those 'who seek beyond what is lawful', and such people have been branded by the Qur'ān as transgressors. (See verse 7.)

This argument appears quite weighty, yet it is marred by the fact that it is difficult to say with absolute certainty that the verse categorically forbids *mut'ah*. The Prophet Muḥammad (peace be upon him) forbade *mut'ah* in a categorical and definitive manner in the year of the conquest of Makka. That *mut'ah* was considered permissible before that is something which is borne out by authentic traditions. Let us suppose that the verse under discussion prohibits *mut'ah*. Now this verse is unanimously considered a Makkan verse, revealed a few years before the *Hijrah*. It seems simply inconceivable that the Prophet (peace be upon him) would have allowed the practice of *mut'ah* (temporary marriage) till the conquest of Makka, even though it had been prohibited by the Qur'ān. It would, therefore, be safer to hold that *mut'ah* was not forbidden by any Qur'ānic verse, but rather by the *Sunnah* of the Prophet (peace be upon him). Had this matter not been clearly resolved by the *Sunnah, mut'ah* could not be forbidden simply on the basis of this verse.

While discussing the question of *mut'ah,* two points need to be clarified here. First, that it had been forbidden by the Prophet (peace be upon him) himself. It is, therefore, incorrect to say that it was 'Umar who forbade it. The fact is that 'Umar was not the one who prohibited *mut'ah,* but the one who enforced the prohibition. *Mut'ah* was prohibited by the Prophet (peace be upon him) himself in the very last stages of his life and, hence, its prohibition was not known to everyone. What 'Umar did was to proclaim the prohibition in such a manner that it became widely known. Moreover, he ensured it was duly executed by recourse to the force of law. Second, as for the legal position of the Shī'ah that *mut'ah* is absolutely lawful, there is no justification for this in any text of the Qur'ān or the *Sunnah*. In the early period of Islam, the few Companions and Successors who held *mut'ah* to be lawful confined its lawfulness to highly exceptional circumstances, to circumstances of extreme compulsion and necessity. None of them believed *mut'ah* to be unconditionally lawful in normal circumstances, i.e. a practice that would be as lawful as say contracting marriage.

'Abd Allāh ibn 'Abbās is mentioned as the leading authority to hold this practice as lawful. It is significant that Ibn 'Abbās mentions the lawfulness of *mut'ah* in the following words: 'It is no different from the carrion which is not lawful for anyone except for him who is compelled to eat it.' (See Jaṣṣāṣ, vol. 2, p. 147 – Ed.) Ibn 'Abbās did, however, recant his position when he observed that some people misused the permission and indulged

(8) who are true to their trusts and their covenants,[8] (9) and who guard their Prayers.[9] ▶	وَٱلَّذِينَ هُمْ لِأَمَـٰنَـٰتِهِمْ وَعَهْدِهِمْ رَٰعُونَ ﴿٨﴾ وَٱلَّذِينَ هُمْ عَلَىٰ صَلَوَٰتِهِمْ يُحَافِظُونَ ﴿٩﴾

in it freely instead of availing of it only under compulsive circumstances. Disregarding whether Ibn 'Abbās and the very small number of like-minded Companions recanted their positions or not, all those who claim to follow the legal position can avail themselves of the lawfulness of *mut'ah* only in very exceptional circumstances. There are no grounds, in any case, to consider it unconditionally lawful, even if one has wives whom one has duly married. Practising *mut'ah* in such a circumstance seems outrageous to a person of sound taste, let alone that its lawfulness be ascribed to the *Sharī'ah* of Muḥammad (peace be upon him) and the *imāms* of the Prophet's family.

I believe that no decent person of the Shī'ah community would be happy if someone were to seek to contract *mut'ah* rather than regular marriage with his sister or daughter. This being the case, if *mut'ah* were practised, it would be necessary to have a fair number of low-class women, say similar to prostitutes. The other possibility is that women of poor families are subjected to *mut'ah* by the rich. However, it is unthinkable that either God or the Prophet (peace be upon him) would endorse a law that is so flagrantly unjust. Is it plausible that the *Sharī'ah* would sanction a practice which no woman could help but view as brazenly dishonourable and shameless?

8. The word *amānāt* (trusts) encompasses all types of trust which either God or society or an individual places in someone else's charge.

As for the word *'ahd* (pledge), it embraces all covenants between man and God, man and man, and one nation and another. One of the distinguishing characteristics of a believer is that he never betrays a trust and never goes back on his committed word. In his sermons, the Prophet (peace be upon him) often used to say: 'He who is not true to his trust is devoid of faith, and he who does not keep to his commitment is devoid of [true] religiosity.' (See Aḥmad ibn Ḥanbal, *Musnad*, vol. 3, p. 135. See also Bayhaqī, *Shu'ab al-Īmān* – Ed.) A tradition in Bukhārī and Muslim states that the Prophet (peace be upon him) said: 'There are four attributes which if they are found in some person [it will be deemed that] he is a full-fledged hypocrite. And if someone has any one of these four attributes [it will be deemed that] he has one attribute of hypocrisy until he abandons it. These attributes are: when he is charged with a trust, he betrays it; when he speaks, he lies; when he makes a commitment, he violates it; and when he quarrels, he transgresses [all limits of morality and truthfulness].' (See Bukhārī and Muslim.)

9. In an earlier verse (see verse 2 above) while referring to *khushū'* it was said that the Believers are those who humble themselves in Prayer (*ṣalāh*). There, the word *ṣalāh* was used in the singular whereas in the present verse, the same word is used in the plural. This is because of a difference in the two

(10) Such are the inheritors (11) that shall inherit Paradise;[10] and in it they shall abide for ever.[11]

(12) We created man out of the extract of clay, (13) then We made him ▸

أُوْلَٰٓئِكَ هُمُ ٱلْوَٰرِثُونَ ﴿١٠﴾ ٱلَّذِينَ
يَرِثُونَ ٱلْفِرْدَوْسَ هُمْ فِيهَا خَٰلِدُونَ ﴿١١﴾
وَلَقَدْ خَلَقْنَا ٱلْإِنسَٰنَ مِن سُلَٰلَةٍ
مِّن طِينٍ ﴿١٢﴾ ثُمَّ جَعَلْنَٰهُ

usages. In the first case, Prayer as such was meant, whereas in the second, the word signifies each single, individual Prayer. Thus, safeguarding Prayers in the second instance means that believers safeguard the appointed time of each Prayer, and safeguard all the rituals of which it is composed; in short, they safeguard everything associated with Prayer. Thus, their safeguarding Prayers means that they take full care to keep their bodies and clothes clean, to perform ablution properly, and remain ever vigilant lest they perform any Prayer without ablution. They should also be mindful of performing Prayers at the right time, rather than lazily, allowing the time to go by. They should also perform all the acts related to Prayers with due concentration and equanimity and not treat them as if they were a burden which they would rather get rid of. Rather than mechanically repeating a set of words that one has committed to memory and which one somehow likes to utter and finish with, everything should be recited with full consciousness and in the manner that a servant entreats his master.

10. *Firdaws*, the most commonly used word for Paradise in the Qur'ān, is common to almost all languages. In Sanskrit, we have the word *Pardisha*, in ancient Kaldian *Pardisa*, in ancient Persian *Pairidaisa*, in Hebrew *Pardis*, in Armenian *Pardiz*, in Syriac *Fardisw*, in Greek *Paradaisus*, in Latin *Paradisus* and in Arabic we have the word *Firdaws*. In all these languages the word signifies a large, enclosed garden adjoining one's residence, a garden that abounds in fruits, especially grapes. In some languages the concept also includes the notion of a garden that abounds in pet birds and animals.

The word *Firdaws* was also used in pre-Islamic Arabic literature. In the Qur'ān, it is used to denote a collection of gardens, such as in the following verse: 'As for those who believe and do good works, the Gardens of Paradise shall be there to welcome them' (*al-Kahf* 18: 107). The image that emerges from this verse is that *Firdaws* is a very spacious garden full of trees, fruits and flowers.

The idea that the believers would inherit Paradise is also mentioned elsewhere in the Qur'ān. For further elaboration, see *Towards Understanding the Qur'ān*, vol. V, *Ṭā Hā* 20, n. 83, p. 226 and *al-Anbiyā'* 21, n. 99, pp. 299–302.

11. These verses make four significant points: first, that those who accept the teaching of the Qur'ān and the Prophet (peace be upon him) as

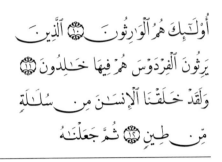

into a drop of life-germ, then We placed it in a safe depository, (14) then We made this drop into a clot, then We made the clot into a lump, then We made the lump into bones, then We clothed the bones with flesh,[12] ▶	نُطْفَةً فِي قَرَارٍ مَّكِينٍ ﴿١٣﴾ ثُمَّ خَلَقْنَا ٱلنُّطْفَةَ عَلَقَةً فَخَلَقْنَا ٱلْعَلَقَةَ مُضْغَةً فَخَلَقْنَا ٱلْمُضْغَةَ عِظَـٰمًا فَكَسَوْنَا ٱلْعِظَـٰمَ لَحْمًا

true and develop the attributes enunciated here, will succeed in the present world and in the World to Come.

Second, true success does not accrue merely by a verbal affirmation of faith, nor merely by developing in oneself some good qualities. True success rather requires a combination of both. When a man accepts God's guidance and cultivates good moral qualities in the light of that guidance, he achieves success.

Third, success does not simply comprise material well-being, nor is it limited to ephemeral worldly success. Instead, man's success consists in a pervasive well-being which embraces unceasing prosperity and well-being both in the present world and in the Hereafter. These can only be attained if one has faith and one is righteous in conduct. This is a universal law and is not negated by the ephemeral prosperity and success of those who are immersed in error. Nor is this law negated by the fact that righteous men of faith are at times temporarily faced with hardship.

Fourth, the attributes of believers are put forward as proof of the truth of Prophet Muḥammad's (pbuh) mission. It is this aspect of the present verses which links them with the discourse that follows until verse 50.

The argument develops in the following manner. It opens with an empirical proof. It says that the teachings of the Prophet (peace be upon him) brought about a moral change in some members of society who had accepted the true faith insofar as they had developed admirable moral qualities. That being the case, it was for the unbelievers to consider how such wholesome changes could have been brought about had the Prophet's teachings not been true.

This is followed by an argument based on observation. It runs as follows: 'There are innumerable signs in the universe around man and within him which conclusively prove the truth of the doctrines of monotheism and of the Hereafter expounded by the Prophet (peace be upon him).' These are followed by arguments drawn from human history.

The historical argument is as follows: the conflict between the Prophets and their opponents had been raging since ancient times and the outcome of this conflict was always the same. This clearly shows which party was in the right, and which in the wrong.

12. For elaboration see *al-Ḥajj* 22, nn. 5, 6 and 9 above.

and then We caused it to grow into another creation.[13] Thus Most Blessed is Allah,[14] the Best of all those that create. (15) Thereafter you are destined to die, (16) and then on the Day of Resurrection you shall certainly be raised up.

ثُمَّ أَنشَأۡنَٰهُ خَلۡقًا ءَاخَرَۚ فَتَبَارَكَ ٱللَّهُ
أَحۡسَنُ ٱلۡخَٰلِقِينَ ﴿١٤﴾ ثُمَّ إِنَّكُم بَعۡدَ
ذَٰلِكَ لَمَيِّتُونَ ﴿١٥﴾ ثُمَّ إِنَّكُمۡ يَوۡمَ
ٱلۡقِيَٰمَةِ تُبۡعَثُونَ ﴿١٦﴾

---

13. Anyone who notes the growth of a foetus in a mother's womb will never be able to anticipate what kind of baby will come into being nor what its mental and physical faculties will be. It is impossible for anyone to predict the marvellous achievements that a child may go on to make in different fields by dint of his intellectual ability, wisdom and skill. For, in the beginning every child is no more than a lump of flesh, which up until its birth is possessed of no more than the most rudimentary attributes of life. In these early stages, the foetus is devoid of the faculties of hearing, sight, speech, understanding and reason. Soon after birth, however, a child becomes something quite different from the foetus it originally was. It now makes its mark as one gifted with the faculties of seeing, hearing, and speaking, and one who gradually acquires knowledge through experience and observation. The child also develops, by and by, an ego of its own which, from the very outset, asserts itself in relation to the things around it, and seeks to establish dominance over them. And as the child grows its ego manifests itself as a factor that constantly becomes more conspicuous and full of impact. Later, when the child grows into youth, he or she becomes totally different from the baby that was. At middle age, we again find another change, and with old age the difference is so great from what was visible in the earlier stages of life that it becomes extremely difficult for the younger ones to imagine what this older person looked like in childhood or during youth. Such extraordinary changes do not occur in any other creature on earth. Let a person look at the powers and abilities of a grown-up and then consider that this was once only a drop of sperm which had been dropped in a mother's womb some fifty or sixty years previously and which had all these astonishing qualities latent in it. When one does actually reflect on this one is forced to utter, with wonder and excitement the words that we find in the verse that follows: 'Blessed is Allah, the Best of all those that create.'

14. The actual words used are فتبارك الله. The full significance and richness of these words are hard to translate. In terms of lexicography and linguistic usage, the expression embraces two meanings. First, that Allah is extremely Holy and is far above all defects, imperfections and limitations. Second, that Allah is so infinitely Good, Bounteous and Munificent that

(17) We have indeed fashioned above you seven paths.[15] Never were We unaware of the task of creation.[16] ▶

وَلَقَدْ خَلَقْنَا فَوْقَكُمْ سَبْعَ طَرَآئِقَ وَمَا كُنَّا عَنِ ٱلْخَلْقِ غَـٰفِلِينَ ﴿١٧﴾

we always find Him higher than whatever estimate we form of Him. (For further elaboration see *al-Furqān* 25, nn. 1 and 19 below.)

When both these meanings are taken into consideration, it is clear that the exclamation 'Blessed is Allah' at the conclusion of the account of the different stages of man's creation by God, serves not only to exalt God, but in fact constitutes the natural conclusion of the argument. What is brought home here is that God, Who develops the extract of clay into a fully-fledged man, is far too Holy to have any partner in His Godhead. Likewise, He is far too great to be incapable of re-creating man whom He created in the first instance. It would also be a very low estimate of God to think that His creative capacities ceased once He created man and that, thereafter, He became bereft of the ability to further create.

15. The actual word used is *ṭarā'iq* which signifies both 'paths' and 'layers'. (See *ṭ-r-q* in *Lisān al-'Arab* – Ed.) If the term is taken in the first sense, it means the orbit of the seven planets. Since man at that time knew only of seven planets, hence only those orbits are mentioned. This statement does not mean that there are no other orbits. On the other hand, if we consider سبع طرائق in the second sense, it means سبع سماوات طباقا an expression used elsewhere in the Qur'ān, 'seven heavens one layer upon the other' (*al-Mulk* 67: 3).

In the present verse it is said that God 'fashioned above you seven paths . . .' Its simple meaning is what the words clearly convey in the first instance. But the statement also seems to emphasize God's greatness insofar as He created the heavens whose creation is a much greater achievement than the creation of man. This is quite in consonance with what the Qur'ān has said elsewhere: 'Indeed the creation of the heavens and the earth is greater than the creation of man' (*al-Mu'min* 40: 57).

16. Alternatively, this verse can be rendered as follows: 'We were never [nor are] oblivious of the creatures.'

The idea expressed here is that it is quite evident from everything God has created that it has neither been created purposelessly nor is it the creation of someone devoid of skill. On the contrary, God's creation conforms to a well-considered plan, with the result that all parts of His creation reveal a high degree of mutual harmony and coordination. Purposiveness is also evident from every aspect of this vast universe and this conclusively points to the wisdom of its Creator.

(18) We sent down water from the sky in right measure, and caused it to stay in the earth,[17] and We have the power ▶	وَأَنزَلْنَا مِنَ ٱلسَّمَآءِ مَآءًۢ بِقَدَرٍ فَأَسْكَنَّٰهُ فِى ٱلْأَرْضِ ۖ وَإِنَّا عَلَىٰ

Alternatively, if the verse is understood in the second sense (namely 'We were never oblivious of the creatures'), it would mean that God has never been negligent of the needs of any of His creatures, nor has He ever been unaware of the state they are in. The result is that God has never allowed anything to go in a direction opposed to His plans, nor has he ever been negligent in providing for the natural requirements of anything. God has always been mindful of all His creation, be it a tiny particle or the leaf of a tree, or anything else.

17. This may be understood to mean seasonal rainfall. When one considers the words of the verse, however, one might be inclined to accept another meaning as well: that at the time of creating the universe, God provided it with water through one huge downpour. Thanks to God's infinite knowledge, He provided through this downpour water in a quantity that would suffice for the earth's needs for all time to come. The water that was so provided accumulated in the recesses of the earth, giving rise to seas, gulfs, and sub-soil water. It is this accumulation of water which is kept rotating through the varying seasons and winds. The original resource of water continues to be distributed through rains, snow-clad mountains, rivers, springs, and wells. This very accumulation of water enters into the process of creation and into the composition of a variety of things. Then it also becomes part of the wind and eventually returns to the same original resource of water. Thus, from the beginning until today the total quantity of water has neither increased nor decreased by as much as a single drop.

What is even more astonishing is that water is composed of two gases, namely hydrogen and oxygen, which were released only once in such quantity and right proportion that a vast quantity of water was produced which continues to fill the seas and oceans and no fresh supply is added to it. So who is it who prevents hydrogen and oxygen from intermingling, even though both gases are found in the world, with the result that not a drop of water has been added to the original reservoir of water? We also know that water evaporates into air. Again who is it who prevents the two gases from separating after this evaporation? Do atheists have any answers to these questions? Or can all this be satisfactorily explained by those who believe in a multiplicity of gods, who believe that there are separate gods of wind and water, of heat and cold?

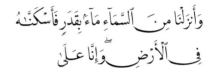

to cause it to vanish (in the manner We please).[18] (19) Then through water We caused gardens of date-palms and vines to grow for you wherein you have an abundance of delicious fruits[19] and from them you derive your livelihood.[20] (20) And We also produced the tree which springs forth from Mount Sinai,[21] containing oil and sauce for those that eat.

ذَهَابٍ بِهِۦ لَقَٰدِرُونَ ﴿١٨﴾ فَأَنشَأْنَا لَكُم
بِهِۦ جَنَّٰتٍ مِّن نَّخِيلٍ وَأَعْنَٰبٍ لَّكُمْ
فِيهَا فَوَٰكِهُ كَثِيرَةٌ وَمِنْهَا تَأْكُلُونَ ﴿١٩﴾
وَشَجَرَةً تَخْرُجُ مِن طُورِ سَيْنَآءَ تَنۢبُتُ
بِٱلدُّهْنِ وَصِبْغٍ لِّلْأَٰكِلِينَ ﴿٢٠﴾

---

18. There are numerous means by which water can be made to disappear: God is quite capable of cutting off the supply of this vital life source by any of these means. Thus, this verse further extends the import of the one which follows: 'What do you consider, if one morning your water were to vanish in the earth who would then supply you with clear flowing water?' (*al-Mulk* 67: 30).

19. This refers to a wide variety of dry and fresh fruits in addition to dates and grapes.

20. Orchards and farms provide man with many forms of livelihood – fruits, grains, timber and much, much more. The words used in the verse are منها تأكلون in which the pronoun منها is related to the word *jannāt* (gardens), rather than to *fawākih* (fruits). As for the word *ta'kulūn* it does not simply mean that 'people eat the fruits of these gardens', it rather conveys the wider meaning of deriving a livelihood from them.

21. This alludes to the olive, the most important product in all the lands around the Mediterranean Sea. The olive tree lasts for one and a half to two thousand years. Olive trees live for so long that on the basis of the height and breadth of some in Palestine it is estimated that they date back to the days of the Prophet Jesus (peace be upon him).

The olive tree is mentioned here in association with Mount Sinai. This presumably is because the original habitat of the olive tree is Mount Sinai which in turn is the most prominent place in that region.

(21) And indeed there is also a lesson for you in cattle. We provide you with drink out of what they have in their bellies;[22] and you have many other benefits in them: you eat of them, (22) and are carried on them and also on ships.[23]

(23) We sent Noah to his people,[24] and he said: "My people! Serve Allah; you have no deity other than He. Do you have no fear?"[25] (24) But the notables among his people had refused to believe, and said:▶

وَإِنَّ لَكُمْ فِى ٱلْأَنْعَـٰمِ لَعِبْرَةً ۖ نُّسْقِيكُم
مِّمَّا فِى بُطُونِهَا وَلَكُمْ فِيهَا مَنَـٰفِعُ
كَثِيرَةٌ وَمِنْهَا تَأْكُلُونَ ﴿٢١﴾ وَعَلَيْهَا
وَعَلَى ٱلْفُلْكِ تُحْمَلُونَ ﴿٢٢﴾ وَلَقَدْ أَرْسَلْنَا
نُوحًا إِلَىٰ قَوْمِهِۦ فَقَالَ يَـٰقَوْمِ ٱعْبُدُوا۟ ٱللَّهَ
مَا لَكُم مِّنْ إِلَـٰهٍ غَيْرُهُۥٓ ۖ أَفَلَا تَتَّقُونَ ﴿٢٣﴾
فَقَالَ ٱلْمَلَؤُا۟ ٱلَّذِينَ كَفَرُوا۟ مِن قَوْمِهِۦ

22. This refers to milk. At another place the Qur'ān speaks of it as something produced from what is within the bodies of animals, between excretion and blood (see *al-Naḥl* 16: 66).

23. Cattle and ships are juxtaposed here because the Arabs mostly used camels for transportation. Now, the camel has been known for a very long time as the 'ship of the desert'. In the poetry of Dhū'l-Rumnah, a pre-Islamic poet of Arabia, we come across the following line:

سفينة برّ تحت خدي زمامها

('The ship of the desert, its rein is under my cheek.')

24. For comparison see *al-A'rāf* 7: 59–64; *Yūnus* 10: 71–3; *Hūd* 11: 25 and 48; *Banī Isrā'īl* 17: 3; and *al-Anbiyā'* 21: 76–7.

25. The unbelievers are asked: do they not have fear when they worship other than their true God? Are they not fearful of the terrible consequences of serving and obeying others than the One True God when they live in the realm of He Who is the true Lord and Master of the whole universe and of themselves as well?

"This is none other than a mortal like yourselves[26] who desires to attain superiority over you.[27] ▶

مَا هَـٰذَآ إِلَّا بَشَرٌ مِّثْلُكُمْ يُرِيدُ أَن يَتَفَضَّلَ عَلَيْكُمْ

26. All those who have wandered away from the True Path share one common error – that a human being cannot become a Prophet; and that Prophets are not human beings. It is for this reason that the Qur'ān repeatedly declared this idea to be altogether false, emphasizing that all the Prophets were human. The Qur'ān also says that in order to carry out the functions of the Prophetic office effectively, he who is sent to human beings should be one of them. (See for further details *al-A'rāf* 7: 63 and 69; *Yūnus* 10: 2; *Hūd* 11: 27 and 31; *Yūsuf* 12: 109; *al-Ra'd* 13: 38; *Ibrāhīm* 14: 10–11; *al-Naḥl* 16: 43; *Banī Isrā'īl* 17: 94–5; *al-Kahf* 18: 110; *al-Anbiyā'* 21: 3 and 34; *al-Mu'minūn* 23: 33 and 47; *Fuṣṣilat* 41: 6 and also the relevant notes.)

27. The enemies of the truth have always been wont to charge that the activity of reformers is actuated by their hunger for power. This very charge was levelled by Pharaoh against Moses and Aaron and was phrased in the form of the following question 'Have you come to turn us away from the way of our forefathers that the two of you might become supreme in the land?' (*Yūnus* 10: 78). The Prophet Jesus (peace be upon him) was also subjected to a similar accusation: that he was striving to become the king of the Jews. The unbelieving Quraysh entertained the same suspicion about the Prophet Muḥammad (peace be upon him). Hence, they made several attempts to entice him into striking a bargain with them. They suggested that if he sought power, they were willing to accept him as their sovereign.

It is inconceivable for those who ceaselessly hanker after worldly benefits, after pomp and glory, to appreciate that anyone can strive simply for the good of mankind, and that all such striving be absolutely sincere and selfless. Such people are wont to come up, every now and then, with catchy slogans and lay false claims to be working for the common welfare of all. They do so even though the true purpose of their effort is nothing else but to achieve power and influence. Furthermore, they regard craftiness and deception as absolutely natural. No wonder then that they tend to believe that no one can call for reform sincerely and altruistically. If someone does call for reform, he must inevitably be prompted, like them, by some ulterior motive. For example, as a subterfuge for the realization of his own selfish designs.

It is also interesting that accusations of hungering after power are always hurled at reformers by those who have been able to entrench themselves in power or by their sycophantic cronies. They seem to believe that the power they enjoy is their birth-right. Hence, if they strive to wrest power from others and to perpetuate their hold on it, all is viewed as perfectly legitimate. But it becomes altogether objectionable if anyone else,

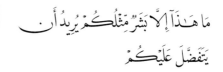

Had Allah wanted (to send any Messengers) He would have sent down angels.[28] We have heard nothing like this in the time of our forebears of old (that humans were sent as Messengers). ▶	وَلَوْ شَآءَ ٱللَّهُ لَأَنزَلَ مَلَـٰٓئِكَةً مَّا سَمِعْنَا بِهَـٰذَا فِىٓ ءَابَآئِنَا ٱلْأَوَّلِينَ ﴿٢٤﴾

someone who has no birth-right to enjoy power, shows the least sign of hungering for it. (For further elaboration see n. 36 below.)

It is pertinent at this stage to point out that whoever rises with the purpose of purging the prevalent order of its evils and expounds a reformist idea and programme is bound to confront the forces that obstruct and oppose such reform. In time, the reformer will naturally make efforts to remove these obstructions, and seek to bring to power those forces that will implement and enforce his ideas and programmes. Additionally, if and when the call for such reform succeeds, that reformer will naturally be invested with leadership and will himself either hold the reins of power, or bring to power some of his supporters and followers. Can we identify any single Prophet or reformer whose efforts were not directed at the implementation of his Message? Who of them did not assume the leadership of his people after his call attained success? Given that, does the mere fact of someone's assuming the leadership of his people suffice to accuse him of being power-hungry? It is only those implacable enemies of the truth who can answer this question in the affirmative.

In point of fact, there is a world of difference between seeking power for its own sake and seeking it for a good cause. This difference can be understood if we compare the dagger of a bandit with the knife of a surgeon. Now, it is possible that someone might claim that there is no difference between the bandit's use of his dagger and the surgeon's use of his instruments, i.e. both pierce another person's body with a sharp instrument. Moreover, both of them acquire money from their action. The preposterousness of this line of argument is all too evident even to be stated. For, the two persons radically differ from each other in respect of their intentions and objectives, their *modus operandi* and their overall role and character. If this were not so, they would not be known by two different names, bandit and surgeon.

28. This statement makes it incontrovertibly clear that the people of Noah (peace be upon him) did not deny the existence of God. Nor did they deny that God is the Lord of the universe Who has all angels subservient to His authority. Thus, Noah's people were guilty of polytheism rather than of atheism; guilty of associating others with the attributes, power and authority of God rather than denying His existence.

(25) He is a person who has been seized with a little madness; so wait for a while (perhaps he will improve)." (26) Noah said: "My Lord! Come to my help at their accusation that I am lying."[29] (27) Thereupon We revealed to him, saying: "Build the Ark under Our eyes and according to Our revelation. And when Our command comes to pass and the oven boils over,[30] take on board a pair each from every species, and also take your household except those of them against whom sentence has already been passed and do not plead to Me on behalf of the wrong-doers. They are doomed to be drowned. ▶

إِنْ هُوَ إِلَّا رَجُلٌۢ بِهِۦ جِنَّةٌ فَتَرَبَّصُوا۟ بِهِۦ حَتَّىٰ
حِينٍ ﴿٢٥﴾ قَالَ رَبِّ ٱنصُرْنِى بِمَا كَذَّبُونِ
﴿٢٦﴾ فَأَوْحَيْنَآ إِلَيْهِ أَنِ ٱصْنَعِ ٱلْفُلْكَ بِأَعْيُنِنَا
وَوَحْيِنَا فَإِذَا جَآءَ أَمْرُنَا وَفَارَ ٱلتَّنُّورُ ۙ فَٱسْلُكْ
فِيهَا مِن كُلٍّ زَوْجَيْنِ ٱثْنَيْنِ وَأَهْلَكَ إِلَّا مَن
سَبَقَ عَلَيْهِ ٱلْقَوْلُ مِنْهُمْ ۖ وَلَا تُخَـٰطِبْنِى فِى
ٱلَّذِينَ ظَلَمُوٓا۟ ۖ إِنَّهُم مُّغْرَقُونَ ﴿٢٧﴾

---

29. The Prophet Noah implored God to punish those who had been accusing him of deceit: 'Then he called on his Lord: "I am one overcome; help me, then, to victory" ' (*al-Qamar* 54: 10). The Qur'ān also mentions that: 'And Noah said: "O my Lord! Leave not any of the unbelievers, not a single one of them on earth! For if You leave any of them, they will but mislead Your servants, and they will breed none but those that are wicked and ungrateful" ' (*Nūḥ* 71: 26–7).

30. Some scholars are inclined to interpret the word *al-tannūr* to mean the earth. Others have considered it to be the highest point of the earth, and others that it means sunrise. Other scholars though set it as a metaphor, the blowing up of *tannūr* being merely a figure of speech such as the expression حمي الوطيس meaning the boiling up of turbulence.

There seems little reason, however, to interpret this word figuratively in disregard of its literal meaning. The verse seems to suggest that a particular oven was indeed designated aforetime as the place from which water would start gushing forth. Such an incident, it was believed, would

(28) And then when you and those accompanying you are firmly seated in the Ark, say: "Thanks be to Allah Who has delivered us from the wrong-doing people."[31] (29) And say: "My Lord! Make my landing a blessed landing, for You are the Best of those Who can cause people to land in safety."[32]

(30) There are great Signs[33] in this story; and ▶

فَإِذَا ٱسْتَوَيْتَ أَنتَ وَمَن مَّعَكَ عَلَى ٱلْفُلْكِ
فَقُلِ ٱلْحَمْدُ لِلَّهِ ٱلَّذِى نَجَّىٰنَا مِنَ ٱلْقَوْمِ
ٱلظَّٰلِمِينَ ﴿٢٨﴾ وَقُل رَّبِّ أَنزِلْنِى مُنزَلًا
مُّبَارَكًا وَأَنتَ خَيْرُ ٱلْمُنزِلِينَ ﴿٢٩﴾ إِنَّ
فِى ذَٰلِكَ لَءَايَٰتٍ

mark the beginning of the Flood. Now, one may feel the need to interpret this word figuratively only if one is not prepared to accept that a flood of such gigantic proportions could have commenced with the eruption of water from an oven. The fact that the starting-point of such an enormous flood was an oven simply shows that the ways of God are indeed strange. Once He decides to inflict a nation with scourge, He strikes from a direction which is even beyond the ken of their imagination.

31. It is significant that God commanded Noah (peace be upon him) to thank Him for the total annihilation of a people. This is clear proof of the extent to which the people of Noah (peace be upon him) were involved in corruption, wickedness and criminal mischief.

32. To make someone land at a certain place, according to Arabic idiom, has the connotation of entertaining and playing host to him. This Prayer, therefore, amounts to saying to God: 'From now on we are Your guests, and You are our hosts.'

33. This story is full of lessons. Through it we learn that the Prophets who called mankind to monotheism were right whereas those who insisted on polytheism were wrong. It is significant that this was also true of Makka in the time of the Prophet (peace be upon him). In fact the Makkan situation at the time of the Prophet Muḥammad closely resembled the situation which obtained in the time of the Prophet Noah (peace be upon them). Additionally, the role of the Prophet Muḥammad was similar to the role of the Prophet Noah (peace be upon them). Likewise, the attitude of the Makkans at the time of Muḥammad (peace be upon him) was similar to that of Noah's people.

surely We do put people to test.[34]

(31) Then, after them, We brought forth another generation;[35] (32) and We sent among them a Messenger from among themselves, ▶

وَإِن كُنَّا لَمُبْتَلِينَ ﴿٣٠﴾ ثُمَّ أَنشَأْنَا مِنۢ بَعْدِهِمْ قَرْنًا ءَاخَرِينَ ﴿٣١﴾ فَأَرْسَلْنَا فِيهِمْ رَسُولًا مِّنْهُمْ

This suggests, in a subtle manner, that the unbelieving Makkans were bound to meet the same fate which had befallen Noah's people. God's Judgement might take some time but it was bound to come and when it did, it would undoubtedly be in favour of the votaries of the truth and against the unbelievers.

34. Alternatively, the verse might be translated as follows: 'We had to put them to test' or 'We have to put them to test.' Whatever be the truly correct translation of the verse, its thrust is to warn people. The warning consisted of bringing home to Noah's people that God does not allow any people whom He has invested with authority and power in any part of His earth to go about doing as they wish, and if they do that God will not hold them to account. On the contrary, it is God's rule that such people are constantly under observation. They are watched in order to establish whether they abuse the power that has been bestowed upon them. What befell Noah's people was strictly according to this rule. No nation is God's favourite to such an extent that He leaves them free to go about pouncing upon the treasures of the world, and never calling them to account for their deeds. All have to go through this process.

35. Some scholars consider this to refer to the Thamūd. For it is said a little later in this *sūrah* that the people of the Thamūd were destroyed by a blast (see verse 41 below). We learn from the Qur'ān that it was indeed the Thamūd who were thus destroyed (*Hūd* 11: 67; *al-Ḥijr* 15: 83; *al-Qamar* 54: 31). According to other scholars, however, this verse refers to the 'Ād since it is they who succeeded Noah's people: 'And do call to mind when He made successors after the people of Noah' (*al-A'rāf* 7: 69). The latter opinion seems more plausible and seems to be corroborated by the words '. . . after the people of Noah'.

As for the reference to the *ṣayḥah* (see, for example, *Hūd* 11: 67 etc.), it was not specific to the Thamūd. For it may be taken, in its general sense, to be the scourge which caused death on a massive scale. Moreover, the word *ṣayḥah* is also used for that hue and cry which takes place at the time of death on a massive scale, whatever its actual cause.

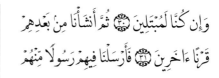

saying: "Serve Allah; you have no god other than He. Do you have no fear?" (33) The notables among his people who had refused to believe and who denied the meeting of the Hereafter, and those whom We had endowed with ease and comfort in this life, cried out:[36] "This is no other than a mortal like yourselves who eats what you eat and drinks what you drink. (34) If you were to obey a human being like yourselves, you will certainly be losers.[37] ▶

أَنِ ٱعۡبُدُواْ ٱللَّهَ مَا لَكُم مِّنۡ إِلَٰهٍ غَيۡرُهُۥٓۚ
أَفَلَا تَتَّقُونَ ٣٢ وَقَالَ ٱلۡمَلَأُ مِن قَوۡمِهِ ٱلَّذِينَ
كَفَرُواْ وَكَذَّبُواْ بِلِقَآءِ ٱلۡأٓخِرَةِ وَأَتۡرَفۡنَٰهُمۡ
فِي ٱلۡحَيَوٰةِ ٱلدُّنۡيَا مَا هَٰذَآ إِلَّا بَشَرٞ
مِّثۡلُكُمۡ يَأۡكُلُ مِمَّا تَأۡكُلُونَ مِنۡهُ
وَيَشۡرَبُ مِمَّا تَشۡرَبُونَ ٣٣ وَلَئِنۡ أَطَعۡتُم بَشَرٗا
مِّثۡلَكُمۡ إِنَّكُمۡ إِذٗا لَّخَٰسِرُونَ ٣٤

---

36. This characterization of the opponents is significant. The ringleaders opposing the Prophet (peace be upon him) were those who held the leadership of their people. The error into which all of them had fallen was their denial of Life after Death. Hence, they had no notion of being accountable or answerable to God. This, in turn, was because of their excessive infatuation with worldly life and their refusal to believe in any value above material well-being. The fact that at that time they enjoyed a considerable degree of prosperity totally swamped them in this erroneous belief. They were so deeply engrossed in worldliness that they considered themselves to be right merely because they thrived materially. They were, thus, in no mood to accept that their beliefs, morality and way of life, which they thought to be the main cause of their success in this world could be mistaken. Human history has repeatedly provided evidence of the fact that the opponents of the truth have always held these three features in common. Little wonder, then, that the same scenario obtained in Makka at the time when the Prophet Muḥammad (peace be upon him) embarked on his reform movement.

37. Some people have misunderstood this verse to mean that the unbelievers made such statements to one another in their private conversations. The fact is, however, that such things were said by the notables of society to the common people. The notables had begun to sense the danger that the commoners might be swayed by the distinctly noble character and appealing discourse of the Prophet (peace be upon him). They considered this possibility a serious threat to their vested interests, to their positions of power, to their privileges and leadership. It was this realization which

(35) Does he promise you that when you are dead and are reduced to dust and bones, you will be brought forth to life? (36) Far-fetched, utterly far-fetched is what you are being promised. (37) There is no other life than the life of the world. We shall live here and here shall we die; and we are not going to be raised again. (38) This man has forged a mere lie in the name of Allah[38] ▶

أَيَعِدُكُمْ أَنَّكُمْ إِذَا مِتُّمْ وَكُنتُمْ تُرَابًا
وَعِظَٰمًا أَنَّكُم مُّخْرَجُونَ ﴿٣٥﴾ ۞ هَيْهَاتَ
هَيْهَاتَ لِمَا تُوعَدُونَ ﴿٣٦﴾ إِنْ هِيَ إِلَّا حَيَاتُنَا
ٱلدُّنْيَا نَمُوتُ وَنَحْيَا وَمَا نَحْنُ بِمَبْعُوثِينَ ﴿٣٧﴾
إِنْ هُوَ إِلَّا رَجُلٌ ٱفْتَرَىٰ عَلَى ٱللَّهِ

prompted them to resort to the vicious propaganda campaign of the kind mentioned earlier, a propaganda deliberately aimed at misleading people.

This represents another aspect of the attitude mentioned earlier with regard to the notables among Noah's people who hurled similar accusations at him (see verse 24 above – Ed.). The notables virtually said that all his claims to be God's Messenger [on the part of Hūd] were merely designed to hood-wink people. All that he was really motivated by was a lust for power. They also claimed that he was in no way different from other people. After all, they said, he too was made of the same flesh and bone as they were. So what justification was there for his wanting to have a position higher than that of anyone else? What was the rationale behind the requirement that others should obey him?

The underlying assumption of their argument, one which these notables took for granted, was that as far as they were concerned, their position of leadership was not open to question. They enjoyed an incontestable status and, hence, no one could raise any question about their authority on the grounds that they were, like everyone else, made of the same flesh and bone. What agitated them was the emerging authority of the Prophet's leadership which seemed to pose a threat to their position. In sum, their arguments were no different from those marshalled by the notables of Noah's community. They too resorted to charging their Prophet with a hunger for power in total disregard of the fact they themselves had not only fully satisfied that hunger, but had stuffed themselves with power well beyond the limit of satiety and were prone to indigestion!

38. These words once again clearly indicate that these people, i.e. the 'Ād, like others before them, did not deny the existence of God. Their

and we shall never believe what he says." (39) The Messenger said: "My Lord! Come to my help at their accusing me of lying." (40) He answered: "A short while, and they shall be repenting." (41) Then a mighty blast quite justly overtook them, and We reduced them to a rubble.[39] So away with the wrong-doing folk!

(42) Then, after them, We brought forth other generations. (43) No nation can outstrip its term, nor can it put it back. (44) Then We sent Our Messengers in succession. Whenever a Messenger came to his people they rejected him, calling him a liar. Thereupon, We made each people to follow the other (to its doom), reducing them to mere tales (of the past). Scourged be the people who do not believe![40]

كَذِبًا وَمَا نَحْنُ لَهُۥ بِمُؤْمِنِينَ ﴿٣٨﴾ قَالَ رَبِّ
ٱنصُرْنِى بِمَا كَذَّبُونِ ﴿٣٩﴾ قَالَ عَمَّا قَلِيلٍ
لَّيُصْبِحُنَّ نَٰدِمِينَ ﴿٤٠﴾ فَأَخَذَتْهُمُ ٱلصَّيْحَةُ
بِٱلْحَقِّ فَجَعَلْنَٰهُمْ غُثَآءً ۚ فَبُعْدًا لِّلْقَوْمِ
ٱلظَّٰلِمِينَ ﴿٤١﴾ ثُمَّ أَنشَأْنَا مِنۢ بَعْدِهِمْ قُرُونًا
ءَاخَرِينَ ﴿٤٢﴾ مَا تَسْبِقُ مِنْ أُمَّةٍ أَجَلَهَا
وَمَا يَسْتَـْٔخِرُونَ ﴿٤٣﴾ ثُمَّ أَرْسَلْنَا رُسُلَنَا
تَتْرَا ۖ كُلَّ مَا جَآءَ أُمَّةً رَّسُولُهَا كَذَّبُوهُ ۚ فَأَتْبَعْنَا
بَعْضَهُم بَعْضًا وَجَعَلْنَٰهُمْ أَحَادِيثَ ۚ فَبُعْدًا
لِّقَوْمٍ لَّا يُؤْمِنُونَ ﴿٤٤﴾

---

main error lay in their succumbing to polytheism. The Qur'ān speaks of this fault on several occasions. (See *al-A'rāf* 7: 70; *Hūd* 11: 53–4; *Fuṣṣilat* 41: 14; *al-Aḥqāf* 46: 21–2.)

39. The word used here is *ghuthā'* which denotes the rubble which accompanies the flood and which accumulates and lies rotting on the coast once the water recedes. (See *g-h-t-h* in *Lisān al-'Arab* – Ed.)

40. Or to put it differently, they refuse to accept the teachings of the Messengers.

(45) Then We sent Moses and his brother Aaron with Our Signs and a clear authority[41] (46) to Pharaoh and to his chiefs, but they behaved superciliously and they were haughty.[42] (47) They said: "Shall we put faith in two mortals like ourselves[43] when their people are slaves to us?"[44] ▶

ثُمَّ أَرْسَلْنَا مُوسَىٰ وَأَخَاهُ هَـٰرُونَ بِـَٔايَـٰتِنَا
وَسُلْطَـٰنٍ مُّبِينٍ ﴿٤٥﴾ إِلَىٰ فِرْعَوْنَ وَمَلَإِيْهِۦ
فَٱسْتَكْبَرُوا۟ وَكَانُوا۟ قَوْمًا عَالِينَ ﴿٤٦﴾
فَقَالُوٓا۟ أَنُؤْمِنُ لِبَشَرَيْنِ مِثْلِنَا وَقَوْمُهُمَا
لَنَا عَـٰبِدُونَ ﴿٤٧﴾

41. The expression 'clear authority' which follows the word 'Signs' signifies that the 'Signs' which had been bestowed upon Moses were sufficient to prove that he indeed was a Messenger who had been raised by God. It is also possible that the word 'Signs' here refers to all Moses' other miracles that were witnessed in Egypt with the exception of the miracle of the rod. As for 'clear authority', this refers to that miracle, i.e. of the rod. Such an expression is understandable because after this miracle it became clear beyond all doubt that the two brothers, Moses and Aaron, had surely been designated by God. (For details see *al-Zukhruf* 43, nn. 43–4.)

42. The words used here, *wa kānū qawman 'ālīn*, mean two things. One is that they were arrogant, iniquitous and oppressive, and the other that they were extremely vain and boastful.

43. For an explanation, see n. 26 above.

44. In this part of the verse the word which is used to characterize the people in question is *'ābid*. In Arabic usage, to accept someone as an object of unquestioned obedience and to worship him are almost synonymous. So whoever unreservedly obeys and serves someone appears as though he worships him.

This sheds significant light on the connotation of the term *'ibādah* (worship). It also highlights the full significance of the teaching of the Prophets to people: that they should shun the *'ibādah* of any other than God and to bind themselves to the *'ibādah* of the One True God alone. This also clearly indicates that *'ibādah*, as conceived by the Prophets, did not merely consist of consecrating the rituals of worship for God alone. Instead, the Prophets also wanted people to become fully devoted to God alone; devoted to Him in worship as well as servitude. It is in this pervasive sense of *'ibādah* that they denied the appropriateness of the *'ibādah* of anyone other

(48) So they rejected them, calling them liars, and they too eventually became of those that were destroyed.[45] (49) And We gave Moses the Book that people might be guided by it.

(50) And We made Mary's son, and his mother, a Sign,[46] ▶

فَكَذَّبُوهُمَا فَكَانُوا۟ مِنَ ٱلْمُهْلَكِينَ ﴿٤٨﴾
وَلَقَدْ ءَاتَيْنَا مُوسَى ٱلْكِتَـٰبَ لَعَلَّهُمْ
يَهْتَدُونَ ﴿٤٩﴾ وَجَعَلْنَا ٱبْنَ مَرْيَمَ وَأُمَّهُۥٓ ءَايَةً

than the One True God. (For further elaboration see *Towards Understanding the Qur'ān*, vol. V, *al-Kahf* 18, n. 50, p. 113.

45. For a more elaborate narration of the story of Moses and Pharaoh see *al-Baqarah* 2: 49–50; *al-A'rāf* 7: 103–36; *Yūnus* 10: 75–92; *Hūd* 11: 96–9; *Banī Isrā'īl* 17: 101–4; and *Ṭā Hā* 20: 9–80.

46. What is said here is not that the son of Mary was a sign of God and that another of His signs was Mary herself. Nor is it being said that Mary and the son of Mary were two signs of God. What is rather said here is that the two of them, taken together, constitute a sign of God. In other words, what is clearly suggested is that it is the extraordinary manner of Jesus' birth, who was born without a father, and the extraordinary way in which Mary conceived him without contact with any male, which combine to make them both a sign of God. All those who, while believing in the Qur'ān, deny the immaculate birth of Jesus, i.e. his birth without a father, would be hard put to explain the Qur'ānic contention that the mother and the son were a sign of God. (For further details see *Towards Understanding the Qur'ān*, vol. I, *Āl 'Imrān* 3, nn. 44 and 53, pp. 252–4 and 260; vol. II, *al-Nisā'* 4, nn. 190 and 212–13, pp. 105 and 116–17; vol. V, *Maryam* 19, nn. 15–22, pp. 152–7 and *al-Anbiyā'* 21, nn. 89–90, pp. 294–5.)

Two other points seem to merit attention. First, that this account of Jesus and his venerable mother betrays another weakness of those steeped in ignorance. The Prophets who have been mentioned earlier were rejected on the grounds that they were mere human beings, and human beings could not be Prophets. By contrast, the followers of Jesus and Mary developed an exaggerated sense of devotion to them so much so that they ended up elevating them from their human status to one of Godhead. Second, there were also others who refused to believe in Jesus even after they had witnessed his miraculous birth and his ability to speak from his cradle. They even went to the extent of calumniating Mary. No wonder God inflicted a severe punishment on them which became an example for all time to come.

and We gave them refuge on a lofty ground, a peaceful site with springs flowing in it.[47]	وَءَاوَيْنَـٰهُمَآ إِلَىٰ رَبْوَةٍ ذَاتِ قَرَارٍ وَمَعِينٍ ﴿٥٠﴾
(51) Messengers![48] Partake of the things that are clean, ▶	يَـٰٓأَيُّهَا ٱلرُّسُلُ كُلُوا۟ مِنَ ٱلطَّيِّبَـٰتِ

47. This place has variously been identified by scholars as Damascus, Ramlah, Jerusalem, and Egypt. According to Christian traditions, Mary had to leave home twice after the birth of Jesus in order to protect him from harm. First she took him to Egypt during the reign of Herod and stayed there until Herod died. Then, in the days of Archelaus, she took Jesus to Nazareth in Galilee (*Matthew* 2: 13–23).

It can hardly be stated with any reasonable degree of certitude which place is alluded to by the Qur'ān here. The word *rabwah* literally means an elevated piece of land which has an even surface and stands out in the surrounding area as a result of its height. Now, since this place is described as *dhāt qarār* (endowed with sedentariness), the place must be one where all necessities of life are found in abundance, such that it is possible for people to live there comfortably. As for the word *ma'īn*, it signifies flowing water or a running stream.

48. After narrating the accounts of several Prophets in the last two sections (i.e. verses 23–50), the discourse is now directed at all Messengers. Quite obviously this does not mean that all Messengers were assembled together at one particular place and addressed collectively. Rather, this manner of address simply signifies that the same directive was given to all the Messengers who were raised at different times and in different places. In this sense, the Messengers represent a single group that had been entrusted with an identical Message. Now, all the Messengers are described as one community, *Ummah,* (see verse 52 and n. 47 below). Therefore, while mentioning the Messengers the Qur'ān adopts a style that suggests that they were so integrated it was as though they were assembled in a single place and received an identical directive.

It is regrettable that the subtlety of the Qur'ānic style has eluded the grasp of some people in our own times. The result being that they have concluded from this verse that the words 'O Messengers' addresses Prophets who will be raised after Muḥammad (peace be upon him). They further infer from this form of address that the institution of Prophethood would continue even after Muḥammad (peace be upon him). It is ironic that those who are so conspicuously incapable of appreciating literary and linguistic subtleties have the audacity to then embark on writing Qur'ānic exegeses.

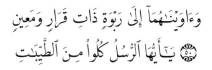

and act righteously.[49] I know well all that you do. (52) This community of yours is one community, and I am your Lord; so hold Me alone in fear.[50]

وَٱعۡمَلُواْ صَٰلِحًاۖ إِنِّي بِمَا تَعۡمَلُونَ عَلِيمٞ ﴿٥١﴾
وَإِنَّ هَٰذِهِۦٓ أُمَّتُكُمۡ أُمَّةٗ وَٰحِدَةٗ
وَأَنَا۠ رَبُّكُمۡ فَٱتَّقُونِ ﴿٥٢﴾

---

49. The word *al-ṭayyibāt* used in the Qur'ān signifies things that are at once clean in themselves and which are obtained through clean and lawful means.

The directive to partake of clean things strikes at the two extremes of monasticism and epicureanism and brings into relief the moderate and balanced approach which characterizes Islam. A Muslim should neither deny himself lawful things, nor should he hanker after everything of the world without distinguishing between that which is lawful and that which is not.

It is also significant that the directive to partake of clean things precedes the directive to act righteously. This suggests that righteous behaviour becomes absolutely meaningless if it is not accompanied with the lawfulness of what one eats and the lawfulness of the earning that enables that eating. The very first condition of being righteous is that man should subsist on what is lawful. According to a *ḥadīth*, the Prophet (peace be upon him) said that God is pure and likes pure things. He followed this statement by reciting the above verse, adding: 'A person undertakes a long journey, his clothes are ridden with dirt and his hair is dishevelled, while the food that he eats is unlawful, the drink that he drinks is unlawful, the dress that he wears is unlawful, and his body has been nourished on what is unlawful, and then he raises his hands to the sky and prays: "O my Lord! O my Lord!" Whence can his Prayer be answered?' (See Muslim, *K. al-Zakāh*, 'Bāb Qubūl al-Ṣadaqah min al-Kasb al-Ṭayyib wa Tarbiyatahā', Tirmidhī, *K. Tafsīr al-Qur'ān*, 'Bāb wa min Sūrah al-Baqarah', and Aḥmad ibn Ḥanbal, *Musnad*, vol. 2, p. 328 – Ed.)

50. The statement that 'this community of yours is one community' implies that all the Prophets belong to one and the same group. As it is, the word *Ummah* signifies a body of people who share a basic principle. The Prophets, even though they belonged to different ages and climes, are designated as one single community, because all shared the same belief, the same religion and the same Message. The words that follow, '. . . I am your Lord', make it quite clear as to what the common basis was that made them one community. (For further details see *al-Baqarah* 2: 130–3 and 213; *Āl 'Imrān* 3: 19–20, 33–4, 64, 73 and 85; *al-Nisā'* 4: 150–2; *al-A'rāf* 7: 59, 65, 73 and 85; *Yūsuf* 12: 37–40; *Maryam* 19: 49 and 59, and *al-Anbiyā'* 21: 71–93.)

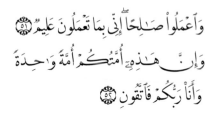

(53) But people later cut up their religion into bits, each group rejoicing in what they have.[51] (54) So leave them immersed in their heedlessness till an appointed time.[52]

فَتَقَطَّعُوٓاْ أَمۡرَهُم بَيۡنَهُمۡ زُبُرٗاۖ كُلُّ حِزۡبِۭ
بِمَا لَدَيۡهِمۡ فَرِحُونَ ٥٣ فَذَرۡهُمۡ فِي غَمۡرَتِهِمۡ
حَتَّىٰ حِينٍ ٥٤

---

51. This is not simply a statement of fact. In addition, it is a part of the argument which runs throughout this *sūrah*. The main point is that all Prophets, right from the Prophet Noah to Jesus, called their respective people to the same teaching – to affirm the Unity of God and the reality of the Hereafter. It is clear, therefore that Islam, meaning submission to the One True God, is the true, primordial religion of the human species. All other religions that we find today are nothing but distorted forms of this primordial religion. They are an ensemble of some truths of the original faith, albeit in distorted form, along with doctrinal accretions that have accumulated over the course of time.

Now, if anyone is in the wrong it is those who follow these distorted religions rather than the Prophet (peace be upon him) who, shunning them called people to embrace the true faith.

52. There is a gap between the two sentences. Rather than filling this gap with an explicit statement, it has been left to the good sense of the reader to complete it since the context itself helps one to realize what is left unsaid.

The background to the discourse is that the Prophet Muḥammad (peace be upon him) had continuously called people to the true faith for a period of five or six years. In so doing he put forward a variety of arguments to establish his point, not least drawing people's attention to several events in human history to emphasize the truth of his Message. He also drew attention to the wholesome impact of his Message on the lives of those who had accepted it, and he proffered it as corroborative evidence in support of the truth of the Message. The pure and spotless conduct of the Prophet (peace be upon him) also made it clear that he was a trustworthy person. Nevertheless, his people continued to exult in the falsehood which they had inherited from their ancestors. Not only did they reject the truth which had been expounded by the Prophet (peace be upon him) with persuasive arguments, they even became sworn enemies of the bearer of that truth. This enmity reached such proportions that they did not shrink from employing any means, howsoever vile and despicable, to frustrate the mission of the Prophet (peace be upon him). They adamantly opposed the Prophet (peace be upon him), taunted and reproached him and used repressive measures including fabricating lies against him.

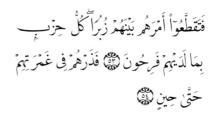

(55) Do they fancy that Our continuing to give them wealth and children (means) that (56) We are busy lavishing on them all kinds of good? Nay, they do not perceive the reality of the matter.[53] ▶

أَيَحْسَبُونَ أَنَّمَا نُمِدُّهُم بِهِۦ مِن مَّالٍ وَبَنِينَ ﴿٥٥﴾
نُسَارِعُ لَهُمْ فِى ٱلْخَيْرَٰتِ ۚ بَل لَّا يَشْعُرُونَ ﴿٥٦﴾

In order to appreciate the statement made here, 'Leave them immersed in their heedlessness', we ought to bear in mind that it was made after it had been fully shown that the true faith has always been one and the same and that those religions invented later are false. In this context, the above statement amounts to saying in a reproachful tone: 'Well, if these people still refuse to accept the truth and wish to exult in their erroneous ways, just leave them alone.'

It is quite obvious that here the use of the imperative 'leave them' cannot be taken in its literal sense, i.e. that the believers should give up preaching the truth to those who are in error. Such an interpretation betrays a total lack of appreciation of the whole tenor of the discourse. A statement such as the above does not imply that preaching of the truth should be abandoned. On the contrary, it is meant to jolt people out of their heedlessness.

Moreover, the use of the words 'till an appointed time' is also meaningful. It amounts to warning people that their exultation will not last for long; that soon they will come to their senses, and that they will wake up and distinguish between the Message that is being given them and the falsehood in which they are jubilating.

53. For a better understanding of what is said here one should glance at the opening verses of this *sūrah*, as the content here is substantially the same, albeit in a different manner. The Makkan unbelievers had a very narrow, materialistic conception of success and well-being. In their view, whoever fed or dressed himself well, lived in good houses, was able to obtain wealth and offspring and fame, prestige and a degree of influence should be reckoned as successful. Conversely, whoever failed to attain these was a failure.

This misconception led them to even larger errors. This consisted in their believing that those who enjoyed material prosperity were definitely in the right, they were God's favourites. For had this not been so, they would not have been able to make all those material achievements. Likewise, those who conspicuously lacked such material attainments, so they thought, were definitely not on the Right Path, neither in regard to their belief nor their practice. Instead they were affected with God's Wrath.

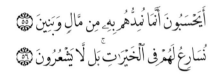

The Qur'ān repeatedly alludes to this serious misconception, one of the most vital causes of those who follow a materialist way of thinking going astray. The Qur'ān also refutes this misconception and explains the truth of the matter in a variety of ways. (See *al-Baqarah* 2: 126 and 212; *al-Tawbah* 9: 55, 69 and 85; *Yūnus* 10: 17; *Hūd* 11: 3, 27–31 and 38–9; *al-Ra'd* 13: 26; *al-Kahf* 18: 28, 32–43, 103 and 105; *Maryam* 19: 77–80; *Ṭā Hā* 20: 131–2, and *al-Anbiyā'* 21: 44, along with the related notes.)

In this connection, there are certain basic points which need to be appreciated for unless they are grasped mental confusion is bound to persist. First, man's success is something more lofty and pervasive than material, or transient worldly achievements.

Second, if those who embrace such a view regard worldly success or lack of it as an index of truth and falsehood, and of good and evil, such a view leads to a basic misconception. In fact, unless one frees oneself from it, one will never be able to find the Straight Way of sound belief and outlook, nor sound conduct and behaviour.

Third, it needs to be emphasized that the present life is meant essentially to test man rather than to recompense him for his works. As far as man's moral acts are concerned, even if there is a recompense for them during this worldly life, that recompense is on a very limited scale and is highly imperfect. Additionally, in the recompense itself there is an ingrained element of test and trial. It would be a misconception of the highest magnitude, rather a folly, if we were to disregard the above and believe that whatever good a person receives here is in reward for his goodness, and that receiving such a reward is an index of the recipient being right, righteous, loved and favoured by God. Likewise, the disposition to regard anyone who is hit by misfortune as one who is necessarily under 'punishment', is in the wrong, unrighteous, and among those who are disapproved of by God is quite unjustified. To believe this is to be totally misconceived, and nothing can have a more disastrous effect on a people's conception of right and wrong, or be more baneful for their moral standards. A seeker of the truth should realize at the very outset that the world is a testing ground for all individuals, communities, indeed the whole of mankind and this in a number of ways. The different circumstances which confront people during the course of this test cannot be regarded as the final judgements of reward and punishment. Nor can they be taken as the criteria for determining which concepts, moral attributes and actions are right and which are wrong. Nor can they be held as the criteria for determining who are loved by God and who are subject to His Wrath.

Fourth, without doubt adherence to the truth and righteousness leads to success and felicity. Likewise, falsehood and evil-doing are bound to result in failure. Nevertheless, we observe that it is possible for falsehood and iniquity to meet with success, even if it be only temporary and apparent. Likewise, we also find that truth and righteousness might encounter failure, even if that too is only temporary and apparent. Now, this phenomenon can often prove to be quite deceptive. Hence, man stands in need of independent criteria to distinguish between good and evil, a criteria that is not susceptible to any delusions. Such criteria are provided by the teachings of the Prophets and the Scriptures, and are endorsed by man's

(57) Surely those who stand in awe for fear of their Lord,[54] (58) who have full faith in the Signs of their Lord;[55] ▶

إِنَّ ٱلَّذِينَ هُم مِّنْ خَشْيَةِ رَبِّهِم مُّشْفِقُونَ ﴿٥٧﴾
وَٱلَّذِينَ هُم بِـَٔايَـٰتِ رَبِّهِمْ يُؤْمِنُونَ ﴿٥٨﴾

common sense. It is also endorsed by the fact that humanity instinctively recognizes, and recognizes unanimously, which acts are essentially good and which are evil.

Fifth, if we find that an individual or community has deviated from the path of truth and is engrossed in sin and corruption, in wrong-doing and transgression, and is nevertheless lavished with bounties, the meaning of all this is quite clear. According to the Qur'ān as well as reason, such an individual or nation has been put to serious test. The bounties that are apparently being lavished on it are not indicative of God's Mercy and Favour; in a way they signify His Wrath. If that person or nation had met with a catastrophe after their wrong-doing, it would have provided impetus for self-reform. But the bestowal of bounties, despite wrong-doing, simply means that the person or nation concerned is being led to their destruction. If the boat carrying that person or nation remains afloat even after iniquity, it means that it has been decided that it should simply be filled with a large amount of water, and then capsized, once and for all.

Conversely, even when there is sincere devotion to God, purity of conduct, honesty in dealings, and benevolence towards His creatures, still the people concerned are confronted with much hardship and suffering, and constantly encounter one calamity after another. This, however, is an indication not of God's Wrath but of His Favour and Mercy. For such a person or community is, thus, being thoroughly purged of impurities in the manner a goldsmith purges gold of all dross so that it comes forth before the world in its pure form. In any case, if such people are not compensated for their good deeds in this world, it does not matter much. The true worth of that pure gold will be recognized by the goldsmith himself, and he will pay its true value. If good people face any hardship or suffering it is not an indication of God's Wrath, rather His Wrath is directed at their enemies, and to the society in which good people are made to suffer and evil-doers are enabled to thrive.

54. Believers are never devoid of fear of God, nor are they heedless of Him. Nor do they act according to the dictates of their whims, disregarding Him above them Who is ever vigilant and Who seizes those who engage in wrong-doing and transgression. The hearts of believers are filled with fear of God, and it is this which prevents them from committing evil.

55. The word 'Signs' embraces two different kinds. On the one hand, it means the signs which are brought forward by the Prophets on God's behalf. On the other hand, it includes those signs that are found within

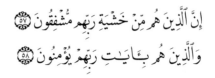

(59) who associate none with their Lord in His Divinity,[56] (60) who give, whatever they give in charity, with their hearts trembling at the thought that they are destined to return to their Lord;[57] ▶

وَٱلَّذِينَ هُم بِرَبِّهِمۡ لَا يُشۡرِكُونَ ﴿٥٩﴾ وَٱلَّذِينَ يُؤۡتُونَ مَآ ءَاتَواْ وَّقُلُوبُهُمۡ وَجِلَةٌ أَنَّهُمۡ إِلَىٰ رَبِّهِمۡ رَٰجِعُونَ ﴿٦٠﴾

man as well as those that are scattered around the universe. Now, to believe in the signs of the Book amounts to confirming their truth. As for belief in the signs in the universe and in man's own being, this suggests having faith in the truths to which these signs testify.

56. Believing in God's signs requires one to believe in the Unity of God. The additional statement that such people do not associate aught with God in His Divinity seems to have been made in view of man's known weaknesses: that occasionally people engage in one form of *shirk* or another, that they associate others with God in His Divinity despite their belief in His signs. One such example of this weakness is *riyā'*, i.e. engaging in acts of religious devotion to impress people with one's piety rather than doing so to exclusively please God. Likewise, excessive veneration of Prophets or saints, at times, also leads people to *shirk*. Other forms of *shirk* include praying to and seeking help from others than God, willingly binding oneself to serve and obey others than the One True Lord, and following man-made laws (in disregard of the Law enjoined by God – Ed.).

Thus, this characterization of the believers as those who do not engage in *shirk* after they are identified as believing in His signs is significant. This would seem to be because believers ought to consecrate their service, obedience and worship exclusively for the One True God in a manner that leaves not even an iota of doubt about it.

57. The word *ītā'* in Arabic usage is not only confined to giving money or something material. It can also be employed to mean giving something non-material. We find, therefore, such expressions in Arabic as: أتيته من نفسي القبول (I have accepted to give him my obedience). Contrariwise, is the expression أتيته من نفسي ألإباءه (I have decided to deny giving him my obedience). Thus giving does not simply mean giving away wealth in the cause of God. It also includes giving oneself to God in obedience and servitude.

In view of the above, the full meaning of the verse is that believers do not gloat at the good deeds they do in obedience to God, at the services they render, at the sacrifices they make. Their piety or their feeling of proximity with God does not generate vanity and arrogance in them. On the

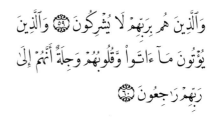

(61) it is these who hasten to do good works and vie in so doing with one another. (62) We do not lay a burden on anyone beyond his capacity.[58] We have a Book ▶

أُوْلَٰٓئِكَ يُسَٰرِعُونَ فِي ٱلۡخَيۡرَٰتِ
وَهُمۡ لَهَا سَٰبِقُونَ ٦١ وَلَا نُكَلِّفُ
نَفۡسًا إِلَّا وُسۡعَهَاۖ وَلَدَيۡنَا كِتَٰبٞ

---

contrary, despite fully exerting themselves in acts of devotion and virtue, they remain anxious for they are unsure whether or not their deeds will find God's acceptance. They are also uncertain about whether their good deeds will outweigh their sins, and whether these good deeds will suffice to earn them God's forgiveness. This very point is explained in the following *ḥadīth* as found in the works of Aḥmad ibn Ḥanbal, Tirmidhī, Ibn Mājah, Ḥākim and Ibn Jarīr al-Ṭabarī. 'Ā'ishah asked the Prophet: 'O Messenger of God! Does this mean that even while committing theft, fornication and drinking wine one should fear God?' It appears that 'Ā'ishah considered يأتون ماأتوا to mean 'whatever they do'. In reply, the Prophet (peace be upon him) clarified: 'No, O daughter of Ṣiddīq. It rather means that he who prays, fasts, pays *Zakāh*, and yet fears God.' (See Ibn Mājah, *K. al-Zuhd*, 'Bāb al-Tawaqqī 'alā al-'Amal' – Ed.)

This, then, identifies that the correct reading of the verse is not *ya'tūna*, but *yu'tūna*. Furthermore, that *yu'tūna* has not been used in the sense of giving away one's wealth, but in the wider sense of giving oneself totally in God's obedience. This verse also points to the inner state of the believer while he is engaged in acts of devotion to God. The best illustration in this regard is a statement made by 'Umar ibn al-Khaṭṭāb close to the time of his death. In spite of his highly distinguished services, throughout his life, in the cause of Islam, he was nonetheless still apprehensive that God would hold him to severe and exacting account. Such was his trepidation that he said: 'If I am reckoned on the Day of Judgement as one whose good and evil deeds are equal, that will be quite fine with me.' Ḥasan al-Baṣrī has also expressed this point beautifully: 'A believer obeys and yet remains fearful, whereas a hypocrite disobeys and is fearless.'

58. This is a vitally significant statement in the context in which it has been made so let us take care to grasp its full import. It was earlier pointed out who those people are who hasten to do good deeds and supersede others in attaining them. This is now followed with a clear reference that God does not place on anyone a burden greater than that which he can bear. In other words, there is nothing superhuman about the character and conduct required of man. All human beings are made of the same flesh and blood, and are capable of establishing very high standards of conduct. Hence, it does not hold water for some people to claim that the kind of character required of them is beyond their capacity. Man is in fact capable

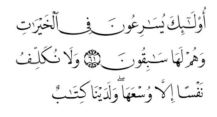

with Us that speaks the truth (about everyone);[59] and they shall in no wise be wronged.[60] (63) Nay, their hearts are lost in ignorance of all this;[61] and their deeds too vary from the way ▶

يَنطِقُ بِٱلْحَقِّ وَهُمْ لَا يُظْلَمُونَ ۝٦٢ بَلْ قُلُوبُهُمْ فِي غَمْرَةٍ مِّنْ هَـٰذَا وَلَهُمْ أَعْمَـٰلٌ مِّن دُونِ ذَٰلِكَ

of following both patterns of behaviour: the one being followed by the generality of people in the time of the Prophet (peace be upon him) as well as the one being followed by the true men of faith from amongst their own people. A person's conduct results from his own choice: which of two acts, each of which he is capable of adopting, does he prefer? If someone makes the wrong choice and, thereafter, devotes his efforts to accumulating evil and distancing himself from good, no amount of false pretension will save him. His plea that good deeds were simply beyond his power will be of no avail and he will be made to suffer the consequences of his wrong choice. If such people do in fact proffer this pretext, saying that the way enjoined by God was beyond their capacity, they are bound to face the question: if that is so, how was it that many people like them were able to follow that way?

59. The 'Book' here means the record of deeds that is being compiled separately for each individual. This record literally embraces everything about a person. All that pertains to a man, every single act, every little movement, every thought and intent, is recorded in minute detail. It is the same 'Book', meaning Record of deeds, about which the following statement is made elsewhere in the Qur'ān: 'And then the "Book", i.e. the Record of their deeds shall be placed before them and you will see the guilty full of fear of what it contains, and will say: "Woe to us! What a 'Book' [i.e. Record of deeds] is this! It leaves nothing, big or small, but encompasses it." They will find their deeds confronting them. Your Lord wrongs no one' (*al-Kahf* 18: 49).

It should be pointed out, however, that some people have understood the word 'Book' here to mean the Qur'ān. This totally confuses the actual meaning of this verse.

60. This is an assurance that no one will be charged with guilt they have not committed. Nor will anyone remain deprived of the reward to which their good deeds entitle them. In short, no one will be unduly punished, nor will anyone be denied the reward that they rightly deserve.

61. That is, they are oblivious of the fact that all their deeds, sayings and thoughts are being recorded and that a time will come when they will be held to account for them.

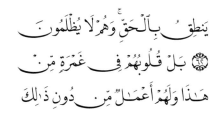

(mentioned above). They will persist in these deeds (64) until We seize with Our chastisement those of them that are given to luxuriant ways.[62] They will then begin to groan.[63] (65) "Put a stop to your groaning now![64] Surely no help shall be provided to you from Us. (66) My Signs were rehearsed to you and you turned back on your heels and took to flight,[65] (67) behaving arrogantly, and making fun, and talking nonsense (about the Book in your nightly chats)."[66]

هُمۡ لَهَا عَـٰمِلُونَ ﴿٦٣﴾ حَتَّىٰٓ إِذَآ أَخَذۡنَا
مُتۡرَفِيهِم بِٱلۡعَذَابِ إِذَا هُمۡ يَجۡـَٔرُونَ ﴿٦٤﴾
لَا تَجۡـَٔرُواْ ٱلۡيَوۡمَۖ إِنَّكُم مِّنَّا لَا تُنصَرُونَ
﴿٦٥﴾ قَدۡ كَانَتۡ ءَايَـٰتِي تُتۡلَىٰ عَلَيۡكُمۡ فَكُنتُمۡ
عَلَىٰٓ أَعۡقَـٰبِكُمۡ تَنكِصُونَ ﴿٦٦﴾ مُسۡتَكۡبِرِينَ
بِهِۦ سَـٰمِرٗا تَهۡجُرُونَ ﴿٦٧﴾

---

62. We have translated the word *mutrafīn* here as 'those given to luxuriant ways'. This word is used for those who, having obtained worldly riches, have immersed themselves in the pursuit of pleasure, and have, thus, become oblivious of their duties to God and to His creatures.

The 'chastisement' which is mentioned in this verse is not the chastisement with which they will be confronted in the Hereafter. Instead, it refers to the chastisement that will seize them here in this world.

63. The verb used here is derived from the word *ju'ār* which signifies the lowing of the oxen produced in a state of severe pain. (See *j-'-r* in *Lisān al-'Arab* – Ed.) In its present usage, the word does not simply denote groaning, but the groaning of one who does not deserve any mercy. The word also carries the nuances of contempt and sarcasm. The meaning conveyed here is: 'You were completely engaged in your misdeeds. But now that the time for the retribution of those deeds has come, you have burst out in piteous lamentation.'

64. This is what the wrong-doers will be told in response to their groaning.

65. These words graphically describe their aversion to the Prophet's message. They were so hostile to the truth that they would not permit their ears even to hear a single word of that message.

66. The word *sāmiran* used in this verse refers to those who engage in *samar*. (See *s-m-r* in *Lisān al-'Arab* – Ed.) It signifies conversations

(68) Did they never ponder over this Word (of God)?[67] Or has he (to wit, the Messenger) brought something the like of which did not come to their forefathers of yore?[68] ▶

أَفَلَمْ يَدَّبَّرُوا۟ ٱلْقَوْلَ أَمْ جَآءَهُم مَّا لَمْ يَأْتِ
ءَابَآءَهُمُ ٱلْأَوَّلِينَ ﴿٦٨﴾

---

people have at night, including gossiping and story-telling. Such light conversations are a part of village life and are held in the late evenings amongst small groups of friends who get together in rural clubs. This practice was also common among the Makkans in the time of the Prophet (peace be upon him).

67. A question is posed here: did the unbelievers reject the Prophet's Message because they failed to comprehend it? Obviously, that was not the case. For, the Qur'ān is far from being a jigsaw puzzle that defies comprehension. Nor has it been revealed in a language alien to the unbelievers. Nor are the contents of the Qur'ān beyond human comprehension. The thrust of the statement then is that the unbelievers fully understood the Message, in fact they understood it even in its complete detail. Their rejection, therefore, is both deliberate and well-considered, and not the result of any deficiency in their understanding.

68. Another possible reason for their rejection of the Qur'ānic Message could be that it expounded something absolutely novel, something altogether unheard of. Obviously, this was not true either. The Prophet (peace be upon him) taught that God had raised many earlier Prophets who brought their Scriptures, called people to monotheism, warned them that they would be held to account in the Life to Come, and expounded well-known principles of morality.

None of these teachings was being expounded for the first time in human history. The neighbouring lands – Iraq, Syria and Egypt – had witnessed the advent of a host of successive Prophets each of whom had expounded substantially the same teachings. Hence, the Arabs were not unfamiliar with the contents of the Prophet's teachings. Apart from the Prophets sent to neighbouring countries, Arabia, itself, had had its share of Prophets. Abraham and Ishmael had come to Arabia. Hūd, Ṣāliḥ and Shu'ayb were also raised there. The names of these Prophets were known to virtually everyone. The unbelievers of Arabia even acknowledged them as those who had been raised by God. They also recognized that these Prophets were not polytheists. On the contrary, they called people to serve the One True God. In sum, their rejection of the Message of the Prophet (peace be upon him) did not arise from their unfamiliarity with what

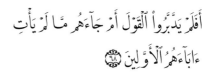

(69) Or is it that they were unaware of their Messenger and were therefore repelled by him for he was a stranger to them?[69] ▶

أَمۡ لَمۡ يَعۡرِفُواْ رَسُولَهُمۡ فَهُمۡ لَهُۥ مُنكِرُونَ ٦٩

he expounded. (For further details see *al-Furqān* 25, n. 84; *al-Sajdah* 32, n. 5; *al-Sabā'* 34, n. 35.)

69. Another question is also posed: did the unbelievers reject the Message of Islam because it was expounded by someone who was a total stranger to them, by one who had suddenly appeared from nowhere and who asked them to believe in his teachings and follow him? Once again, this could not be the reason for their rejection. For the bearer of this Message was a member of their own community. The nobility of his lineage was not unknown to them. They were also thoroughly familiar with his distinguished personal character for they had known him as a child, and had witnessed him grow to youth before their very eyes. They subsequently also witnessed his youth enter the precincts of manhood. All of them were well aware that he was truthful and veracious, that he was absolutely trustworthy, that he possessed an unblemished character. Thanks to these qualities, his compatriots called him *al-amīn* (the trustworthy one). Even his worst enemies conceded that he had never lied. He was a model of chastity and purity, known to be honourable and virtuous. They knew him to be forbearing, truth-loving and peacefully disposed, one who had always kept aloof from all manner of feuds and squabbles. They also knew that he was a straightforward person, and that his dealings with others were transparent. They also knew that he honoured his word and was faithful to his commitments. They knew that he was neither disposed to engage in wrong-doing nor supported others in their wrong-doing. They knew that his door was open for everyone in distress, for everyone who required help, for everyone who was in need, and that he greeted such people with the utmost compassion, tenderness and sympathy.

They also knew that never before had he declared himself to be a Prophet, had not even uttered a word that would suggest that he was preparing the ground to make such a claim. Moreover, ever since the day he declared himself to be a Prophet, he had consistently preached one and the same Message. Not once did he deviate. Not once did he modify his claim or change the content of his Message. Nor could one detect any evolution in his claims, an evolution that could lend him to be suspected of proceeding gradually towards self-exaltation – an evolution whose start was marked, as is the case with imposters, by first making a modest claim, and then proceeding to make ever taller claims after having consolidated his position. Not only that, his life also bore witness to the fact that he

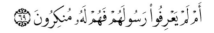

(70) Or do they say that there is madness in him?[70] Nay, he has brought them the Truth and it is the Truth that most of them disdain. (71) Were the Truth to follow their desires, the order of the heavens and the earth and those who dwell in them would have been ruined.[71] ▶

أَمْ يَقُولُونَ بِهِۦ جِنَّةٌۢ ۚ بَلْ جَآءَهُم بِٱلْحَقِّ
وَأَكْثَرُهُمْ لِلْحَقِّ كَـٰرِهُونَ ﴿٧٠﴾
وَلَوِ ٱتَّبَعَ ٱلْحَقُّ أَهْوَآءَهُمْ لَفَسَدَتِ
ٱلسَّمَـٰوَٰتُ وَٱلْأَرْضُ وَمَن فِيهِنَّ ۚ

---

not only practised all that he preached to others, but he rather practised it before he preached it.

It was also quite evident that there was no contradiction between his word and deed. Nor was there any trace of hypocrisy in his conduct. Nor did he have a different set of weights and measures for himself and for others.

It was thus difficult for the Makkan unbelievers to say of someone who was so well known, so tried and tested among his fellow-beings, that he was crafty, and having won over peoples' hearts with his captivating words, then threw away the mask he had been wearing only to reveal his true colours. Essentially his detractors were unable to accuse him of playing tricks with them in order to promote his covert evil designs. (For further elaboration see *Towards Understanding the Qur'ān*, vol. II, *al-An'ām* 6, n. 21, pp. 226–7; vol. IV, *Yūnus* 10, n. 21, pp. 19–21; and vol. V, *Banī Isrā'īl* 17, n. 105, pp. 71–2.)

70. Another possible reason for the unbelievers rejecting the Prophet's teaching is mentioned here in the form of a query: did they reject his teaching because they believed that he was mad? Again, quite obviously this was not the reason for their intransigence. For regardless of whatever they might have said publicly about the Prophet, they recognized in their heart of hearts that he was sharp-witted, wise and sagacious. For, after all, the difference between sanity and insanity is quite obvious and hence there was no question of their being confused on this issue. It is only those who are brazenly obstinate who could say that he who brought them the Qur'ān was insane. Could anyone who knew anything about the life of the Prophet (peace be upon him) believe that it was the life of someone who was mentally deranged? For strange indeed is that insanity, or for that matter the fits of epilepsy mentioned with such gusto by Orientalists, which leads to a work like the Qur'ān! What kind of insanity is it that enabled the Prophet to successfully lead a movement that changed not only the destiny of his own land but also of the whole world?

71. This pithy sentence embodies a statement of great significance, and we should make every effort to understand it. It is customary for foolish

Nay, the fact is that We have brought to them their own remembrance; and yet it is from their own remembrance that they are turning away.[72]	بَلْ أَتَيْنَٰهُم بِذِكْرِهِمْ فَهُمْ عَن ذِكْرِهِم مُّعْرِضُونَ ﴿٧١﴾

people to become angry with those who tell them the truth. Such people wish to hear whatever best suits their interests rather than what is true and what accords with the facts. Such men tend to forget that the truth remains the truth regardless of whether people like it or not. Even if all people combine to negate a fact or change a truth into a falsehood, they will fail to do so.

When such is the case, how can facts and truths be so altered as to make them conform to the wishes of an individual? Alternatively, how can facts constantly conform to a myriad of mutually conflicting wishes? Foolish people fail to appreciate that if there is any discordance between their wishful thinking and reality, then it is their wishful thinking that is to blame rather than reality. In denying reality, such people cause no harm to it *per se*, instead they only harm themselves.

This immense system of the universe is based on well-established realities and inalterable laws. Living in the framework of such a universe, it is imperative that man strive to bring his thoughts, wishes and conduct in conformity with reality. He should constantly apply himself, with the help of rational argument, experience and observation, to what reality indeed is. It is only the puerile who, at both mental and practical levels, adamantly cling to their preconceptions, wishes and biases and who attempt to show those realities as conforming to their preconceived ideas. Once they embark on this course, they turn a blind eye to every piece of argument, howsoever weighty and reasonable it might be.

72. The word *dhikr* used here has three possible meanings, each of which seems to be correct in the present context:

(1). *Dhikr*, in the first place, might be regarded as a synonym about human nature. Taken in this sense, the present verse would mean that the Qur'ān is not speaking about some other world that is unrelated to them. On the contrary, the Qur'ān is concerned with expounding the reality of man's being, with explaining his nature and his urges. The Qur'ān does so in order to remind man of the lesson that he is ever disposed to forget, a lesson that he is averse to learning. Such an escapist attitude is not an escape from matters unrelated to man. It is rather man's escape from the truth about himself.

(2). The word *dhikr* may also be taken to mean admonition and good counsel. In this case the verse in question would mean that the Message of

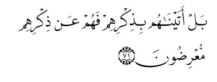

(72) Are you asking them for something? What Allah has given you is the best. He is the Best of providers.[73] ▶	أَمْ تَسْـَٔلُهُمْ خَرْجًا فَخَرَاجُ رَبِّكَ خَيْرٌ وَهُوَ خَيْرُ ٱلرَّٰزِقِينَ ﴿٧٢﴾

the Qur'ān constitutes an admonition which is in their own best interests. Hence, if they flee from it, it would amount to fleeing from something that is conducive to their own good.

(3). *Dhikr* may also be used in the sense of honour. If this sense is accepted, the verse means that if the unbelievers accept the Message that has been brought to them, they will be endowed with honour. On the contrary, if they turn away from it, it will amount to denying themselves a golden opportunity for their own growth and exaltation.

73. This is another argument in support of the Prophet's claim to have been designated by God as a Prophet. The argument demonstrates that the Prophet (peace be upon him) was quite evidently most selfless in his mission. No one could honestly accuse him of facing all the hassle involved in his work in order to fulfil any selfish design. Before embarking on his mission as the Message-bearer of Islam, he was a fairly prosperous trader. After becoming involved in Islam, he began to face want and privation. Before he was designated as God's Messenger, he was held in high esteem by his people. Thereafter, however, he was subjected to both verbal abuse and even physical hurt; and even his life was at risk. In the past, he had lived a happy life with his family, but thanks to his mission, he became engaged in a struggle which left him little time for rest and peace. Moreover, the cause that he was expounding yielded no advantages to him directly. On the contrary, it antagonized virtually every element of his people so much so that his own kith and kin seemed bent on the utmost hostility towards him. In view of all this, who in his right mind would say that the work of the Prophet (peace be upon him) was that of a self-seeker?

Self-seekers are wont to come forward as champions of tribal and national chauvinism. They use their ability and craftiness in a manner that enables them to assume the leadership of their people. Self-seekers are never advocates of unpopular causes; they are never the proponents of an idea that would frontally challenge the chauvinistic biases and prejudices of their people, let alone espouse an idea that negates the very foundation on which the tribal pre-eminence of the Makkan unbelievers rested. This argument is put forward by the Qur'ān not only in support of the truth of Muḥammad's claim, but in order to prove the truth of all Prophets (peace be upon all of them). (For further details see *al-An'ām* 6: 9; *Yūnus* 10: 72; *Hūd* 11: 29 and 51; *Yūsuf* 12: 104; *al-Furqān* 25: 57; *al-Shu'arā'* 26: 109, 127, 145, 164 and 180; *Sabā'* 34: 34; *Yā Sīn* 36: 21; *Ṣād* 38: 86; *al-Shūrā* 42: 23; and *al-Najm* 53: 40, along with the relevant notes.)

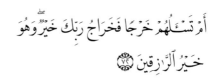

(73) You are calling them to a Straight Way,[74] (74) but those who do not believe in the Hereafter are ever prone to deviate from the Right Way.

(75) Were We to be merciful to them and remove from them their present afflictions, they would persist in their transgression, blindly wandering on.[75] ▶

وَإِنَّكَ لَتَدْعُوهُمْ إِلَىٰ صِرَٰطٍ مُّسْتَقِيمٍ ﴿٧٣﴾
وَإِنَّ ٱلَّذِينَ لَا يُؤْمِنُونَ بِٱلْءَاخِرَةِ عَنِ
ٱلصِّرَٰطِ لَنَٰكِبُونَ ﴿٧٤﴾ ۞ وَلَوْ رَحِمْنَٰهُمْ
وَكَشَفْنَا مَا بِهِم مِّن ضُرٍّ لَّلَجُّوا۟ فِى
طُغْيَٰنِهِمْ يَعْمَهُونَ ﴿٧٥﴾

---

74. The unbelievers denied the After-Life and this made them bereft of all sense of responsibility. Basically, they were easygoing and carefree. Since they did not believe that this life had any other purpose, or that they were accountable for their deeds before a higher authority, why should they be concerned about what is good and what is evil? Like animals, their only concern was with the optimal fulfilment of their physical and sensual desires. If these needs were fulfilled, all else, even questions of good and evil, right and wrong, could be dismissed as altogether irrelevant. On the other hand, if in the pursuit of their material goals they discovered something wrong, something which served as an obstacle to their self-gratification, they would consider what had caused that wrong and how it could be rectified. Such people are naturally not interested in finding out the true path that human beings ought to follow.

75. This alludes to the hardship and suffering experienced by the Makkans as a result of the then raging famine. Some narrators, however, have mixed up the two famines which afflicted the Makkans. The result being that the average reader is unclear about which famine is being alluded to here. One of these famines occurred some time after Prophethood was bestowed upon Muḥammad (peace be upon him), and the other took place a few years after *Hijrah*. This second famine was caused by Thumāmah ibn Uthāl who stopped the export of food grains from Yamāmah to Makka. The present verse, though, refers to the first rather than the second famine. According to a tradition in both Bukhārī and Muslim, on the authority of 'Abd Allāh ibn Mas'ūd, when the Quraysh repeatedly refused to accept the Prophet's Message and placed numerous obstacles in his way, he prayed to God: 'O God, help me against them with a seven-year famine as You helped Joseph with a seven-year famine.' (See Bukhārī, *K. al-Da'wāt*, 'Bāb al-Du'ā' 'alā al-Mushrikīn', and Tirmidhī, *K. Tafsīr al-Qur'ān*, 'Bāb wa min Sūrah al-Dukhān' – Ed.) Consequently, a very severe famine took hold of

(76) (They are such) that We seized them with chastisement (and yet) they did not humble themselves before their Lord, nor do they entreat (77) until We opened upon them the door of a severe chastisement. Then lo, in this state they become utterly despaired of any good.[76]

(78) It is He Who has endowed you with the faculties of hearing and sight and has given you hearts (to think). Scarcely do you give thanks.[77] ▶

وَلَقَدْ أَخَذْنَٰهُم بِٱلْعَذَابِ فَمَا ٱسْتَكَانُوا۟
لِرَبِّهِمْ وَمَا يَتَضَرَّعُونَ ﴿٧٦﴾ حَتَّىٰٓ إِذَا
فَتَحْنَا عَلَيْهِم بَابًا ذَا عَذَابٍ شَدِيدٍ إِذَا
هُمْ فِيهِ مُبْلِسُونَ ﴿٧٧﴾ وَهُوَ ٱلَّذِىٓ أَنشَأَ
لَكُمُ ٱلسَّمْعَ وَٱلْأَبْصَٰرَ وَٱلْأَفْـِٔدَةَ ۚ
قَلِيلًا مَّا تَشْكُرُونَ ﴿٧٨﴾

Makka, so much so that the Makkans resorted to eating carrion. There are several allusions to this famine in the Makkan *sūrahs*. (See, for example, *al-An'ām* 6: 42–4; *al-A'rāf* 7: 94–9; *Yūnus* 10: 11–12 and 21; *al-Naḥl* 16: 112–13; and *al-Dukhān* 44: 10 and 16, along with the relevant notes.)

76. The word *mublisūn* used in this verse is very rich in meaning so that the expression: 'they will utterly despair of all good', does not express the full import of the statement. The root *b-l-s* from which the verbal form *iblīs* is derived, embraces several meanings. It denotes a person's being wonder-struck, aghast with fear, heart-broken with grief and sorrow, utterly frustrated after suffering a succession of reverses. Since the word signifies desperation arising from loss of all hope, Satan has been named *Iblīs*. (See *b-l-s* in *Lisān al-'Arab* – Ed.) This word is chosen for Satan because in states of utter frustration his injured pride is so provoked that he seeks to wreak every possible havoc and commit every kind of crime.

77. The unbelievers are being asked: did God not endow human beings with eyes, ears, and the faculties of head and heart so that they might use them in the manner of animals? Do these faculties have no other purpose than that human beings become engrossed in scheming as to how they can best employ them in the fulfilment of their biological needs, and for the constant improvement of their standards of living? Can there be any greater ingratitude on man's part than that he makes himself indistinct from

(79) It is He Who has dispersed you all around the earth, and it is unto Him that you shall all be mustered. (80) It is He Who gives life and causes death, and He holds mastery over the alternation of night and day.[78] Do you not understand this?[79] ▶

وَهُوَ ٱلَّذِى ذَرَأَكُمْ فِى ٱلْأَرْضِ وَإِلَيْهِ تُحْشَرُونَ ﴿٧٩﴾ وَهُوَ ٱلَّذِى يُحْىِۦ وَيُمِيتُ وَلَهُ ٱخْتِلَٰفُ ٱلَّيْلِ وَٱلنَّهَارِ ۚ أَفَلَا تَعْقِلُونَ ﴿٨٠﴾

animals, and this despite the fact he was created as a species distinct from animals? The result is that people are prone to use their eyes to observe everything except those signposts which lead to a comprehension of reality. They make use of their ears to hear everything except that which enables them to comprehend the truth. They employ their heads and hearts to reflect on literally everything except the fundamental question of how did they come into being and for what purpose. What a pity that those who abuse their God-given faculties live in our midst and are reckoned as human beings rather than brutes!

78. The previous verse drew man's attention to the fact of his using his faculties to obtain knowledge – through his senses and reason – as quite inappropriate. After arousing man from this state of heedlessness, the present verse proceeds to emphasize that there are a myriad of signs around him. If man could only observe them properly or derive from them proper inferences, he would be able to reach the truth. Thanks to those signs, it is quite possible for man to realize that this well-regulated universe could neither have come into existence without God Who created it, nor could it have been created by a plethora of gods. Overwhelming evidence is available to lead a reasonable person to believe that the universe rests on the solid bedrock of the Unity of God. Furthermore, the evidence which exists around man should suffice to convince him that this universe is neither devoid of purpose, nor is it an act of play and sport, nor a set of meaningless talismans. On the contrary, the universe is based on an order that is full of wisdom. Is it conceivable that man, who enjoys free-will, should have been placed in such a universe and not be held to account, be simply reduced to dust after death?

79. Evidence is being marshalled here to confirm the cardinal doctrines of the Unity of God and the After-Life. The signs to which attention is being drawn in the verses that follow provide sufficient proof to refute both polytheism and any denial of the After-Life.

(81) Nay, but they say the like of what their predecessors of yore had said. (82) They say: "Is it that when we are dead and have been reduced to dust and bones, shall we then be raised up again? (83) We were promised such things and so were our forefathers before us. All these are no more than tales of the past."[80]

(84) Ask them: "Whose is the earth and those who are in it?" Tell us if you know (85) They will surely say: "Allah's." Say: "Then why do you not take heed?"[81] (86) Ask them: "Who is the Lord of the seven heavens, the Lord of the Great Throne?" (87) They will surely say: "Allah."[82] Say: "Will you not, then, fear (Allah)?"[83] ▶

بَلْ قَالُوا۟ مِثْلَ مَا قَالَ ٱلْأَوَّلُونَ ﴿٨١﴾
قَالُوٓا۟ أَءِذَا مِتْنَا وَكُنَّا تُرَابًا وَعِظَـٰمًا أَءِنَّا
لَمَبْعُوثُونَ ﴿٨٢﴾ لَقَدْ وُعِدْنَا نَحْنُ وَءَابَآؤُنَا
هَـٰذَا مِن قَبْلُ إِنْ هَـٰذَآ إِلَّآ أَسَـٰطِيرُ
ٱلْأَوَّلِينَ ﴿٨٣﴾ قُل لِّمَنِ ٱلْأَرْضُ وَمَن فِيهَآ
إِن كُنتُمْ تَعْلَمُونَ ﴿٨٤﴾ سَيَقُولُونَ لِلَّهِ ۚ
قُلْ أَفَلَا تَذَكَّرُونَ ﴿٨٥﴾ قُلْ مَن رَّبُّ
ٱلسَّمَـٰوَٰتِ ٱلسَّبْعِ وَرَبُّ ٱلْعَرْشِ ٱلْعَظِيمِ
﴿٨٦﴾ سَيَقُولُونَ لِلَّهِ ۚ قُلْ أَفَلَا تَتَّقُونَ ﴿٨٧﴾

---

80. In this respect, one should remember that the unbelievers who rejected the After-Life as something impossible, were not simply denying that After-Life. They were, in fact, also denying God's omnipotence and wisdom.

81. If God is the sole creator of the earth and all who dwell on it, what prevents people from comprehending the simple truth that He, and none but He, deserves to be served? Likewise, if God created all the human beings who ever lived on the earth, what difficulty would He face were He to Will that all of them be brought back to life?

82. The actual word used in the verse is *li Allāh*, which should literally be rendered: 'Allah's' or 'belonging to Allah'. In deference to English usage, however, we have translated it simply as 'Allah'.

83. The proposition that God is Lord of the universe was acknowledged even by the unbelievers. Given that is the case, why are people not afraid

(88) Ask them: "Say, if you indeed know, to whom belongs the dominion over all things;[84] (Who is it) that grants asylum, but against Whom no asylum is available?" (89) They will surely say: "(The dominion over all things) belongs to Allah." Say: "Whence are you then deluded?"[85] ▶

قُلْ مَنۢ بِيَدِهِۦ مَلَكُوتُ كُلِّ شَيْءٍ وَهُوَ
يُجِيرُ وَلَا يُجَارُ عَلَيْهِ إِن كُنتُمْ تَعْلَمُونَ ﴿٨٨﴾
سَيَقُولُونَ لِلَّهِ ۚ قُلْ فَأَنَّىٰ تُسْحَرُونَ ﴿٨٩﴾

of acting rebelliously towards God and associating others with Him in His Divinity? Why are they not worried about when they will be called to account by the Lord of the heavens and the earth about their behaviour? What justification will they be able to put forward to Him for their actions?

84. The word *malakūt* combines two meanings: *mulk* (kingship, dominion) and *milk* (ownership). At the same time, it also carries the nuance of intensity. Taking all these things into account, the verse seems to pose the question: who is it who has absolute power over, and total ownership of, everything?

85. The unbelievers are asked: أنّى تسحرون. The literal translation of this is: 'Whence are you then bewitched?' The essence of magic and sorcery is to show a thing to be different from what it really is. The magician, thus, creates a false impression in the minds of onlookers, making them believe things to be contrary to what they actually are. Thus the question posed by the verse amounts to asking people: who is it who has bewitched these people so that even though they are aware of disparate facts, they are nonetheless unable to comprehend reality? What kind of spell has been cast upon them such that those who are not their lords appear to them either to be their lords, or the partners of their lords? What kind of magic has made them look upon those who have no power as worthy of being served as the One True God should be served; in fact they consider them to be even more deserving of service and worship than He Who has all power? Who has blinded them to well-known facts so that they are treacherous and faithless to the One True God about Whom they themselves recognize that against Him no one can provide any refuge? Are they doing this in the hope that they will be provided refuge by those who have no power to do so? Who has deluded them into believing that He Who is the True Master of everything will never hold them to account, that He will never question them in what manner they used the things which truly belonged to Him?

(90) We have brought before them the Truth, and there is no doubt that they are lying.[86] (91) Never did Allah take unto Himself any son,[87] nor is there any god other than He. ▶	بَلْ أَتَيْنَٰهُم بِٱلْحَقِّ وَإِنَّهُمْ لَكَٰذِبُونَ ﴿٩٠﴾ مَا ٱتَّخَذَ ٱللَّهُ مِن وَلَدٍ وَمَا كَانَ مَعَهُۥ مِنْ إِلَٰهٍ

How have they succumbed to the erroneous belief that the Sovereign of the universe will never question them as to what right they had to claim their own sovereignty or to accept the sovereignty of others in His realm?

These questions assume greater meaning in view of the fact that the unbelieving Quraysh were wont to accuse the Prophet (peace be upon him) of being a magician. So saying the Qur'ān turns the tables on the unbelievers, virtually telling them that they mistake the person who guides them to the truth, a truth they also recognize, for a magician. Conversely, those who truly delude them into believing what is contrary to reason and logic, what is altogether opposed to their experience and observation, even opposed to their own statements concerning the truth, are unquestioningly accepted by them as their guides. This without there arising the least suspicion in their minds that such are the real magicians.

86. Their assertion that aught other than the One True God partakes of Divinity (that is, shares with God any of His attributes or authority, or His rights *vis-à-vis* His creatures) is a lie. They also lie when they say that there will be no After-Life. This lie can even be shown to be so by virtue of their own statements. For, on the one hand, they themselves concede that God is the Lord of the heavens and the earth, and that He has absolute control over everything in the universe. On the other, they contend that godhead is not exclusively God's but rests with others too – with those who are bound to be His creatures and servants and, thus, under His omnipotent control. Quite evidently these two positions totally contradict each other.

The same applies to the unbelievers' contention regarding the After-Life. On the one hand, they concede that God has created both human beings and this enormous universe. On the other, they contend that God is unable to resurrect those whom He once created. Such an assertion is most patently irrational. Thus, both their doctrines, polytheism and denial of the After-Life, are altogether inconsistent with their own stated positions.

87. This statement should not be regarded as one that simply refutes the Christian doctrine that Jesus was the son of God. It refutes similar doctrines held by other religious groups as well. The Arab polytheists of the time also claimed that their deities were God's offspring. Most polytheists the world over have in one way or another succumbed to this error. However, since the Christian doctrine that Jesus was the son of God

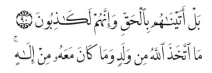

(Had there been any other gods) each god would have taken his creatures away with him, and each would have rushed to overpower the other.[88] Glory be to Allah from all that they characterize Him with! (92) He knows both what is visible and what is not visible.[89] ▶

إِذًا لَّذَهَبَ كُلُّ إِلَٰهٍۭ بِمَا خَلَقَ وَلَعَلَا بَعْضُهُمْ عَلَىٰ بَعْضٍ ۚ سُبْحَٰنَ ٱللَّهِ عَمَّا يَصِفُونَ ﴿٩١﴾ عَٰلِمِ ٱلْغَيْبِ وَٱلشَّهَٰدَةِ

gained much currency, even some leading Muslim commentators of the Qur'ān are of the opinion that the present verse was revealed to refute this false Christian belief.

It should be recalled, however, that the entirety of this discourse is addressed to the Makkan unbelievers, that is from beginning to end. It would be rather odd then if the discourse suddenly began to direct itself at the Christians. However, the Qur'ānic assertion is couched in such terms that it refutes all those who trace the pedigree of their deities to God, whether such a doctrine is held by Christians, Arab polytheists or for that matter by anyone else.

88. This statement means that it is simply impossible for different forces and spheres of the universe to have different creators and gods and that those gods enjoy the absolute cooperation and harmony among themselves which is reflected in the whole. The regularity in the system of the universe and the absolute harmony found among its different components indicates that they are all in the grip of one central authority. Had the authority governing the universe been divided among several holders, disagreement among them would be inevitable, and as such would lead to conflict and fighting. This point has also been emphasized elsewhere in the Qur'ān:

> Had there been many gods in the heavens and the earth beside Allah, the order of both the heavens and the earth would have gone to ruin (*al-Anbiyā'* 21: 22).
>
> Say: (O Muḥammad!): 'Had there been other gods with Him, as they claim, they would surely have attempted to find a way to the Lord of the Throne' (*Banī Isrā'īl* 17: 42).

(For further elaboration see *Towards Understanding the Qur'ān*, vol. V, *Banī Isrā'īl* 17, n. 47, p. 45; and *al-Anbiyā'* 21: 22.)

89. This is a subtle allusion to a certain form of polytheism which first gave rise to the polytheistic version of intercession, and later on, to the

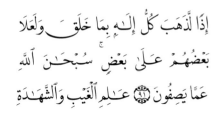

Exalted is Allah above all that they associate with Him.

(93) Pray, (O Muḥammad): "My Lord, if You should bring the scourge of which they had been warned in my presence, (94) then do not include me, my Lord, among these wrong-doing people."[90] (95) Surely We are able to show you what We warn them against.

(96) (O Muḥammad)! Repel evil in the best manner. We are well aware of all that they say about you. (97) And pray: "My Lord! I seek Your refuge from the suggestions of the evil ones;▶

فَتَعَـٰلَىٰ عَمَّا يُشۡرِكُونَ ﴿٩٢﴾ قُل رَّبِّ
إِمَّا تُرِيَنِّي مَا يُوعَدُونَ ﴿٩٣﴾ رَبِّ فَلَا تَجۡعَلۡنِي
فِي ٱلۡقَوۡمِ ٱلظَّـٰلِمِينَ ﴿٩٤﴾ وَإِنَّا عَلَىٰٓ أَن
نُّرِيَكَ مَا نَعِدُهُمۡ لَقَٰدِرُونَ ﴿٩٥﴾ ٱدۡفَعۡ
بِٱلَّتِي هِيَ أَحۡسَنُ ٱلسَّيِّئَةَۚ نَحۡنُ أَعۡلَمُ
بِمَا يَصِفُونَ ﴿٩٦﴾ وَقُل رَّبِّ أَعُوذُ بِكَ مِنۡ
هَمَزَٰتِ ٱلشَّيَٰطِينِ ﴿٩٧﴾

---

fallacious belief that someone other than God possesses knowledge of things that lie beyond the ken of sense-perception (*ghayb*) – the knowledge of all that was and all that will be. The present verse refutes both these erroneous notions of polytheism. (For further elaboration see *Towards Understanding the Qur'ān*, vol. V, *Ṭā Hā* 20, nn. 85–6, pp. 227–9 and *al-Anbiyā'* 21, n. 27, p. 262.)

90. This, of course, does not mean that there was any danger that the Prophet (peace be upon him) would become one of the wrong-doers. Nor was there any possibility that he would succumb to iniquity if he did not make the Prayer mentioned here. Rather, the point that is made emphasizes that God's punishment is something to be dreaded. It is certainly not something that a person should invite upon himself. Additionally, if God defers His punishment, as a result of His Mercy and Forbearance, this should not prompt a person to persist with impunity in acts of iniquity and disobedience against God. God's punishment is so horrendous that even the righteous will seek refuge from it, this despite all the good deeds they might have done, so what hope is there for the sinners?

This also indicates that when God's punishment comes upon a people as retribution for their collective misdeeds, it is not only the evil-doers but also the righteous who are often struck by it. Hence, the righteous who live

(98) I even seek Your refuge, my Lord, lest they should approach me."[91]

(99) (They shall persist in their deeds) until when death comes to anyone of them he will say: "My Lord, send me back to the world[92] (100) that I have left behind. I am likely to do good."[93] ▶

وَأَعُوذُ بِكَ رَبِّ أَن يَحْضُرُونِ ﴿٩٨﴾ حَتَّىٰٓ
إِذَا جَآءَ أَحَدَهُمُ ٱلْمَوْتُ قَالَ رَبِّ ٱرْجِعُونِ
﴿٩٩﴾ لَعَلِّىٓ أَعْمَلُ صَـٰلِحًا فِيمَا تَرَكْتُ

in a misguided and wicked milieu should always seek God's refuge from His punishment. For one never knows when God's scourge will seize the wrong-doers, and whom it will include.

91. For further elaboration see *Towards Understanding the Qur'ān*, vol. II, *al-An'ām* 6, nn. 71–2, pp. 262–3; vol. III, *al-A'rāf* 7, nn. 138 and 150–3, pp. 101–2 and 112–15; vol. IV, *Yūnus* 10, n. 39, p. 32; *al-Ḥijr* 15, n. 48, p. 302; and *al-Naḥl* 16, nn. 122–4, pp. 375–7; and vol. V, *Banī Isrā'īl* 17, nn. 58–63, pp. 51–3. Also see *Fuṣṣilat* 41, nn. 36–41.

92. The expression ربي ارجعون has a plural form. One possible meaning is that the plural of respect adopted here addresses one who is worthy of it. The use of the plural form as a show of respect is common to virtually all languages. The other possible reason for use of the plural might be to emphasize that this Prayer was to be made over and over again. In other words, it conveys the idea that they should pray repeatedly: 'Send me back; send me back.' Additionally, some commentators have expressed the opinion that in the first part of this sentence the words 'My Lord!' are addressed to God, whereas the second part of the sentence ارجعون ('send me back') is a pleading addressed to those angels who seize the soul of a sinner. In other words, the verse would mean: O my Lord! [O angels!] send me back.

93. That sinners would constantly pray to God to grant them another chance, right from the time of their death until they are hurled into Hell on the Day of Judgement, is a recurrent idea in the Qur'ān. In fact they will continue to so plead even after they have been consigned to Hell, but if their plea is heard, they will never disobey God but from thereon in follow the Right Path instead. (For further elaboration see *al-An'ām* 6: 27–8; *al-A'rāf* 7: 53; *Ibrāhīm* 14: 44–5; *al-Mu'minūn* 23: 105–15; *al-Shu'arā'* 26: 102; *al-Sajdah* 32: 12–14; *al-Fāṭir* 35: 37; *al-Zumar* 39: 58–9; *al-Mu'min* 40: 10; *al-Shūrā* 42: 44, along with the relevant notes.)

Nay,[94] it is merely a word that he is uttering.[95] There is a barrier behind all of them (who are dead) until the Day when they will be raised up.[96] ▶

كَلَّآ إِنَّهَا كَلِمَةٌ هُوَ قَآئِلُهَا وَمِن وَرَآئِهِم بَرْزَخٌ إِلَىٰ يَوْمِ يُبْعَثُونَ ﴿١٠٠﴾

94. Despite their pleading, the sinners will not be sent back to the world. No one will be allowed to start his life afresh. The reason being that if a person is granted a fresh lease of life for the same purpose, that is, to test him, one of two conditions will obtain. Either all that he witnessed after his death will remain preserved in his memory or he will be restored to life devoid of any memory as was the case at the time of his first birth. In the former situation, the whole purpose of testing him would be lost. For this test consists in whether one discovers the truth by appropriately using one's mental faculties and accepts it or not; or whether without directly observing ultimate realities, one chooses obedience rather than disobedience even though one has had the freedom to choose between the two. But once the ultimate realities are shown to man and he witnesses the dire consequences of his disobedience, then this almost amounts to depriving him of the opportunity to disobey. Once man observes with his own eyes the horrible consequences of disobedience, how is it possible that he would not believe and not be obedient?

Let us now consider the second possibility, namely that man is recreated exactly as he was before, that is, bereft of any memory of past misdeeds and without having directly observed the ultimate consequences of disobedience to God. This would be tantamount to repeating something unnecessarily. For if someone failed the test earlier, what point is there in subjecting them to the same test again, for they are bound to perform exactly as previously? (For further elaboration see *Towards Understanding the Qur'ān*, vol. I, *al-Baqarah* 2, n. 228, pp. 163–4; vol. II, *al-An'ām* 6, n. 6, pp. 217–18 and nn. 139–40, pp. 296–7; and vol. IV, *Yūnus* 10, n. 26, pp. 24–5.)

95. It may, alternatively, be translated as: 'It is a statement he is now bound to make.' In other words, his utterance is not worth considering. For, faced with God's punishment, he is bound to say so. Yet, given another chance, he would behave exactly as he did earlier. Hence, his utterance merits no attention and he need not be sent back to life.

96. The word *barzakh* is an Arabized form of the Persian word *pardah* (signifying a barrier). According to this verse, there is presently a barrier between those who are dead and the present world. This barrier prevents the dead from returning to life, and so they will stay where they are till the Day of Judgement.

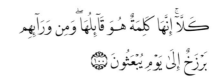

(101) And then no sooner the Trumpet is blown than there will remain no kinship among them that Day, nor will they ask one another.[97] (102) When those whose scales are heavy,[98] they alone will attain success; (103) and those whose scales are light, those will be the ones who will have courted loss.[99] They will abide in Hell. (104) The Fire shall scorch their faces, exposing their jaws.[100] ▶

فَإِذَا نُفِخَ فِى ٱلصُّورِ فَلَآ أَنسَابَ بَيْنَهُمْ يَوْمَئِذٍ
وَلَا يَتَسَآءَلُونَ ﴿١٠١﴾ فَمَن ثَقُلَتْ مَوَٰزِينُهُۥ
فَأُو۟لَٰٓئِكَ هُمُ ٱلْمُفْلِحُونَ ﴿١٠٢﴾ وَمَنْ خَفَّتْ
مَوَٰزِينُهُۥ فَأُو۟لَٰٓئِكَ ٱلَّذِينَ خَسِرُوٓا۟ أَنفُسَهُمْ
فِى جَهَنَّمَ خَٰلِدُونَ ﴿١٠٣﴾ تَلْفَحُ وُجُوهَهُمُ
ٱلنَّارُ وَهُمْ فِيهَا كَٰلِحُونَ ﴿١٠٤﴾

---

97. This does not mean that a father will cease to be a father, and a son cease to be a son. Rather, it means that neither a father will be of any avail to his son, nor a son of any avail to his father. Everyone will be too engrossed in their own plight to be able to think of their kindred, let alone show them any sympathy or aid. This state of affairs is mentioned at several places in the Qur'ān:

> No friend shall inquire about another friend (*al-Ma'ārij* 70: 10).
>
> To redeem himself from the torment of that day the sinner will gladly sacrifice his children, his wife, his brother, his kindred who had provided him shelter, and all the people of the earth (*al-Ma'ārij* 70: 11–14).
>
> On that Day each person shall flee from his own brother, and from his mother and his father, and from his wife and his children. Each one of them, that Day, will have enough concern of his own to make him indifferent to the others (*'Abasa* 80: 34–7).

98. This is a reference to those whose good deeds will outweigh their evil ones.

99. These verses should be read in conjunction with the Qur'ānic account of true prosperity and failure as outlined in the opening verses (1 ff.) and verses 51 ff. of the present *sūrah*.

100. The word used here is *kāliḥūn*, signifying those whose face is so scorched that their skin is tattered and their teeth are protruding just as though they are the burnt head of a goat. Someone asked 'Abd Allāh ibn

(105) "Are you not those to whom My revelations were recited, and you dubbed them as lies?" (106) They will say: "Our Lord! Our misfortune prevailed over us. We were indeed an erring people. (107) Our Lord! Take us out of this. Then if we revert (to evil-doing) we shall indeed be wrong-doers." (108) Allah will say: "Away from Me; stay where you are and do not address Me.[101] (109) You are those that when a party of My servants said: 'Our Lord, we believe, so forgive us, and have mercy on us, for You are the Best of those that are merciful,' (110) you made a laughing-stock of them and your hostility to them caused you to forget Me, and you simply kept laughing. ▶

أَلَمْ تَكُنْ ءَايَٰتِى تُتْلَىٰ عَلَيْكُمْ فَكُنتُم بِهَا
تُكَذِّبُونَ ﴿١٠٥﴾ قَالُوا۟ رَبَّنَا غَلَبَتْ عَلَيْنَا شِقْوَتُنَا
وَكُنَّا قَوْمًا ضَآلِّينَ ﴿١٠٦﴾ رَبَّنَآ أَخْرِجْنَا مِنْهَا
فَإِنْ عُدْنَا فَإِنَّا ظَٰلِمُونَ ﴿١٠٧﴾ قَالَ ٱخْسَـُٔوا۟
فِيهَا وَلَا تُكَلِّمُونِ ﴿١٠٨﴾ إِنَّهُۥ كَانَ فَرِيقٌ مِّنْ
عِبَادِى يَقُولُونَ رَبَّنَآ ءَامَنَّا فَٱغْفِرْ لَنَا وَٱرْحَمْنَا
وَأَنتَ خَيْرُ ٱلرَّٰحِمِينَ ﴿١٠٩﴾ فَٱتَّخَذْتُمُوهُمْ
سِخْرِيًّا حَتَّىٰٓ أَنسَوْكُمْ ذِكْرِى وَكُنتُم
مِّنْهُمْ تَضْحَكُونَ ﴿١١٠﴾

Mas'ūd the meaning of the root word *k-l-ḥ*. To this he replied: 'Have you not seen the burnt head of an animal?'

101. The unbelievers are told not to plead to be free; nor to put forth any excuses. This does not mean, however, that they will become mute and disabled from such pleading for themselves. True, some traditions suggest that this will be their very last utterance. But this view is, however, discordant with the Qur'ānic account. For the Qur'ān subsequently recounts the conversation that will take place between the unbelievers and God in the Next Life (see verse 112 ff. below – Ed.). Obviously, either these traditions are untrue or they mean that thereafter the unbelievers will not be able to plead for their redemption, (rather, they will be unable to speak altogether. – Ed.).

(111) Lo! I have rewarded them this Day for their steadfastness, so that they, and they alone, are triumphant."[102] (112) Then Allah will ask them: "For how many years did you stay on earth?" (113) They will say: "We stayed for a day or part of a day.[103] Ask of those who keep count of this." (114) He will say: "You stayed only for a while, if you only knew that.[104] ▶

إِنِّى جَزَيْتُهُمُ ٱلْيَوْمَ بِمَا صَبَرُوٓا۟ أَنَّهُمْ هُمُ
ٱلْفَآئِزُونَ ﴿١١١﴾ قَٰلَ كَمْ لَبِثْتُمْ فِى ٱلْأَرْضِ
عَدَدَ سِنِينَ ﴿١١٢﴾ قَالُوا۟ لَبِثْنَا يَوْمًا أَوْ بَعْضَ
يَوْمٍ فَسْـَٔلِ ٱلْعَآدِّينَ ﴿١١٣﴾ قَٰلَ إِن لَّبِثْتُمْ
إِلَّا قَلِيلًا ۖ لَّوْ أَنَّكُمْ كُنتُمْ تَعْلَمُونَ ﴿١١٤﴾

102. Once again the Qur'ānic concepts pertaining to success and failure are being clearly stated in the present verse.

103. For details see *Towards Understanding the Qur'ān,* vol. V, *Ṭā Hā* 20, n. 80, pp. 224–5.

104. The Messengers used to tell the unbelievers that the life of the world was meant merely to test them. It was a life so ephemeral that they should not consider it to be their real life. They were told in unequivocal terms that the real abode will be in the World to Come wherein they will remain forever. They were, therefore, counselled not to engage in deeds which whilst yielding some transient pleasure, will nonetheless destroy all their prospects in the eternal life of the Hereafter. Yet the unbelievers did not pay any heed to the Messengers. They were bent on denying the Hereafter and believed that the Next Life was simply a figment of the Messengers' imaginations. They suffered from the illusion that the life of the world was all that there was and, hence, is ought to be enjoyed to the maximum. The unbelievers' remorse later on though will be to no avail. They should have realized while they were alive that the After-Life is a reality. Instead, they wasted the opportunity that was made available to them, totally ruining their prospects in the never-ending life of the Hereafter for the sake of the advantages and pleasures of the present life.

(115) Did you imagine that We created you without any purpose,[105] and that you will not be brought back to Us?"

(116) So, exalted be Allah,[106] the True King! There is no god but He, the Lord of the Great Throne. (117) He who invokes any other god along with Allah – one for whom he has no evidence[107] – his reckoning is with his Lord alone.[108] Indeed, these unbelievers shall not prosper.[109]

أَفَحَسِبۡتُمۡ أَنَّمَا خَلَقۡنَٰكُمۡ عَبَثٗا وَأَنَّكُمۡ
إِلَيۡنَا لَا تُرۡجَعُونَ ١١٥ فَتَعَٰلَى ٱللَّهُ ٱلۡمَلِكُ
ٱلۡحَقُّۖ لَآ إِلَٰهَ إِلَّا هُوَ رَبُّ ٱلۡعَرۡشِ
ٱلۡكَرِيمِ ١١٦ وَمَن يَدۡعُ مَعَ ٱللَّهِ إِلَٰهًا
ءَاخَرَ لَا بُرۡهَٰنَ لَهُۥ بِهِۦ فَإِنَّمَا حِسَابُهُۥ عِندَ
رَبِّهِۦٓۚ إِنَّهُۥ لَا يُفۡلِحُ ٱلۡكَٰفِرُونَ ١١٧

105. The word *'abathan* used here may be taken to mean either 'by way of sport and play' or 'for the sake of sport and play'. In the former sense, the verse means: 'Do you believe that man was created simply by way of jest and amusement, that his creation was devoid of any purpose, and that God had dispersed a species on earth without requiring it to achieve any object?' If the word *'abathan* is understood in the latter sense, it means: 'Do you think that you have been created merely to devote all your time to frivolous things such as sport, play and entertainment, to activities that lead to no worthwhile results?'

106. That is, He is far too exalted to do anything that is purposeless. Also, He is far too exalted to make it possible for any of His creatures to partake of His Divinity.

107. An alternative rendering of the above could be: 'He who invokes any other God along with Allah has no sanction to do so.'

108. That is, there will be no way for such people to escape from being called to account, from being questioned about their deeds.

109. This is a reiteration of the point made earlier; a statement about those who will truly prosper and those who will be the losers. (See, for example, verses 102–3 above – Ed.)

(118) And say, (O Muḥammad): "My Lord, forgive us and have mercy on us, for You are the Best of those that are merciful."[110]	وَقُل رَّبِّ ٱغْفِرْ وَٱرْحَمْ وَأَنتَ خَيْرُ ٱلرَّٰحِمِينَ ﴿١١٨﴾

110. The subtlety of this supplication should not be missed. It was earlier pointed out that God would not pardon those who had made a laughing-stock of the Prophet (peace be upon him) and the believers when they made this Prayer (see verses 105–10). Now the Prophet (peace be upon him) and by implication the Companions, are also being directed to make the same Prayer mentioned above. The implication being that if the unbelievers persist in this mocking of them, they will earn strong evidence against themselves in the Hereafter. This despite the clear warning they have been given here.

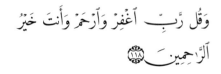

Sūrah 24

Al-Nūr

(The Light)

(Madinan Period)

Title

The title is derived from verse 35 of this *sūrah*: 'Allah is the Light of the heavens and the earth.'

Period of Revelation

There is agreement that this *sūrah* was revealed after Ghazwat Banū al-Muṣṭaliq. It is evident from the Qur'ān itself that it was revealed in the context of the well-known incident of slander (*ifk*) which is mentioned in detail in verses 11–20. Moreover, it is established by authentic traditions that this incident took place while the Muslims were on the move in connection with the campaign against the Banū al-Muṣṭaliq.

There is, however, disagreement about whether this expedition took place before the Battle of Aḥzāb in 5 A.H. or after the battle in 6 A.H. This matter needs to be investigated because the injunctions regarding *ḥijāb* are to be found in only two *sūrahs* of the Qur'ān: *al-Aḥzāb* and the present *sūrah*, *al-Nūr*. As far as *Sūrah al-Aḥzāb* is concerned, there is complete agreement that it was revealed on the occasion of the Battle of Aḥzāb. Now, if the Battle of Aḥzāb predates the expedition of the Banū al-Muṣṭaliq, it obviously means that the earlier injunctions about *ḥijāb* are those that are embodied in *Sūrah al-Aḥzāb*, and that these have been supplemented by the current ones in *Sūrah al-Nūr*. Conversely, if the campaign against the Banū al-Muṣṭaliq took place before the Battle of Aḥzāb, the sequence would be reversed, meaning thereby that the injunctions pertaining to *ḥijāb* commenced with those found in *Sūrah al-Nūr* and that they were given their final touch in *Sūrah al-Aḥzāb*. Since confusion on this issue might cloud our understanding regarding the wisdom underlying the injunctions about *ḥijāb*, it is necessary to ascertain the date of the revelation of *Sūrah al-Nūr* before proceeding any further.

According to Ibn Sa'd, Ghazwat Banū al-Muṣṭaliq took place in Sha'bān 5 A.H. and Ghazwat al-Aḥzāb in Dhū al-Qa'dah of the same year. (See Ibn Sa'd, *Ṭabaqāt*, vol. 2, pp. 63–5 – Ed.) This view is supported by the traditions cited on the authority of 'Ā'ishah which are narrated in connection with the incident of slander. These traditions mention the quarrel between Sa'd ibn 'Ubādah and Sa'd ibn Mu'ādh. (See Bukhārī, *K. Tafsīr al-Qur'ān*, *Sūrah al-Nūr*, 'Bāb law lā idh . . . al-Kādhībūn' (verses 12–13) – Ed.) All authentic traditions, however, affirm that Sa'd ibn Mu'ādh had died in Ghazwat Banū Qurayẓah which took place immediately after Ghazwat al-Aḥzāb. (See Ibn Sa'd, *Ṭabaqāt*, vol. 2, p. 78 – Ed.) Hence, there is no question that Sa'd ibn Mu'ādh was alive in 6 A.H.

On the other hand, Muḥammad ibn Iṣḥāq narrates that Ghazwat al-Aḥzāb took place in Shawwāl 5 A.H. and Ghazwat Banū al-Muṣṭaliq in Sha'bān 6 A.H. (See Ibn Hishām, vol. 2, pp. 214 and 289 – Ed.) Again, this account is corroborated by a large number of traditions narrated from 'Ā'ishah and others. We learn from these traditions that the injunctions about *ḥijāb* had already been revealed before the incident of slander, and that they can be found in *Sūrah al-Aḥzāb*. These traditions also inform us that Zaynab was married to the Prophet Muḥammad (peace be upon him) by then, the marriage having taken place after Ghazwat al-Aḥzāb in Dhū al-Qa'dah 5 A.H. This incident, as we know, is mentioned in *Sūrah al-Aḥzāb*. Furthermore, it appears from these traditions that Ḥamnah, Zaynab's sister, took a leading part in the slander incident because she regarded 'Ā'ishah as her sister's rival insofar as 'Ā'ishah was another of the Prophet's wives. (See Bukhārī, *K. Tafsīr al-Qur'ān*, *Sūrah al-Nūr*, 'Bāb law lā idh . . . al-Kādhībūn' (verses 12–13) – Ed.) Obviously, it must have taken some time for Ḥamnah's negative feelings towards 'Ā'ishah to develop after the marriage between the Prophet (peace be upon him) and Zaynab took place. All these traditions, therefore, reinforce Ibn Isḥāq's account of the incident.

What is, however, difficult to accept is that the name of Sa'd ibn Mu'ādh figures in the slander incident. This difficulty though is resolved by the fact that while some of the traditions narrated from

'Ā'ishah regarding the incident mention Sa'd ibn Mu'ādh, other traditions mention Usayd ibn Ḥuḍayr. (See Ibn Hishām, vol. 2, p. 254 – Ed.) Additionally, these latter traditions are fully consistent with the traditions narrated from 'Ā'ishah. If an attempt was made to reconcile the chronology of events with the assumption that the slander incident took place while Sa'd ibn Mu'ādh was alive, and to believe for that reason that both Ghazwat Banū al-Muṣṭaliq and the slander incident took place before the Battle of Aḥzāb and the expedition against the Qurayẓah, we would be confronted with an insolubly complex problem. Such an assumption would require that we consider the revelation of the verse pertaining to *ḥijāb* to have taken place even before the Battle of Aḥzāb and the expedition against the Qurayẓah. This, however, is directly opposed to the statements of the Qur'ān and several authentic traditions which fully establish that both the Prophet's marriage with Zaynab and the injunction pertaining to *ḥijāb* belong to the period after the Battle of Aḥzāb and the expedition against the Qurayẓah. It is for this reason that Ibn Ḥazm, Ibn al-Qayyim and several other scholars have considered Muḥammad ibn Isḥāq's account to be the correct one, and we too are of the same opinion.

Historical Background

Having ascertained that *Sūrah al-Nūr* was revealed in the later half of 6 A.H., a few months after the revelation of *Sūrah al-Aḥzāb*, let us now consider the background against which it was revealed.

The rise of the Islamic movement beginning with the Muslims' victory at the Battle of Badr had reached a high point by the time of Ghazwat al-Aḥzāb. The Jews, the hypocrites and the wavering Muslims had all begun to realize that it would be impossible to thwart this nascent movement merely by force of arms. On the occasion of Ghazwat al-Aḥzāb all these hostile elements forged a united front and a massive army of 10,000 invaded Madina. These opponents of Islam maintained their siege of Madina for one full month and then at long last they retreated in utter frustration. No sooner had they retreated than the Prophet (peace be upon him) proclaimed: 'The Quraysh shall never invade you after this year; but it is you who will be in a position to invade them' (Ibn Hishām, vol. 3, p. 266).

This in fact signified that the anti-Islamic forces had lost their capacity to launch any offensive against the Muslims. It also signified that the time when Islam had to fight a defensive war was over. From now on Islam would be on the offensive and any anti-Islamic forces on the defensive. The view expressed by the Prophet (peace be upon him) was a totally correct assessment of the situation. Furthermore, this fact was also fully recognized by the other party.

The increasing number of Muslims was, however, not the main reason for the ever-growing rise of Islam's power. As far as numbers are concerned, right from the Battle of Badr – the first battle – to that of Aḥzāb, the non-Muslims always greatly outnumbered the Muslims. In fact, the Muslims represented at that time barely one-tenth of Arabia's total population. Nor did the Muslims have any advantage over their adversaries in terms of arms. For the unbelievers excelled the Muslims in every kind of weaponry. Likewise, in respect of economic power and political influence the Muslims were no match for the unbelievers. The latter virtually had control over all of Arabia's economic resources whereas the Muslims were hard put to make both ends meet. Polytheists from all over Arabia as well as the Jews and Christians supported the Makkan unbelievers against the Muslims who, since they called people to embrace a new faith, had lost the support of all those who were loyal to the status quo ante.

Under these circumstances there was one factor that mainly enabled the Muslims to constantly move ahead. In essence, this was nothing less than their moral superiority, and this was an element which even their enemies acknowledged. For they quite clearly observed the unblemished character and conduct of Muḥammad (peace be upon him) and his Companions. On the one hand, this strength, purity and sterling character won the hearts of others to their faith. On the other, these same outstanding qualities infused in them a high degree of unity, discipline and solidarity. These qualities invested the Muslims with an almost insurmountable power. Hence, when the Jews and polytheists were confronted with the Muslims whose body politic was characterized with inner cohesion, solidarity and discipline they proved no match for them, neither in times of peace nor of war.

People who are wicked and mean by nature display a strange characteristic when they observe the good qualities of others. Even when they realize that the good qualities of others are conducive to their success and their own weaknesses cause them to suffer loss, they are still hardly inclined to purge themselves of their weaknesses or adopt the good qualities found among others. On the contrary, they concentrate all their attention on manipulations aimed at promoting the same weaknesses from which they suffer.

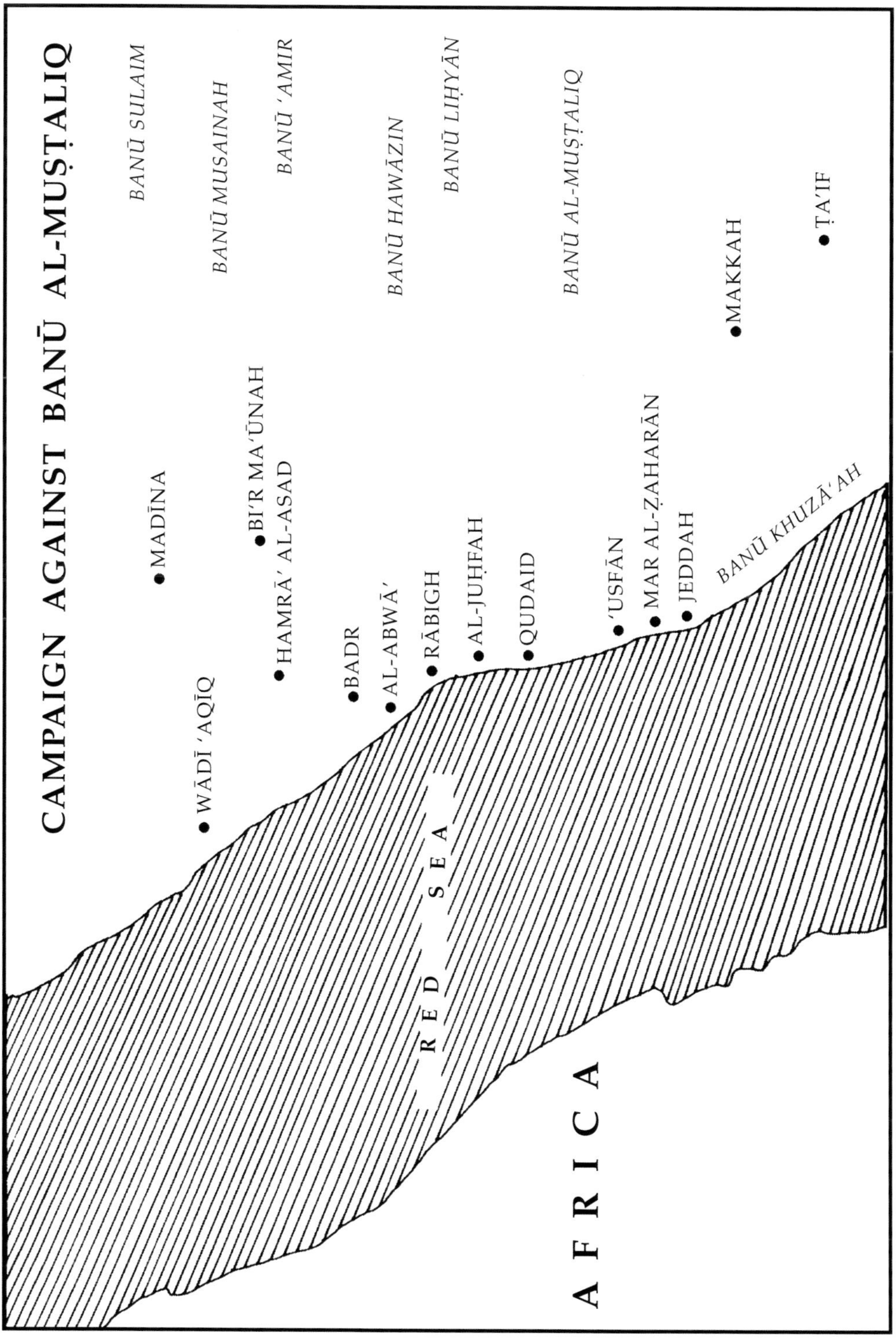
CAMPAIGN AGAINST BANŪ AL-MUṢṬALIQ
BANŪ SULAIM
BANŪ MUSAINAH
BANŪ ʻAMIR
BANŪ HAWĀZIN
BANŪ LIḤYĀN
BANŪ AL-MUṢṬALIQ
MAKKAH
ṬAʼIF
MADĪNA
BIʼR MAʻŪNAH
HAMRĀʼ AL-ASAD
WĀDĪ ʻAQĪQ
BADR
AL-ABWĀʼ
RĀBIGH
AL-JUḤFAH
QUDAID
ʻUSFĀN
MAR AL-ẒAHARĀN
JEDDAH
BANŪ KHUZĀʻAH
RED SEA
AFRICA

In this respect, the anti-Islamic forces resolved to launch a campaign to malign the Muslims. They thought that as a result of this campaign, the world would look at the Muslims as not significantly different from them, that the former too were not completely free from blemishes. As a result of this mentality, instead of engaging the Muslims in armed battle, the enemies of Islam directed their efforts at launching vicious and mean campaigns against them. This was in addition to attempts to sow discord in their ranks.

This purpose could be accomplished by the hypocrites who were apparently a part of the Muslim community. They could prove far more effective in carrying out this task than the enemies of Islam outside the Muslim ranks. It was decided, therefore, that the hypocrites of Madina should first foment trouble from within, and that the external enemies – the Jews and the polytheists – should subsequently exploit this to their utmost. This conspiracy of the enemies of Islam first manifested itself in Dhū al-Qa'dah 5 A.H. This was occasioned by the decision to extirpate the pre-Islamic custom of adoption.[1] The Prophet (peace be upon him) embarked on an effort to eradicate this custom by his own personal example. He did so by marrying Zaynab bint Jaḥsh, the divorced wife of his adopted son Zayd ibn Ḥārithah. The hypocrites of Madina seized this opportunity to raise a storm of hostile propaganda against the Prophet (peace be upon him). The Jews and the polytheists joined hands with them. Thereafter, all the forces hostile to Islam unanimously embarked on a similar course and resorted to a campaign of slander and calumny. They invented stories of how Muḥammad (peace be upon him) had fallen in love with the wife of his adopted son, how Zayd had found out about this and divorced his wife, and how the Prophet (peace be upon him) had subsequently married his own daughter-in-law.

These stories were spread on such a scale that even the minds of some Muslims could not remain altogether immune from their influence. The result is that we find vestiges of these stories in the traditions about the Prophet's marriage to Zaynab even in the works of some scholars of *Ḥadīth* and *Tafsīr*. This material was subsequently also much exploited by Orientalists who added a lot of vigour to the traditional material when they narrated this incident in their own works.

The fact of the matter, however, is that Zaynab was the daughter of the Prophet's paternal aunt, Umaymah, the daughter of 'Abd

---

1. The custom of adoption in vogue in Arabia at that time consisted of designating someone else's child as one's own and then assigning to him the same position as one's own issue – Ed.

al-Muṭṭalib. The Prophet (peace be upon him) thus knew her well from her childhood onwards. Thus, it is preposterous to say that the Prophet (peace be upon him) having accidentally seen her instantly fell in love with her because of her physical attractiveness.

It may also be recalled that only the previous year the Prophet (peace be upon him) had himself persuaded her to marry Zayd. It may further be recalled that Zaynab's brother, 'Abd Allāh ibn Jaḥsh, who was opposed to this proposal was angry that the marriage took place. Zaynab too was not very happy about it, for it can well be appreciated that a girl who belonged to the noblest family of the Quraysh would not welcome becoming the wife of a freed slave. However, since the Prophet (peace be upon him) wished to set the precedent of equality in the Muslim community, he felt that it should begin with his own family. Therefore, he virtually directed Zaynab to marry Zayd. Likewise, it was well known that it was mainly because of Zaynab's pride in her lineage that she could not live happily with Zayd, and that it was this factor which eventually led to their divorce. Even in the face of these well-known facts the enemies of Islam brazenly used this incident as a pretext to malign the Prophet (peace be upon him). Their design was so well-conceived and well-executed that the incident continues to cast its shadow to this day.

Another act of character-assassination was committed on the occasion of the expedition of Banū al-Muṣṭaliq. This time the slander campaign was even more fierce.

The Banū al-Muṣṭaliq are a branch of the Khuzā'ah tribe who lived in Qudyad which lies on the Red Sea coast between Jeddah and Rābigh. There was a spring called Muraysī' in the area where all the families of Banū al-Muṣṭaliq lived. The military expedition that was launched is, therefore, also referred to in the traditions as the Expedition of Muraysī'. The exact location of the campaign is delineated on the map entitled Ghazwat Banū al-Muṣṭaliq (see p. 135).

In Sha'bān 6 A.H. the Prophet (peace be upon him) learned that the Banū al-Muṣṭaliq, in collaboration with some other tribes, were preparing to mount an attack on the Muslims. As soon as the Prophet (peace be upon him) came to know this, he marched in their direction at the head of an armed force so that the evil might be nipped in the bud. 'Abd Allāh ibn Ubayy joined the Prophet (peace be upon him) on this expedition along with a large number of hypocrites. Ibn Sa'd has mentioned that never before had the hypocrites joined the Prophet (peace be upon him) in any expedition in such large numbers. The Prophet (peace be upon him), however, surprised the enemy by the speed at which he reached al-Muraysī'. After very limited fighting, the whole tribe was taken captive and the goods in their possession seized. Soon after the completion of this mission, while the Muslim army was still encamped at Muraysī', an altercation broke out about water between a servant of 'Umar named Jahjāh ibn Mas'ūd al-Ghifārī and Sinān ibn Wabar al-Juhanī, who was an ally of the Khazraj. One group called upon the *Anṣār* for help and the other asked the *Muhājirūn* to come to their aid. Though people from both groups responded somehow the matter was resolved.

'Abd Allāh ibn Ubayy, who belonged to the Khazraj, made an issue of this minor incident seeking to exploit it to the full. He began to incite the *Anṣār*, telling them: 'These *Muhājirūn* have now pounced upon us and have become our enemies. Our example in relation to these Qurayshī destitute is that of a person who takes good care of a dog with the result that eventually the dog mangles him. You brought these people here and made them share your wealth and property. If you were to just withdraw your support from them even today, they would be forced out.' He then swore, declaring that after the return to Madina, 'Those who are honourable among us will drive away those that are degraded.'[2]

When these disturbing reports reached the Prophet (peace be upon him), 'Umar proposed that 'Abd Allāh ibn Ubayy be put to the sword. The Prophet (peace be upon him), however, decided otherwise, saying that if such a thing were done, people would go about saying that he, Muḥammad, kills his own Companions. So saying, the Prophet (peace be upon him) asked the army to immediately march ahead of that place. He did not stop until noon the next day, this so that his people were too exhausted to indulge in gossip. On the way, Usayd ibn Ḥuḍayr asked: 'O Messenger of God! Today you ordered us to march at a time quite different from the time you used to choose for it in the past.' The Prophet (peace be upon him) replied: 'Did you not hear what your friend is talking about?' Usayd ibn Ḥuḍayr then asked the Prophet (peace be upon him) who that person was. The Prophet (peace be upon him) replied that it was 'Abd Allāh ibn Ubayy. Thereupon he submitted: 'O Messenger of God! Please be indulgent with him. At the time when you arrived in Madina we had already decided to appoint him our ruler. We were in fact having a crown prepared for him. Your coming to Madina spoiled his game. He is merely giving vent to his spite.' (See Wāqidī, *al-Maghāzī*, vol. 2, p. 419 – Ed.)

---

2. This statement by 'Abd Allāh ibn Ubayy is reproduced in the Qur'ān itself: 'If we return to Madina, surely the more honourable element will expel the meaner one' (*al-Munāfiqūn* 63: 8).

'Abd Allāh ibn Ubayy's mischief did not abate for he then came forth with something even graver. It was so grave that had the Prophet (peace be upon him) and his Companions not acted with the utmost restraint and wisdom, a civil war could have flared up in the nascent Muslim community of Madina. The mischief to which we are referring is the campaign of slander launched against 'Ā'ishah.

It is appropriate if here we consider the account of the whole incident in 'Ā'ishah's own words. We have attempted to fill any gaps that might be found in 'Ā'ishah's account by recourse to other authentic traditions pertaining to the incident. This material, however, has been added to the account within square brackets so that the continuity of the narrative is not interrupted. What follows brings out the whole content and context of the incident:

> It was the practice of the Prophet (peace be upon him) to decide which of his wives would accompany him on a journey by drawing lots.[3] For the expedition of Banū al-Muṣṭaliq, the lot fell in my name and so I accompanied him. On our return while we were approaching Madina, the Prophet (peace be upon him) camped for the night at a place. Some time before dawn, preparations were made to set out. I had gone to attend the call of nature and as I was about to return to the camp, I felt that my necklace broke and fell down somewhere. I started to look around for it. Meanwhile, the caravan proceeded. It was customary that I would sit in a litter which was then put on a camel by four persons. Since we women were very lean and thin in those days because of paucity of food, the carriers of my litter did not even realize that I was not in it. They placed the litter on the camel and set off. When I returned [to the camp] after having traced my necklace, I could not find anyone there. I covered myself up with a sheet and lay there assuming that when people discovered my absence, they would try to trace me and so eventually return to the same spot. Meanwhile, I fell asleep. When morning arrived, Ṣafwān

3. This drawing of lots should not be misconstrued as some form of lottery prevalent at the time. The Prophet (peace be upon him) resorted to this practice since all his wives had equal rights and there was evidently no grounds for preferring one over and above another. Had the Prophet (peace be upon him) himself chosen some in preference to others this might have injured their feelings. He, therefore, resolved the issue by drawing lots. The *Sharī'ah* allows this mode of selection if all concerned are equally and legitimately entitled to something and there is no other plausible way of preferring one to another, the circumstances obviously not allowing all such persons to benefit from the opportunity.

> ibn Mu'aṭṭal al-Salamī passed by the spot where I lay asleep. He immediately recognized me since he had seen me often before the injunction relating to *ḥijāb* was revealed. Ṣafwān was one of the Companions who had participated in the Battle of Badr. He was in the habit of sleeping till late in the morning.[4] Hence, he had been left behind and lay asleep somewhere in the camp when the caravan set off for Madina. He halted his camel on observing me and exclaimed: 'To Allah do we belong and to Him we are destined to return.[5] Oh! The Prophet's wife has been left behind.' As he uttered these words, I woke up and immediately covered my face with the sheet. Without saying a word to me, he made his camel kneel down beside me while he himself stood aside. I rode the camel and he [i.e. Ṣafwān] began to move ahead, leading the camel by the nose-string. Around noon, we joined the army when it was about to camp. Even then nobody had realized that I had been left behind. This provided the slanderers an opportunity to hurl all kinds of calumnies. 'Abd Allāh ibn Ubayy took a leading role in this slander campaign. I was, however, totally ignorant of the raging storm of calumny directed at me.

According to some other reports, when 'Ā'ishah reached the camp on Ṣafwān's camel and it became known that she had been left behind, 'Abd Allāh ibn Ubayy instantly exclaimed: 'By God! She has not returned untouched. Look! The wife of your Prophet spent the night with another person and now he is publicly bringing her back.'

We now revert to 'Ā'ishah's account:

> On reaching Madina, I fell ill and was bed-ridden for a month. Calumnious reports were in circulation and even reached the Prophet's ears, but I knew nothing about that. Nonetheless, what worried me was the Prophet's lack of attention towards me, which he was wont to show to me during my illness.

---

4. Abū Dā'ūd's *Sunan* and other collections of *aḥādīth* mention that Ṣafwān's wife complained to the Prophet (peace be upon him) about the fact that Ṣafwān never offered *Fajr* Prayers on time. In his defence Ṣafwān pleaded that it was a family trait and that he could not help over-sleeping in the morning. The Prophet (peace be upon him) told him to pray whenever he got up. (See Abū Dā'ūd, *K. al-Ṣawm*, 'Bāb al-Mar'ah taṣūmu bi ghayr idhn Zawjihā' – Ed.) Some scholars of *Ḥadīth* cite this [habit of oversleeping] as the reason for his missing the caravan. Others, however, state that the Prophet (peace be upon him) had assigned him the duty to retrieve whatever articles might have been left in the morning after the army had decamped.

5. This is a verse from the Qur'ān, and is usually uttered in exclamation on knowing that something tragic or awful has taken place – Ed.

When he entered the house he went no further than asking some member of the family: 'How is she?' As for myself, he would not speak to me. This made me suspect that there was something behind it. Eventually I obtained his permission to move out to my mother's house so that she might look after me properly.

One night I went out of Madina to attend to the call of nature. Up till that time there were no toilets in our houses and we used to go into open fields for this purpose. I was accompanied by the mother of Misṭaḥ ibn Uthāthah who was the maternal cousin of my father. [One learns from other traditions that Abū Bakr[6] used to support the whole of Misṭaḥ's family. Notwithstanding this favour, he joined with those who were engaged in spreading slanderous accusations about 'Ā'ishah.] Along the way Misṭaḥ's mother stumbled and exclaimed: 'May Misṭaḥ be undone!' I asked her: 'What kind of mother are you that you are cursing your son who participated in the Battle of Badr?' Then she narrated the whole story: how scandal-mongers had launched a campaign of slander against me. Apart from the hypocrites, some Muslims had also become a party to this vicious campaign, the leading ones among them being Misṭaḥ, Ḥassān ibn Thābit and Ḥamnah bint Jaḥsh, Zaynab's sister. On hearing this I was horrified. I even forgot the purpose for which I had gone there and immediately returned to my house and spent the whole night crying.

In my absence the Prophet (peace be upon him) summoned 'Alī and Usāmah ibn Zayd and sought their advice. Usāmah spoke highly of me, saying: 'O Messenger of God! We have seen in your wife nothing but goodness. It is a sheer lie and falsehood which is being disseminated against her.' 'Alī said: 'O Messenger of God! There is no dearth of women. You can replace her with another wife. Should you like to find out, send for the slave-girl who serves her and ask her about the matter.' Hence the slave-girl was summoned and interrogated. In her reply she said: 'By God, Who has sent you with truth, I have never observed anything bad in her. The only lapse I can think of is that sometimes I knead flour and while I attend to something else and request her to look after the flour, she falls asleep and goats eat the flour up.'

---

6. Who was 'Ā'ishah's father – Ed.

That same day, the Prophet (peace be upon him) addressed the Muslims, saying: 'O Muslims! Who is there to defend my honour against the assaults of the person who has hurled false accusations against my family and has thus agonized me? By God, I have never seen anything bad in my wife nor in the person who is subjected to slander and calumny; he is a person who never visited my house in my absence.' On hearing this Usayd ibn Ḥuḍayr [according to other reports, Sa'd ibn Mu'ādh][7] rose and said: 'O Messenger of Allah! If that man is from our tribe we will put him to the sword. And if he is from our brothers, the Khazraj, then order us and we are here to carry out your order.' No sooner was this said than Sa'd ibn 'Ubādah,[8] the chief of the Khazraj, contributed his position: 'You are lying. You will not kill him. You are talking of putting this man to the sword because he belongs to the Khazraj. Had he been from your own tribe you would have never said that you would put him to the sword.' Thereupon Usayd ibn Ḥuḍayr responded, saying: 'You are a hypocrite and for that reason you are supporting other hypocrites.' This created pandemonium in the Mosque of the Prophet (peace be upon him) even though the Prophet himself was at the time sitting on the pulpit. The Aws and Khazraj tribes were on the verge of exchanging blows but the Prophet (peace be upon him) pacified them, whereafter he descended from the pulpit. (See Bukhārī, *K. Tafsīr al-Qur'ān*, *Sūrah al-Nūr*, 'Bāb law lā idh . . . al-Kādhibūn' (verses 12–13) and *ibid.*, *K. al-Maghāzī*, 'Bāb Ḥadīth al-Ifk' – Ed.)

---

7. This might possibly be because instead of using the name 'Ā'ishah used the appellation: 'The chief of Aws'. Some narrators of this tradition might have considered this appellation to refer to Sa'd ibn Mu'ādh because during his life-time he was chief of the Aws and he is generally known historically in this capacity. However, at the time of the incident under discussion, Sa'd's paternal cousin, Usayd ibn Ḥuḍayr was chief of the Aws.

8. Although Sa'd ibn 'Ubādah was a pious and sincere Muslim who had tremendous love and regard for the Prophet (peace be upon him) and was instrumental in the spread of Islam in Madina, he was excessively attached to his tribe. Prompted by this tribal fraternity he defends 'Abd Allāh ibn Ubayy. The same bias surfaced in his exclamation on the day of the conquest of Makka: 'This is the day of massacre. Whatever is forbidden would be lawful today.' (See Ibn Hishām, vol. 2, pp. 406–7 – Ed.) The Prophet (peace be upon him) asked him to surrender the banner of his contingent as punishment for this outburst. This also explains his insistence, after the Prophet's death, that the Caliphate was the right of the *Anṣār*. When he failed in his move and all the *Anṣār* and *Muhājirūn* pledged their allegiance to Abū Bakr, his was the lone voice of dissent. He refused to take the oath of allegiance to the Caliph who was from the Quraysh. (See *al-Iṣābah* by Ibn Ḥajar and *al-Istī'āb* by Ibn 'Abd al-Barr about Sa'd ibn 'Ubādah, pp. 10–11 – Ed.)

The remaining details of the incident are mentioned in our explanatory notes which pertain to the Qur'ānic verses that exonerate 'Ā'ishah from the charges levelled against her (see verses 11 ff.). The point made above is that 'Abd Allāh ibn Ubayy by initiating this mischief attempted to kill several birds with one stone. On the one hand, he attacked the honour of the households of both the Prophet (peace be upon him) and Abū Bakr. On the other, he sought to lower the moral prestige of the Islamic movement which was then at its pinnacle. Furthermore, had Islam not brought about the moral transformation of its followers, the mischief created by him would have provoked a civil war between the *Muhājirūn* and the *Anṣār*, let alone between the two tribes of the *Anṣār* themselves who might have engaged in gory acts of fratricide.

Subject Matter and Main Themes

The above account provides the background against which the last six sections of *Sūrah al-Aḥzāb* were revealed, this at a time when the first major propaganda campaign against Islam was launched. This was on the occasion of the Prophet's marriage with the divorced wife of his adopted son, Zayd. (See *al-Aḥzāb* 33: 28–73 – Ed.) As for *Sūrah al-Nūr*, it was revealed at the time of the second major propaganda campaign against Islam. If one systematically studies both *sūrahs* against this background, it facilitates an understanding of the underlying wisdom of the injunctions expounded in them.

The hypocrites had intended to defeat the Muslims in that very field in which the latter enjoyed superiority. Rather than engage in an emotionally-charged disquisition against the conspiracies of the hypocrites, the Muslims were asked to fill in the gaps in their own moral conduct. In short, they were required to fortify themselves on the moral front.

We have already taken note of the storm of mischief that the hypocrites and unbelievers raised on the occasion of the Prophet's marriage to Zaynab. It was during those turbulent days that *Sūrah al-Aḥzāb* was revealed and the following directives laid down in that *sūrah* especially with respect to social relations:

i. The wives of the Prophet (peace be upon him) were asked to stay indoors with grace and dignity and not to go about making a public display of their attractions. They were also directed that whenever they happened to converse with men who did not fall into the category of *maḥram*, they should avoid any mannerism that would lead such men to entertain any uncalled-for expectations. (See verses 32–3 of *Sūrah al-Aḥzāb*.)

ii. Those Muslims who did not have any ties of kinship with the Prophet's family were barred from entering his house unless they were specially granted permission to do so. If they needed to ask anything of the Prophet's wives, they were to do so from behind a screen (verse 53).

iii. A distinction was drawn between *maḥram* relatives and those who were not *maḥram*. In this respect, an injunction was issued (verse 55) directing that only *maḥram* relatives could freely enter the house(s) of the Prophet (peace be upon him).

iv. It was impressed upon the Muslims that the Prophet's wives were their mothers and, hence, no one could marry them after the Prophet (peace be upon him) just as no person may marry his mother. Hence, the Muslims were asked to have nothing but the purest of intentions with regard to the Prophet's wives (verses 53–4).

v. The Muslims were also warned that causing any offence to the Prophet (peace be upon him) would incur God's curse upon them both in this life and in the Next, and that it would render them liable to a humiliating punishment in the Hereafter. Likewise, those who cause an unjustified hurt to the Muslims, be they men or women, or who calumniate them, commit a grave sin (verses 57–8).

vi. All Muslim women were directed that whenever they have to go out they should properly cover their bodies with their outer garments and cast their mantle over their faces (verse 59).

Subsequently, when the same slander campaign again rocked the Madinan society, *Sūrah al-Nūr* was revealed. It also embodied injunctions that are relevant to the realms of morality, social life and law. The purpose of those injunctions was to protect Muslim society from the rise and spread of social evils. If social evils were to raise their ugly heads, then certain measures are documented as a means of curbing them. What follows is a summary of the injunctions and directives given in the same sequence in which they appear in this *sūrah*. This so that one has a fairly clear idea about the whole range of measures – legal, moral and social – that were prescribed by the Qur'ān. These were prescribed at the appropriate psychological moment as assistance in the reform and development of human society:

i. Illicit sex, which had already been denounced as a social evil (*al-Nisā'* 4: 15–16), was now declared a cognizable criminal offence. The specific punishment of one hundred lashes was laid down with regard to those so convicted.
ii. People were directed to refrain from having social relations with those who were morally corrupt. The believers were furthermore especially asked not to enter into matrimonial relations with the morally bankrupt.
iii. Anyone who accuses another of unlawful sexual intercourse (*zinā*) and fails to produce four witnesses to substantiate such a charge is liable to a punishment of eighty lashes.
iv. The procedure of *li'ān* was laid down in respect of the husband who accused his wife of having committed unlawful sexual intercourse. (For an explanation of *li'ān* see Glossary of Terms.)
v. While refuting the false allegations of the hypocrites against 'Ā'ishah, it was laid down that people should not blindly accept slanderous charges levelled against persons of honourable character nor should they go about spreading them themselves. Instead people should seek to curb the circulation of such outrageous reports rather than go about narrating them to others.

   In this connection a general principle was expounded: that men of clean character are suitable for matrimonial relations with women of clean character. In fact it is quite difficult for such people to feel at home with corrupt women even for a few days. The same is true about women of clean character. The soul of a good-charactered woman will find peace and harmony with a good-charactered man alone and she will be totally out of place if she makes a life-partner of a corrupt man. Given that the Prophet (peace be upon him) was a person of clean moral character – in fact he was possessed of the cleanest possible character – does it stand to reason that he would make a corrupt woman his favourite wife? How can it even be imagined that anyone as pious and righteous as the Prophet Muḥammad (peace be upon him) would take and keep a woman of disreputable character as his wife, one who goes to the extent of committing adultery? Thus, the accusation that was levelled against 'Ā'ishah was no more than a slanderous lie fabricated by a depraved person. The whole account of the incident was so outrageously false that no one could possibly believe it. The people should have used their brains and seen with open eyes what kind of person levelled such an outrageous accusation.

vi. Those who are guilty of spreading malicious rumours and seek to spread moral corruption in Muslim society deserve punishment rather than encouragement.

vii. As a general rule, it was prescribed that relations in the Muslim society should be based on the principle that people should have good faith with regard to one another. Everyone was to be considered innocent until proved otherwise, rather than vice versa.

viii. A general directive was given that people should not enter one another's house freely. They may do so only when they are expressly permitted by the owners to so enter their homes.

ix. Both men and women were asked to restrain themselves from intentionally looking at, let alone ogling, members of the opposite sex.

x. Women were directed to cover their heads and bosoms even in their own homes.

xi. Women were also directed not to display their attractions before anyone other than their husbands, their *maḥram* relatives and the servants of the house.

xii. They were directed not only to cover their personal adornments, but also not to go out of their homes while wearing tinkling ornaments.

xiii. The practice of remaining unmarried was declared to be undesirable both for men and women. A general directive was given that unmarried persons, including slave men and women, should marry. This because to remain unmarried often makes people instrumental in the spread of corruption or makes them vulnerable to the same. Those who are unmarried, even when they themselves do not directly engage in moral corruption, are at least more amenable to lending their ears to rumours of moral corruption and to spreading those rumours around.

xiv. A device, namely *mukātabah*, was found for the emancipation of slaves, both male and female. (See Glossary of Terms –

Ed.) The masters of slaves were urged to provide financial assistance to those slaves who had made *mukātabah* contracts in order that they might be able to emancipate themselves.

xv. The use of slave-girls for prostitution was henceforth prohibited. Up until this time it had been customary for slave-girls to belong to this profession. Hence, the prohibition of this practice was aimed at extirpating prostitution.

xvi. Domestic servants and minor children were directed not to enter unannounced the bedrooms of any male or female of the house during the hours of privacy (i.e. in the early hours of the morning and afternoon, and at night). Even children were required to seek permission before entering anyone's bedroom.

xvii. Old women were granted the concession to take off their headscarves in their own homes. They were, nevertheless, asked not to make a deliberate display of their attractiveness. Moreover, they were told that it was preferable if they continued to wear headscarves to cover themselves.

xviii. The blind, the lame, the maimed and the sick were granted leave to eat anything at anyone's house and the same would not be considered as theft or embezzlement. In other words, such persons would not be taken to task for so doing.

xix. Close relatives and friends were allowed to eat freely at one another's homes, even without obtaining formal permission, and that doing so was to be considered the same as eating at one's own place. Thus, members of society were brought closer to each other and the barriers of estrangement removed. This was done in order to foster mutual affection and a sincere warmth between people so that any mischief-mongers might be hard put to find gaps they could exploit to achieve their own nefarious designs.

Along with providing these directives, this *sūrah* also outlines those features which distinguish the hypocrites from the true believers. Moreover, measures were prescribed so as to introduce greater discipline in the collective life of the Muslims. Steps were also taken to reinforce the inner strength of Muslim society.

What is most remarkable is that this whole *sūrah* is absolutely free from the bitterness caused by vulgar and obscene accusations. Consider the context in which the *sūrah* was revealed on the one hand, and note its contents and style on the other. Even though the atmosphere was highly charged, both the content and the tenor of this *sūrah* rise above what would normally be expected of any discourse on such an occasion. Take into account the provocative background of the events and note the restrained dignity in which the laws were laid down, the reformative directives given, the guidance provided, and the instruction and admonition imparted. This indicates that even when Muslims encounter mischievous hostility they should always act with wisdom and restraint and be magnanimous despite all provocation. The tone and tenor of this *sūrah*'s discourse also conclusively prove that the Qur'ān was in no way composed by Muḥammad (peace be upon him). For had it been so, it would have carried some reflection – notwithstanding the loftiness of the Prophet's vision and the greatness of his character – of the bitterness that an innocent person feels when his own honour and dignity are subjected to outrageous attack. On the contrary, there is every indication in the *sūrah* that it is the work of One Who is looking at the human situation from a great height. One Who is providing valuable guidance to mankind without being affected by any personal or narrow considerations, or by the conditions obtaining at a given time and place.

In the name of Allah, the Most Merciful, the Most Compassionate.

(1) This is a *sūrah* which We have revealed, and which We have made obligatory; We have revealed in it clear instructions[1] so that you may take heed.

(2) Those who fornicate – whether female or male – flog each one of them with a hundred lashes.[2] ▶

بِسْمِ ٱللَّهِ ٱلرَّحْمَٰنِ ٱلرَّحِيمِ

سُورَةٌ أَنزَلْنَٰهَا وَفَرَضْنَٰهَا وَأَنزَلْنَا فِيهَآ
ءَايَٰتٍۭ بَيِّنَٰتٍ لَّعَلَّكُمْ تَذَكَّرُونَ ﴿١﴾
ٱلزَّانِيَةُ وَٱلزَّانِى فَٱجْلِدُوا۟ كُلَّ وَٰحِدٍ
مِّنْهُمَا مِا۟ئَةَ جَلْدَةٍ ۖ

---

1. The opening verse persistently stresses 'We'. The purpose behind this is to vehemently emphasize that this *sūrah* was revealed by 'Us' [i.e. by God] rather than anyone else. Hence, it ought not to be taken lightly, as something coming from one who lacks power and authority. It should be appreciated that He Who has revealed this *sūrah* is One Who holds everyone's lives in His grip, Who is so overwhelmingly powerful that no one can go beyond His control.

It is further clarified in the later part of the verse that whatever has been said in this *sūrah* is not in the nature of 'recommendations' or 'suggestions', that may or may not be followed by a person, depending on his own will. They are, instead, categorical commands which must be followed. If someone believes in and wants to submit himself to God, it is imperative that he acts in conformity with these commands. Furthermore, far from being ambiguous, these commands are couched in terms which are both clear and categorical. As a result, it is not justifiable to make excuses and contend that since the injunctions were incomprehensible it was not possible to act upon them.

This preamble is followed by the commands themselves. The preamble seems to underscore how important the commands are in the sight of God. It is pertinent to point out here that no other *sūrah* of the Qur'ān has such a forceful preamble.

2. The issue under discussion is hedged in by several legal, moral and historical aspects which need to be explained and elaborated upon. If these aspects were not mentioned in detail, it would be extremely difficult for a person of our own time to appreciate the Qur'ānic legislation expounded

here. Hence, what follows is an attempt to shed light on different aspects of the Qur'ānic legislation in question:

(i) As it is, everyone knows what *zinā* (unlawful sexual intercourse) means, namely that a male and a female have sexual relations without there being any legal sanction for the same. There has been absolute agreement among human beings from very early times that this act is morally wrong, religiously sinful, socially reprehensible and on the whole, condemnable. The only ones who see the matter differently are those who have allowed their carnal desires to overwhelm their reason or who have elevated their eccentricities into philosophy.

What accounts for this universal condemnation of unlawful sexual intercourse is that human nature itself is prompted by an inner impulse to regard it as forbidden. For the very survival of the human species and the sustenance of human society demands that men and women should not come together merely for sensual pleasure and then part company when that purpose has been fulfilled. Rather, such a relationship should be based on a covenant of mutual fidelity of a durable and abiding nature, a covenant that is well known and enjoys the sanction of society.

Without stable relations of marriage the human race cannot survive even for a day. This is so because the human baby requires, for its survival and growth, continual compassionate care and nurture for several years in the early part of its life. Now, a woman is not likely to be ready to single-handedly bear the burden of a child's upbringing unless the male, who was equally responsible for that birth, also shares that burden. Likewise, a society cannot survive without that covenant which creates ties between a man and a woman. In fact, human society cannot even come into being without the matrimonial tie which makes a man and a woman live together and, thus, found a family and thereafter foster further relationships between other families, which in turn gives birth to a community and a society. If a man and a woman were to start freely meeting each other just for the purpose of mutual enjoyment in total disregard of the objective of establishing a family, then this would strike a fatal blow to man's collective life and demolish the very foundation on which society is built. Hence, uninhibited relations between men and women which are not based on any known and accepted covenant of mutual fidelity are against the very nature of man. It is precisely because of these considerations that fornication has always been looked upon as a grave vice, an act of immorality, and in religious terms, a sin.

This also explains why those who have endeavoured to encourage people to marry have also sought to prevent the incidence of unlawful sexual intercourse by one means or another. These endeavours, however, differ from one legal, moral, social and religious system to another. This variation stems from the fact that some societies have a strong and clear consciousness about the harmfulness of unlawful sexual intercourse for the human species and human society while the perception of other societies is, relatively speaking, weak and hazy.

(ii) Although there has been general agreement that unlawful sexual intercourse is forbidden, there has been disagreement as to whether it is also a crime which calls for punishment. It is precisely on this point that the Islamic position radically differs from a number of other religious and legal systems. Those societies which have been close to human nature have always regarded unlawful relations between a male and a female to be a crime, and have prescribed severe punishments for the same.

As moral corruption made inroads into human society, there developed a lenient attitude, one of tolerance, towards this offence. The first lapse in this regard was to make a sharp distinction between fornication and adultery and to consider the former to be an ordinary offence and the latter a punishable one. For this reason, several legal systems define fornication as the act of sexual intercourse between a male (regardless of whether he is married or not) and a female who is not one's wife.

This definition focuses only on the marital status of the woman, and not that of the man. If the woman is without a husband, it is simply a case of fornication rather than adultery, and it is regarded so irrespective of whether the man who commits the act has a wife or not. In ancient Egypt, Babylon, Assyria and India, fornication carried a very light sentence. The same was the case in Greece and Rome and it also influenced Judaic thought. According to the Bible, this offence entails only a monetary compensation. The relevant Biblical command is:

> If a man seduces a virgin that is not betrothed, and he lies with her, he shall give the marriage present for her, and make her his wife. If her father utterly refuses to give her to him, he shall pay money equivalent to the marriage present for virgins (*Exodus* 22: 16–17).

The same command is laid down in *Deuteronomy*, though here it is phrased somewhat differently. It clarifies that the man should pay the woman's father fifty shekels of silver (*Deuteronomy* 22: 28–9). However, if a man fornicates with the daughter of a priest, according to Judaic law, he is to be hanged until dead, whereas the girl is to be burnt alive (*Everyman's Talmud*, pp. 319–20).

That this view is almost identical with the Hindu code can be seen when we compare it with the laws (*Dharma Shastra*) of Manu. He says: 'Anybody who commits fornication with an unmarried girl of his own caste with her consent, does not deserve any punishment. If the father of the girl is willing, the man should compensate him and marry the girl. However, if the girl belongs to a higher caste and the man is of a lower caste, the girl should be driven away from home and the limbs of the man should be amputated' (Chapter 8, stanza 365, 366).

If the girl is a Brahmin, the punishment would be to burn the man alive (stanza 377).

The fact is that in all these legal systems, adultery which denotes a man's sexual relations, be he married or unmarried, with a woman who is someone's wife, is considered the major crime. Once again, what renders this act as a crime is not the mere fact that it is an unlawful sexual act. Rather, the main consideration is that this act would compel another man to bring up a child who is not his. In other words, fornication as such is not considered a serious offence. Rather, the mixing-up of the parentage of one's children with those of others is reckoned to be the serious offence which deserves punishment, both in the case of the man and the woman.

According to the Egyptians, in such a case the man should be severely beaten with sticks and the woman's nose amputated. Similar punishments were prescribed in Babylon, Assyria and Persia. In Hinduism, the woman involved in such an act was required to be thrown to the hounds to be torn to pieces and the man put on a hot iron bed and a fire lit all around him. In Ancient Greece and Rome the husband had the right either to kill the man whom he found having sexual intercourse with his wife or receive damages from him. Subsequently, in the first century B.C., Augustus Caesar decreed that half the property of a man guilty of adultery should be confiscated and that additionally he be exiled.

As for the woman, it was laid down that she would forfeit half her dowry and that one-third of her assets be confiscated and she be banished to a remote part of the Empire. Constantine changed this law and instead laid down capital punishment for both men and women who are guilty of adultery. In the days of Leo and Marcian, the punishment was changed to life imprisonment. Justinian reduced the punishment further and laid down that the woman be flogged and confined to a monastery. Her husband had the right either to obtain her release within two years or leave her there to suffer life-long confinement.

The following represent the legal provisions in Judaic Law pertaining to unlawful sexual relations:

> If a man lies carnally with a woman, who is a slave, betrothed to another man and not yet ransomed or given her freedom, an inquiry shall be held. They shall not be put to death, because she was not free (*Leviticus* 19: 20).
>
> If a man commits adultery with the wife of his neighbour both the adulterer and the adulteress shall be put to death (*Leviticus* 20: 10).
>
> If a man is found lying with the wife of another man, both of them shall die, the man who lay with the woman, and the woman; so you shall purge the evil from Israel (*Deuteronomy* 22: 22).
>
> If there is a betrothed virgin, and a man meets her in the city and lies with her, then you shall bring them both out to the gate of that city,

> and you shall stone them to death with stones, the young woman because she did not cry for help though she was in the city, and the man because he violated his neighbour's wife; so you shall purge the evil from the midst of you. But if in the open country a man meets a young woman who is betrothed and the man seizes her and lies with her, then only the man who lay with her shall die. But to the young woman you shall do nothing; in the young woman there is no offence punishable by death . . . (*Deuteronomy* 22: 23–6).

By the time of Jesus' advent, the Jewish rabbis, lawyers, and general public, literally everyone, had consigned this law to oblivion. Even though the law existed, was documented in the Scriptures and considered to be God's command, still nobody cared to follow it. There is not a single report in Jewish history to suggest that it was ever enforced. When Jesus (peace be upon him) embarked on calling people to the truth, he soon attracted a large number of followers, and the different means that were adopted to put a stop to the spread of his Message proved ineffectual.

Faced with this situation, the Jewish leaders and hypocrites thought of a ruse to embarrass Jesus. They brought to him a woman who was guilty of adultery, and asked him to decide her case (see *John* 8: 1–11).

In so doing, they intended to drive Jesus into one of two difficult positions. If he pronounced any sentence other than stoning to death, he would be accused of tampering with God's Law for the sake of worldly exigencies. On the other hand, if he sentenced the woman to stoning, he would put himself in a situation where he could be accused of taking a position that was in flagrant contradiction with the prevailing Roman Law. Moreover, any strict adherence to Mosaic Law by Jesus could be exploited insofar as people would be scared that he would strictly enforce the whole corpus of the Torah.

Jesus (peace be upon him), however, turned the tables on his detractors by uttering a short sentence: 'Let him who is without sin among you be the first to throw a stone at her' (*John* 8: 7). On hearing this, the rabbis quietly dispersed, their moral depravity, thus, laid bare. As the guilty woman stood alone, Jesus made her repent. After she repented, he asked her to depart. He did so because in that situation Jesus (peace be upon him) was in no position to act as judge, nor had the judicial procedure (such as having witnesses testify to the offence) been followed. Moreover, an Islamic State did not exist at the time which would have enforced the Law of God.

Christians are wont to base themselves on this and a few other statements that Jesus (peace be upon him) made on a variety of occasions. In Christian societies an entirely different concept is entertained about unlawful sex. For them, if sexual relations take place between an unmarried man and an unmarried woman (by mutual consent – Ed.) it is certainly a sin but it is not a cognizable offence. However, if either of the two persons who engage in unlawful sexual relations is married, or if both of them are married, their sexual relations are considered a cognizable offence. Nonetheless, what makes the act a sin is the violation of the marriage contract, rather than the mere fact of unlawful sex, and this makes the act an offence in the legal sense. According to Christian doctrine, the married man who engages in unlawful sex is a criminal because he has violated the marital vow which he solemnly made with his spouse at the altar of the church through a priest. However, the only legal consequence of such an act is that the wife of the man so guilty might secure separation from him by charging her husband with being unfaithful to the covenant he made with her. The same is also true of a woman who engages in sexual relations outside of her marriage covenant. At the same time, the husband of the woman who is a party to adultery, also has the right to claim damages from the man who subjected his wife to adultery.

This is the only punishment that Christian Law lays down with respect to married persons, both men and women, who are guilty of adultery. Unfortunately, this punishment is a double-edged sword. For if a woman secures separation from her husband who is guilty of infidelity, she would doubtless be released from him according to Christian Law which stipulates that she may not marry again. The same holds true for the husband who secures separation from his wife who is guilty of infidelity. According to the Christian Law, he too may not marry again. In other words, only those who are prepared to lead the solitary life of monks should brand one's spouse with infidelity and take the matter to a Christian court.

The modern Western legal enactments in regard to this question, which are enforced at the present time in most Muslim countries, are based on the very concepts mentioned above. According to Western legal concepts, fornication is regarded at most as a blemish, as an act of immorality, or a sin, but it is certainly not a cognizable offence. It becomes an offence only if one party has resorted to the use of force so that the sexual act took place against the will of the other. As for having sexual intercourse with someone else's married partner, the aggrieved party can file for a divorce from the offending party. If adultery is proved, the husband may obtain divorce from his wife and also receive monetary compensation from the man guilty of adultery.

(iii) As distinguished from these concepts, Islam regards the act of illegitimate sexual intercourse as a penal crime *per se*. Moreover, if such an act is committed by a married person, the severity of the offence increases. This severity does not emanate from the fact that the adulterer has broken the marital vow, or has violated the sanctity of another person's bedroom. The offence becomes more severe because of the fact that a legitimate means was available to a married person to satisfy his sexual urge, but he still resorted to unlawful means to so satisfy himself.

Unlawful sex is viewed by Islam as a crime which, if no steps are taken to curb it, strikes at the very root of humanity and civilization. Both the survival of the human race and the continuity of man's collective existence make it imperative that sexual relations between men and women are confined to their lawful forms alone. Now, such a goal cannot be achieved if such relations between men and women are left to everyone's own will. For, if the opportunity to satisfy one's sexual urge is available without being attendant to the responsibility of rearing a family, it would be impossible to confine people to lawful relationships alone. This can be well illustrated by an example from our own day-to-day life. If people are given the option to travel with or without buying a ticket, how many people would still volunteer to buy such tickets? If carrying a proper ticket is considered a necessary condition for travelling then it is obvious that travelling without a ticket should be treated as an offence. However, if someone travels without a ticket owing to his resourcelessness, he may be regarded as an offender of a lesser order. Conversely, if a wealthy person simply refuses to buy a ticket even though he has the means to do so, he should certainly be regarded as a greater culprit.

(iv) In order to protect society from the harmful effects of unlawful sex, Islam does not confine itself to legal sanctions. Instead, it makes use of a number of reformative and preventive measures as well. Legal sanctions are in fact used as a last resort.

Quite obviously, in the Islamic scheme of things it is not at all desirable that people be subjected to flogging for having committed unlawful sexual intercourse. What Islam truly aims at is that people refrain from indulging in unlawful sex so that recourse to penal measures does not arise. Hence, Islam seeks, first of all, to purify people's lives; seeks to infuse people's hearts with fear of the Omniscient and Omnipotent Lord of the heavens and earth, makes man conscious of his accountability in the Hereafter, thereby making him realize that he cannot escape the consequences of his actions even in the Next Life, thus, creating a disposition in man to obey God's Law as a necessary corollary of faith. Moreover, Islam repeatedly reminds man that unlawful sex and unchasteness are mortal sins for which man will have to face a very strict reckoning from God in the Next Life. This is an idea that recurs time and again in the Qur'ān. Furthermore, Islam takes every step to create the conditions that facilitate marriage. If a man does not feel satisfied for some reason by having just one wife, Islam provides him with the opportunity to have a maximum of four wives. If the spouses find their matrimonial relations incompatible, the male partner may resort to *ṭalāq* (repudiation of the marriage by the husband) and the female partner may have recourse to *khul'* (separation at the initiative of the wife). If there are serious differences between a husband and a wife, Islam provides that the two may either approach other relatives with a request that they serve as arbitrators or they may refer their problems to a court of law. This may be done in order to achieve a reconciliation between them, or the two may be freed of their marital tie such that it becomes possible for them to remarry whomsoever they wish.

These points are clearly expressed in *Sūrahs al-Baqarah, al-Nisā'* and *al-Ṭalāq*. It should also be noted that the present *sūrah* expresses its disapproval of those men and women who abstain from marriage, and that it calls upon them instead to marry. This injunction embraces both the free person and the slave, male and female. Islam also seeks to remove factors which prompt or provoke people into illegitimate sexual relations or which provide opportunities for engaging in the same. Hence, one year before laying down the punishment for unlawful sexual intercourse, women were directed in *Sūrah al-Aḥzāb* to cover themselves with their mantles and draw their outer garments about themselves. The wives of the Prophet (peace be upon him), who were the role models for all Muslim women, were directed to stay indoors and not go about displaying their charms. If people wanted to ask anything of them, they were to do so from behind a screen. Muslim women look up to the wives and daughters of the Prophet (peace be upon him) rather than the women of pre-Islamic times who were devoid of the concepts just expressed.

Even before the enforcement of the penal laws pertaining to unlawful sexual relations, free-mixing between the sexes had ceased to be the norm in Muslim society. Women too had given up parading their charms in public. Furthermore, those conditions which create opportunities for and facilitate indulgence in unlawful sex had been done away with.

It was, then, after these measures had been taken that the penalty for unlawful sexual intercourse was prescribed. Thereafter, it was in this very *sūrah* that deterrent measures were laid down so that the spread of *faḥsh* (obscenity) would be prevented. Likewise, prostitution was outlawed and those guilty of accusing others of involvement in unlawful sexual relations were liable to a severe punishment if they were unable to substantiate their accusations with due evidence. Moreover, both men and women were asked to lower their gaze so as to put an end to ogling, which all too quickly leads to admiration of beauty and which, in turn, gives rise to love affairs. Women were also told to distinguish between their male relatives, treating their *maḥram* relatives differently from their non-*maḥram* relatives, and to abstain from meeting relatives of the latter category in a state that would make a display of their adornments.

When one takes note of all this, one appreciates the pervasive scheme of reform envisioned by Islam whereby the punishment prescribed for unlawful sexual acts is only one aspect. The idea underlying these penalties is that exemplary punishment should be meted out to the incorrigibly wicked who ignore all reform measures. These are the ones who are so deeply immersed in evil that they fail to mend their ways despite all the different measures adopted by Islam to mobilize their inner resources to bring about changes in people's attitude and behaviour. Moreover, Islam adopted a number of measures facilitating marriage and the like so that legitimate opportunities were provided to people for satisfying their sexual urges. Now, if after all this some insist upon satisfying those urges in an unlawful manner, then they deserve to be met with an exemplary punishment.

If even one such individual in a society is duly punished, several others with similar propensities will realize how such culprits are treated, and presumably this will act as something of a deterrent. This penalty is not simply meant to chastise an offender, but also declares that Muslim society is not an entertainment park for those bent upon unfettered sexual self-indulgences. It is not a pasture for those who, impervious to all moral restraints, are inclined to let their lasciviousness loose.

When one considers the reformative scheme of Islam it is evident that it is both coherent and well-conceived. Each part is so vital that none can be dispensed with and nothing added. Ideas for altering this scheme often enter the heads of naïve simpletons who are wont to throw down the mantle of reform without even comprehending Islam's own scheme of reform. Alternatively, such ideas come to the minds of those, who out of their own perversity, deliberately seek to subvert the Islamic scheme of things.

(v) Unlawful sexual intercourse was declared an offence in 3 A.H. Nevertheless, it was not the kind of offence against which the Islamic State, or its police, or its courts could take action. By and large unlawful sexual intercourse was considered an offence against the family, or at best against society. Hence, it was members of the family concerned who were entitled to mete out punishment to offenders. The operative injunction at this stage was that if four witnesses testified to seeing a man and a woman engaged in unlawful sex, then both of them should be beaten and the woman confined to the house. This injunction was to remain in operation until the revelation of any further injunction on the subject. (See *al-Nisā'* 4: 15–16 and *Towards Understanding the Qur'ān*, vol. II, *al-Nisā'* 4, n. 26, pp.17–19.) The actual injunction which laid down a specific penalty for fornication was revealed about three years after the revelation of this initial injunction. This latter injunction abrogated the former and henceforth made fornication a cognizable offence.

(vi) The punishment laid down in this verse pertains to unlawful sexual intercourse *per se*. It is not the punishment which is prescribed for those who are convicted of unlawful post-marital sexual intercourse which is a very grave offence in the sight of Islamic Law. It is evident from the Qur'ān that the punishment which is being prescribed here is meant for those unmarried persons who are guilty of unlawful sexual intercourse as indicated by the Qur'ān itself. For it was earlier stated in *Sūrah al-Nisā'*: 'As for those of your women who are guilty of immoral conduct, call upon four from amongst you to bear witness against them. And if four men do bear witness, confine those women to their houses until either death takes them away or Allah opens some way for them' (*Towards Understanding the Qur'ān*, vol. II, *al-Nisā'* 4: 15, p. 17).

A further command was laid down in the same *sūrah*: 'And those of you who cannot afford to marry free believing women (*muḥṣanāt*), then marry such believing women whom your right hands possess . . . Then if they become guilty of immoral conduct after they have entered into wedlock, they shall be liable to half the penalty to which free women (*muḥṣanāt*) are liable' (*Towards Understanding the Qur'ān*, vol. II, *al-Nisā'* 4: 25, p. 28).

The former verse indicates that God would ordain some other commandment for women guilty of fornication and who had, therefore, been sentenced to confinement in their houses till death or until Allah 'opens some way for them' (*al-Nisā'* 4: 15). It is clear, then, that the present verse of *Sūrah al-Nūr* is the command which is alluded to in *Sūrah al-Nisā'*. The second verse of *Sūrah al-Nisā'* quoted above mentions the punishment for married slave-girls who are guilty of fornication. The word *muḥṣanāt* (free believing women) is used twice in the verse and in both cases it occurs in the same context. Obviously it carries the same meaning in both places. In the second instance, (*al-Nisā'* 4: 25), while laying down the punishment for married slave-girls reference is also made to those who cannot 'afford to marry free believing women' (*al-Nisā'* 4: 25). This expression clearly excludes married women and is specifically directed at free believing women who are unmarried. Moreover, at the conclusion of verse 25 of *Sūrah al-Nisā'*, it is stated that if a married slave-girl commits unlawful sexual intercourse, she would receive half the penalty meted out to a free believing woman guilty of the same offence. It is evident from the context that the expression *muḥṣanāt* carries the same meaning as in the other verse. In other words, the reference is not to a married woman, but to an unmarried free woman. Taken together, both these verses of *Sūrah al-Nisā'* suggest that the injunction conveyed through this verse of *Sūrah al-Nūr* prescribes the punishment to be inflicted on unmarried persons who are guilty of unlawful sexual intercourse. (For further details see *Towards Understanding the Qur'ān*, vol. II, *al-Nisā'* 4, n. 46, p. 29.)

(vii) Let us now look at the question of what the punishment is for unlawful sexual intercourse committed by a free woman. The Qur'ān, itself, is silent about this. A number of authentic traditions, however, fully establish the point that not only did the Prophet (peace be upon him) specify lapidation as its punishment, but he himself put that punishment into effect in a few instances. This practice was also followed by each of the four Rightly-Guided Caliphs during their respective periods of rule. Besides, they openly declared this to be the punishment for such an offence. The Companions and Successors were completely unanimous in their views on this verse. Not a single statement was made by anyone which might lead one to conclude that anyone in the early period of Islam had any doubts about the validity of this punishment. Even in later times, leading Muslim jurists in different parts of the world were unanimous that this punishment was a well-established practice of the Prophet (peace be upon him). The reason being that the evidence for its validity is so numerous and so weighty that no scholar worth the name would dare deny it. In fact, in the whole history of the *Ummah* none except the Khawārij and some Mu'tazilah have considered it otherwise. Even then they did not reject it on the grounds that it did not have the Prophet's sanction, but rather because they held it to be contrary to the Qur'ān.

Their objection, however, was ill-founded and rested on their misunderstanding of the Qur'ān. Such people claimed that the words *zāniyah* and *zānī* (those who commit 'unlawful sexual intercourse – whether female or male') were used in an absolute (*muṭlaq*) sense. Hence, they considered the Qur'ānic prescription of flogging each of them with a hundred lashes an addition to the punishment prescribed by the Qur'ān with regard to all those who indulge in unlawful sexual relations, regardless of their marital status. They did not see any justification in distinguishing between married and unmarried persons who commit unlawful sex nor in prescribing a different punishment for those who fall into the former category. They considered such a distinction to be opposed to the Law of God.

This line of argument is seriously flawed. It disregards the fact that the Prophet's explanations of the Qur'ān carry the same weight as the Qur'ān itself. This is evident from the following example: the Qur'ān makes an absolute statement about men and women who commit theft, and prescribes the punishment of cutting off his or her offending hand. If this Qur'ānic command is not interpreted in light of its explanation by the Prophet (peace be upon him), we will not be able to make any distinction between thieves, and the hand of every thief will be amputated even if he stole only a needle or a fruit. This is bound to happen if we do not restrict the absoluteness of the Qur'ānic statement in light of its explanation by the Prophet (peace be upon him). On the other hand, if someone who steals millions of rupees and, when arrested, contends that he has repented and mended his ways and that he should, therefore, be set free on the grounds of the Qur'ānic verse which makes this absolute statement: 'But he who repents after he has committed wrong, and makes amends, Allah will graciously turn to him. Truly Allah is All-Forgiving, All-Compassionate' (*al-Mā'idah* 5: 39). Obviously, this apparently absolute statement has got to be qualified by other considerations, especially by the traditions which have a bearing on the subject.

To take another case, we find that the Qur'ān forbids a man to marry his foster mother or foster sister (*al-Nisā'* 4: 23) but it does not so forbid marriage to one's foster daughter. If the above line of argument is followed consistently, one would be justified in contending that forbidding marriage with one's foster-daughter is opposed to the Qur'ān. The Qur'ān also forbids a man from marrying two sisters at the same time (*al-Nisā'* 4: 23), but it does not specify that he cannot marry two women one of whom is a maternal aunt and the other her niece; or one whom is a paternal aunt and the other her niece. Now, anyone who pursues this argument, is bound to say that to regard the above-mentioned marital ties as forbidden is opposed to the Qur'ān. Likewise, marriage with one's step-daughter is only prohibited if she has been brought up in her step-father's house (*al-Nisā'* 4: 23). However, if someone were to consider marriage with his step-daughter to be forbidden *in toto*, he would be regarded, according to the line of argument mentioned above, as holding an opinion in opposition to the Qur'ān.

Likewise, the Qur'ān grants permission to pledge one's property in terms which create the impression that this permission is dependent upon the person being a traveller and to whom no scribe is available to commit the loan document to writing (*al-Baqarah* 2: 2 and 3). If one follows this line of argument, one would consider pledging one's property while still at home and when a scribe becomes available then commit the loan document to writing.

To consider another example, the Qur'ān states in quite general terms: 'Take witnesses when you sell and buy something' (*al-Baqarah* 2: 282). According to this logic, all transactions which take place day in and day out would be regarded as unlawful since no witnesses are brought forth to prove them.

These examples establish the fallacious position of those who regard lapidation as contrary to the Qur'ān. It is undeniable that in the Islamic scheme of things the Prophet (peace be upon him) was required not only to convey God's commandments, but also to explain their true purpose, illustrating how they are to be applied, and whether any exception may be made in their application. Anyone who denies this role of the Prophet (peace be upon him) goes against the very fundamentals of faith itself. Moreover, such a view would land us in awkward situations which are just too many to enumerate here.

(viii) Muslim jurists are at variance with one another as regards what constitutes *zinā* (unlawful sexual intercourse). According to Ḥanafī scholars, it consists of 'a man's frontal sexual intercourse with a woman to whom he is neither married, nor whom is his slave-girl, nor about whom there is any reasonable ground for him to assume that she is his wife or slave-girl'. This definition of *zinā* excludes sodomy as well as sexual intercourse with animals. It is only sexual intercourse in the vagina of a woman which is reckoned as *zinā* provided it is not done with legal title or under the misunderstanding that one is entitled to it.

By contrast, Shāfi'ī jurists define *zinā* as follows: 'Unlawful sexual intercourse (*zinā*) consists of the act of penetration of a person's private part into the private part of another provided that it is unlawful to do so but to which people are instinctively inclined.'

According to the Mālikīs, *zinā* consists in having sexual intercourse, either vaginal or anal, be it with a man or a woman, when one does not have the right to do so, and when there is no ground to assume that one has such a right. According to the last two schools, *zinā* also covers sodomy.

The fact of the matter is that these latter two definitions do not conform with the well-known definition of *zinā* and the Qur'ān always uses a term in its widely familiar meaning. Should a particular word be employed as a special term, the Qur'ān itself explains its connotation. There is, however, nothing in the above verse to indicate that the word *zinā* is used for some special rather than its ordinary meaning. Hence, the word should be taken in its general, widely-known sense. In other words, it should be deemed to stand only for what is normally considered as unlawful sexual intercourse between a man and a woman. Other forms of sexual perversion, therefore, lie beyond the scope of this above definition. Moreover, it is common knowledge that there was some difference of opinion among the Prophet's Companions regarding the punishment that ought to be meted out to those guilty of sodomy. Had sodomy been considered a part of *zinā*, there would have been no reason for any disagreement among the Companions on this question.

(ix) Legally speaking, a man's mere penetration of his penis into a woman's vagina, provided it is unlawful for him to do so, is enough to constitute *zinā* and make him liable for punishment. Full penetration of the penis or having full sexual intercourse are not the necessary constituents of *zinā*. However, if the penetration of a man's penis does not take place, the mere fact that a man and woman are found lying on the same bed, or that they are engaged in love-play, or are found together in a nude position, none of these suffice to convict them of *zinā*. If a man and a woman are found in such compromising positions, the *Sharī'ah* does not prescribe that they be subjected to a medical examination so as to determine whether sexual intercourse actually took place, and to punish them if it is so established. Those who are found in such shamelessly compromising positions would, however, be subjected to the punishment that might be decided upon by the *qāḍī*, depending on the circumstances of each particular case. It is also possible that the *Shūrā* of an Islamic State might determine the punishment to be meted out in such cases. However, if it is decided that the punishment consists of flogging, this may not exceed ten lashes. This because of a *ḥadīth* in which it is specified that a person may not be subjected to more than ten lashes in cases which do not involve *ḥadd* punishment. (See Bukhārī, *K. al-Ḥudūd*, 'Bāb kam al-Ta'zīr wa al-Adab', Muslim, *K. al-Ḥudūd*, 'Bāb Qadr Aswaṭ al-Ta'zīr' and Abū Dā'ūd, *K. al-Ḥudūd*, 'Bāb fī al-Ta'zīr' – Ed.)

Conversely, if someone is not caught committing such an objectionable act [i.e. one which is short of *zinā*] but voluntarily confesses the same from a feeling of remorse, it suffices to exhort him to repent. It is narrated by

'Abd Allāh ibn Mas'ūd that someone came and confessed that he had everything possible with a woman in the countryside short of sexual intercourse. So saying, he offered himself for punishment in the manner that was considered appropriate. In response, 'Umar said to him: 'When God has concealed what you had done, you should not have made it public.' The Prophet (peace be upon him) remained quiet all along and the person departed. He then called for him and recited the following Qur'ānic verse: 'And establish the Prayer at the two ends of the day and in the first hours of the night. Indeed the good deeds drive away the evil deeds.' (*Towards Understanding the Qur'ān*, vol. IV, *Hūd* 11: 114, p. 137.) Someone asked whether this ruling was meant specifically for that person alone. To this the Prophet (peace be upon him) replied: 'No, it is a general ruling.' (See Bukhārī, *K. Tafsīr al-Qur'ān*, 'Bāb Qawlihī: wa aqim al-Ṣalāh ṭarafai al-nahār wa zulfan min al-layl . . . (*Hūd* 11: 114)' and Tirmidhī, *K. Tafsīr al-Qur'ān*, 'Bāb wa min *Sūrah Hūd*' – Ed.) Not only that but if a person voluntarily admits to having committed an offence without specifying it, the *Sharī'ah* does not permit probing the offence he committed. In this respect, someone once appeared before the Prophet (peace be upon him) stating that he was liable to *ḥadd* punishment and asking that the Prophet enforce the same. The Prophet (peace be upon him) did not ask about the *ḥadd* to which the man was liable. After finishing the Prayer the man rose once again, saying: 'I am guilty. Punish me.' Thereupon the Prophet (peace be upon him) said: 'Have you not offered Prayers with us just now?' He said: 'Yes.' The Prophet (peace be upon him) said: 'Allah has pardoned your misdeed.' (See Bukhārī, *K. al-Ḥudūd*, 'Bāb idhā aqarra bi al-Ḥadd ... hal li al-Imām an yastura 'alayh' – Ed.)

(x) According to Islamic teachings, a man may not be convicted of *zinā* unless certain conditions, which we shall explain below, are fulfilled. In this regard a distinction is made between conviction for *zinā* as such, and someone's commitment of that offence after marriage. With regard to someone's conviction merely for *zinā*, it is necessary that the person be adult and sane. If a minor or an insane person commits *zinā*, he is not liable for the *ḥadd* punishment laid down.

As for convicting someone of *zinā* after *iḥṣān* (marriage), some additional conditions have to be met apart from those of adulthood and sanity. These conditions are as follows: first, that the said person be free. There is unanimity among scholars – and this on the grounds that the Qur'ān itself indicates (*al-Nisā'* 4: 25 – Ed.) – that a slave is not liable to lapidation. We have mentioned earlier that if a slave-girl is convicted of unlawful sexual intercourse, she is liable to half the punishment prescribed for an unmarried free woman. Jurists are unanimous that this also applies to male slaves. Second, such a person should have been duly married. There is unanimity of opinion on this question as well. In accordance with this condition, if a man has had sexual relations with his slave-girl or he has contracted a defective marriage, he is not reckoned as a married person. In other words, if such a person is convicted of unlawful sexual intercourse, he is liable to be flogged rather than lapidated. Third, such a person should not only have been married but should also have had privacy (*khalwah ṣaḥīḥah*) with his wife [that is, he should have consummated his marriage]. The mere contract of marriage does not place a man or woman in the category of *muḥṣan* so that were he or she to commit unlawful sexual intercourse, they might be punished with lapidation. Most jurists are agreed on this point as well.

Abū Ḥanīfah and Muḥammad ibn al-Ḥasan al-Shaybānī have further added that a man or woman will be considered *muḥṣan* only if both of them were free, sane and adult at the time of the marriage and their enjoyment of consummation of the marriage. The difference caused by this additional condition is that if someone married a slave-girl, a female minor or an insane woman and then had sexual intercourse with her, he will still not be lapidated even if he commits unlawful sexual intercourse thereafter. The same applies to women in similar circumstances. That is, if a woman has had sexual intercourse with a minor, insane or slave husband, she will not be lapidated even if she is guilty of unlawful sexual intercourse thereafter. Even a little reflection on this enables one to appreciate that these two authorities, renowned for their intellectual maturity, added something which perfectly stands to reason.

The fourth condition in this regard is that the culprit concerned should be a Muslim. There is, however, considerable disagreement among jurists on this point. Shāfi'ī, Abū Yūsuf and Aḥmad ibn Ḥanbal do not consider this to be a requisite condition. For them, even if a *dhimmī* commits unlawful sexual intercourse, he will be lapidated. However, Abū Ḥanīfah and Mālik are agreed that lapidation should only be applied to Muslims who commit unlawful sexual intercourse after *iḥṣān* (marriage). Among their arguments, the most reasonable and weighty is that in order for such a severe punishment as lapidation to be inflicted, the culprit should be proved as having committed the error even though he was in a full state of *iḥṣān*.

Iḥṣān means to be fortified so that one may be able to fully protect oneself. This is achieved by three things. The first of these fortifications consists of belief in God and in the accountability of the Hereafter and the acceptance of God's commands as the binding norms of one's behaviour. The second consists of one being free, rather than a slave, so that one is immune from any other person's constraint which might prevent one from making use of the lawful means of gratifying one's instinctive desires. In other words, a person is not faced with a state of compulsion and helplessness that prompts him to commit sin. Likewise, such a person should also not be devoid of the support that a person receives from his family in safeguarding his morals and honour. The third fortification consists of wedlock, which provides a person with the lawful means to satisfy his desires. It is only when one has these three protective fortifications that one becomes fully secure. It is only after these three conditions have been fulfilled that a person deserves to be lapidated for having merely gratified his lust.

If, however, someone does not believe in God, or in the Hereafter, or in a set of Laws prescribed by God, he is obviously not in a state of *iḥṣān*. Hence, committing such an otherwise outrageous act of immorality does not attain the same degree of graveness that warrants his lapidation. This opinion is endorsed by a tradition on the authority of 'Abd Allāh ibn 'Umar which was narrated by Isḥāq ibn Rāhawayh in his *Musnad* and by Dāraquṭnī in his *Sunan*: 'He who associates aught with God in His Divinity is not a *muḥṣan*.'

There is, however, disagreement as to whether the sentence mentioned in this tradition is a saying of the Prophet (peace be upon him) or simply that of 'Abd Allāh ibn 'Umar. Despite this weakness in the tradition, its content seems perfectly sound. It is possible though to controvert this view by reference to one case which involved a Jew as the culprit whereby the Prophet (peace be upon him) decreed that he be lapidated. Such a contention, however, would not be tenable. For if we bring together the authentic traditions relating to this case it becomes evident that the Prophet (peace be upon him) did not enforce this provision of Islamic Law on the grounds of it being the law of the land, he rather enforced upon the Jew his own religious law. We learn from an authentic tradition in Bukhārī and Muslim that when this case was put before the Prophet (peace be upon him), he asked the Jews present: 'What is the relevant provision for this [offence] in your Scripture, the Torah?' (See Muslim, *K. al-Ḥudūd*, 'Bāb Rajm al-Yahūd Ahl al-Dhimmah'. There is, however, a slight discrepancy between the words of *ḥadīth* quoted by the learned author here. He quotes the words: ماتجدون في التوراة في شأن الرجم {أو ماتجدون في كتابكم في شأن الرجم}. We have found that the actual words in Muslim are ماتجدون في شأن الزنا – Ed.) When it became clear that the Torah prescribed lapidation, the Prophet (peace be upon him) said: 'So I decide according to what is laid down in the Torah.' (See Abū Dā'ūd, *K. al-Ḥudūd*, 'Bāb fī Rajm al-Yahūdīyīn' – Ed.) According to another tradition, while giving his verdict on this case the Prophet (peace be upon him) remarked: 'O Allah, I am the first person to revive Your command which they [the Jews] caused to die.' (See Muslim, *K. al-Ḥudūd*, 'Bāb Rajm al-Yahūd Ahl al-Dhimmah' and Abū Dā'ūd, *K. al-Ḥudūd*, 'Bāb fī Rajm al-Yahūdīyīn' – Ed.)

(xi) In order to convict someone of unlawful sexual intercourse, it is not only necessary to make sure that he committed that act, but also that he committed it of his own free-will. If someone is compelled into that act, he is neither guilty nor deserving of punishment. In such cases, the person is not liable to punishment in view of the general principle of the *Sharī'ah* which states: 'A man is acquit of responsibility for acts to which he has been compelled.' In verse 33 of the present *sūrah* we should note God's forgiveness of women who have been subjected to sexual intercourse under duress. Several traditions also establish that in case of rape, it was only the rapist who was punished whereas the victim was spared. According to one tradition a woman who was proceeding to perform Prayers in the darkness of night was overpowered and raped. When she cried for help people came to her rescue and the rapist was arrested. The Prophet (peace be upon him) had the rapist flogged while the woman was set free. (See Tirmidhī, *K. al-Ḥudūd*, 'Bāb mā jā' fī al-Mar'ah idhā ustukrihat 'alā al-zinā' and Abū Dā'ūd, *K. al-Ḥudūd*, 'Bāb fī Ṣāḥib al-Ḥadd yajī'u fa yuqirr' – Ed.) According to another tradition, someone raped a girl during the days of 'Umar. 'Umar had the rapist flogged while the girl was free to go. (See Bukhārī, *K. al-Ikrāh*, 'Bāb idhā ustukrihat al-Mar'ah 'alā al-zinā fā lā Ḥadd 'alayhā' – Ed.)

In view of these authentic traditions there is a unanimous ruling that women subjected to the sexual act under duress ought not to be considered guilty. There remains disagreement among scholars, however, on the question of whether a male who is compelled to commit unlawful sexual intercourse is guilty or not. Abū Yūsuf, Muḥammad ibn al-Ḥasan al-Shaybānī, Shāfi'ī and Ḥasan ibn Ṣāliḥ are of the opinion that if a man is forced into having sexual intercourse he should also be forgiven. Zufar, however, is of the opinion that such a person ought not to be forgiven on the grounds that sexual intercourse cannot be performed without penile erection and the fact that erection took place shows that the person was motivated by sexual passion. Abū Ḥanīfah is of the opinion that if the State or any magistrate appointed by the State forces someone to have unlawful sexual intercourse, he will not be punished. For if the State itself forces someone to commit a crime, it forfeits the authority to enforce the punishment laid down for it. If, however, someone other than the State forces a person to commit unlawful sexual intercourse, he will be punished. This is so because the culprit could not have committed the crime without sexual passion, and sexual passion cannot be forced on anyone from without.

Of these three, the first position, namely that of the male who is compelled to commit unlawful sexual intercourse, is the most sound. What makes it so is that though erection may indicate the sexual arousal of the person concerned, it does not necessarily show his consent and desire to engage in unlawful sexual intercourse. Suppose a tyrant forcibly casts a person of good moral character into prison, confines him in a room, and then sends to that room a young and beautiful woman, stark naked and forcibly keeps the two confined in that room under lock and key, refusing to release that person until he commits the sexual act with her. Let us suppose that under such circumstances the two do have sexual intercourse and the tyrant is able to produce four witnesses to that effect. Would it be fair to stone them to death in disregard of the circumstances in which that act was committed? Would it be fair even to have them flogged? It stands to reason and also accords with human behaviour that at times a person's sexual passion might be aroused without his intention having any hand in the matter.

Alternatively, suppose a person is imprisoned and is allowed to partake of nothing except wine. Now, if he were to drink wine in such a situation, would it be fair to punish him for drinking wine even though he drank it under compulsive circumstances? Should we consider him deserving of punishment merely on the grounds that wine could not have gone down his throat unless he had willed it? For a man can be convicted of a crime not merely because of his will, but also because of his free-will which accompanied the crime. If someone is forcibly placed under circumstances which virtually compel him to engage in a criminal act, he should be absolved of all guilt in certain cases, and in others the extenuating circumstances should lighten his offence.

(xii) The *Sharī'ah* does not permit anyone other than the State to prosecute those who commit unlawful sexual intercourse, be they men or women. Nor is anyone besides the court empowered to punish them. All jurists of the *Ummah* are agreed that the demand to execute the Qur'ānic command of flogging such persons is not given to ordinary people. It is rather directed to the magistrates and judges of the Islamic State. There is, however, disagreement over the question of whether a master has the right to enforce *ḥadd* punishment on his slave. All leading jurists of the Ḥanafī school are agreed that he is not empowered to do so. The Shāfi'īs, however, are of the opinion that he has such authority. According to the Mālikīs, a master is not authorized to amputate the hand of a slave who is guilty of theft. He can, however, enforce the *ḥadd* punishment on a slave who is found guilty of *zinā* or *qadhf* (unsubstantiated accusations of unlawful sexual intercourse) or drinking.

(xiii) Islamic Law declares the punishment for unlawful sexual intercourse to be a part of the law of the State. Hence, this punishment is enforced on all subjects of the State, be they Muslim or non-Muslim. Except for Mālik all leading jurists share this opinion. Abū Ḥanīfah though, is of the opinion that non-Muslims cannot be stoned to death. The reason behind not so enforcing this punishment on non-Muslims is that one of the conditions for the enforcement of stoning is that the person concerned be a fully-fledged *muḥṣan*. Now, since a person does not become a full *muḥṣan* unless he is a Muslim, so non-Muslims cannot be stoned to death. Mālik, however, argues that the command to punish those who commit unlawful sexual intercourse is addressed exclusively to Muslims, i.e. the punishment laid down in Islamic Law for this offence is a part of the personal law of the

Muslims. A *musta'min* (the non-Muslim who enters *Dār al-Islām* with the assurance of security) who commits unlawful sexual intercourse, according to Shāfi'ī and Abū Yūsuf, is to be subjected to a *ḥadd* punishment. But Abū Ḥanīfah and Muḥammad ibn al-Ḥasan al-Shaybānī are of the opinion that he should be spared even this.

(xiv) Islamic Law does not make it obligatory for people to confess their crimes. Nor does it make it obligatory for them to report offences committed by others to the authorities. However, once the authorities are informed that such an offence has been committed, there remains no room to spare the culprit the required punishment. According to a *ḥadīth*, the Prophet (peace be upon him) said: 'He who commits any of these filthy acts, should keep it concealed under the cover that God has placed over it. However, if he exposes it, we will enforce on him the punishment laid down in the Book of God.' (See Mālik, *Muwaṭṭa'*, *K. al-Ḥudūd* – Ed.) Abū Dā'ūd recorded with regard to Mā'iz ibn Mālik al-Aslamī that after he had committed unlawful sexual intercourse, he was told by Hazzāl ibn Nu'aym to go to the Prophet (peace be upon him) and confess his offence. He accordingly went to the Prophet and confessed what he had done. Thereupon, the Prophet (peace be upon him) subjected him to death by stoning. At the same time, the Prophet (peace be upon him) said to Hazzāl: 'Had you covered his crime by your garment, it would have been better for you.' (See Abū Dā'ūd, *K. al-Ḥudūd*, 'Bāb fī al-Satr 'alā Ahl al-Ḥudūd' – Ed.) There is also a *ḥadīth* that the Prophet (peace be upon him) said: 'Better pardon one another with regard to *ḥudūd*, because when it reaches me, it becomes obligatory to enforce it.' (See Abū Dā'ūd, *K. al-Ḥudūd*, 'Bāb al-'Afw 'an al-Ḥudūd mā lam tablugh al-Sulṭān' and al-Nasā'ī, *K. Qaṭ' al-Sāriq*, 'Bāb mā yakūnu Ḥirzan wa mā lā yakūn' – Ed.)

(xv) As far as the offence of unlawful sexual intercourse is concerned, it is not liable to mutual settlement. The following incident is found in almost all collections of *Ḥadīth*. A young man who worked as a labourer for someone committed unlawful sexual intercourse with that person's wife. The father of the young man obtained the affected person's consent in lieu of a hundred goats and a slave-girl. However, when the case was put before the Prophet (peace be upon him), he said: 'Your goats and your slave-girl are returned to you.' (See Bukhārī, *K. al-Ṣulḥ*, 'Bāb idhā Iṣṭalahū 'alā Ṣulḥ jawr fa al-Ṣulḥ Mardūd' – Ed.) Thereafter, he enforced on both the convicted man and the woman the punishment laid down for unlawful sexual intercourse. This not only indicates that this question may not be settled by mutual agreement, but also that it does not provide for paying damages in cases which involve the violation of a woman's honour.

(xvi) In an Islamic State, no one can be subjected to any punishment for committing unlawful sexual intercourse unless that charge can be established by due evidence. Unless there is definite evidence against someone that he/she was guilty of unlawful sexual intercourse, he/she may not be subjected to the *ḥadd* punishment regardless of the number of sources from which the rulers come to know about the occurrence of that offence. There was a woman in Madina about whom it was generally said that her sexual immorality was widely known. According to a tradition, she made a display of her wickedness even after embracing Islam. (See Bukhārī, *K. al-Tamannī*, 'Bāb mā yajūz . . . wa qawlahū Ta'ā lā 'law anna lī bikum quwwah' (*Hūd* 11: 80) – Ed.) In another tradition, it is said that she made her immorality known publicly. (See Bukhārī, *K. al-Ḥudūd*, 'Bāb man aẓhar al-Fāḥishah' – Ed.) According to these traditions 'suspicion was attached to her because of her way of talking, her demeanour and because of the kind of people who frequented her. Nevertheless, since there was no definite proof of her being guilty of this act, she was not punished. This despite the fact that the Prophet (peace be upon him) said about her: 'If I had to stone someone to death without proof, I would certainly have had her stoned.' (See Ibn Mājah, *K. al-Ḥudūd*, 'Bāb al-satr 'alā al-Mu'min wa Daf' al-Ḥudūd bi al-Shubuhāt.' There is a slight variation between the words quoted by the author and the text we have found in Ibn Mājah. The text, according to the author is ادفعوا الحدود ما وجدتم لها مدفعا whereas we have found لها instead of له – Ed.)

(xvii) The first possible proof of the offence is that there should be witnesses who affirm that the crime was committed by the people in question. What follows represents some of the important aspects of Islamic Law on this question:

a. The Qur'ān specifies that as far as the proof required in connection with sexual intercourse is concerned, there should be at least four eye-witnesses to the act. This point was made in *al-Nisā'* 4: 15 and also in the present *sūrah* (see verse 13). Without witnesses, a judge cannot decide the case on the basis of his personal information, so much so that he cannot even decide the case had he seen the offence with his own eyes.
b. Moreover, the testimony of only those witnesses who fulfil the conditions laid down by Islamic Law as being trustworthy can be accepted. These conditions include that the person has not been convicted of making a false testimony or of fraud and cheating; nor should he be a convicted criminal; nor someone well-known for his enmity towards the accused, etc. In any case, no person can be stoned to death or even flogged on the basis of evidence which is not fully reliable.
c. The witnesses should testify that they saw the man and the woman concerned engaged in the actual state of sexual intercourse,

i.e. they saw the act as clearly as a staining needle in a collyrium, or a rope immersed in a well.

d. The witnesses should be agreed about the time, place and identity of the persons engaged in the act of sexual intercourse. Any variance in their statements on these vital aspects would render their testimony void.

These conditions of evidence clearly show that Islamic Law does not want that tripods be fixed here, there and everywhere and that the flogging of people become a daily spectacle. Instead, punishments are to be inflicted only when, and despite the efforts made to reform people and deter them from such criminal acts, there remains in an Islamic society those who shamelessly commit sexual intercourse before the eyes of at least four other people.

(xviii) There is a difference of opinion on the question of a woman being found pregnant even though she has no husband, or of a slave-girl being pregnant without her having a known master. In this respect, the question is does their pregnancy provide sufficient grounds for them to be prosecuted for unlawful sexual intercourse? 'Umar considered this sufficient ground as did the Mālikīs. The majority of jurists, however, do not consider the mere fact of pregnancy a sufficiently strong ground to subject anyone to lapidation or flogging. In order that such a severe punishment be awarded, it is necessary that either the accused should admit guilt or the witnesses bear testimony that the offence was committed.

One of the basic guiding principles of Islamic Law is that the accused be granted the benefit of doubt. The Prophet (peace be upon him) said: 'Avoid enforcing *ḥudūd* as much as you can' (Ibn Mājah). There is another *ḥadīth* of similar import: 'Keep *ḥudūd* away from Muslims as much as possible. If there is any way to spare people from punishment, let them go. For it is much better that an *imām* (i.e. ruler) should err in acquitting someone rather than that he should err in punishing someone [who is not guilty]. (See Tirmidhī, *K. al-Ḥudūd*, 'Bāb mā jā' fī Dar' al-Ḥudūd – Ed.)

In light of these principles, pregnancy might be a very strong ground for suspecting someone of being involved in unlawful sex, but it is certainly not conclusive proof of the same. For there is a one in a million chance that the male sperm might have reached a woman's womb leading to conception even though sexual intercourse had not taken place. Even this remote possibility is sufficient to save the accused woman from being subjected to severe punishment.

(xix) There is also disagreement among jurists as to what should be done with those who level a charge of unlawful sexual intercourse when witnesses disagree in their statements, or when their testimonies fail to establish the charge. Should those witnesses who testified to the offence be convicted of making false testimony? Some jurists are of the opinion that in such a case false witnesses should be held guilty of slander (*qadhf*) and as such flogged with eighty lashes. According to other jurists, they should not be punished for they only appeared as witnesses and not as plaintiffs. Their reasoning being that if such witnesses were liable to punishment then it would deter them from appearing before the courts to testify. In other words, who would take the risk of testifying when a person cannot be sure that his testimony will be considered true by the court, or when the possibility exists that any of the four witnesses might change his mind?

In our opinion, this latter view is more reasonable for it allows the same benefit of doubt which is granted the accused to be extended to the witnesses as well. If the evidence of a witness does not necessarily lead to a person's conviction, it should nonetheless not lead to the prosecution of that witness for slander (*qadhf*) unless it is conclusively established that he wilfully lied.

Two arguments are, however, generally advanced in support of the view that a witness who testifies that someone committed unlawful sexual intercourse but where the crime is not established would be convicted of *qadhf*. First, that the Qur'ān itself holds slander to be a punishable offence. This argument, however, is not tenable because the Qur'ān itself draws a distinction between a slanderer and a witness. A witness cannot be taken as a slanderer simply because his testimony was not considered sufficient by the court to convict the accused.

The second argument is that 'Umar convicted Abū Bakrah and two other witnesses of slander in the case pertaining to Mughīrah ibn Shu'bah. However, when one studies the details of this case it becomes clear that it cannot be taken as a precedent for cases relating to insufficient evidence for conviction. The following represent some relevant details pertaining to the above incident. Relations between Mughīrah ibn Shu'bah, the Governor of Baṣrah, and Abū Bakrah had been strained for quite some time. The houses of both were situated on the same street, each facing the other. One day the windows of their houses were forced open by gusts of wind. As Abū Bakrah rose to shut his window, he glanced at the house opposite and saw Mughīrah engaged in sexual intercourse. At that time, three of Abū Bakrah's friends – Nāfi' ibn Kaladah, Ziyād and Shibl ibn Ma'bad – were sitting with Abū Bakrah. He called to them, saying: 'Look and be witness to what Mughīrah is doing.' His friends asked him about the identity of the woman. Abū Bakrah told them she was Umm Jamīl.

The very next day, the matter was reported to 'Umar who immediately suspended Mughīrah and appointed Abū Mūsā al-Ash'arī, as Governor of Baṣrah. 'Umar summoned both the accused and the witnesses to Madina. In their testimony, Abū Bakrah and the two other witnesses declared that they had seen Mughīrah having sexual intercourse with Umm Jamīl. Ziyād, however, said that the woman was not fully observable so he could not say with certainty that she was Umm Jamīl.

During cross-examination, Mughīrah established that it would not be possible for the witnesses to be completely sure about the identity of the woman they had seen through the window because of the distance between them and the objects of their observation. He also established that his wife and Umm Jamīl resembled each other.

It was evident from the circumstances that the Governor of a province in the days of 'Umar could not have asked a woman to let him commit adultery with her in his official residence where his own wife also lived. The accusation made by Abū Bakrah and his friends about Mughīrah that he was seen committing adultery was thus more of a slander than a testimony of what they had observed. So, not only did 'Umar acquit Mughīrah but also subjected Abū Bakrah, Nāfi' and Shibl to the punishment prescribed for *qadhf* (slander). This judgement was obviously specific to the circumstances of this particular case. It cannot be considered as a basis for laying down the general rule that witnesses whose evidence does not lead to the conviction of the accused in a case of *zinā* should necessarily be punished. (For details of this case see Ibn al-'Arabī, *Aḥkām al-Qur'ān*, vol. 2, pp. 88–9.)

(xx) Apart from the testimony of witnesses, the confession of the accused can also lead to conviction. This confession should be couched in clear, unequivocal terms affirming that the person committed sexual intercourse with a woman with whom he was not so permitted to do. The court should also ensure that the culprit made the statement without any external pressure and that he was in full control of his senses at the time. Furthermore, this confession should be made four times and on each occasion the person should clearly admit his guilt. This opinion is held by Abū Ḥanīfah, Aḥmad ibn Ḥanbal, Ibn Abī Laylā, Isḥāq ibn Rāhawayh and Ḥasan ibn Ṣāliḥ. Other jurists, however, consider a single confession sufficient for conviction. This opinion is maintained by Mālik, Shāfi'ī, 'Uthmān al-Battī and Ḥasan al-Baṣrī. In a case where a person is convicted only on the grounds of his own confession and where no other evidence is available, revocation of the confession at a later stage should lead to suspension of the punishment. This is so even though it may be evident that such a revocation is made so as to escape the punishment in question.

The judicial precedents from which these rulings have been derived are found in different works of *Ḥadīth*. The most outstanding precedent of all though is the case of Mā'iz ibn Mālik al-Aslamī which was reported by a large number of narrators on the authority of several Companions, and which is contained in most *Ḥadīth* collections. Mā'iz was an orphan who belonged to the tribe of Aslam, and was brought up by Hazzāl ibn Nu'aym. Mā'iz had unlawful sexual intercourse with a freed slave-girl.

Hazzāl asked Mā'iz to go to the Prophet (peace be upon him) and inform him of the incident. So Mā'iz went to the Prophet's Mosque and said to the Prophet (peace be upon him): 'O Messenger of Allah! Purify me. I have committed unlawful sexual intercourse.' The Prophet (peace be upon him) turned his face away from him, saying: 'Woe unto you. Go back and seek God's pardon.' Mā'iz appeared again before the Prophet (peace be upon him) and repeated his plea, but the Prophet (peace be upon him) once again turned his face away. Exactly the same thing happened a third time, and at this stage Abū Bakr warned Mā'iz that if he confessed for a fourth time, the Prophet (peace be upon him) would have him stoned to death. Undeterred even by this Mā'iz appeared again before the Prophet and repeated his request. The Prophet (peace be upon him) on this occasion turned to him, saying: 'Perhaps you kissed her, or amorously vexed her, or looked at her with sexual passion.' Mā'iz replied that that was not the case. The Prophet (peace be upon him) then asked him: 'Did you lie with her in the same bed?' He said: 'Yes.' The Prophet (peace be upon him) then asked him again: 'Did you have *mubāsharah* with her?'[1] Mā'iz replied in the affirmative. The Prophet (peace be upon him) once again made the same query of him. Then the Prophet (peace be upon him) asked him if he had had *mujāma'ah* with her, a term which clearly means 'sexual intercourse' in Arabic usage. He again replied in the affirmative. The Prophet (peace be upon him) asked him once again, using a term which means nothing but sexual intercourse and one which even has a somewhat unseemly nuance. This was a term which the Prophet had never used before, nor did he use it again afterwards. Had a person's life not been at stake, the Prophet (peace be upon him) would never have uttered such a word. Mā'iz, however, once again replied in the affirmative. The Prophet (peace be upon him) then asked him again in these words: 'Did you approach her in such manner that your organ disappeared into her organ?' He again said: 'Yes!' The Prophet (peace be upon him) further asked him: 'Did it disappear as does the staining needle in the collyrium or a rope disappears in a well?' He said: 'Yes.' The Prophet (peace be upon him) asked him further: 'Do you know what *zinā* is?' To this he replied: 'Yes! I did with her unlawfully what one does legitimately with one's wife.' The Prophet (peace be upon him) asked him whether he was married. He replied in the affirmative. The Prophet (peace be upon him) then asked him: 'Are you drunk?' This Mā'iz denied. A person stood up and checked his breath and confirmed that he was not drunk. The Prophet (peace be upon him) then inquired of his neighbours about Mā'iz whether he was insane. This was also denied by them. The Prophet (peace be upon him) then said to Hazzāl, who was responsible for bringing the incident to the Prophet's notice: 'If you had left this matter covered with your garment, it would have been much better for you.'

1. The word used here could mean sexual intercourse as well as something less than that.

After all this, the Prophet (peace be upon him) then directed that Mā'iz be stoned to death. Mā'iz was taken out of the town and there he was stoned. When the stones began to hit him, he ran for his life, saying: 'Take me back to the Messenger of God. My tribesmen have put me up to this. They betrayed me by telling me that he would not put me to death.' Yet those who were stoning him continued until he was dead. When this matter was reported to the Prophet (peace be upon him) he said: 'Why did you not release him? You should have brought him to me. Maybe he would have repented and Allah would have accepted his repentance.' (See Abū Dā'ūd, *K. al-Ḥudūd*, 'Bāb Rajm Mā'iz ibn Mālik', Bukhārī, *K. al-Ḥudūd*, 'Bāb Hal Yaqūlu al-Imām li al-Muqirr la'allaka lamazta aw ghamazta' and Muslim, *K. al-Ḥudūd*, 'Bāb man I'tarafa 'alā nafsihī bi al-zinā' – Ed.)

Another incident relates to a woman from the clan of Ghāmid, a branch of the Juhaynah tribe. She too confessed that she had been guilty of unlawful sexual intercourse, that she was pregnant, and that she was carrying an unlawful baby in her womb. She also confessed on four different occasions that she had been guilty of unlawful sexual intercourse and that she was unlawfully pregnant. When she confessed for the first time, the Prophet (peace be upon him) said to her: 'Woe to you. Go back and seek pardon from God and repent to Him.' She replied: 'Do you want to defer me as you did with Mā'iz? I am pregnant as a result of unlawful sexual intercourse.' Since her confession was supported by her pregnancy, the Prophet (peace be upon him) did not cross-examine her as thoroughly as he had done Mā'iz. The Prophet (peace be upon him) then said: 'If you insist, go back now and return to me after you have delivered the child.' After delivering the child she returned with the baby and asked the Prophet (peace be upon him) to purify her by carrying out the punishment. The Prophet (peace be upon him) again told her to go back, feed the baby, and return after weaning. She again returned to the Prophet (peace be upon him) after she had finished weaning the child. She was also carrying a piece of bread with which she fed the child whilst saying to the Prophet: 'O Messenger of God! His suckling is now complete. Look, he is now taking bread.' The Prophet (peace be upon him) then directed someone to look after the child and bring him up and he further ordered that the woman be stoned to death.

Common to both these incidents is the point that the culprit unequivocally confessed on four occasions. The *ḥadīth* narrated by Buraydah mentions that the Companions generally felt that if Mā'iz and the woman of the Ghāmid clan had not confessed their offence four times they would not have been lapidated. (See Abū Dā'ūd, *K. al-Ḥudūd*, 'Bāb Rajm Mā'iz ibn Mālik' – Ed.) However, in another instance, we find the following statement made by the Prophet (peace be upon him): 'Go and ask his wife. If she confesses, stone her to death.' (See Muslim, *K. al-Ḥudūd*, 'Bāb man I'tarafa 'alā nafsihī bi al-zinā' – Ed.) There is no mention in this tradition of four confessions. Hence a group of jurists have inferred that one single confession is sufficient to enforce the punishment prescribed for unlawful sexual intercourse.

(xxi) The three cases mentioned above prove that anyone who confesses to having committed an unlawful sexual act will not be asked about the identity of their partner, for that would entail the punishment of two people and the *Sharī'ah* is not at all eager to so punish people. If the culprit, however, voluntarily discloses the identity of their partner, the other person will be interrogated about the matter. If they too confess, then they also will be subjected to the punishment laid down for the offence. Conversely, if they deny it, only the person who confesses to the offence will be punished.

There is some disagreement among jurists when the second party denies having been involved in unlawful sexual intercourse. In this respect, should the person who confessed be punished for *zinā* or *qadhf* (unsubstantiated unlawful sexual intercourse)? According to Mālik and Shāfi'ī, the person concerned should receive the punishment prescribed for unlawful sexual intercourse because by their own confession they are definitely guilty of *zinā* regardless of whether the other person's involvement in the offence is established or not. Abū Ḥanīfah and Awzā'ī, however, are of the opinion that the confessor should be punished for *qadhf*. This because the denial of the other party makes it doubtful that unlawful sexual intercourse actually took place. What is beyond all doubt though is the fact that they accused a person of involvement in *zinā* which they then failed to prove. Hence the *qadhf* punishment. This view is endorsed by Muḥammad ibn al-Ḥasan al-Shaybānī, and according to at least one report, also by Shāfi'ī. Muḥammad ibn al-Ḥasan al-Shaybānī expressed the opinion – and Shāfi'ī, according to one version, endorsed this – that such a person should be punished for both *zinā* and *qadhf*, for they admitted to the former offence but could not establish the involvement of the other party in it.

A similar case was once brought before the Prophet (peace be upon him). According to a tradition regarding this incident, as recorded in Abū Dā'ūd and Aḥmad ibn Ḥanbal on the authority of Sahl ibn Sa'd: 'Someone came to the Prophet (peace be upon him) and confessed that he had committed unlawful sexual intercourse with a certain woman. The Prophet sent for the woman and asked her. She denied the incident altogether. The Prophet (peace be upon him) punished the man but spared the woman.'

This tradition, however, does not specify the exact punishment meted out to the man. According to another tradition on this question, one based on the authority of 'Abd Allāh ibn 'Abbās, the Prophet (peace be upon him) punished the man for unlawful sexual intercourse because he had confessed to the offence. He then asked the woman, and upon her denial he inflicted upon the man the flogging prescribed with regard to *qadhf*. (See Abū Dā'ūd, *K. al-Ḥudūd*, 'Bāb: Idhā aqarr al-Rajul bi al-zinā wa lam tuqirr al-Mar'ah' – Ed.) This tradition is rated as weak in respect of its chain of narration: one of its narrators, Qāsim ibn Fayyāḍ, has been declared untrustworthy by several leading scholars of *Ḥadīth*. Additionally, the tradition does not seem to stand to reason. One finds it hard to believe that the Prophet (peace be upon him) would have a person flogged and then go about inquiring about the truth of the incident. Both reason and justice required that the Prophet (peace be upon him) should not decide the case without referring the matter to the woman who was allegedly the other party. This view is supported by the tradition narrated by Sahl ibn Sa'd we mentioned above. In view of this, the second tradition cannot then be regarded as trustworthy.

(xxii) Jurists hold different views on the question of what punishment is to be meted out to those men and women who are convicted of unlawful sexual intercourse. The following is a summary of the leading jurists' main opinions.

Punishment for Married Men and Women Convicted of Unlawful Sexual Intercourse

Aḥmad ibn Ḥanbal, Dā'ūd al-Ẓāhirī and Isḥāq ibn Rāhawayh are of the opinion that they should first be lashed a hundred times and then be stoned to death. All other jurists, however, think that stoning to death should be their only punishment, i.e. the two punishments cannot be combined.

Punishment for Unmarried Persons Guilty of Unlawful Sexual Intercourse

According to Shāfi'ī, Aḥmad, Isḥāq, Dā'ūd al-Ẓāhirī, Sufyān al-Thawrī, Ibn Abī Laylā, Isḥāq ibn Rāhawayh, and Ḥasan ibn Ṣāliḥ, the punishment is a hundred lashes and one year's banishment for both the man and the woman.

According to Mālik and Awzā'ī, however, the man is to be lashed a hundred times and banished for a year while the woman is to be subjected to only one punishment, namely a hundred lashes. (All the jurists are of the opinion that banishment in this context denotes that the culprit be driven away from his town to such a distance that it makes it incumbent on him to shorten the Prayer. However, Zayd ibn 'Alī and Ja'far al-Ṣādiq are of the opinion that imprisonment serves the purpose of banishment.)

Abū Ḥanīfah and his disciples, especially Abū Yūsuf, Zufar and Muḥammad ibn al-Ḥasan al-Shaybānī are of the opinion that the *ḥadd* punishment for unlawful sexual intercourse for both males and females is a hundred lashes, and that alone. If any punishment is added to that prescription, such as imprisonment or banishment, then this is *ta'zīr* rather than *ḥadd*. The judge may look at each case on the basis of its merit and if he finds that the culprit is a highly immoral person, or that the amorous relations between the two parties convicted of unlawful sexual intercourse are unusually strong, then the judge may add to the *ḥadd* punishment as he finds necessary, such as with banishment or imprisonment.

Ḥadd is the prescribed punishment that must be awarded to those who deserve to receive that punishment if the required evidence is available. *Ta'zīr*, on the other hand, is a punishment which is not specifically provided for in the Law – neither its kind nor its quantity. It is made more or less severe depending on the merits of each case which may be determined by the court.

Jurists have supported these variant opinions by adducing different traditions on the question. These are as follows:

> A tradition has been narrated by 'Ubādah ibn Ṣāmit (see Muslim, Abū Dā'ūd, Ibn Mājah, Tirmidhī and Aḥmad ibn Ḥanbal) according to which the Prophet (peace be upon him) said: 'Take it from me. Take it from me. God has prescribed the ruling for the woman who is guilty of unlawful sexual intercourse. For unlawful sexual intercourse committed by an unmarried man or an unmarried woman the punishment is one hundred lashes and one year of banishment, while the punishment for a married man and a married woman is a hundred lashes and stoning.' (See Abū Dā'ūd, *K. al-Ḥudūd*, 'Bāb fī al-Rajm', Ibn Mājah, *K. al-Ḥudūd*, 'Bāb Ḥadd al-Zinā', Tirmidhī, *K. al-Ḥudūd*, 'Bāb mā jā' fī al-Rajm 'alā al-Thayyib' and Muslim, *K. al-Ḥudūd*, 'Bāb Ḥadd al-Zinā' – Ed.)
>
> Although this *ḥadīth* has come down through a sound chain of narrators, there are nevertheless many sound traditions which prove that the *ḥadīth* was never applied either in the days of the Prophet (peace be upon him) or of the Rightly-Guided Caliphs. Furthermore, no jurist has issued any ruling which accords with this tradition. What is, however, beyond doubt is that Islamic Law distinguishes between those who are married and those who are not when awarding punishment for *zinā*. An unmarried man who engages in unlawful sexual intercourse with a married or unmarried woman will be awarded the same punishment, regardless of the marital status of his partner. Likewise, if a married man commits unlawful sexual intercourse with a woman he will be awarded the same punishment regardless of the marital status of his female partner in that act. The same applies to the woman who is guilty of this offence. If she is married she will be awarded the same punishment regardless of whether the male partner to the act is married or not.

A tradition narrated by Zayd ibn Khālid al-Juhanī (see Bukhārī, Muslim, Abū Dā'ūd, Tirmidhī, Nasā'ī, Ibn Mājah and Aḥmad ibn Ḥanbal), states that two bedouin appeared before the Prophet (peace be upon him). One of them said: 'My son used to work as a labourer in this person's house. He had unlawful sexual relations with his wife. I gave him one hundred goats and a slave-girl by way of compensation. I am, however, told by scholars that this is opposed to the Book of God.' The other person also made the same plea. The Prophet (peace be upon him) said: 'I will decide the case exactly according to the Book of God. Take back your goats and the slave-girl. Your son will be lashed a hundred times and be exiled for one year.' He then asked Unays, a member of the Aslam tribe, to ascertain the truth of this report by asking the woman concerned. He further directed that the woman be stoned to death if she admitted to the crime. She confessed and was so lapidated. (See Bukhārī, *K. al-Muḥāribīn min Ahl al-Kufr wa al-Riddah*, 'Bāb al-I'tirāf bi al-zinā', Muslim, *K. al-Ḥudūd*, 'Bāb man i'tarafa 'alā nafsihī fī al-zinā' and Abū Dā'ūd, *K. al-Ḥudūd*, 'Bāb fī al-Mar'ah al-latī amara al-Nabiyu . . . bi Rajmihā min al-Juhaynah' – Ed.) (This tradition does not mention that the woman was lashed before being stoned to death.) The unmarried man was flogged as well as exiled for having had unlawful sexual intercourse with a married woman.

None of the traditions relating to the cases of Mā'iz and the woman of the Ghāmid clan, as found in the different collections of *Ḥadīth*, mention that the culprits were lashed before being stoned to death. Nor is there even a single tradition which indicates that the Prophet (peace be upon him) ever combined the two punishments. In all cases where a person was convicted of unlawful sexual intercourse, the Prophet (peace be upon him) awarded only one punishment, namely that of stoning to death. (See Bukhārī, *K. al-Muḥāribīn* . . . 'Bāb Rajm al-Ḥablā min al-zinā idhā aḥṣanat' and Muslim, *K. al-Ḥudūd*, 'Bāb Rajm al-Thayyib fī al-zinā' – Ed.) The famous sermon of 'Umar in which he forcefully argued for the punishment of lapidation for a married person, a tradition which is found in the works of Bukhārī, Muslim, Tirmidhī and Aḥmad ibn Ḥanbal with a variety of chains of narration, also does not mention that lashing was combined with stoning to death.

Among the Rightly-Guided Caliphs only 'Alī combined the two punishments in a case. This incident was reported by Aḥmad ibn Ḥanbal and Bukhārī on the authority of 'Āmir Sha'bī. A woman named Shurāḥah confessed that she had become pregnant as a result of unlawful sexual intercourse. 'Alī had her lashed on a Thursday and stoned to death on a Friday, saying that he had inflicted the former punishment in accordance with the Qur'ān and the latter in accordance with the Prophet's *Sunnah*. (See Bukhārī, *K. al-Muḥāribīn* . . . 'Bāb Rajm al-Muḥṣin . . .' and Aḥmad ibn Ḥanbal, *Musnad*, vol. 1, p. 107 – Ed.) This is the only incident where the two punishments were combined.

According to a tradition narrated by Jābir ibn 'Abd Allāh, a person committed unlawful sexual intercourse and the Prophet (peace be upon him) awarded him only lashes. It later transpired that the man was married whereupon the Prophet (peace be upon him) had him stoned to death. (See Abū Dā'ūd, *K. al-Ḥudūd*, 'Bāb Rajm Mā'iz ibn Mālik' – Ed.) We have already narrated several traditions which show that in the case of unmarried women the Prophet (peace be upon him) awarded only the punishment of lashing. This is evident from the example of a man who raped a woman while she was on her way to Prayers (see Abū Dā'ūd, *K. al-Ḥudūd*, 'Bāb Rajm Mā'iz ibn Mālik' – Ed.), as it is of the man who confessed to the crime whereas the woman denied it.

When 'Umar exiled Rabī'ah ibn Umayyah ibn Khalaf for drinking the latter joined ranks with the Romans. When 'Umar heard of this he decided that in future he would never exile anyone. Likewise, he refused to exile unmarried men or women who were convicted of unlawful sexual intercourse, saying that it would cause greater harm. (See Ibn al-'Arabī, *Aḥkām al-Qur'ān*, vol. 2, p. 1324, *Sūrah al-Nūr* and Jaṣṣāṣ, *Aḥkām al-Qur'ān*, vol. 3, p. 261.)

When we consider all these traditions together it becomes evident that the opinion of Abū Ḥanīfah and his disciples is the most sound. If a person commits unlawful sexual intercourse after marrying (*iḥṣān*), the only prescribed punishment for this offence is stoning to death, whereas if a person commits this act before marrying, the only prescribed punishment is a hundred lashes. These two punishments were never combined right from the time of the Prophet (peace be upon him) until the time of 'Uthmān. As for combining lashing with exile, we find that on some occasions this did happen but not on others. This further illustrates the soundness of the Ḥanafī doctrine on this question.

(xxiii) Insofar as the kind of lashing that is required, a clue to the same is provided by the Qur'ān itself. The imperative used in the Qur'ān – *fa ijladū* – is derived from the root *j-l-d* which itself is derived from the word *jild* (skin). All linguists and commentators on the Qur'ān consider it to mean that flogging whose effect is confined to the skin and which does not reach the flesh. Thus, a flogging that tears the flesh into pieces is contrary to the Qur'ānic command.

Irrespective of whether a lash or a cane is used for flogging, the instrument should neither be too thick and hard nor too light and soft. According to a tradition in Mālik's *Muwaṭṭa'*, the Prophet (peace be upon him) once called for a lash with which to flog someone. The one he was given had been used many times and had thus become soft. The Prophet (peace be upon him), therefore, asked for a harder lash. A new lash was presented to him which had not become soft because it had not been used. He then directed that another lash be given him, one that was midway between the two and which had been used before. The Prophet (peace be upon him) then had the person in question flogged with that lash. A tradition of similar import is narrated by Abū 'Uthmān al-Nahdī of 'Umar which says that he also used an average lash. (See Jaṣṣāṣ, *Aḥkām al-Qur'ān*, vol. 3.) Note that a whip with knots or one with two or three prongs cannot be used for this purpose. (See Abū Dā'ūd, 'Bāb fī Ḍarb al-Wajh fī al-Ḥadd' – Ed.)

As for the flogging itself, it should be of average intensity. 'Umar used to direct the flogger: 'Strike in such manner that your armpit is not revealed'. (Ibn al-'Arabī, *Aḥkām al-Qur'ān*, vol. 2, p. 84; Jaṣṣāṣ, *Aḥkām al-Qur'ān*, vol. 3.) In other words, the arm should not be stretched fully nor the flogging be done with full force. Moreover, flogging should not cause any wound and should not be concentrated on any particular part of the body. It should rather be spread all over. Only the face, the private parts and, according to the Ḥanafīs the head, should be spared while all other parts of the body should be subjected to the flogging. While having someone flogged 'Alī said: 'Give each part of the body its due except the face and the private parts.' According to another tradition, he instructed: 'Spare the head and the private parts.' (Jaṣṣāṣ, *Aḥkām al-Qur'ān*, vol. 3.) In this respect the Prophet (peace be upon him) directed: 'If anyone of you hits someone, he should avoid the face.' (Abū Dā'ūd.)

Men should be flogged in a standing position whereas women should be flogged whilst sitting. In the days of Abū Ḥanīfah, Ibn Abī Laylā, the Judge of Kūfah, had a woman flogged while she was standing. Abū Ḥanīfah took strong exception to this and publicly declared this practice to be wrong. This, incidentally, also sheds light on his position regarding the idea of contempt of court. During a flogging, a woman was to remain fully dressed; indeed her clothes were to be so folded and bound that during the flogging no part of her body was to be exposed. All that was required of such a woman was that she cast aside clothes that were extraordinarily thick. There is some difference of opinion regarding the dress of male culprits. According to some jurists, they should be allowed to wear only such dress as covers their body up to the waist while other jurists insist that their shirts should also not be taken off. Abū 'Ubaydah once ordered a person who was convicted of unlawful sexual intercourse to be flogged. The culprit said: 'Let my sinful body be punished fully.' So saying, he started to take off his shirt. Abū 'Ubaydah, however, saw to it that he did not do so. (See Jaṣṣāṣ, *Aḥkām al-Qur'ān*, vol. 3, p. 262.) In the time of 'Alī someone was even flogged while he was wearing a sheet of cloth.

It is further forbidden to flog someone when it is either very hot or very cold. During winter, flogging can be carried out only when it is relatively warm, and during summer, when it is relatively cool.

It is not permissible to flog someone after tying him up with something. An exception may, however, be made in the case of a person who tries to flee from his punishment. According to 'Abd Allāh ibn Mas'ūd, it is not permissible to flog someone either after having stripped him naked or after tying him to a tripod.

Jurists consider it lawful that a culprit be flogged at least twenty times a day. It is, however, preferable that the full punishment be inflicted in one go.

Flogging should not be entrusted to rough executioners. It should rather be entrusted to persons of knowledge and understanding who are well aware as to what kind of beating accords with the requirements of the *Sharī'ah*. As reported in the *Zād al-Ma'ād* of Ibn al-Qayyim, 'Alī, Zubayr, Miqdād ibn 'Amr, Muḥammad ibn Maslamah, 'Āṣim ibn Thābit and Ḍaḥḥāk ibn Sufyān used to perform this duty in the time of the Prophet (peace be upon him). (See Ibn al-Qayyim, *Zād al-Ma'ād*, vol. 1, pp. 44–5.)

Should the culprit be so sick that there is no reasonable chance of recovery, or if he is too old, he should be hit only once with a branch with a hundred twigs, or with a broom with a hundred straws so as to meet the formal requirements of the Law. In the time of the Prophet (peace be upon him), a sick and old person was apprehended for unlawful sexual intercourse and he was awarded the above-mentioned punishment. (See Abū Dā'ūd, *K. al-Ḥudūd*, 'Bāb fī Iqāmat al-Ḥadd 'alā al-Marīḍ' – Ed.) If a pregnant woman is to be flogged, her punishment should be deferred until she has delivered the child and completed the period of perinatal haemorrhage. If she is to be stoned to death, she cannot be punished before the baby is fully weaned. If the case of unlawful sexual intercourse is supported by due evidence, the witnesses would initiate the flogging, whereas in the case of the culprit's confession, the judge himself would initiate it. This mechanism was devised to instil into the minds of both witnesses and judges the gravity of the matter. When 'Alī decided the case of Shurāḥah and sentenced her to be stoned to death, he said: 'Had there been a witness to this offence, he should have initiated the strike. However, as she has been sentenced in view of her own confession, I will initiate it.' According to the Ḥanafīs, it is obligatory for punishments to be performed in this manner. The Shāfi'īs, however, do not consider it obligatory.

When one examines these detailed rules about the execution of flogging as prescribed by Islamic Law, one is struck by the temerity of those who brand the Law as savage and barbaric. Yet, these very same people have no qualms about the flogging which is common in prisons today. According to present-day laws, not only the courts but even the superintendent of a prison is authorized to award a sentence of thirty cane lashes to a prisoner for mere disobedience or insolent behaviour. Harrowing indeed is the manner in which cane-lashing is practised today for special kinds of cane are even selected for the purpose. The cane is then soaked in water such that when a criminal is lashed, his flesh will be cut into pieces. Moreover, a professional flogger is hired to execute the punishment, the requirement being that he constantly practise the art of flogging so that he might be able to do an efficient job whenever it is required. Furthermore, the prisoner is tied to a tripod in order to ensure that he does not budge even an inch in this state of immense pain. The flogger approaches him at full speed and hits him with all the force possible. The culprit is flogged consistently on his buttocks, as a result of which the flesh is torn into pieces, exposing his bones. The flogging is executed with such vehemence that even the healthiest person falls into unconsciousness before he has received thirty lashes. The wounds thus caused often take a long time to heal. This 'civilized' mode of punishment is very much in force in today's prisons. It is ironic that those very persons who are responsible for the enforcement of this kind of punishment have the cheek to criticize the Islamic Law of flogging and denounce it as barbaric. We are also all well aware that it is not only criminals who are punished in the above manner, but even suspects, especially those suspected of political 'crimes', who are subjected to this highly savage torture during interrogation in our prisons today.

(xxiv) When the culprit who has been sentenced to stoning dies as a result of that punishment he has to be buried honourably in a Muslim cemetery following the correct funeral services. No one has the right to speak ill of him. According to a tradition, 'Abd Allāh al-Anṣārī narrates that when Mā'iz ibn Mālik died as a result of stoning, the Prophet (peace be upon him) spoke well of him and himself led his funeral Prayer. (See Bukhārī, *K. al-Muḥārībīn min Ahl al-Riddah wa al-Kufr*, 'Bāb al-Rajm bi al-Muṣallī' – Ed.) There is another tradition which is narrated by Buraydah to the effect that the Prophet (peace be upon him) said: 'Seek forgiveness for Mā'iz. He made a repentance which, were it to be divided over the whole community, it would suffice for everyone.' (Muslim.) The same tradition mentions that when the woman of the Ghāmid tribe died as a result of stoning, the Prophet (peace be upon him) also led her funeral Prayer. And when Khālid ibn al-Walīd spoke ill of her, the Prophet (peace be upon him) said: 'Restrain yourself, Khālid. By the Being Who holds my life in His Hand, she made such a true repentance that had the collector of [unlawful] imposts repented as she did he too would have been forgiven.' (See *loc. cit.* – Ed.) A tradition is narrated by Abū Hurayrah that as the Prophet (peace be upon him) was going somewhere a few days after the stoning of Mā'iz he overheard two persons speaking ill of him. As the Prophet (peace be upon him) continued on his way, he came across the carcass of a donkey. He halted and said to those two people: 'Eat some of it [i.e. the carcass of the donkey].' They said: 'O Messenger of God, who can eat of it?' He replied: 'What you were eating just now was worse than eating this carcass.' (See Abū Dā'ūd, *K. al-Ḥudūd*, 'Bāb Rajm Mā'iz ibn Malīk – Ed.) In another tradition it is stated that on the occasion of the funeral Prayer of the woman of Ghāmid, 'Imrān ibn Ḥuṣayn asked the Prophet (peace be upon him) if the funeral Prayer would be made for a person who was guilty of unlawful sexual intercourse? The Prophet (peace be upon him) replied: 'She has made a repentance that were it to be distributed over all the inhabitants of Madina, it would suffice for everyone.' (See Muslim, *K. al-Ḥudūd*, 'Bāb man i'tarafa 'alā nafsihī bi al-Zinā' – Ed.) Another tradition on the authority of Abū Hurayrah says: 'While someone was being punished for having taken intoxicating drinks a person exclaimed: "May Allah disgrace you." On hearing this, the Prophet (peace be upon him) said: "Do not say so. Do not help Satan against him."'

And let not tenderness for them deter you from what pertains to Allah's religion, if you do truly believe in Allah and the Last Day;[3] ▶

وَلَا تَأْخُذْكُم بِهِمَا رَأْفَةٌ فِي دِينِ ٱللَّهِ إِن كُنتُمْ تُؤْمِنُونَ بِٱللَّهِ وَٱلْيَوْمِ ٱلْآخِرِ

(See Bukhārī, *K. al-Ḥudūd*, 'Bāb al-Ḍarb bi-al-Jarīd wa al-Ni'āl – Ed.) In the tradition as recorded in Abū Dā'ūd, one finds an additional sentence to that which is found in the above tradition. This additional sentence was a statement made by the Prophet (peace be upon him) to the effect that: 'You should rather say: "O Allah pardon him and be merciful to him." ' (See Abū Dā'ūd, *K. al-Ḥudūd*, 'Bāb fī al-Ḥadd fī al-Khamr' – Ed.)

This, then, encapsulates the spirit of punishment in Islam. From an Islamic viewpoint, even the punishment that is meted out to the worst kind of criminal is motivated by good-will for all, including the culprit, rather than by any feeling of hostility or vengefulness. Hence, after the culprit is punished, he is treated with compassion and kindness. It remains for the present civilization to have the unique distinction of taking petty-mindedness to its current heights. It is possible under this civilization alone for someone to be killed by the police or the army, a killing which a judicial inquiry of sorts validates, but not for him to be given a decent burial or for anyone to say a good word about him.

(xxv) We have already mentioned the rules of the *Sharī'ah* in cases involving sexual intercourse with a woman within the prohibited degrees of marriage. (See *Tafhīm al-Qur'ān*, vol. 1, p. 336.) Likewise, we have mentioned the viewpoint of the *Sharī'ah* pertaining to sodomy. (See *Tafhīm al-Qur'ān*, vol. 2, pp. 51–4.) As for sexual intercourse with animals, some Muslim jurists prescribe the same punishment as laid down for unlawful sexual intercourse between humans. However, Abū Ḥanīfah, Abū Yūsuf, Mālik, Zufar, Muḥammad ibn al-Ḥasan al-Shaybānī and Shāfi'ī do not equate this act with unlawful sexual intercourse; they are of the opinion that the culprit should be subjected to *ta'zīr* rather than *ḥadd* and that the punishment meted out be left to the discretion of the judge. It is also possible that the *Majlis al-Shūrā* (consultative council) of the State may prescribe a punishment for this offence if it so desires.

3. What is most striking in the verse is that the expression used for a provision of the criminal law is 'Allah's religion'. One, thus, learns that Prayer, fasting, *Ḥajj*, and *Zakāh* alone do not subsume 'religion'. Religion, instead, also embraces law. Hence the Qur'ānic expression 'to establish true religion' does not mean merely to establish Prayer, etc. but also to

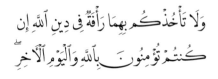

implement the Laws of God and the system of life promulgated by the *Sharī'ah*. If this is not done and Prayer alone is established, this amounts to only a partial establishment of the true religion. Furthermore, if the Laws ordained by God are spurned in favour of other laws, this amounts to rejecting the religion of God.

It is also noteworthy that God warns the believers against that misplaced compassion which prevents them from enforcing the punishment of men and women who indulge in unlawful sexual intercourse. This is expressed in clearer terms by the Prophet (peace be upon him) in the following *ḥadīth*: 'A ruler who has waived off even a single lash out of the prescribed punishment will be brought on the Day of Judgement and asked: "Why did you do so?" In reply he will say: "I did so out of mercy for Your servants." It will be said to him: "Are you more merciful than Me?" He will then be ordered to be cast into Hell-Fire. Then he who added one single lash to those prescribed will be asked: "Why did you do so?" In reply he will say: "In order that they cease indulging in acts of disobedience to You." It will then be said to him: "Are you wiser than Me in regard to them?" Then it will be commanded that he be cast into Hell-Fire.' (*Tafsīr Kabīr*, vol. 6, p. 225.)

This will happen when someone either increases or decreases the punishment laid down by God, either because of compassion or in order to deter people from committing acts of disobedience. If someone, however, were to alter God's Laws in consideration of the culprit's social position, this would surely be considered the very worst kind of offence. There is a statement from the Prophet (peace be upon him) which has been narrated by 'Ā'ishah to this effect. In the course of a sermon the Prophet (peace be upon him) said: 'O people! The communities before you perished because when a respectable person of the community committed theft, people spared him and punished him as if he was a weak person.' (See Bukhārī, *K. al-Ḥudūd*, 'Bāb Iqāmat al-Ḥudūd 'alā al-Sharīf wa al-Waḍī'' and 'Bāb Karāhīyat al-Shāfā'ah fī al-Ḥadd idhā rufi'a ilā al-Sulṭān' and Muslim, *K. al-Ḥudūd*, 'Bāb Qaṭ' al-sāriq al-Sharīf wa Ghayrih wa al-Nahy 'an al-Shāfā'ah fī al-Ḥudūd' – Ed.) According to another tradition, the Prophet (peace be upon him) said: 'To enforce one prescribed punishment (*ḥadd*) is much more beneficial for the inhabitants of the earth than forty days of rainfall.' (See Ibn Mājah, *K. al-Ḥudūd*, 'Bāb Iqāmat al-Ḥudūd' and Nasā'ī, *K. Qaṭ' al-Sāriq*, 'Bāb Targhīb fī Iqāmat al-Ḥadd' – Ed.)

Some commentators on the Qur'ān take the present verse to mean that no one who has been convicted should be released without enforcing the prescribed punishment of a hundred lashes. Other scholars, however, interpret this to mean that the flogging should not be so light that the culprit would not experience any pain. Moreover, it unequivocally makes the point that anyone who is convicted for unlawful sexual intercourse should receive the punishment prescribed for it by God, and that it should not be changed to any punishment other than flogging out of compassion or mercy.

and let a party of believers witness their punishment.[4]

(3) Let the fornicator not marry any except a fornicatress or idolatress and let the fornicatress not marry any except a fornicator or an idolater. That is forbidden to the believers.[5]

وَلْيَشْهَدْ عَذَابَهُمَا طَآئِفَةٌ مِّنَ ٱلْمُؤْمِنِينَ ﴿٢﴾
ٱلزَّانِى لَا يَنكِحُ إِلَّا زَانِيَةً أَوْ مُشْرِكَةً وَٱلزَّانِيَةُ
لَا يَنكِحُهَآ إِلَّا زَانٍ أَوْ مُشْرِكٌ ۚ وَحُرِّمَ
ذَٰلِكَ عَلَى ٱلْمُؤْمِنِينَ ﴿٣﴾

To regard flogging as a barbaric punishment is tantamount to unbelief itself. Such an outrageous opinion is altogether inconsistent with faith. Only the worst hypocrites can believe in God and at the same time regard a punishment prescribed by Him as barbaric.

4. This means that the punishment should be carried out publicly. This would, on the one hand, arouse in the culprit a feeling of shame and on the other serve as a lesson to others.

This throws further light on the Islamic concept of punishment. While laying down the punishment for stealing, the Qur'ān adds: 'This is a recompense for what they have done, an exemplary punishment from Allah.' (*al-Mā'idah* 5: 38.)

In the same vein, people are being directed in the present verse to publicly enforce the punishment on those guilty of unlawful sexual intercourse. This highlights the three main objectives of punishment in Islam. First, it is to make the culprit suffer for the evil he has perpetrated on some of his fellow human beings or society as a whole. Second, it seeks to deter the people who are inclined towards evil so that they are dissuaded from committing the same offence again. Third, punishment is to be meted out to culprits in order that those members of society who are disposed to criminal acts should be deterred from actually committing them. Moreover, one advantage of publicly enforcing punishments is that those in authority are likely to shrink from acting either too leniently or with undue harshness with offenders.

5. A befitting match for a person who is guilty of unlawful sexual intercourse and who does not subsequently repeat the offence could only be either a woman who does not mind unlawful sexual relations or a polytheist. A believing woman of good moral character cannot be a good match for such a dissolute person. It is in fact prohibited for believers to wilfully give their daughters in marriage to such persons. Therefore, as

far as those women who are guilty of unlawful sex and who do not repent thereafter are concerned, it is in men of the same character or polytheists where they will find appropriate spouses. For quite obviously such women are not befitting spouses for believers of good character.

In fact it is not only inappropriate but also forbidden for a good-charactered believer to marry a woman who is known to be morally dissolute, especially in matters pertaining to sex. It is obvious then that this injunction applies to those men and women who persist in their evil ways. As for those who repent and mend their ways after some lapse, this verse is not applicable to them. For those who repent and subsequently mend their ways can no longer be treated as tainted with the guilt of unlawful sexual intercourse.

This verse, which interdicts marriage with a man guilty of unlawful sexual intercourse, is understood by Aḥmad ibn Ḥanbal to mean that such a marriage, even if it is contracted, will be deemed void. The appropriate meaning, however, is that people should not contract such marriages. The verse does not mean that if someone actually contracts such a marriage despite the injunction, that the contract is void and that the contractees would be charged with unlawful sexual intercourse. The Prophet (peace be upon him) laid down a general rule, saying: 'An unlawful act does not render lawful acts unlawful.' (Ṭabarānī and Dāraquṭnī.) In other words, an illegal act does not nullify other legal acts. Hence, if someone who committed unlawful sexual intercourse in the past marries someone later on, this does not mean that the relationship between the spouses is unlawful or that the partner in the marriage contract who did not commit unlawful sexual intercourse is guilty of the other person's earlier offence. As a matter of principle, no illegal act other than open rebellion renders a person an outlaw.

If we consider this verse in light of what has been said above, it is quite clear that its true purpose is to emphasize to believers that deliberately choosing those who are known for sexual immorality as marriage partners is an act of sin which they should stay away from. This because choosing such persons in marriage encourages persons of dissolute character. This is not appropriate because the *Sharī'ah* likes such people to be worthy of censure and condemnation.

This verse does not lend itself to the conclusion that a sexually deviant Muslim's marriage with a polytheist woman or that of a sexually deviant Muslim woman's marriage with a polytheist man is legitimate. Rather, the verse underscores the fact that unlawful sex is an outrageous act and a Muslim who is guilty of it is no longer worthy of having matrimonial relations with good-charactered persons of the Muslim society. If there is any such dissolute person, he should better turn his attention to those of his own ilk – either those who are guilty of sexual immorality like himself, or polytheists who do not consider themselves bound by God's commands. (See Aḥmad ibn Ḥanbal, *Musnad*, vol. 2, p. 159 – Ed.)

(4) Those who accuse honourable women (of unchastity) but do not produce four witnesses, flog them with eighty lashes, and do not admit their testimony ever after. They are indeed transgressors, ▶	وَٱلَّذِينَ يَرْمُونَ ٱلْمُحْصَنَٰتِ ثُمَّ لَمْ يَأْتُوا۟ بِأَرْبَعَةِ شُهَدَآءَ فَٱجْلِدُوهُمْ ثَمَٰنِينَ جَلْدَةً وَلَا تَقْبَلُوا۟ لَهُمْ شَهَٰدَةً أَبَدًا ۚ وَأُو۟لَٰٓئِكَ هُمُ ٱلْفَٰسِقُونَ ﴿٤﴾

This verse can properly be understood in light of the traditions of the Prophet (peace be upon him) on this question. In this respect, there is a tradition on the authority of ʿAbd Allāh ibn ʿAmr ibn al-ʿĀṣ that there was a woman called Umm Mahzūl who was a prostitute. A Muslim intended to marry her and sought the Prophet's permission to do so. The Prophet (peace be upon him) remained silent at his questioning twice, but when he was questioned for the third time he responded in the negative and recited this verse. (See Aḥmad ibn Ḥanbal, *Musnad* and Nasāʾī.) According to another tradition, there was a Companion named Marthad ibn Abī Marthad who had unlawful sexual relations with a Makkan prostitute before the advent of Islam. Later on, he intended to marry her and sought the Prophet's permission. He asked the Prophet (peace be upon him) twice, but he remained silent on this issue. When he put the same question to him for the third time, the Prophet (peace be upon him) recited this verse, saying: 'Therefore, do not marry her.' (See Abū Dāʾūd, *K. al-Ḥudūd*, 'Bāb al-Nikāḥ, 'Bāb fī Qawlihī Taʿālā: al-Zānī lā yankiḥu illā zāniyah' and Tirmidhī, *K. Tafsīr al-Qurʾān*, 'Bāb wa min Sūrah al-Nūr' – Ed.)

There are also several other traditions on the authority of ʿAbd Allāh ibn ʿUmar and ʿAmmār ibn Yāsir to the effect that the Prophet (peace be upon him) said: 'A cuckold can never enter Paradise.' (See Aḥmad ibn Ḥanbal, *Musnad*, vol. 2, p. 134 and Nasāʾī, *K. al-Zakāh*, 'Bāb al-Mannān bi mā aʿṭa' – Ed.) Both Abū Bakr and ʿUmar used to flog unmarried men and women who were guilty of unlawful sex and would then have them married to each other. It is narrated by ʿAbd Allāh ibn ʿUmar that someone approached Abū Bakr in a state of panic. He was in such a state that he could not speak properly. Abū Bakr directed ʿUmar to talk to him in private. On being gently questioned he said that someone had been staying with him as a guest and had developed sexual relations with his daughter. ʿUmar exclaimed: 'Fie upon you! Why did you not cover up your daughter?' Eventually a case was brought against the two. Both were punished, then married to each other, and Abū Bakr sent them into exile for one year. Some other traditions of similar import are found in Qurṭubī's *Aḥkām al-Qurʾān*, vol. 2, p. 86. (See Ibn al-ʿArabī, *Aḥkām al-Qurʾān*, vol. 2, p. 1331 – Ed.)

(5) except those of them that repent thereafter and mend their behaviour. For surely Allah is Most Forgiving, Ever Compassionate.[6]

(6) As for those who accuse their wives (of unchastity), and have no witnesses except themselves: the testimony of such a one is that he testify, swearing by Allah four times, that he is truthful (in his accusation), ▶

إِلَّا ٱلَّذِينَ تَابُوا۟ مِنۢ بَعْدِ ذَٰلِكَ وَأَصْلَحُوا۟
فَإِنَّ ٱللَّهَ غَفُورٌ رَّحِيمٌ ﴿٥﴾ وَٱلَّذِينَ يَرْمُونَ
أَزْوَٰجَهُمْ وَلَمْ يَكُن لَّهُمْ شُهَدَآءُ إِلَّآ أَنفُسُهُمْ
فَشَهَٰدَةُ أَحَدِهِمْ أَرْبَعُ شَهَٰدَٰتٍۭ بِٱللَّهِ ۙ
إِنَّهُۥ لَمِنَ ٱلصَّٰدِقِينَ ﴿٦﴾

---

6. This directive aims at putting an end to salacious talk and gossip in society about illicit sexual relations between people. People are required to abstain from the same because it leads to numerous other evils. The worst effect is that it creates an atmosphere conducive to illicit sex. A person relates to another person the illicit sexual adventures of another person. These tales naturally circulate and in due course a lot of exciting material is added to the original stories. This arouses sexual passions all round. Those inclined to evil ways thus come to know through whom their sexual passions can be gratified.

The *Sharī'ah,* however, aims to nip this evil in the bud. Therefore, on the one hand, it prescribes that a person convicted of unlawful sexual intercourse be subjected to the most severe punishment to which any criminal would be subjected. On the other hand, it also ensures that the person who accuses others of this grave offence be able to conclusively prove it, and if he fails to do so that he be severely punished with 80 lashes.

This so as to deter people from irresponsibly slandering others. Even if one observes someone actually indulging in unlawful sex before one's own eyes, one should not publicize it, this to prevent corruption from spreading. If one can secure the required number of witnesses one may report the matter to the authorities concerned, but one should certainly not go about publicizing it. Only in this manner can one duly prove the person concerned to be guilty and thereby have the authorities punish him.

For a fuller understanding of this provision of Islamic Law, one should take note of the following rulings which pertain to the question:

i. The words used in the verse are: *wa al-ladhīna yarmūna* (and those who accuse). The context, however, makes it clear that not all but only a special kind of accusation is meant here, i.e. that of unlawful sexual intercourse. If we examine the verses from the very beginning of this *sūrah*, we note that the punishment for unlawful sexual intercourse was first laid down. A little later, we come across injunctions pertaining to *li'ān*. The mention of accusation in between the statements about the two matters mentioned above, makes the nature of the accusation quite clear. Moreover, since the verse speaks of accusing chaste women, it implies that the accusation is one that pertains to their chastity. Moreover, the accusers are asked to produce four witnesses in support of their charge. It is common knowledge that this type of evidence is required only in the case of unlawful sexual intercourse. In view of this, there is a consensus among scholars that the above verse aims specifically at enunciating the rules that ought to be followed when someone accuses the other of having committed unlawful sexual intercourse. A special term, *qadhf*, was used to signify this kind of accusation. Thanks to this term, it became possible to distinguish between accusations to do with sexual conduct and accusations regarding other offences such as theft, drinking alcohol, usury, or disbelief in Islam. Accusations other than *qadhf* could be decided upon by the judge at his discretion, or a suitable penalty could be fixed by the consultative assembly of the Islamic State by promulgating a law dealing with cases of libel and contempt.

ii. Although the verse speaks only of accusing chaste and honourable women, jurists are agreed that it also covers accusations against chaste and honourable men. By the same token, although the statement *yarmūn al-muḥṣanāt* would ordinarily suggest that the accusers are male, women too can be accusers. Women who are guilty of such an accusation will also be dealt with according to the same Law; gender being of no consequence in *qadhf* offences. As a matter of Law, whoever slanders a chaste and honourable person will be prosecuted.

It is also worth clarifying that the word *muḥṣanāt* used here signifies chaste and honourable women rather than just married women although the term is quite often used in this sense. The emphasis here is on the chastity and purity of people subjected to accusations of sexual misconduct, rather than any women with their marital status.

iii. This penal injunction will be executed only when the accusation is directed at either men or women who are *muḥṣan*, that is chaste and honourable, but not otherwise. If a non-*muḥṣan*, one notorious for sexual misconduct is charged with such unlawful conduct, this cannot be considered an act of slander (*qadhf*). But if someone who is of good moral character is accused of sexual misconduct, the judge may punish the accuser who is unable to duly substantiate it. The consultative assembly of the Islamic State may also enact a suitable law on this question.

iv. If someone simply accuses a person of committing unlawful sexual intercourse, without providing any evidence for the accusation, this in itself does not necessarily warrant that the accuser be awarded the punishment laid down for *qadhf*.

In order that this punishment be awarded, certain conditions must be fulfilled. These conditions relate to (a) the accuser, (b) the accused, and (c) the offence of which someone has been accused.

As for the conditions which must be found in the accuser in order that he be punished for *qadhf*, they are as follows: First, the accuser should be an adult. If a minor is guilty of this offence, he may be punished but not subjected to the *ḥadd* (prescribed) punishment. Second, the accuser should be a sane person. An insane person may not be subjected to *ḥadd* punishment. Likewise, anyone who is under the effect of intoxication by any agent other than wine, for example a person under the influence of anesthetic etc., may not be held guilty. Third, the accuser should have made the accusation of his own free-will. If someone compelled him into unjustifiably accusing someone else of unlawful sexual intercourse, he cannot be held guilty. Fourth, the accuser should neither be the father nor the grandfather of the accused since in such a case he cannot be awarded the *ḥadd* punishment for *qadhf*.

The Ḥanafīs add one more condition to these, namely that the accuser be capable of speech. A dumb person who accuses another of unlawful sexual intercourse by gesture is not liable to the *ḥadd* punishment for *qadhf*. Shāfi'ī, however, disagrees on this point. In his opinion, if the gestures of the accuser are clear enough to make everyone fully understand what he means, he will be considered to have committed *qadhf*. This because accusing someone by gesture is as damaging to his reputation as accusing him by word of mouth. On the contrary, the Ḥanafīs believe that gestures are an insufficient means of communicating the accusation and so they lay down a *ta'zīr* rather than a *ḥadd* punishment for such people.

As for the conditions which pertain to the person at whom the accusation is directed, these are as follows: First, that he be sane, i.e. he should be charged with unlawful sexual intercourse at a time when he is in a state of sanity. A person cannot be convicted of *qadhf* if he accuses an insane person of committing unlawful sexual intercourse, not even if the person accused becomes sane at some later date. For an insane person cannot be expected to guard his chastity. Hence, if it is established by evidence that he committed unlawful sexual intercourse, he will not be awarded the *ḥadd* punishment prescribed for *zinā*. Nor will the accusation of unchastity damage that person's reputation owing to his insanity. The accuser will, therefore, not be punished for *qadhf*. Mālik and Layth ibn Sa'd, however, are of the opinion that anyone who accuses an insane person of unlawful sexual intercourse should also be punished for *qadhf* because he brought a grave charge against someone without providing due evidence.

Second, that the accusation is directed at a person who has attained his majority. If the accusation is directed at a minor, or at someone who later comes of age but who was subjected to a charge of unlawful sexual intercourse at a time when he was still a minor, the accuser will not be liable for the punishment laid down for *qadhf*. The reason being that like the insane person, a minor too cannot guard his chastity, nor is he liable to the punishment for *zinā* if he committed this offence when he was a minor, nor is the reputation of a minor damaged by this accusation. However, Mālik is of the opinion that if a boy who is close to the age of majority is accused of unlawful sexual intercourse, the accuser will not be punished for *qadhf*. But, if a girl who is close to the age of maturity is accused of having had unlawful sexual intercourse, the accuser will be subjected to the *qadhf* punishment. The reason for this being that such an accusation seriously damages the girl's reputation. In fact, it damages the honour of the whole family, and furthermore the girl's future is jeopardized.

Third, that the accused be a Muslim. That is, the accuser will be convicted of *qadhf* if he lays a charge of *zinā* against a person who is a Muslim. If the charge is brought against a non-Muslim, or against a Muslim who was charged with the offence whilst not being a Muslim, the accuser will not be convicted of *qadhf*.

Fourth, that the accused should be a free person. If a charge of *zinā* is laid against a slave, whether male or female, or if a free person is charged with *zinā* before acquiring their freedom, the accuser will not be convicted of *qadhf*. This because the helplessness associated with slavery makes it difficult for the person concerned to guard his chastity. It is also significant that the Qur'ān uses the expression *muḥṣanāt* in contrast to slave-girls in *Sūrah al-Nisā'* (4: 24–5). This is, however, contested by Dā'ūd al-Ẓāhirī who is of the opinion that the person who accuses a slave, whether male or female, should also be punished for *qadhf*.

Fifth, that the accused be a chaste person. That is, he should neither have been convicted of the act of *zinā*, nor acts which might be considered to create a suspicion of *zinā* such as follows: that he contracted a defective marriage, or that he married someone secretly, or that he had sexual intercourse with some slave-girl under the misunderstanding that he had ownership rights over her, or that he had sexual intercourse with someone on the wrong assumption that he had contracted marriage with her. Nor should his lifestyle be such that a charge of sexual misconduct could, with some justification, apply to him. Nor should he ever have been convicted of acts of sexual misconduct, even if they be of a lesser order than fully-fledged *zinā*. For if any of these circumstances exist, his chastity no longer remains above board. As a consequence, if anyone accuses a person of such doubtful sexual conduct, he cannot be subjected to the punishment of 80 lashes. For even if evidence for *zinā* is brought against the accused any time prior to his having received the punishment for *qadhf*, the latter will be exempted from the punishment. This because the person against whom he laid the charge could no longer be considered a chaste person.

To say that the accuser in the five instances cited above is not liable for the *ḥadd* punishment for *qadhf* does not mean, however, that the person who charges an insane person or a minor, or a non-Muslim, or a slave, or a person not known to be of chaste character with sexual misconduct, cannot be subjected to any kind of punishment. For such persons may indeed he awarded a *ta'zīr* punishment.

Let us now turn to the conditions which should obtain in the act of *qadhf* itself. If a person accuses someone of committing unlawful sexual intercourse, he is liable to a *qadhf* conviction if either of the following conditions obtain: (a) that the accused is charged with the kind of sexual act which, if substantiated, renders him liable for the *ḥadd* punishment for *zinā*; or (b) that the accused is described as an illegitimate child.

In either case, the accusation should be couched in clear and explicit terms. An accusation which is expressed in metaphorical terms or in allusions will be disregarded. Likewise, the charge should not be expressed in a phraseology which can be construed to mean unlawful sex or illegitimate birth only if it is assumed that the accuser intended those words to mean so. For instance, if someone identifies a person as sinful and dissolute, or calls a woman a prostitute, or calls a *Sayyid* [i.e. descendant of the Prophet] a Pathan [implying that he was not so descended] such statements may not be regarded as *qadhf*. Likewise, those words and expressions which people resort to by way of abuse, for example bastard, etc., cannot be considered clear statements which amount to *qadhf*.

There is, however, disagreement among jurists with regard to innuendoes. For example, a person may say: 'Yes, but I am not an adulterer'; or that: 'But my mother did not give birth to me by adultery.' In such cases, Mālik is of the opinion that if the statement clearly means that the person concerned is accused of having committed *zinā* or of being an illegitimate child then this amounts to *qadhf* and entails *ḥadd* punishment. However, Abū Ḥanīfah and his disciples as also Shāfi'ī, Sufyān al-Thawrī, Ibn Shubrumah and Ḥasan ibn Ṣāliḥ grant the benefit of doubt to the accuser on the grounds that the statement is in the nature of a veiled attack rather than a clear accusation. As there is some room for doubt, *ḥadd* punishment cannot be awarded in such cases.

Aḥmad ibn Ḥanbal and Isḥāq ibn Rāhawayh are of the opinion that if such a statement is made in the course of a quarrel, it amounts to *qadhf* while if such a remark is made in jest, it does not constitute *qadhf*. However, among the Rightly-Guided Caliphs, 'Umar and 'Alī enforced *ḥadd* punishment in such cases. In the days of 'Umar there ensued a fight between two people whereby one said to the other: 'Neither my father was an adulterer nor my mother an adulteress.' The matter was brought before 'Umar. He asked the audience what they made of the comment. Some said that the person concerned had paid a compliment to his own parents, without necessarily calling into question the character of the adversary's parents. Others, however, disagreed and took strong exception to the words in which the statement was made. For them, the statement implied that the parents of his adversary were guilty of adultery. 'Umar concurred with the latter view and awarded the *ḥadd* punishment for *qadhf* to the accuser. (See Jaṣṣāṣ, *Aḥkām al-Qur'ān*, vol. 3.)

There is a difference of opinion about whether one becomes guilty of *qadhf* when one accuses someone of sodomy. Abū Ḥanīfah does not consider this accusation to be *qadhf* whereas Abū Yūsuf, Muḥammad ibn al-Ḥasan al-Shaybānī and Shāfi'ī do so.

(v) There is disagreement among jurists about whether *qadhf* is a cognizable offence or not. Ibn Abī Laylā is of the opinion that a person guilty of *qadhf* should be punished regardless of whether the victim of the accusation makes the plea for the accuser's punishment or not. However, Abū Ḥanīfah and others of his school are of the opinion that once someone is convicted of *qadhf*, he will be awarded the same punishment. The initiation of judicial proceedings against the accuser, however, is contingent upon the wish of the victim. The same view is held by Shāfi'ī, Aḥmad ibn Ḥanbal and Awzā'ī. As for Mālik, he considers it a cognizable offence if it is committed in the presence of the judge; otherwise the prosecution of the accuser depends upon the victim's claim.

(vi) *Qadhf* is not a compoundable offence. If the victim does not ask for the initiation of legal proceedings, then such proceedings will not be initiated. However, once the complaint is admitted, the accuser will be required to substantiate his charge by providing due evidence. If he fails to do so, he will be punished for *qadhf*. But once legal proceedings start, neither the court nor the accused may pardon the accuser. Nor will the payment of damages be admissible. Nor will the culprit be spared *ḥadd* punishment by his repenting or tendering an apology for his offence. We have already mentioned the ruling of the Prophet (peace be upon him) in this respect: 'Settle cognizable offences among yourselves. However, if a case involving *ḥadd* is brought to my attention, [a decision on the matter] becomes obligatory.' (See Abū Dā'ūd, *K. al-Ḥudūd*, 'Bāb al-'Afw 'an al-Ḥudūd mā lam tabligh al-Sulṭān' – Ed.)

vii. According to the Ḥanafīs, the plea to enforce *ḥadd* punishment for *qadhf* may either be made by the victim himself, or in his absence by those whose descent and lineage are adversely affected, for example by his parents, children or grandchildren. Muḥammad ibn al-Ḥasan al-Shaybānī and Shāfi'ī, however, consider it a hereditary right. Hence, if the victim dies, any of his heirs may plead that the prescribed punishment be awarded the offender. It is somewhat strange that Shāfi'ī excludes husband and wife from his category of legitimate claimants on the grounds that death severs the matrimonial tie and that if any of the spouses is subjected to *qadhf*, the other's descent is not damaged.

Both these points are hardly convincing. Once this claim is recognized as a hereditary right, the contention that death brings the relationship between husband and wife to an end is contrary to the Qur'ān itself. For the Qur'ān considers each of the two spouses to inherit the other. It is contended that if a spouse is slandered, this does not damage the descent of the other spouse. This may be correct in the case of the husband, but it is certainly not correct in the case of the wife. For if a woman is slandered, the descent of all her children becomes doubtful. Moreover, it is inappropriate to think that the punishment for *qadhf* is prescribed only in consideration of the adverse impact it has on some people. An accusation of unlawful sexual intercourse damages the descent, honour and reputation of the victims to the accusation. It is indeed absolutely dishonourable for a decent person to find that his/her life-partner be branded as morally dissolute and profligate. In short, since the claim for *qadhf* punishment is a hereditary right, there seems no valid ground to exclude spouses from the category of its legitimate claimants.

viii. Once someone is convicted of *qadhf*, the only thing which can redeem and save him from the *ḥadd* punishment is that he be able to produce four witnesses who testify that they saw the person accused of unchastity actually commit unlawful sexual intercourse with such and such a person. According to the Ḥanafī school, these four witnesses should appear in court together and testify to the same. If they appear one by one, each would be guilty of *qadhf*, and the acquital of each would again require a set of four witnesses.

This, however, does not seem that persuasive. The correct legal position is the one held by Shāfi'ī and 'Uthmān al-Battī who state that all that is required of the four witnesses is that they should corroborate the accusation that has been made. Whether these witnesses testify together or separately does not make any material difference. In fact, they are of the opinion that it is even preferable if the witnesses appear and testify separately, one after the other as is usual in other cases. The Ḥanafīs are of the opinion that in order for the accuser not to be punished for *qadhf*, he is required to produce four witnesses, but it is not essential that they be upright. As long as the accuser is able to produce four witnesses, even four *fāsiq* witnesses, he will be acquitted of *qadhf*. Similarly, a victim of an unchastity charge will also not be subjected to *ḥadd* punishment for *zinā* just because the witnesses were not *'ādil* (upright). However, he who is guilty of *qadhf* may not escape *ḥadd* punishment if he produces as witnesses those who are either non-Muslims, blind, slaves, or are of those who have been convicted of *qadhf* in the past.

Shāfi'ī is of the opinion that if a person accuses someone of committing unlawful sexual intercourse and produces only *fāsiq* persons as witnesses, both the accuser and his witnesses should be awarded the *ḥadd* punishment for *qadhf*. This opinion is also shared by Mālik.

The Ḥanafī position on this question, however, seems more plausible: if the witnesses are upright (*'ādil*) the accuser will be acquitted of the *qadhf* charge and the charge of unlawful sexual intercourse will be established against the person so accused. But if the witnesses are not upright, their testimonies become doubtful. Hence, it is no longer certain that the accuser committed *qadhf*, that the person accused of unchastity committed *zinā*, or that the statements made by the witnesses are necessarily true or false. Because of this element of doubt none will be considered liable to *ḥadd* punishments.

ix. If the accuser fails to produce the evidence required to bring about his acquittal from *qadhf*, the Qur'ān lays down three penalties: (a) that he who is guilty of *qadhf* be flogged 80 lashes; (b) that his testimony not be accepted ever after; and (c) that he be branded as a transgressor (*fāsiq*). This mention of the punishment is followed by the statement: 'Except those of them that repent thereafter and mend their behaviour. For surely Allah is Most-Forgiving, Ever Compassionate.'

This naturally raises the question which of the three above-mentioned punishments will be waived if the person convicted of *qadhf* repents and mends his ways? Jurists are agreed that if a person repents and reforms himself, the first consequence of *qadhf* definitely applies; that is, the *ḥadd* punishment of 80 lashes will not be voided by the culprit's repentance and self-reform. There is also a consensus among jurists that the exception mentioned in the verse pertains to the last-mentioned consequence of *qadhf*.

In other words, he who repents and mends his behaviour will no longer be considered a *fāsiq* (transgressor), and that God will indeed pardon him.

The only difference of opinion on this question among jurists relates to whether a person becomes guilty of *qadhf* as soon as he commits that offence or when the charge of *qadhf* is established against him. Shāfi'ī and Layth ibn Sa'd are of the opinion that by the mere commitment of *qadhf* a person renders himself unfit to testify. On the other hand, Abū Ḥanīfah and the jurists of his school as well as Mālik believe that a person is to be regarded as a transgressor (*fāsiq*) only after he is convicted. Before such a conviction, he may testify. It seems more plausible that one becomes a transgressor (*fāsiq*) in the sight of God as a result of indulging in *qadhf*, but only after being convicted of *qadhf* does a person become a transgressor in the eyes of the general public.

Now we come to the injunction whereby the testimony of the person found guilty of *qadhf* should ever, in the future, be accepted. There is considerable disagreement among jurists on whether this applies even to those who repented and reformed themselves after being convicted of *qadhf*. Some hold the view that while such persons no longer remain transgressors (*fāsiq*) in the sight of God and men, nevertheless the first two commandments mentioned here will be applied to them: namely that they will be awarded the *ḥadd* punishment for *qadhf* and their testimony will, henceforth, never be accepted.

This opinion is held by Shurayḥ, Sa'id ibn al-Musayyab, Ḥasan al-Baṣrī, Ibrāhīm al-Nakha'ī, Muḥammad ibn Sīrīn, Makḥūl, 'Abd al-Raḥmān ibn Zayd, Abū Ḥanīfah, Abū Yūsuf, Zufar, Muḥammad ibn al-Ḥasan al-Shaybānī, Sufyān al-Thawrī and Ḥasan ibn Ṣāliḥ.

Another group of jurists, however, take a different view. According to them, the person guilty of *qadhf* will be subjected to *ḥadd* punishment despite his repenting and reforming himself. However, because of his repentance and self-reform, he will neither be regarded as a *fāsiq*, nor will his testimony be rejected. Those who subscribe to this opinion include 'Aṭā', Ṭā'ūs, Mujāhid, Sha'bī, Qāsim ibn Muḥammad, Sālim, Zuhrī, 'Ikrimah, 'Umar ibn 'Abd al-'Azīz, Ibn Abī Nujayḥ, Sulaymān ibn Yasār, Masrūq, Ḍaḥḥāk, Mālik ibn Anas, 'Uthmān al-Battī, Layth ibn Sa'd, Shāfi'ī, Aḥmad ibn Ḥanbal and Ibn Jarīr al-Ṭabarī.

In substantiating their viewpoint the latter group adduce, apart from other arguments, the judgement pronounced by 'Umar ibn al-Khaṭṭāb in the case of Mughīrah ibn Shu'bah. There are some traditions which mention that after the *ḥadd* punishment was meted out to the guilty, 'Umar said to Abū Bakrah and his two associates: 'If you repent [or, in a variant version, if you admit that you had levelled a false charge], I will accept your testimony in the future; but if you do not, I will not accept your testimony.' The other two confessed that they had indeed levelled a false charge, but Abū Bakrah stuck to his original position.

Apparently this is a weighty argument in favour of this legal opinion. However, when we carefully consider the available account of this particular case, it becomes quite clear that it is not appropriate to cite the above precedent on the question under discussion. For in this particular case there was no disagreement with regard to the incident concerned and even Mughīrah ibn Shu'bah did not deny it.

The matter under dispute concerned the identity of the woman involved in the incident. Mughīrah mistook her for Umm Jamīl. It was well established that there was a great deal of resemblance between the two women, i.e. Mughīrah's wife and Umm Jamīl, and since the person observed them from some distance and at a time when the light was poor, it was difficult for him to make out who the woman concerned was. Hence, there was some ground to believe that the person concerned was Umm Jamīl.

As for the circumstantial evidence, this supported Mughīrah's contention. One of the prosecution witnesses also acknowledged that it was difficult to clearly make out the identity of the woman in question. It was on this basis that 'Umar decided the case in favour of Mughīrah ibn Shu'bah and not Abū Bakrah. In these circumstances, it can be appreciated that 'Umar's intention was to impress upon the accusers that they had levelled a serious charge on the basis of a misperception. He also wanted to drive home to them that they should repent for their actions and come forth with the assurance that they would desist from such acts in the future, or their testimony would never again be admitted.

This does not justify the conclusion that even the testimony of the person who is proved to be lying in his charge of unchastity against others will be accepted if he repents. The fact is that on this question the opinion of the former group of jurists seems to carry greater weight. For the truth of a person's repentance is known only to God. Hence, if a person publicly repents, all that we can do is not call him a *fāsiq* in the future. It would be inappropriate though to start trusting the word of the person who proved himself to be untrustworthy simply on the grounds that he publicly uttered the words: 'I repent.'

Moreover, if we consider the manner in which the relevant Qur'ānic verse is phrased, the exception expressed by the words 'except those of them that repent thereafter' only pertains to them being called *fāsiq*. We are led to this conclusion by the fact that the command to flog those convicted of *qadhf* with 80 lashes, and not to admit their testimony thereafter have been expressed in the imperative form. On the other hand, the statement that those who repent of falsely accusing people of sexual misconduct is given as a piece of information: namely that they are 'transgressors except those of them that repent and mend their behaviour'.

The sequence of these statements clearly indicates that the exception that is made relates to their being transgressors. That is, had they not repented they would be considered as transgressors. But since they did repent, they cease to be transgressors. Even if we concede that the exception is not strictly confined to the last part of the verse, we can find no reasonable grounds to believe that the exception should apply only to the command to 'never admit their testimony' but not to the command to flog them.

x. Here one may ask: why should the exception expressed by the words 'those who repent and mend their behaviour' not apply to all three things mentioned in the verse: namely, meting out the punishment of flogging, not accepting the testimony of the person guilty of *qadhf*, and regarding him as *fāsiq*?

It may be argued that since *qadhf* amounts to defaming someone, why should the false accuser not be fully acquitted after (a) he confesses his guilt, (b) he tenders an apology to the victim of *qadhf*, (c) he repents of the wrong that he has done and assures everyone that he will never do the same again? This line of argument is apparently strengthened by the following words of the Qur'ān: 'They are indeed transgressors except those of them that repent thereafter and mend their behaviour. For surely Allah is Most Forgiving, Ever Compassionate.' One may say to this that it would be strange indeed for God to pardon such persons while His creatures should refuse to do so.

In response, it should be pointed out that repentance does not simply consist of uttering a few words of remorse. Instead, it consists of a man's sincere feelings of grief at his fault, combined with a resolve to adopt righteous conduct in the future. Hence, repentance does not enable a man to escape worldly punishments; it may, however, lead him to escape the punishment of the Hereafter. Hence God does not say [in the Qur'ān] that if a criminal repents, he need not be punished. What is said instead is that in respect of those who repent, God will be 'Most Forgiving, Ever Compassionate.'

xi. It is pertinent to point out that if someone fails to substantiate his charge by due evidence, this does not necessarily mean that he was lying. For it is possible that even though his charge is correct he might be unable to furnish the evidence required to establish it. Is it fair that such a person be held as a transgressor (fasiq) not only in the sight of men but also in the sight of God simply because he was unable to back up his charge, one which might have been true, with the evidence required?

The explanation for this is that even if a person saw an act of moral corruption being committed, he is still sinful if he goes about publicizing it or if he accuses the person concerned of the offence without being able to establish it with due evidence. If some act of corruption is confined to a little corner of life, the *Sharī'ah* does not approve of someone embarking on a campaign to bring that knowledge to everyone's attention. If a person knows that such corruption exists, two options are available to him. First, he should let it remain where it is; and second, he should establish with due evidence to the rulers of the Islamic State that corruption exists so that they may be able to root it out. There are, however, only these two options, no more. If someone were to start publicizing such things, he would be guilty of spreading that corruption all around. Furthermore, if he charges someone with an offence as grave as *zinā* without providing due evidence his failure to establish the charge leads to further spread of corruption and it also emboldens the corrupt to engage in acts of corruption. Hence, he who charges someone with unchastity without providing due evidence is certainly a *fāsiq* even though in point of fact he may be telling the truth.

xii. As regards the punishment for qadhf, Hanafi jurists are of the opinion that a person so convicted be flogged more lightly than the person convicted for *zinā*. The number of lashes though should remain 80. This is understandable since it is not absolutely certain that the accuser was a liar.

xiii. What should the punishment be for the person who commits qadhf more than once? The Hanafis and the majority of jurists are of the opinion that he should only be punished once, regardless of the number of times that he levels the charge against the person concerned before he is punished or during the time that he is punished. Not only that, if he persists in his charge even after the execution of the sentence of punishment against him, the *ḥadd* once meted out is deemed enough. However, if he levels the charge of another act of unlawful sexual intercourse against the same person after the punishment has been meted out, a new case will be instituted against him. After being subjected to *ḥadd* punishment in Mughirah's case, Abu Bakrah continued to say publicly: 'I affirm that Mughirah had committed unlawful sexual intercourse.' 'Umar considered prosecuting him again. However, since Abu Bakrah was reiterating the same charge he had levelled earlier, 'Ali expressed the view that a new case could not be instituted against him. 'Umar accepted this advice of 'Ali's. Subsequently, there developed a near consensus among jurists that a qadhif, who had been punished for failing to prove his charge of unchastity could not be prosecuted for repeating the charge for which he had been punished. He may be prosecuted afresh only if he levelled a new charge.

xiv. There is disagreement among jurists about what punishment ought to be awarded to the person who, instead of accusing just one other, accuses a group of people of *zinā*. According to the Ḥanafīs, if someone charges several people with unchastity, regardless of whether he uses one word or several words to level

(7) and a fifth time, that the curse of Allah be on him if he be lying (in his accusation). (8) And the punishment shall be averted from the woman if she were to testify, swearing by Allah four times that the man was lying, (9) and a fifth time that the wrath of Allah be on her if the man be truthful (in his accusation).[7] ▶

وَٱلْخَٰمِسَةُ أَنَّ لَعْنَتَ ٱللَّهِ عَلَيْهِ إِن
كَانَ مِنَ ٱلْكَٰذِبِينَ ﴿٧﴾ وَيَدْرَؤُا۟ عَنْهَا
ٱلْعَذَابَ أَن تَشْهَدَ أَرْبَعَ شَهَٰدَٰتٍۭ بِٱللَّهِ
إِنَّهُۥ لَمِنَ ٱلْكَٰذِبِينَ ﴿٨﴾ وَٱلْخَٰمِسَةَ
أَنَّ غَضَبَ ٱللَّهِ عَلَيْهَآ إِن كَانَ
مِنَ ٱلصَّٰدِقِينَ ﴿٩﴾

that charge, he should be punished only once. This providing he does not come forward with a new charge to the same effect. This accords with the following words of the verse: 'Those who accuse chaste, honourable women [of unchastity] . . .' (*al-Nūr* 24: 4). We, thus, learn that he who slanders a whole group of people will be punished only once. This is significant in view of the fact that unlawful sexual intercourse involves at least two people. Despite the involvement of those two people, the *Sharī'ah* prescribes no more than a single *ḥadd* punishment rather than one *ḥadd* for accusing a man and another *ḥadd* for accusing a woman. Nonetheless, Shāfi'ī is of the opinion that anyone who is guilty of slandering a group of people, either in one or several words, should be punished separately for each and every accusation against all those who comprise that group. The same opinion is held by 'Uthmān al-Battī. However, Ibn Abī Laylā holds the same view as Sha'bī and 'Awzā'ī, namely that if someone charges in a single statement a group of people with unlawful sexual intercourse he will be subjected to a single punishment. However, anyone who makes separate statements regarding each member of the group, accusing each of them of committing unlawful sexual intercourse, will be liable to a punishment in respect of each person whom he has accused.

7. There is a time lapse between the revelation of the preceding verses and the present ones. After the punishment for *qadhf* was laid down in the Qur'ān the minds of the people were vexed by a question. They said that when someone observes that a man and a woman unrelated to him are engaged in acts of immorality, it is not difficult for him to be patient. In other words, someone can easily restrain himself from speaking about

the whole incident, indeed disregard it entirely, when no witnesses are available to testify to it. Yet what should be done if this person were to see his own wife engaged in unlawful sex? If he killed her, he would be liable to punishment. If he decided to go and find four witnesses to observe the offence, it is inconceivable that the culprit would stay around long enough to enable this observation to occur. It is not easy, though, for someone to observe such a thing with regard to his wife and still remain patient. True, in such a case, the husband certainly can exercise his option to divorce his wife. But were he to do so neither that perverse woman nor her partner in the adultery would have suffered any punishment whether moral or material. Additionally, if the woman becomes pregnant as a result of that unlawful act, the husband would have to assume responsibility for bringing up that child. This hypothesis was first put forward by Sa'd ibn 'Ubādah, i.e. what would he do if he were placed in such an unenviable position? He said that if he so found his wife involved in an act of adultery he would not go about finding witnesses to the act. He would rather bring the matter to an end by having recourse to his sword. (Bukhārī, *K. al-Ḥudūd*, 'Bāb man ra'ā ma' Imra'tih Rajulan fa qatalah' – Ed.)

Shortly after this, several cases arose whereby husbands found themselves in such a position and these instances were reported to the Prophet (peace be upon him). It is narrated on the authority of 'Abd Allāh ibn Mas'ūd and 'Abd Allāh ibn 'Umar that one of the *Anṣār*, perhaps 'Uwaymir al-'Ajlānī, came to the Prophet (peace be upon him) and said: 'O Messenger of God! If someone finds another person with his wife and reports it, you will subject him to the punishment for *qadhf*. If he kills her, you will put him to death. If he remains silent, he will be consumed by rage. What should he do then?' Thereupon the Prophet (peace be upon him) prayed to God for guidance. (Bukhārī, *K. al-Tafsīr*, *Sūrah al-Nūr*, 'Bāb wa al-Khāmisah anna la'nat Allāh 'alayh in kāna min al-Kādhibīn' and Muslim, *K. al-Li'ān* – Ed.) It is narrated by 'Abd Allāh ibn 'Abbās that Hilāl ibn Umayyah reported that he had personally seen his wife commit adultery. Upon this the Prophet (peace be upon him) said: 'Bring witnesses or else you will be prosecuted for *qadhf*.' This agitated the Companions. Hilāl said: 'By God Who has sent you as a Messenger to us, I am telling the truth. I saw this incident with my own eyes, and heard it with my ears. I am sure that God will reveal an injunction in my case that will save my back [from flogging].' The present verse was revealed on this particular occasion. (Bukhārī, *K. al-Tafsīr al-Qur'ān*, *Sūrah al-Nūr*, 'Bāb wa yudra' 'anhā al-'Adhāb an-tashhad Araba'a'h Shahādāt bi Allāh innahū la-min al-Kādhibīn' – Ed.)

The method of dealing with this problem is known as *li'ān*. After revelation of this rule the Prophet (peace be upon him) dealt with similar cases in accordance with it and detailed reports about the same can be found in works of *Ḥadīth*. The *Ḥadīth*, in any case, are the best source of information on the detailed rules and procedures pertaining to *li'ān*.

The details of Hilāl ibn Umayyah's case are available in *Ḥadīth* works and Ṭabarī's *Tafsīr.* It is related on the authority of 'Abd Allāh ibn 'Abbās and Anas ibn Mālik that after this verse was revealed both Hilāl and his wife were brought to the Prophet (peace be upon him). The Prophet (peace be upon him) first mentioned God's command which had been revealed, adding: 'Do you realize that the punishment in the Hereafter is much more grievous than the one in this life?' Hilāl said: 'My charge against her is absolutely true.' Hilāl's wife, however, totally denied it. The Prophet (peace be upon him) then said that the two should take an oath. Accordingly, Hilāl rose first, taking the oath in accordance with the Qur'ānic rule. While he was so doing the Prophet (peace be upon him) repeatedly said: 'God knows that one of you is certainly a liar. Then will either of you repent?' Before Hilāl took the oath for the fifth time, those present said to him: 'Fear God. Punishment in this life is lighter than the one in the Next. This fifth oath will incur God's punishment on you.' Yet Hilāl said: 'God Who has saved me here will not punish me in the Hereafter', and so saying, he took the final oath.

It was then his wife's turn. Just as she was about to take the final oath, she was interrupted with the following words: 'Fear God. It is easier to bear punishment in this life than in the Next. This final oath will incur God's punishment on you.' On hearing this, she paused, hesitating a little. The audience at this point thought that she was about to confess her sin but instead she said: 'I will not bring abiding dishonour to my tribe.' So saying, she took the final oath.

The Prophet (peace be upon him) then effected a separation between them and resolved that her child, whom she had recently conceived, would be known as her child, and not as the child of her husband. Yet no one would be able to accuse her of not being chaste or her child of being illegitimate. If anyone were to do so they would be awarded the punishment for *qadhf*. Hilāl's wife would not be entitled to maintenance or the right of residence in her husband's house during the period of *'iddah* for she was now separated from her husband without this being caused by either divorce or his death. The Prophet (peace be upon him) then told people to closely observe the features of the child after its delivery. If it resembled Hilāl, it would thus be his child. Conversely, if it resembled the person accused of adultery, it would be his. After the child's birth, it was found that it resembled the person accused of adultery. On learning this, the Prophet (peace be upon him) exclaimed: 'But for these oaths [or the Qur'ānic command which has already decided the matter], I would have dealt very differently with this woman.' (See Bukhārī, *K. Tafsīr al-Qur'ān*, *Sūrah al-Nūr*, 'Bāb wa yudra' 'anhā al-'Adhāb an-tashhad Araba'a'h Shahādāt bi Allāh innahū la-min al-Kādhibīn' – Ed.)

Detailed proceedings of another case which relates to Uwaymir al-'Ajlānī are recorded in Bukhārī, Muslim, Abū Dā'ūd, Nasā'ī, Ibn Mājah and Aḥmad ibn Ḥanbal on the authority of Sahl ibn Sa'd al-Sā'idī and 'Abd Allāh ibn 'Umar. According to these traditions, 'Uwaymir al-'Ajlānī and his wife were both called to the Prophet's Mosque. Before they were asked to take an oath against each other, the Prophet (peace be upon him) warned them three times: 'God knows full well that one of you is certainly a liar. Will then either of you repent?' When neither did so, both were made to take oaths and 'Uwaymir further said: 'O Messenger of God, if I ever keep this woman I will be lying.' Saying this he divorced her even before the Prophet (peace be upon him) had effected a separation between them. As reported by Sahl ibn Sa'd, the Prophet (peace be upon him) then said: 'This separation is for each such couple that resorts to *li'ān* (mutual cursing).'

Since then it has been the practice that couples who resort to *li'ān* are separated with the stipulation that they may never remarry. 'Abd Allāh ibn 'Umar, however, says only that the Prophet (peace be upon him) effected a separation between the two. There is an additional piece of information in Sahl ibn Sa'd's account that the woman was pregnant and 'Uwaymir claimed that the conception was not a result of any act of his. (See Bukhārī, *K. Tafsīr al-Qur'ān, Sūrah al-Nūr*, 'Bāb wa al-Khāmisah anna La'nat Allāh 'alayh in kāna min al-Kādhibīn' and 'Bāb Qawlih 'azza wa jalla: Wa al-ladhīna yarmūna Azwājahum wa lam yakun lahum Shuhadā' . . .' Ed.) Accordingly, the child was ascribed to the mother alone. The legal doctrine since then has been that such a child, to wit, a child whose mother's husband disowns being the father of that child, inherits only his mother and that she alone inherits him (i.e. to the exclusion of the woman's husband).

Several other such cases are reported in works of *Ḥadīth*. These traditions, however, do not specify the names of the parties concerned. Possibly some are related to the two cases already cited. Some traditions, however, mention additional cases and shed light on important points pertaining to *li'ān*.

In reporting one case, 'Abd Allāh ibn 'Umar adds that after the couple had resorted to *li'ān*, the Prophet (peace be upon him) effected a separation between them. (See Bukhārī, *K. al-Tafsīr al-Qur'ān*, *Sūrah al-Nūr*, 'Bāb Qawlih ta'ālā anna Ghaḍab Allāh 'alayhā in kāna min al-Ṣādiqīn' – Ed.) There is another tradition from the same authority, 'Abd Allāh ibn 'Umar, to the effect that a husband and wife took the oaths of *li'ān*. The husband contended that his wife's pregnancy was not by him. Here, too, the Prophet (peace be upon him) effected a separation between them, declaring that the child would be ascribed to the mother alone.

There is yet another tradition on the authority of 'Abd Allāh ibn 'Umar whereby after the *li'ān* proceedings, the Prophet (peace be upon him) said: 'Both of you are accountable to God, and one of you is certainly a liar.' He then said to the husband: 'She is not yours any longer. You have no [conjugal] rights with respect to her. Nor may you commit any excesses nor take any vindictive action against her.' The husband said: 'O Messenger of God! Help me get back my money [i.e. the bridal-due which he paid her].' The Prophet replied: 'You have no right to reclaim your money. If you are true in your charge, then that money is the recompense for the pleasure you legitimately derived from her. On the other hand, if you have lied against her, you are even farther removed from your money; that money is now farther from you than it is from her.' (Bukhārī, *K. al-Ṭalāq*, 'Qawl al-Imām li al-Mutalā'inayn inna Aḥadakumā Kādhib fa hal minkumā Tā'ib min' – Ed.)

Dāraquṭnī has quoted the following opinion of 'Alī ibn Abī Ṭālib and 'Abd Allāh ibn Mas'ūd: 'The principle that has been established is that spouses who resort to *li'ān* may never come together again [i.e. they may never remarry].' Dāraquṭnī also narrates a tradition from 'Abd Allāh ibn 'Abbās that the Prophet (peace be upon him) himself said: 'Such a couple may never come together again [that is they may never remarry].'

It is reported by Qabīṣah ibn Dhuwayb that someone declared that his wife's pregnancy was not by him. Later he retracted his statement. After the child was born he again claimed that the child was not his. The case was put before 'Umar ibn al-Khaṭṭāb who prosecuted him for *qadhf* and then issued a judgement that the child would be ascribed to him (Dāraquṭnī and Bayhaqī).

'Abd Allāh ibn 'Abbās reported that someone came to the Prophet (peace be upon him) and submitted: 'I have a wife whom I love very much but she does not shrug away anyone's hand.' It is noteworthy that this was a metaphorical expression meaning either adultery on the part of the wife or something rather less. The Prophet (peace be upon him) asked him to divorce her. In response, he said that he could not live without her. The Prophet (peace be upon him) then told him to keep her and did not ask him to elaborate upon the implication of his earlier statement. Thus, the Prophet (peace be upon him) did not necessarily accept the statement to mean that the person concerned charged his wife with adultery, nor did he order *li'ān* in this case.

Abū Hurayrah reports that a bedouin came to the Prophet (peace be upon him) saying: 'My wife has given birth to a child of dark complexion. I do not think it is my child.' The bedouin's suspicion was based merely on the child's complexion. He did not have any other grounds to suspect his wife of adultery. The Prophet (peace be upon him) asked him: 'Do you have any camels?' He replied in the affirmative. The Prophet then asked him to specify the colour of his camels. He said that they were of a reddish colour. The Prophet then further asked him if he also had any brown camels, and the bedouin replied in the affirmative. The Prophet (peace be upon him) then asked him to explain how the colour of the camels had become different from one another. To this the man replied that it might be an hereditary consequence. The Prophet (peace be upon him) responded that the dark complexion of his child could also be an hereditary factor. The Prophet (peace be upon him) thus, did not allow the bedouin to disown the paternity of the child. (See Bukhārī, *K. al-Ḥudūd*, 'Bāb mā jā' fī al-Tawlīd' – Ed.)

There is another tradition on the authority of Abū Hurayrah that the Prophet (peace be upon him) while commenting on the Qur'ānic verse relating to *li'ān*, said: 'God has nothing to do with a woman who conceives an unlawful child and makes him part of the family though he does not belong to it. God will not admit her to Paradise. In like manner, the husband who disowns the paternity of his child, the while the child looks on at him, God will conceal Himself from such a person on the Day of Judgement and will humiliate him before the creatures of all times.' (See Abū Dā'ūd, *K. al-Ṭalāq*, 'Bāb al-Taghlīz fī al-Intifā' – Ed.)

The Islamic Law of *li'ān* is based on the present verse along with the above-mentioned statements of the Prophet (peace be upon him) and the general principles of the *Sharī'ah*. In light of the above, jurists have elaborated a set of laws on this question, the most mentionable of which are as follows:

i. There is disagreement among jurists with regard to the husband who personally observes his wife commit adultery and kills her rather than taking recourse to *li'ān* oaths. One group says that capital punishment will be meted out to him because he was not authorized to execute the punishment of his own accord. Another group, however, say that he is not to be awarded capital punishment. Nor will he be blamed providing his charge is proved to be true. In other words, if it is established that the person concerned murdered his wife and he was provoked into so doing by having observed his wife commit adultery. Aḥmad ibn Ḥanbal and Isḥāq ibn Rāhawayh are of the opinion that the person concerned will have to produce two witnesses to testify that the reason for killing his wife was her act of adultery. Among the Mālikīs, Ibn al-Qāsim and Ibn Ḥabīb mention another condition as well, namely that the person so murdered should be married. If an unmarried person is so killed, the murderer will be subjected to *qiṣāṣ*. However, the majority of jurists are of the view that he would be spared *qiṣāṣ* only if he produces four witnesses who testify to the adultery. The accuser may also be spared *qiṣāṣ* if the person whom the accused had killed after observing him commit adultery with his wife admits commiting adultery with the accuser's wife or that the person so killed, provided they are unmarried, confessed during their life-time that they had been guilty of unlawful sexual intercourse with that person's wife.

ii. *Li'ān* is only effective when it is made under the aegis of the court rather than by the parties concerned via their mutual consent.

iii. If a husband accuses his wife of unlawful sex or disowns the paternity of the child, she has the right to seek the intervention of the court and have her husband take the *li'ān* oath. In this respect her right is the same as her husband's.

iv. Can there be *li'ān* between every couple, or is it subject to certain conditions? Jurists have different opinions on this question. According to Shāfi'ī, anyone whose oath is legally admissible and who has the right to pronounce divorce may proceed with *li'ān*. In other words, in order to initiate *li'ān* proceedings it is enough that the person concerned be sane and adult. This irrespective of whether the husband and wife are Muslims or non-Muslims, whether they are free or slave, whether their testimony is trustworthy or not, and whether the wife of a Muslim husband is herself a Muslim or a *dhimmī*. The views of Mālik and Aḥmad ibn Ḥanbal on this question are more or less the same. The Ḥanafīs, however, contend that recourse to *li'ān* may be made only in cases of those free Muslim couples who have not been convicted of *qadhf*. If both the husband and the wife are unbelievers, slaves, or have been convicted of *qadhf*, then recourse to *li'ān* may not be made. Moreover, if the wife was previously involved in a relationship which was either clearly of a prohibited nature, or if she is of a doubtful character, then recourse to *li'ān* is not available.

Ḥanafī jurists prescribe these conditions in view of the difference between *li'ān* and *qadhf*. That is that if any person other than the husband commits *qadhf*, he is liable to *ḥadd* punishment, but if the husband makes the same accusation, he may save himself from the *ḥadd* punishment for *qadhf* by having recourse to *li'ān*. In all other respects, the laws relating to *li'ān* and *qadhf* are exactly alike. Moreover, the Ḥanafīs believe that since the oaths in *li'ān* have the same status as evidence then those who are not eligible to testify are also ineligible to take the *li'ān* oaths.

On this question the Ḥanafī position seems weak whereas the Shāfi'ī position appears sound. The first reason for this is that the Qur'ān does not make the question of slandering one's wife a part of the verse which lays down the law of *qadhf*. Instead, the Qur'ān lays down a separate rule for this. Hence, it is not appropriate to treat *li'ān* as a part of the law of *qadhf* and subject it to the conditions pertaining to *qadhf*. The words of the verse dealing with *li'ān* differ from those used in the verse on *qadhf*. The legal rules of the two also vary. Hence, the provisions relating to *li'ān* should only be derived from that verse which deals with *li'ān*. For example, the verse on *qadhf* rules that all those who charge chaste and honourable women with unlawful sex deserve to be punished. *Per contra*, there is no reference to a chaste wife in the verse about *li'ān*.

Let us suppose that some woman had at one time been guilty of sexual misconduct after which she repented and married another man. Now, if her husband makes a false charge of sexual misconduct against her, the Qur'ān does not grant him the licence to accuse his wife of unchasteness, nor to deny the paternity of the child borne by that woman on the grounds that she had once been guilty of unlawful sex. The other highly important reason is that there is a vast difference between one's own wife and any other woman as far as levelling a charge of unlawful sex is concerned. It is natural, therefore, that the spirit of the law with regard to both is bound to vary. For, if a person accuses an unrelated woman with unchasteness, the case is pretty simple because the person has no emotional involvement or emotional ties with her. Furthermore, the charge that he makes against her in no way damages his honour. Nor is there any question of social ties, mutuality of rights and obligations, nor of lineage and descent between him and that woman. If a man is concerned with the moral conduct of such a woman, he is at best moved by the desire to see society free of moral corruption.

On the contrary, a man's relations with his wife exist on a variety of levels and are of a very profound nature. For his wife is a repository of his pedigree and honour, of his property and his home. Being his life partner, his wife is well aware of many of his secrets. This in addition to the fact that the two are bound together by some very profound and fine emotional ties. Were a wife to commit an act of sexual misconduct, this injures her husband's honour and dignity, hurts his most vital interests, and jeopardizes the future of his coming generations. Since the two cases are poles apart, they cannot be governed by the same law. In fact, a person's relationship with his wife is such that even his religious, social and legal status hardly make any difference.

There seems no justification, therefore to distinguish between Muslims and *dhimmīs*, between the free person and the slave, between those whose testimonies are accepted by the court and those whose testimonies are not accepted.

Now, if a *dhimmī*, a slave or anyone who has previously been convicted of *qadhf* observes his wife engage in the sexual act with someone else, or if he comes to believe that his wife has become pregnant as a result of sexual intercourse with some other man, is there any reasonable ground to deny him the right to initiate *li'ān* proceedings? If this right is denied him, what legal remedy exists for such people for the redress of their grievance?

The intent of the Qur'ān is clear enough: it seeks to provide a way out for a couple who have landed themselves in a highly unenviable state. This might either consist of the husband being tormented by belief that his wife is guilty of adultery and/or that she is pregnant as a result of her illicit relations with someone else. Alternatively, the wife might be agonized by her husband's charge of unchasteness against her, or his denial, without justification, of the paternity of her child fathered by him. Such a situation calls for a way out for all those concerned and not only for those who are free, Muslims, and whose evidence is admissible in court. Now, can we find any indication in the Qur'ān that restricts the application of the *li'ān* law to any particular group of people to the exclusion of others?

It is also argued that the Qur'ān has characterized the oath of *li'ān* as testimony (see verses 6–9). It is contended, therefore, that the conditions of testimony have to be fulfilled in the case of *li'ān* as well. In view of the above, if an *'ādil* (trustworthy) husband whose testimony is admissible in court were to take the oath of *li'ān* while his wife failed to do so, the woman should be lapidated since due evidence has been provided that she was guilty of adultery. It is astonishing that the Ḥanafīs do not believe that in such a case lapidation should be carried out. This goes to show that the Ḥanafīs do not regard the *li'ān* oath as equivalent to testimony. The fact is that the Qur'ān, notwithstanding its use of the word *shahādah* for these oaths (see verses 6–9), does not regard them as evidence in the strict sense of the word or else it would have asked the woman to take the oath eight rather than four times.

v. *Li'ān* is not required in cases where a charge is made only in a figurative sense, or when it is expressed as something that one suspects rather than something which one is fully sure about. It is required only if the husband clearly and unambiguously charges his wife with adultery, or unequivocally disowns the child borne by his wife to be his. Mālik and Layth ibn Sa'd suggest an additional condition: that at the time of taking the oath the husband should say that he himself saw his wife commit adultery. This addition, however, has no sound basis. Moreover, it is supported neither by the Qur'ān nor any *ḥadīth*.

vi. According to Abū Ḥanīfah and other jurists of his school, if the husband who has charged his wife with adultery refrains from taking the *li'ān* oaths, he should be imprisoned until he confesses that he has levelled a false charge. He should not be released unless he does so, and once he has he will be awarded the *ḥadd* punishment for *qadhf*. On the other hand, Mālik, Shāfi'ī, Ḥasan ibn Ṣāliḥ and Layth ibn Sa'd are of the opinion that his refraining from taking the oath amounts to his admitting that he was lying, and this requires that the person concerned be subjected to the *ḥadd* punishment for *qadhf*.

vii. According to the Ḥanafīs, if the wife declines to take the *li'ān* oaths after her husband has done so, she should be imprisoned and not released until she either takes the required oaths or confesses that she committed adultery. In the latter case, she should be lapidated. The Ḥanafīs justify this on the basis of the Qur'ānic statement that the woman will be spared punishment only if she takes an oath (see verses 7–9). However, since she declines to take the oath, she must of necessity be punished.

This view though is flawed since the Qur'ān does not specify any particular punishment. It only speaks of punishment as such. As for the opinion that it can only mean *ḥadd* punishment for *zinā*, it should be pointed out that the Qur'ān lays down the condition of four witnesses for such a punishment to be awarded. This condition is not met by the oaths taken by a single person even if they be taken four times. The husband's oaths suffice to save him from the *ḥadd* punishment for *qadhf* and that the laws of *li'ān* be applied to his wife. Yet, these oaths are not sufficient in themselves to establish that the wife was guilty of adultery. Were she to take counter oaths, this would cast serious doubt on the whole case. Now, as we know, whenever there is any doubt, *ḥadd* punishment cannot be awarded.

Such a case should not be considered analogous to the *qadhf* committed by the husband, for that *qadhf* is fully established. It is precisely because there is no doubt about his having committed *qadhf* that he is required to take *li'ān* oaths. However, the oaths of the husband are not sufficient to prove that the wife committed adultery. Such a case can only be conclusively established by her own confession or by the testimony of four witnesses.

viii. According to Aḥmad ibn Ḥanbal, if the wife is pregnant at the time of *li'ān*, the act of *li'ān* itself suffices to release the husband from the responsibility of the pregnancy and the child subsequently borne by his wife will not be reckoned as his child, regardless of whether the husband explicitly denied his role in his wife's pregnancy or not. Shāfi'ī, however, is of the opinion that the husband's charge of adultery against his wife and his disowning responsibility for his wife's pregnancy are not one and the same. Unless the husband disowns the pregnancy, the child will be reckoned as his notwithstanding the charge of adultery he levelled against his wife. For even if the wife is found to have committed adultery, this does not prove *ipso facto* that she conceived the child as a result of that adultery.

ix. Mālik, Shāfi'ī and Aḥmad ibn Ḥanbal grant the husband the right to disown his responsibility from pregnancy during the period of that pregnancy, and permit *li'ān* on that basis. Abū Ḥanīfah, however, believes that if the husband does not specifically accuse his wife of adultery, but simply claims that he found his wife pregnant in such circumstances that the pregnancy could not have been via him, then *li'ān* proceedings should be deferred until the child is born. For occasionally cases of false or phantom pregnancy arise.

x. In case a father disowns paternity of the child, this is unanimously considered to warrant *li'ān*. Likewise, there is a consensus among jurists that if a father accepts paternity of the child, even once, whether explicitly or implicitly, he forfeits the right to disown the child later on. If he does so, he incurs the punishment prescribed for *qadhf*. How long the father has the right to do so, however, is a disputed matter. According to Mālik, if the father was present during the period of his wife's pregnancy, he has the right to disown the child during this period. Thereafter, he ceases to have such a right. However, if he was away from his wife and the baby was born during his absence, he may disown the child on learning about its birth. In Abū Ḥanīfah's view, if he disowns the child a day or two after its birth and initiates *li'ān* proceedings, the husband will be exempt from the responsibility of bringing up the child. However, if he disowns the child after some considerable period, for example one year after the child's birth, the responsibility of bringing up that child remains his. In Abū Yūsuf's opinion, the father has the right to disown the child up until 40 days after its birth, or up until 40 days after his knowing about its birth. But he loses that right thereafter. The specific limit of 40 days that has been fixed in this connection, however, is pointless. The sound position on this question seems to be Abū Ḥanīfah's, namely that the father should disown the child within a day or two after its birth or after receiving such news. This period may be extended on grounds that are plausible.

xi. If after divorcing his wife the ex-husband still accuses her of adultery, this does not warrant *li'ān*. Instead he will be prosecuted for *qadhf*. Since *li'ān* is a provision for spouses and the divorced wife has ceased to be a spouse, *li'ān* rules do not apply to her. The only exeption that can be allowed in this connection is in the case of a revocable divorce, provided that such a charge was levelled within the period during which the husband had the right to revoke the divorce. According to Mālik, *qadhf* only arises if the question of pregnancy or parentage is not at issue. For, in such a case, the husband retains the right to initiate *li'ān* proceedings even after *ṭalāq bā'in* (divorce that nullifies the marriage). He may have recourse to *li'ān* not to bring his divorced wife into disrepute, but only in order to be relieved from the responsibility of bringing up a child which he does not consider his own. Almost the same view is held by Shāfi'ī.

xii. There is consensus among jurists in the cases of *li'ān* that the spouses become immune from any punishment. They also concur that if the husband disowns the paternity of the child then the

> child is ascribed to the wife alone. In such a case, it will not be regarded as its father's child, nor will it inherit him. It will inherit its mother and its mother will inherit it. Jurists also agree that no one will be allowed to call that woman an adulteress, or the child illegitimate even though the circumstances obtaining at the time of *li'ān* might indicate that the woman was indeed guilty of adultery.

Other areas of agreement among jurists are as follows. First, if anyone reiterates the old charge of adultery against the woman, or brands the child as illegitimate after *li'ān*, he will receive the *ḥadd* punishment for *qadhf*. Second, the wife does not forfeit her bridal-money as a result *of li'ān*. She is, however, not entitled to maintenance and accommodation which are prerequisites during her *'iddah*. Third, the wife is no longer lawful for her husband; i.e. he no longer has any right to conjugal relations with her.

As regards areas where jurists disagree with one another, the first is as to how the separation between husband and wife comes into effect after *li'ān*. The next disputed question is whether the couple can remarry after having been separated as a result of *li'ān*.

As regards the former question, namely how the separation between the spouses comes into effect after *li'ān*, Shāfi'ī is of the opinion that once the husband completes the *li'ān* proceedings, the wife stands separated from him regardless of whether she has taken the counter oaths or not. According to Mālik, Layth ibn Sa'd and Zufar, however, the separation comes into effect after both the husband and wife have completed the *li'ān* procedures. Abū Ḥanīfah, Abū Yūsuf and Muḥammad ibn al-Ḥasan al-Shaybānī believe that *li'ān* does not in itself bring about separation. It is rather the courts that effect separation. It is better if the husband himself divorces his wife or else the judge will announce such a separation.

Let us consider the question as to whether the spouses who are separated as a result of *li'ān* can ever remarry. Mālik, Abū Yūsuf, Zufar, Sufyān al-Thawrī, Isḥāq ibn Rāhawayh, Shāfi'ī, Aḥmad ibn Ḥanbal and Ḥasan ibn Ziyād are of the opinion that they stand forbidden for each other for ever. Even if they mutually agree on remarriage, they are not entitled to do so. 'Umar, 'Alī and 'Abd Allāh ibn Mas'ūd also share the same opinion. On the contrary, Sa'īd ibn al-Musayyab, Ibrāhīm al-Nakha'ī, Sa'īd ibn Jubayr, Abū Ḥanīfah and Muḥammad ibn al-Ḥasan al-Shaybānī argue that if the husband subsequently admitted that his earlier statement was false, and if he received the *ḥadd* punishment for *qadhf*, then they could remarry. In their opinion, what makes the former husband and wife forbidden is *li'ān*. Hence, they remain forbidden for each other as long as the *li'ān* lasts. However, once the husband admits that he made a false statement and receives his due punishment for the same, the *li'ān* is voided, and, thus, the restriction on their remarrying ends.

(10) Were it not for Allah's Bounty and His Mercy unto you and that Allah is much prone to accept repentance and is Wise, (you would have landed yourselves into great difficulty on the question of unsubstantiated accusation of your spouses).

(11) Surely those who invented this calumny[8] ▶

وَلَوْلَا فَضْلُ ٱللَّهِ عَلَيْكُمْ وَرَحْمَتُهُۥ
وَأَنَّ ٱللَّهَ تَوَّابٌ حَكِيمٌ ۝١٠ إِنَّ
ٱلَّذِينَ جَآءُو بِٱلْإِفْكِ

8. This alludes to the charge levelled against 'Ā'ishah. The use of the word *ifk* (calumny) amounts to the total negation of the charge by God Himself. For *ifk* literally means to revert a statement, or to alter something making it divergent from the fact. Hence, this word is a synonym for a blatant lie or slander. Employed in the context of a charge, it denotes fabricating a calumny against someone.

The present verse marks the beginning of the discourse which relates to the incident which prompted this *sūrah*'s revelation. In the introduction to the *sūrah*, we have presented a detailed account of the incident in 'Ā'ishah's own words. That account, however, related to the earlier part of the incident. What follows now is the later part of the narration, and it is again given in 'Ā'ishah's own words:

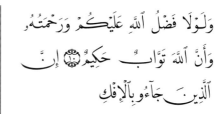

> Reports about the slander had been in circulation in Madina for almost a month. It made the Prophet (peace be upon him) suffer great anguish. I and my parents too were in great distress and felt much disturbed. Finally, the Prophet (peace be upon him) came and sat beside me. During all this period he had not sat beside me. [My parents] Abū Bakr and Umm Rūmān both felt that some decision was at hand. Hence, they too joined me. The Prophet (peace be upon him) said: 'O 'Ā'ishah, I have received such and such report about you. If you are innocent, I hope God will proclaim your innocence. If you have committed a sin, you should turn to God and seek His pardon. When a servant of God confesses his sin and repents, God pardons him.' On hearing this my tears dried up. I requested my father to say something on my behalf. He said that he did not know what to say. I made the same request to my mother who said that she was too perplexed to say anything. Then I said: 'Something has reached your ears which seems to have convinced you. If I plead my innocence – and God knows that I am innocent – you will not believe me.

> And if I confess something which I have not done – and God knows that I did not do any such thing – you will believe me.' [I tried to recall the name of Prophet Jacob (peace be upon him) but could not do so]. Then I said that in such circumstances I have no other option but to say what had been said by the Prophet Joseph's father: 'So I will be graciously patient' (*Yūsuf* 12: 83). [This statement alludes to the false charge of stealing against Jacob's son Benjamin.] After saying this, I lay down and turned my side to the other direction. I told myself that since God knows my innocence, He will make the truth evident. It had not occurred to me though that God would proclaim my innocence by revealing a *sūrah* which would be recited till the Last Day. I did not consider myself worthy enough to be exonerated by God [in such a manner]. What I thought was that the Prophet (peace be upon him) would see in a dream that God had exonerated me. In the meanwhile, the Prophet was observed to be in the state in which he received the revelation. Even in extreme cold his face used to be covered with sweat. All of us became quiet. I was devoid of all fear. However, my parents were extremely anxious. They were fearful about the revelation, fearing what would come out of it. When the Prophet (peace be upon him) recovered from this state he was much delighted. Smiling, he exclaimed: 'Congratulations 'Ā'ishah! God has exonerated you.' Then the Prophet recited ten verses of this *sūrah* [i.e. verses 11–21]. My mother asked me to rise and thank the Prophet (peace be upon him). To this I replied: 'I will neither thank him nor you [my parents]; I thank God Who has proclaimed my innocence. You never even repudiated the slander against me.'

It is worth clarifying that the above account is not drawn from a single tradition; rather it is a summary of all the traditions about this incident narrated by 'Ā'ishah and recorded in various works of *Ḥadīth* and *Sīrah*. (See Bukhārī, *K. Tafsīr al-Qur'ān*, *Sūrah al-Nūr*, 'Bāb law lā idh sami'tumūh ẓann al-Mu'minūn wa al-Mu'mināt bi Anfusihim Khayrā' (verse 12) – Ed.)

At this point attention should be drawn to a point that is somewhat subtle. The proclamation of 'Ā'ishah's innocence was preceded by a whole section devoted to injunctions pertaining to *zinā, qadhf* and *li'ān*. This seems to intend that accusations against anyone regarding their sexual misconduct should not be taken lightly. It is far too grave an allegation to be used for social entertainment. Anyone who accuses another person of adultery should be ready to produce the required number of witnesses to testify to it. If he does so, those convicted of unlawful sexual relations – be they men or women – will be severely punished. But if the accuser is lying, then he certainly deserves to receive 80 lashes so that he and others like him are deterred from making such false statements. In case such a charge is levelled by the husband, he will have to go through the procedure of

are a band from among you.[9] Do not deem this incident an evil for you; nay, it is good for you.[10] Every one of them has accumulated sin in proportion to his share in this guilt; ▶	عُصۡبَةٌ مِّنكُمۡۚ لَا تَحۡسَبُوهُ شَرًّا لَّكُمۖ بَلۡ هُوَ خَيۡرٌ لَّكُمۡۚ لِكُلِّ ٱمۡرِيٕٖ مِّنۡهُم مَّا ٱكۡتَسَبَ مِنَ ٱلۡإِثۡمِۚ

li'ān in the courts. In other words, no one can hurl such an accusation at others and go about lightly as if nothing serious had happened.

9. Only a few people have been identified in the traditions as those who went about spreading rumours. These are 'Abd Allāh ibn Ubayy, Zayd ibn Rifā'ah (who was probably the son of Rifā'ah ibn Zayd, a Jewish hypocrite), Misṭaḥ ibn Uthāthah, Ḥassān ibn Thābit, and Ḥamnah bint Jaḥsh. Two of these, namely 'Abd Allāh ibn Ubayy and Zayd ibn Rifā'ah were hypocrites. The rest, however, were believers who out of some weakness or error became a party to this mischief. As for any others who might have had a hand in this affair, the works of *Ḥadīth* and *Sīrah* fail to identify them or the roles they might have played.

10. This is intended to comfort the Prophet (peace be upon him). He is being assured that this malicious campaign of slander, which had been engineered by the hypocrites, is bound to boomerang upon them. They, themselves, thought that this would be a significant blow to the Prophet. In point of fact, however, it was destined to hurt the enemies of the Prophet and to prove useful for his cause.

As we have pointed out in the introductory part of this *sūrah*, the hypocrites deliberately mounted this onslaught, seeking to damage the moral esteem of the Muslims, and it is in this very domain that the superiority of the Muslims was incontrovertible. In fact, it was precisely because of their moral superiority that the Muslims had excelled their rivals in every field. God in His Wisdom turned the tables on the enemies of Islam and made even this incident a blessing for the Muslims. On this occasion, the conduct of the Prophet as well as Abū Bakr's and the members of his family and the Muslims at large proved beyond any shadow of a doubt how far removed the Muslims were from moral evil, how restrained, forbearing, gracious and strongly disposed they were to fairness and justice. The Muslims were so strongly devoted to the Prophet (peace be upon him) that even a slight hint from him would have made them behead those who had dared to launch a malicious attack against his honour. Thereafter, after God's proclamation had been made, the Prophet had only three Muslims punished on the grounds that they were guilty of *qadhf*.

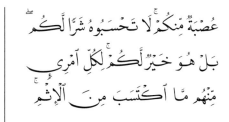

As for the hypocrites, he took no action against them. Misṭaḥ, who was a relative of Abū Bakr and from whom he used to receive financial support, had taken a leading part in this slander campaign and yet Abū Bakr proved his graciousness and magnanimity by not severing his familial and social ties with him. Nor did he stop his financial aid to Misṭaḥ and his family. The other wives of the Prophet (peace be upon him) neither provided any encouragement to the slander campaign against 'Ā'ishah nor did they endorse it. Even Zaynab, whose sister Ḥamnah bint Jaḥsh was a party to this campaign, if at all she uttered any words about the matter, they were words of praise and appreciation of 'Ā'ishah. According to 'Ā'ishah's own account, among all the wives of the Prophet it was with Zaynab whom her relations were mutually rivalrous. Nevertheless, during this period the Prophet once asked Zaynab's opinion about 'Ā'ishah, and Zaynab's reply was: 'O Messenger of God, by God I know nothing in 'Ā'ishah except goodness.' (See Bukhārī, *K. Tafsīr al-Qur'ān*, *Sūrah al-Nūr*, 'Bāb law lā idh sami'tumūh . . .' (verse 12) – Ed.)

'Ā'ishah's own graciousness is evident from the fact that she always treated Ḥassān ibn Thābit with much respect and consideration. This despite that fact that he had played a prominent role in the campaign launched against her. When some people drew her attention to Ḥassān's role in maligning her, she silenced them by saying that Ḥassān's verses had effectively warded off the attacks of the enemies against Islam and the Prophet (peace be upon him). (See Bukhārī, *K. Tafsīr al-Qur'ān*, *Sūrah al-Nūr*, 'Bāb . . . yubayyinu Allāh lakum al-Āyāt' (verse 18) – Ed.)

We have so far discussed the role of those people directly involved in the incident. Let us now turn to the generality of Muslims. Their excellent moral standards are brought into sharp relief in the following report about Abū Ayyūb al-Anṣārī and his wife. When she told him about the slanderous charges that were in circulation, Abū Ayyūb said: 'O mother of Ayyūb, had you been in 'Ā'ishah's place, would you have done such a thing?' To this she replied: 'By God, I would have never done so.' Abū Ayyūb continued: ' 'Ā'ishah is much better than you. Had I been in place of Ṣafwān, such an outrageous thought would not have even crossed my mind. And Ṣafwān is a much better Muslim than I.'

Thus, the hypocrites' hopes were dashed to the ground. Contrary to their expectations, the moral superiority of the Muslims shone even more brightly in the wake of this incident.

Another redeeming feature occasioned by the incident was the addition of several injunctions, laws and social regulations. Thanks to these, it lies within the power of the Muslim society to keep itself immune from the rise and spread of evil and to expeditiously curb such evil if and when it does raise its head.

Another good that ensued from this incident was that it made the Muslims realize that the Prophet (peace be upon him), with all his spiritual and he who has the greater part of it[11] shall suffer a mighty chastisement. ▶

وَالَّذِي تَوَلَّىٰ كِبْرَهُۥ مِنْهُمْ لَهُۥ عَذَابٌ عَظِيمٌ ﴿١١﴾

loftiness and the very special mission bestowed upon him by God, did not have access to the realm that lies beyond sense-perception. All that he knew pertaining to this realm consisted of what God Himself chose to acquaint him with. Unless God revealed anything pertaining to this realm, the Prophet's knowledge was like that of any other human being. We note that for one full month the Prophet (peace be upon him) remained in great anguish. Sometimes he would ask his maid servant, then his other wives, and then 'Alī and Usāmah about the matter. Likewise, he told 'Ā'ishah: 'If you have committed this act, you should repent and if you are not guilty, God will proclaim your innocence.' If he had known the Unseen, he would not have conducted such an investigation, nor would he have asked 'Ā'ishah to repent. It was only God Who clarified the whole matter and the Prophet (peace be upon him) came to know – thanks to His revelation – what he had been unable to know for a whole month.

This enabled the Muslims to learn by direct experience that they should abstain from that exaggerated and excessive veneration which had characterized the attitude of the followers of other religions towards their religious leaders. Presumably God had delayed revealing the truth of this matter for one full month in order to drive this point home to the Muslims. Had the whole matter been instantly revealed this lesson would probably not have been imparted so effectively.

11. This is an allusion to 'Abd Allāh ibn Ubayy who had concocted the calumnious allegation and who was the master-mind behind the slander campaign. Some traditions mistakenly identify Ḥassān ibn Thābit as the one to whom this verse alludes. However, such a view stems from a misunderstanding on the part of the narrators of those traditions. As for Ḥassān ibn Thābit, at the very most his lapse constituted no more than his being carried away by the propaganda campaign launched by the hypocrites. Ibn Kathīr is quite right in saying that had there not been a tradition in Bukhārī on this matter implicating Ḥassān ibn Thābit it would not even have been worth considering.

The greatest lie, rather the greatest calumny in this connection is the statement by Hishām ibn 'Abd al-Malik, the Umayyad Caliph, that the present verse refers to 'Alī. It is reported in Bukhārī, Ṭabarānī and Bayhaqī that Hishām ibn 'Abd al-Malik considered the words *al-ladhī tawallā kibrahū* to refer to 'Alī ibn Abī Ṭālib. However, 'Alī was not at all involved in the incident. All that happened was that 'Alī found the Prophet (peace be upon him)

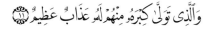

(12) When you heard of it, why did the believing men and women not think well of their own folk[12] ▶	لَّوْلَآ إِذْ سَمِعْتُمُوهُ ظَنَّ ٱلْمُؤْمِنُونَ وَٱلْمُؤْمِنَٰتُ بِأَنفُسِهِمْ خَيْرًا

highly agitated about the matter and that he asked 'Alī for advice. On this occasion 'Alī said that God had placed no restriction on the Prophet (peace be upon him) in this matter. There were many women and if he so wished, he might divorce 'Ā'ishah and marry some other woman. This did not mean at all that 'Alī endorsed the slanderous charge that had been made against 'Ā'ishah. 'Alī's only concern was that the distress of the Prophet (peace be upon him) should come to an end.

12. Alternatively, this may be translated as 'why did believing men and women not think well of their own folk'. Both translations seem equally sound. Moreover, there seems a subtlety in the phrasing of the verse which we should attempt to grasp. The bare facts of the incident relating to 'Ā'ishah and Ṣafwān ibn al-Mu'aṭṭal are as follows: A lady,[1] who was a member of a caravan, was left behind and so was a male member of the caravan, who later saw her and asked her to mount his camel. Now, for someone to believe that the two necessarily engaged in a sinful relationship assumes other things. First, that if he (or she) had been placed in the same position he/she would necessarily have committed that sin, because if he/she did not commit that sinful act it was because no member of the other sex was available to him/her in a similar circumstance. Had that been available, he/she would certainly have availed himself/herself of the opportunity to engage in sinful conduct. Second, that his/her impression about the society to which he/she belongs is that all its members, male or female, are so degenerate that they would not shrink from making use of any opportunity to act sinfully.

This would be the presupposition if the man and woman were strangers to one another. But the matter becomes far more grave if they happened to come from the same place. For in such a case the woman who was accidentally left behind by the caravan would either be the wife, sister or daughter of one of the man's friends, relatives, neighbours or acquaintances. In that case, it would mean that the accuser holds a very poor opinion of his own society – a society that is absolutely devoid of moral values. For it is unthinkable for a decent person to come across a woman belonging to the family of a friend, relative or acquaintance, and that the first thing he does is violate her honour.

In this particular case, such an assumption is in fact far more outrageous. For the woman in question was none other than a wife of the Prophet (peace be upon him) and every Muslim regards the wives of the Prophet as

and say: "This is a manifest calumny?"[13] (13) Why did they not bring four witnesses ▶	وَقَالُواْ هَـٰذَآ إِفۡكٌ مُّبِينٌ ﴿١٢﴾ لَّوۡلَا جَآءُو عَلَيۡهِ بِأَرۡبَعَةِ شُهَدَآءَ

even more honourable than his own mother. In fact, all the wives of the Prophet had been made absolutely forbidden to the Muslims, forbidden in the same way as their own mothers. Moreover, such an assumption was being entertained about a person who was in the same caravan, who was a soldier of the same army, and who was an inhabitant of the same town. Above all, he was a Muslim who believed that the husband of the woman in question was none other than the Messenger of God, one upon whom he looked as his guide and leader, one at whose command he had put his own life at stake in a battle as dangerous as that of Badr.

Viewed against this background, the utter outrageousness of the mental disposition which prompted this accusation can be seen in its full starkness. Hardly anything could have been more degrading and despicable. It is for this reason that God characterizes those who levelled this accusation as those who form a very poor estimate of themselves as well as a very poor estimate of the character and conduct of other members of their society.

13. That is, the idea was too ignoble even to be considered for a moment. Every Muslim should have dismissed it outright as a blatant lie, as a piece of mischievous fabrication, as an outrageous calumny. It might well be asked then, that if it was such an outrageous lie, why did the Prophet (peace be upon him) and Abū Bakr not deny it on the very first day and why did they attach such importance to it?

A husband and a father in such a situation have a position that is different from that of others. No one knows a woman better than her husband, and a sane husband cannot be misled by a slander campaign against his righteous and pious wife. However, if his wife is made the target of such a campaign, he is not in the best position to dismiss it out of hand, branding it a baseless calumny. Such an attitude is likely to provide grounds for the false notion that the husband is too hen-pecked to be able to dispassionately consider the relevant facts about his wife.

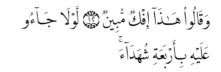

In like manner, parents are also exposed to the same difficulty. Their out-of-hand dismissal of an accusation against their daughter helps little to clarify their daughter's position. For their rejection of the charge is likely to be taken as a mere expression of parental love and affection. This then is what consumed the Prophet (peace be upon him) as also Abū Bakr and his wife Umm Rūmān. Obviously, they did not have the slightest doubt about 'Ā'ishah's character and conduct. As for the Prophet (peace be upon him), he publicly declared, in his address, that he had seen nothing bad in support of their accusation? Now that they have brought no witnesses, it is indeed they who are liars in the sight of Allah.[14] (14) Were it not for Allah's Bounty and His Mercy unto you in the world and in the Hereafter a grievous chastisement would have seized you on account of what you indulged in. (15) (Just think, how wrong you were) when one tongue received it from another and you uttered with your mouths something you knew nothing about. You deemed it to be a trifle while in the sight of Allah it was a serious matter.

فَإِذْ لَمْ يَأْتُوا۟ بِٱلشُّهَدَآءِ فَأُو۟لَـٰٓئِكَ عِندَ ٱللَّهِ
هُمُ ٱلْكَـٰذِبُونَ ﴿١٣﴾ وَلَوْلَا فَضْلُ ٱللَّهِ
عَلَيْكُمْ وَرَحْمَتُهُۥ فِى ٱلدُّنْيَا وَٱلْـَٔاخِرَةِ
لَمَسَّكُمْ فِى مَآ أَفَضْتُمْ فِيهِ عَذَابٌ عَظِيمٌ
﴿١٤﴾ إِذْ تَلَقَّوْنَهُۥ بِأَلْسِنَتِكُمْ وَتَقُولُونَ
بِأَفْوَاهِكُم مَّا لَيْسَ لَكُم بِهِۦ عِلْمٌ وَتَحْسَبُونَهُۥ
هَيِّنًا وَهُوَ عِندَ ٱللَّهِ عَظِيمٌ ﴿١٥﴾

either in 'Ā'ishah's character or in Ṣafwān's. (See Bukhārī, *K. al-Maghāzī*, 'Bāb Ḥadīth al-Ifk' – Ed.)

14. 'In the sight of Allah' here means 'according to the Law of Allah'. For God obviously knew full well that the accusation was absolutely false. The falsity of the accusation did not rest on the fact that the accusers failed to produce witnesses.

There should be no misunderstanding at this stage that the charge was rejected just on the grounds that it was not substantiated by the evidence of witnesses. Nor are Muslims being asked to regard that charge as a calumnious slander merely on the grounds that it was not borne out by the testimony of four witnesses. Such a misunderstanding could arise if one fails to grasp the nature of the incident. The accusers had not levelled the allegation because they themselves, or any others, had observed the monstrosity which they claimed had taken place. They built up such a large charge merely on the grounds that 'Ā'ishah, who had been left behind, was subsequently brought back by Ṣafwān on his camel.

No sensible person can even consider that 'Ā'ishah's being left behind was part of some pre-arranged scheme. Anyone who contrived such a

(16) And why, no sooner than you had heard it, did you not say: "It becomes us not even to utter such a thing? Holy are You (O Allah)! This is a mighty calumny." (17) Allah admonishes you: If you are true believers, never repeat the like of what you did. (18) Allah clearly expounds to you His instructions. Allah is All-Knowing, All-Wise.[15]

(19) Verily those who love that indecency should spread among the believers deserve a painful chastisement in the world and the Hereafter.[16] ▶

وَلَوْلَآ إِذْ سَمِعْتُمُوهُ قُلْتُم مَّا يَكُونُ لَنَآ أَن
نَّتَكَلَّمَ بِهَٰذَا سُبْحَٰنَكَ هَٰذَا بُهْتَٰنٌ
عَظِيمٌ ﴿١٦﴾ يَعِظُكُمُ ٱللَّهُ أَن تَعُودُوا۟ لِمِثْلِهِۦٓ
أَبَدًا إِن كُنتُم مُّؤْمِنِينَ ﴿١٧﴾ وَيُبَيِّنُ ٱللَّهُ
لَكُمُ ٱلْءَايَٰتِ ۚ وَٱللَّهُ عَلِيمٌ حَكِيمٌ ﴿١٨﴾ إِنَّ
ٱلَّذِينَ يُحِبُّونَ أَن تَشِيعَ ٱلْفَٰحِشَةُ فِى ٱلَّذِينَ
ءَامَنُوا۟ لَهُمْ عَذَابٌ أَلِيمٌ فِى ٱلدُّنْيَا وَٱلْءَاخِرَةِ ۚ

---

scheme would not have committed the obvious mistake of appearing with 'Ā'ishah in broad daylight to rejoin the caravan which had by then pitched camp. The actual chain of events itself points to the innocence of both 'Ā'ishah and Ṣafwān. In such circumstances if any charge could have been so levelled it would have been only on the grounds of first-hand observation of the incident. For there was absolutely no *prima facie* ground, no circumstantial evidence, to support such a serious charge.

15. These verses, and especially God's reproach embodied in these words: '. . . why did the believing men and women not think well of themselves . . . ?' are very significant. In fact they provide an important general principle: that all affairs of the Muslim society be based on the reciprocity of good faith. What this means is that unless proved otherwise, a Muslim should hold a good opinion about other Muslims. The basic principle is that a person should be deemed innocent unless there are reasonable grounds to believe that he is guilty, or at least that there are grounds to suspect him of being guilty. Likewise, every person is true in whatever he says unless there exist grounds to believe otherwise.

16. In this context the meaning of the verse is that those who engage in fabricating and publicizing shameful allegations so that Muslim society

Allah knows, but you do not know.[17] (20) Were it not for Allah's Bounty and His Mercy unto you, and that Allah is Most Forgiving and Wise, (the evil that had been spread among you would have led to terrible consequences).

(21) Believers! Do not follow in Satan's footsteps. Let him who follows in Satan's foot-steps (remember that) Satan bids people to indecency and evil. Were it not for Allah's Bounty and His Mercy unto you, ▶

وَٱللَّهُ يَعْلَمُ وَأَنتُمْ لَا تَعْلَمُونَ ﴿١٩﴾ وَلَوْلَا
فَضْلُ ٱللَّهِ عَلَيْكُمْ وَرَحْمَتُهُۥ وَأَنَّ ٱللَّهَ
رَءُوفٌ رَّحِيمٌ ﴿٢٠﴾ ۞ يَٰٓأَيُّهَا ٱلَّذِينَ ءَامَنُوا۟
لَا تَتَّبِعُوا۟ خُطُوَٰتِ ٱلشَّيْطَٰنِ ۚ وَمَن يَتَّبِعْ
خُطُوَٰتِ ٱلشَّيْطَٰنِ فَإِنَّهُۥ يَأْمُرُ بِٱلْفَحْشَآءِ
وَٱلْمُنكَرِ ۚ وَلَوْلَا فَضْلُ ٱللَّهِ عَلَيْكُمْ وَرَحْمَتُهُۥ

succumbs to immoral ways and its moral stature is undermined, deserve to be punished. The words used in the verse embrace all the various forms that might be used to spread moral corruption and lewd behaviour including those means employed to awaken sexual passion, be they poetry, song, fiction, pictures, plays and drama. These also include clubs and hotels which provide dancing and other forms of obscene entertainment involving the mixed participation of men and women. The Qur'ān declares such people to be criminals, those who deserve punishment not only in the Hereafter but also in this world. It is, therefore, the responsibility of an Islamic State to extirpate all the means which promote obscenity. The penal law of an Islamic State should declare these as cognizable offences since the Qur'ān characterizes them as crimes against public order. In the same vein, the Qur'ān prescribes punishments for all those who are guilty of such offences.

17. Man might not know, but God certainly does, the adverse effects such acts have on society and Muslims should, therefore, trust God and devote all their energy and resources to putting an end to the evils which have been identified by Him. These are not minor offences which might be overlooked. Rather, they are grave and those guilty of them should be severely punished.

not one of you would have ever attained purity.[18] But Allah enables whomsoever He wills to attain purity. Allah is All-Hearing, All-Knowing.[19]

(22) Let those among you who are bounteous and resourceful not swear to withhold giving to the kindred, to the needy, and to those who have forsaken their homes in the cause of Allah; rather, let them forgive and forbear. Do you not wish that Allah should forgive you? Allah is Ever Forgiving, Most Merciful.[20]

مَا زَكَىٰ مِنكُم مِّنْ أَحَدٍ أَبَدًا وَلَٰكِنَّ ٱللَّهَ
يُزَكِّي مَن يَشَآءُ ۗ وَٱللَّهُ سَمِيعٌ عَلِيمٌ ﴿٢١﴾
وَلَا يَأْتَلِ أُو۟لُوا۟ ٱلْفَضْلِ مِنكُمْ وَٱلسَّعَةِ
أَن يُؤْتُوٓا۟ أُو۟لِى ٱلْقُرْبَىٰ وَٱلْمَسَٰكِينَ
وَٱلْمُهَٰجِرِينَ فِى سَبِيلِ ٱللَّهِ ۖ وَلْيَعْفُوا۟
وَلْيَصْفَحُوٓا۟ ۗ أَلَا تُحِبُّونَ أَن يَغْفِرَ ٱللَّهُ
لَكُمْ ۗ وَٱللَّهُ غَفُورٌ رَّحِيمٌ ﴿٢٢﴾

---

18. Satan is determined to bog man down in the filth of evil. Had God, out of His sheer Grace and Benevolence, not made what is good distinct from what is evil and had He not shown man the Right Way and enabled him to reform himself accordingly, no one would have been able to purify his own life merely on the basis of his native endowments.

19. God does not arbitrarily endow people with the ability to purify themselves. Rather, He does so on the basis of His knowledge as to who sincerely seeks the Right Way and who seeks error. So pervasive is God's knowledge that He hears what people say in their own privacy and He knows the ideas that cross a man's mind. Hence, God decides on a sound and solid basis whom He enables to purify himself and whom He does not.

20. 'Ā'ishah reports that after her exoneration by the Qur'ān, Abū Bakr discontinued the financial help he provided to Misṭaḥ ibn Uthāthah. This he did because Misṭaḥ showed neither consideration for kinship nor felt ashamed in acting so wickedly towards his daughter despite Abū Bakr's munificence to him and his family. It was against this backdrop that the above verse was revealed. On hearing it Abū Bakr instantly cried out: 'Yes, Allah! We do want You, Our Lord, to forgive us.' (See Bukhārī, *K. Tafsīr al-Qur'ān, Sūrah al-Nūr*, 'Bāb inna al-ladhīna yuḥibbūn 'an tashī'

(23) Those that accuse chaste, unwary,[21] believing women, have been cursed in the world and the Hereafter, ▶	إِنَّ ٱلَّذِينَ يَرْمُونَ ٱلْمُحْصَنَٰتِ ٱلْغَٰفِلَٰتِ ٱلْمُؤْمِنَٰتِ لُعِنُوا۟ فِى ٱلدُّنْيَا وَٱلْءَاخِرَةِ

al-Fāḥishah' – Ed.) He then resumed his financial help to Misṭaḥ and did so on an even bigger scale.

According to 'Abd Allāh ibn 'Abbās, some other Companions, in addition to Abū Bakr, vowed not to extend any help to those who had taken part in the slander campaign. But after the revelation of this verse they too recanted their vow. Thus the bitterness and hostility which had been engendered by the slander campaign instantly dissipated.

Here we may also consider a legal question: if someone takes a vow and later realizes that there is no good in it, should he honour the vow or break it and make expiation for it? According to some jurists such expiation (*kaffārah*) is not required. That a person opts for that which is good in itself constitutes the expiation for breaking the vow. They support this opinion by referring to this verse and point out that God directed Abū Bakr to break his vow without asking him to make any expiation for so doing. Moreover, they cite the following statement made by the Prophet (peace be upon him) in support of their view: 'If someone vows and later realizes that the other option is better, he should go for the better option and that constitutes its expiation.'

Another group of jurists, however, refer to the categorical injunctions of the Qur'ān about breaking a vow (see *al-Baqarah* 2: 225 and *al-Mā'idah* 5: 89). The verse under discussion neither abrogates nor categorically modifies this injunction. Hence, it should be considered as still being in force. Moreover, in the verse under discussion God asked Abū Bakr to break his vow but He did not specify that he was exempt from the expiation necessitated by such an act. As for the Prophet's statement, it implies that the sin incurred by making an improper vow is atoned for by opting for that which is better. The statement does not mean though that if one adopts the preferable option, one need not expiate oneself for breaking the vow. In another *ḥadīth* the Prophet (peace be upon him) says: 'He who vows and later realizes that something is better than that, he should follow what is better and make expiation for his broken vow.' We thus learn that expiation for breaking a vow is one thing, but expiation for the sin of not doing good is quite another. Taking a better option when one realizes that such is available in preference to what one had vowed constitutes the expiation for the earlier mistake. As for the expiation for breaking one's vow, this is laid down in the Qur'ān. (See *Tafhīm al-Qur'ān*, vol. 4, *Sūrah Ṣād* 38, n. 46.)

21. The word *ghāfilāt* is used in this verse to characterize believing women [who have been subjected, despite their excellent character, to outrageous accusations]. They are described here as simple, straightforward,

وَلَهُمْ عَذَابٌ عَظِيمٌ ﴿٢٣﴾ يَوْمَ تَشْهَدُ عَلَيْهِمْ
أَلْسِنَتُهُمْ وَأَيْدِيهِمْ وَأَرْجُلُهُم بِمَا كَانُوا يَعْمَلُونَ
﴿٢٤﴾ يَوْمَئِذٍ يُوَفِّيهِمُ اللَّهُ دِينَهُمُ الْحَقَّ
وَيَعْلَمُونَ أَنَّ اللَّهَ هُوَ الْحَقُّ الْمُبِينُ ﴿٢٥﴾
الْخَبِيثَاتُ لِلْخَبِيثِينَ وَالْخَبِيثُونَ لِلْخَبِيثَاتِ ۖ
وَالطَّيِّبَاتُ لِلطَّيِّبِينَ وَالطَّيِّبُونَ لِلطَّيِّبَاتِ ۚ
أُولَٰئِكَ مُبَرَّءُونَ مِمَّا يَقُولُونَ ۖ

and a mighty chastisement awaits them. (24) (Let them not be heedless of) the Day when their own tongues, their hands, and their feet shall all bear witness against them as to what they have been doing.[22] (25) On that Day Allah will justly requite them, and they will come to know that Allah – and He alone – is the Truth, the One Who makes the Truth manifest. (26) Corrupt women are for corrupt men, and corrupt men for corrupt women. Good women are for good men, and good men for good women. They are innocent of the calumnies people utter.[23] ▶

honourable and decent women who are void of all the cunning that characterizes women of bad character. They are essentially so good that they are not even aware of devious ways of corruption and how people go about them. Being essentially good they are unable to imagine that people would make them targets of outrageous accusations of sexual misconduct. The Prophet (peace be upon him) branded the slandering of chaste women as among the seven deadly sins. A tradition in Ṭabarānī on the authority of Ḥudhayfah mentions that the Prophet (peace be upon him) said: 'To slander a chaste woman nullifies all one's good deeds of one hundred years.'

22. For further details see *Tafhīm al-Qur'ān*, vol. 4, *Yā Sīn* 36, n. 55 and *Fuṣṣilat* 41, n. 25.

23. This verse expounds a general principle: that evil men and evil women make a good match. Likewise, righteous men are instinctively drawn towards righteous women in their choice of life-partners. Anyone who is disposed towards evil, never stops at doing just one evil act. Instead, his conduct and habits embrace the whole gamut of evil that supports and nourishes him. For it is not possible for evil to overtake someone who is

There shall be forgiveness for them and a generous provision.	لَهُم مَّغْفِرَةٌ وَرِزْقٌ كَرِيمٌ ﴿٢٦﴾

otherwise a good person. It is inconceivable for evil to suddenly burst forth from a man whose general conduct and pattern of behaviour display no indications of it.

This psychological fact about people is well known. Now, how can anyone believe that a man of such outstandingly excellent character as the Prophet would put up with and have tender feelings for a woman guilty of gross sexual misconduct? It is, therefore, all the more surprising that some Muslims gave credence to a report which insinuated that someone as pure as the Prophet (peace be upon him) had put up with such a woman. How could the Prophet spend such a long time with her and yet her ways, her gait, her mode of conversation and her gestures not betray her true character? By the same token, is it conceivable that a man possessed of purity of soul and excellent moral character would live happily with a woman of such low character?

This point is made so as to caution Muslims against blindly accepting similar charges in the future. In other words, they would be well advised to critically look into the conduct of the accused, to consider the nature of the accusation and to arrive at some judgement as to whether the incident reported could indeed have taken place or not. There should at least be some *prima facie* ground for the charge that is made. A report cannot be given credence simply on the basis that it has been narrated by someone. If there is some ground for the accusation one may believe it, or at any rate regard it as within the range of possibilities. But if something strange is reported – something for which there seems no supporting basis – it should not be accepted merely because someone – who at any rate might be a fool or scoundrel – has reported it.

Some commentators of the Qur'ān interpret the present verse to mean that evil things are for evil people, meaning thereby that evil things are worthy of evil people. Conversely, good things behove good people, implying that they are to be exonerated of the evil acts attributed to them by their opponents. Other scholars consider this verse to mean that evil deeds are done by evil people whereas good deeds are worthy of being done by good people. Good people are far above the level of evil conduct that is ascribed to them by evil people.

Other scholars interpret the verse to mean that evil deeds are committed by evil people and good deeds by good people. Good people cannot engage in the evil deeds which are ascribed to them by slanderers.

All these meanings may be derived from this verse. It appears, however, that the first meaning is the correct one, especially in view of the context in which it occurs.

(27) Believers![24] Enter not houses other than your own houses until ▶	يَـٰٓأَيُّهَا ٱلَّذِينَ ءَامَنُوا۟ لَا تَدْخُلُوا۟ بُيُوتًا غَيْرَ بُيُوتِكُمْ حَتَّىٰ

24. The injunctions laid down in the early part of this *sūrah* aimed at remedying evils after they had appeared in society. They suggest how to deal with mischief once it has erupted. The injunctions that follow, those laid down in the present and following verses, aim at preventing the rise of evil and mischief. They aim at reforming man's collective life and at removing the causes which give rise to such evil.

Before studying these injunctions, it is necessary to clearly grasp the following points:

i. The laying down of these injunctions immediately after commenting on the slander incident clearly indicates that God viewed the levelling of an utterly false accusation against a person as august as the Prophet's wife and the spread of that accusation to be related to the social milieu, i.e. one which was charged with excessive sexuality. In order to change this sexually-charged milieu, it was necessary that people no longer be free to enter each other's houses; that men and women who were not related to each other should no longer be free to mix with each other; that women not be allowed to appear before unrelated males in a state that might allure the latter; that prostitution be altogether banned; that both men and women be discouraged from leading unmarried lives, and that even slaves, male and female, should be encouraged to marry. In other words, in God's sight the public appearance of women in an alluring manner and the presence of a large number of unmarried people in society were the two main causes which endowed the social milieu with excessive sexuality. (See Abū Dā'ūd, *K. al-Ādāb*, 'Bāb fī al-Isti'dhān' – Ed.) Precisely because of these reasons, people were more willing to indulge in and enjoy scandals, be they real or imaginary. So in order to reform this situation, God in His wisdom laid down injunctions that were most appropriate, most suitable, and most effective.

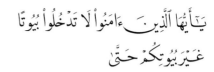

ii. The concerns of the *Sharī'ah* are not confined to forbidding evil and prescribing punishment for those who so commit evil. The *Sharī'ah* rather seeks to remove the causes which either prompt, or create opportunities, or even compel people to indulge in those evils. Apart from forbidding offences, the *Sharī'ah* also seeks to do away with the causes of those offences, as also with the factors that prompt people to commit them. This is done in order to prevent men from getting even close to evil. The role of the *Sharī'ah* is not simply that of a prosecutor, but also of a sincere you have obtained the permission[25] of the inmates of those houses and have greeted them with peace. This is better for you. It is expected that you will observe this.[26] ▶

تَسْتَأْنِسُوا۟ وَتُسَلِّمُوا۟ عَلَىٰٓ أَهْلِهَا ۚ ذَٰلِكُمْ خَيْرٌ لَّكُمْ لَعَلَّكُمْ تَذَكَّرُونَ ﴿٢٧﴾

guide and counsellor. It, therefore, has recourse to all possible educational, moral and social measures so as to help people stay away from evil.

25. The words that are actually used in this verse are *ḥattā tasta'nisū*. They are, however, generally taken to mean *ḥattā tasta'dhinū*. There is, however, a subtle difference between the two expressions which should not be overlooked. Had the Qur'ān used the latter expression it would have meant: 'Do not enter others' houses unless you have obtained the permission of those who live in them.' The Qur'ān, however, opted for the former expression: *ḥattā tasta'nisū*. As it is, the expression is derived from the root word (*alif nūn sīn*), and signifies one's having become familiar and friendly. Taken in this sense, the verse means: 'Do not enter others' houses unless you have become familiar with the inmates of those houses, or until you have ascertained that they feel at ease [at your entering their houses].' In other words, before entering a house one should make sure that the host is favourably disposed to oneself and one's visit. Our translation makes allowance for this subtle nuance. Moreover, in our opinion this interpretation is closer to the import of the verse.

26. In the days of *Jāhilīyah*, the Arabs were accustomed to greeting the occupants of a house with expressions such as حييتم صباحا or حييتم مساء ('good morning' or 'good evening'). So saying, they would barge into each other's houses. Because of this sudden entry into the houses of others, accusationally they would find the occupants, especially women, in improper states. In order to avoid this, God laid down the rule that everyone has a right to privacy in his own house and it is not lawful to enter anyone's private quarters without the latter's consent.

Soon after the revelation of this verse the Prophet (peace be upon him) promulgated certain laws and rules of behaviour, which are mentioned below:

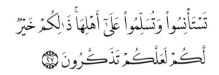

i. The Prophet (peace be upon him) declared the right to privacy a general rule. The result is that a person may not enter someone else's house without the prior consent of its occupant. This right to privacy became quite pervasive. As a result, people were also forbidden to peep into others' houses, or to look at them from the outside, so much so that people were not allowed to read letters addressed to anyone else without his/her permission. According to Thawbān, a freed slave of the Prophet, the Prophet said: 'If someone's sight enters [a person's house] then there remains no occasion for seeking permission [to enter the house].' (Abū Dā'ūd, see *loc. cit.* – Ed.) According to Huzayl ibn Shuraḥbīl, someone came to the Prophet's house and sought permission while standing right in front of the door to the house. The Prophet (peace be upon him) said: 'Stand aside. The permission solicited is the permission to see' (Abū Dā'ūd). When the Prophet (peace be upon him) visited someone he used to make a point of not standing in front of the door for in those days there used to be no curtains at the doors. He would stand on either side of the door and seek permission to enter. (See Abū Dā'ūd, *K. al-Ādāb*, 'Bāb al-kam Marrah yusuallim al-Rajul fī al-Isti'dhān' – Ed.) Anas, who had the honour of serving the Prophet, says that once someone peeped into the Prophet's chamber and that at that moment the Prophet (peace be upon him) had an arrow in his hand. The Prophet advanced towards him as though he was about to pierce the arrow into his belly. (See Abū Dā'ūd, *K. al-Ādāb*, 'Bāb fī al-Isti'dhān' – Ed.) It is also reported by 'Abd Allāh ibn 'Abbās that the Prophet (peace be upon him) said: 'Whoever looks at the letter of his brother without his permission, it is as though he was peeping at the fire.' (See Abū Dā'ūd, *K. al-Ṣalāh*, 'Bāb al-Du'ā' – Ed.)

In works of *Ḥadīth* one also finds the following tradition from the Prophet (peace be upon him): 'If someone peeps into the living quarters of others, and if the latter knocks out his eye by throwing grit, they will not be taken to task for the loss of that person's eye.' (See Bukhārī, *K. al-Diyāt*, 'Bāb man iṭṭala'a fī Bayt Qawm fa faqa'ū 'Aynah . . .' and Muslim, *K. al-Ādāb*, 'Bāb Taḥrīm al-Naẓar fi Bayt Ghayrih' – Ed.) Another *ḥadīth* makes almost the same point: 'If a man peeps into a house, and the dwellers of the house gouge out his eye, they will not be held accountable for the loss of the eye.' (See Abū Dā'ūd, *K. al-Ādāb*, 'Bāb fi al-Isti'dhān' – Ed.)

Shāfi'ī takes this *ḥadīth* in its literal sense, considering it permissible to gouge out the eye of one who peeps into your house. The Ḥanafīs, however, interpret the verse somewhat differently. They contend that the Qur'ānic injunction is not applicable in the case of simply casting a glance. Rather, if someone enters a house without permission and fails to stop though asked to do so by the members of that household, it is permissible for them to restrain him and they will not be taken to task if, during the course of their efforts his eye or any limb is damaged (Jaṣṣāṣ, *Aḥkām al-Qur'ān*, vol. 3).

ii. Some jurists are of the opinion that the interdiction against looking into someone's house also applies to trying to hear conversations which take place in that house. For example, if a blind person enters someone's house without the latter's permission, he would, of course, not be able to see anything but he could listen to the householder's conversation without their permission. This too constitutes a violation of another's privacy.

iii. The injunction to seek permission before entering is not specific to entering the houses of strangers. One is required to do the same while entering the homes of close relatives. In fact one is required to seek permission even from such close relatives as one's mother and sister. Someone asked the Prophet (peace be upon him): 'Should I seek the permission of my mother when I visit her?' The Prophet (peace be upon him) replied in the affirmative. He again submitted: 'There is no one besides me to attend to her. Should I seek her permission every time I visit her?' The Prophet (peace be upon him) replied: 'Would you like to see your mother naked?' (Ibn Jarīr al-Ṭabarī has cited this *mursal* tradition on the authority of 'Aṭā' ibn Yasār, *Muwaṭṭa'*, *K. al-Isti'dhān* – Ed.) 'Abd Allāh ibn Mas'ūd's own opinion about the question is as follows: 'One should seek permission while visiting one's mother and sister' (Ibn Kathīr). 'Abd Allāh ibn Mas'ūd also says that even when one goes to one's wife in one's own house one should give some indication of one's approach, by for example, clearing one's throat before entering. His wife, Zaynab, reports that before entering the house 'Abd Allāh ibn Mas'ūd used to indicate that he was about to enter, thus avoiding any suddenness (Ibn Jarīr al-Ṭabarī).

iv. The only exemption from the requirement to obtain prior permission before entering someone's house is in situations of emergency. For example, in the event of fire or burglary, etc., one may enter a house without seeking prior permission.

v. When the practice of seeking permission to enter someone's house was introduced, people were not familiar with its niceties. Once someone visited the Prophet (peace be upon him) and while standing at the door he yelled: 'Should I enter?' The Prophet (peace be upon him) told his slave-girl that the visitor was not aware of the proper way of seeking permission to enter someone's house. He asked her to tell the visitor that the proper way to seek permission was to say: '*Al-Salāmu 'Alaykum*. May I enter?' (See Abū Dā'ūd, *K. al-Ādāb*, 'Bāb kayfa al-Isti'dhān' – Ed.) Jābir ibn 'Abd Allāh narrates that once he went to the Prophet's house in connection with the debts of his late father and as he knocked at the Prophet's door the latter asked: 'Who are you?' I replied: 'This is me.' The Prophet (peace be upon him) repeated the statement 'This is me', two or three times, meaning that it could not be made out from such a statement who the visitor was. (See Abū Dā'ūd, *K. al-Ādāb*, 'Bāb al-Rajul yasta'dhin bi al-Daqq' – Ed.) Kaldah ibn Ḥanbal visited the Prophet (peace be upon him) and took his seat without greeting him. The Prophet asked him to go out and re-enter after a proper greeting. (See Abū Dā'ūd, *K. al-Ādāb*, 'Bāb kayfa al-Isti'dhān' – Ed.) The correct way to seek permission is to first mention one's name and then seek permission to enter the house. It is said that whenever 'Umar came to the Prophet (peace be upon him) he would say: 'Peace be upon you, O Messenger of God! May 'Umar enter?' (See Abū Dā'ūd, *K. al-Ādāb*, 'Bāb fī al-Rajul yufāriq al-Rajul thumma yalqāh a-yusallim 'alayh' – Ed.) The Prophet (peace be upon him) also stated that a person should seek permission no more than three times. If there was no response after that, the visitor should go away. (See Abū Dā'ūd, *K. al-Ādāb*, 'Bāb kam Marrah yusallim al-Rajul fī al-Isti'dhān' – Ed.) The Prophet (peace be upon him) himself followed this practice. Once he went to visit Sa'd ibn 'Ubādah and sought permission twice after greeting him. Still there was no response. When the Prophet (peace be upon him) repeated the same for a third time and there was no response, he was about to leave. It was then that Sa'd ibn 'Ubādah rushed out, saying: 'O Messenger of God! I was listening. I thought that the greater the number of times that your blessed tongue mentions the Prayer of peace and mercy for me, the better it is. I, therefore, answered you in an almost inaudible voice.' (See Abū Dā'ūd, *K. al-Ādāb*, 'Bāb kam Marrah yusallim al-Rajul fī al-Isti'dhān' – Ed.) Likewise, one should not seek permission intermittently. There should rather be a pause after the permission is sought so that if the host is preoccupied with something, there is enough time for him to free himself of it and respond.

vi. The owner of the house or any other person authorized by him, such as a servant or any other responsible person, should grant the visitor permission to enter. If only a child tells the visitor to enter, the latter should not enter on that basis.

vii. It is not proper for a visitor to insist that permission necessarily be granted; indeed one should go away if permission is refused. If one seeks permission three times and yet fails to obtain it, or if the host refuses to meet with one, the visitor should better return at some later date.

(28) Then if you find no one in them, do not enter until you have been given permission (to enter).[27] And if you are told to go back, then do go back. This is a purer way for you.[28] Allah knows all what you do. (29) However, it is not blameworthy for you if you enter houses that are uninhabited but wherein there is something of use to you.[29] Allah is well aware of what you disclose and what you conceal.

(30) (O Prophet), enjoin believing men to cast down their looks[30] and ▶

فَإِن لَّمْ تَجِدُوا فِيهَا أَحَدًا فَلَا تَدْخُلُوهَا حَتَّىٰ
يُؤْذَنَ لَكُمْ ۖ وَإِن قِيلَ لَكُمُ ارْجِعُوا
فَارْجِعُوا ۖ هُوَ أَزْكَىٰ لَكُمْ ۚ وَاللَّهُ بِمَا تَعْمَلُونَ
عَلِيمٌ ﴿٢٨﴾ لَّيْسَ عَلَيْكُمْ جُنَاحٌ أَن تَدْخُلُوا
بُيُوتًا غَيْرَ مَسْكُونَةٍ فِيهَا مَتَاعٌ لَّكُمْ ۚ
وَاللَّهُ يَعْلَمُ مَا تُبْدُونَ وَمَا تَكْتُمُونَ ﴿٢٩﴾
قُل لِّلْمُؤْمِنِينَ يَغُضُّوا مِنْ أَبْصَارِهِمْ

27. It is not permissible to enter someone's house unless the master of the house has granted prior permission to do so. For example, it would even be proper for a visitor to enter a house if the master of the house were absent providing such permission had been granted. However, it would not be proper for a visitor to enter a house without obtaining due permission from the master.

28. A person should not feel offended if someone refuses a meeting. For a person is perfectly within his rights to refuse meeting someone or to excuse himself from such a meeting if he is preoccupied with something else. According to jurists, once permission is refused, the visitor should not remain standing in front of the house. He should rather move away. No one has the right to force anyone to meet with him or to bother him by adamantly standing at his door.

29. This refers to public places such as hotels, guest houses, shops and other places which everyone is entitled to enter without obtaining any specific permission to do so.

30. The words used here are *yaghuḍḍū min abṣārihim*. Literally the word *ghaḍḍ* denotes reducing or lowering something. The words *ghaḍḍ al-baṣar*,

therefore, are usually translated as 'lowering one's gaze' or 'keeping one's gaze downwards'. This Qur'ānic directive does not mean, however, that one should always gaze downwards. What it really means is that one should not look thoroughly at a certain thing; that one should not allow one's eyes to be unfettered in looking. In other words, one should avoid looking at things which it is improper to look at. This may be achieved either by avoiding looking at something by turning one's gaze away or by lowering it. Once again, the words *min abṣārihim* signify that some, rather than every kind of looking needs to be avoided. The use of the preposition *min* implies this. In other words, God does not intend that people should not look thoroughly at anything. God only wants that they should exercise restraint in looking at certain things. It becomes evident from the context that this directive is addressed to those men who focus their gaze on women, or who cast their glances at others' private parts, or who intentionally look at obscene objects.

Let us see then how this Qur'ānic injunction is explained by the *Sunnah* of the Prophet (peace be upon him):

i. It is not permissible for a male to fix his gaze on a woman other than his wife or on women who are forbidden him in marriage. If he sees someone accidentally, then he is not blameworthy. What is reprehensible, however, is that he should cast his gaze at women towards whom he feels attracted, and that he repeats this act. In the Prophet's view, this is tantamount to adultery of the eye. He said that a person can indulge in unlawful sex through all his senses. To fix one's gaze on someone is the unlawful sex of the eye. To woo and cajole a woman constitutes an act of unlawful sex by the tongue. To seek enjoyment via a woman's charming voice is adultery of the ears. To touch someone with sexual passion and to proceed towards someone under the influence of sexual passion represents adultery of the hands and feet. After these preliminary acts comes the role of the sexual organs: they either go forth to the stage of culmination of the sexual act or they abstain from doing so. (See Bukhārī, *K. al-Isti'dhān*, 'Bāb Zinā at-Jawāriḥ dūn al-Farj', Muslim, *K. al-Qadar*, 'Bāb Qadar 'alā ibn Ādam Khaṭar min al-Zinā wa Ghayrih' and Abū Dā'ūd, *K. al-Nikāḥ*, 'Bāb fī mā yu'mar bih min Ghaḍḍ al-Baṣar' – Ed.)

   According to a tradition narrated by Buraydah, the Prophet (peace be upon him) told 'Alī ibn Abī Ṭālib: 'O 'Alī! Let the first glance not be followed by the other. You may cast the first glance, not the second.' (See Abū Dā'ūd, *K. al-Nikāḥ*, 'Bāb fī mā yu'mar bih min Ghaḍḍ al-Baṣar' and Tirmidhī, *K. al-Ādāb*, 'Bāb mā jā' fī' al-Naẓar min al-Mufāja'ah' – Ed.) Jarīr ibn 'Abd Allāh said that he asked the Prophet (peace be upon him): 'What should I do if I see a woman by sheer chance?' He replied: 'Turn your gaze away or lower it.' (See Abū Dā'ūd, *K. al-Nikāḥ*, 'Bāb fī mā yu'mar bih min Ghaḍḍ al-Baṣar', Tirmidhī, *K. al-Ādāb*, 'Bāb mā jā' fī al-Naẓar min al-Mufāja'ah' and Muslim, *K. al-Ādāb*, 'Bāb Naẓar al-Faj'ah' – Ed.) It is narrated on the authority of 'Abd Allāh ibn Mas'ūd that the Prophet (peace be upon him) said: 'God says: "Glance is one of the deadly arrows of Satan. He who forsakes it out of fear for Me, I shall grant him in lieu of that a faith whose sweetness he shall find in his heart".' (Ṭabarānī.) Abū Umāmah narrates that the Prophet (peace be upon him) said: 'There is not a Muslim who, after observing the attractions of a woman turns his gaze away, but Allah will cause his worship to become palatable to him.' (See Aḥmad ibn Ḥanbal, *Musnad*, vol. 5, p. 264 – Ed.) According to a tradition on the authority of Jābir ibn 'Abd Allāh al-Anṣārī narrated by al-Ṣādiq and his father, Muḥammad al-Bāqir, the Prophet's cousin, Faḍl ibn 'Abbās, who was a young man at that time, was riding a camel with the Prophet while returning from al-Mash'ar al-Ḥarām on the occasion of the Prophet's Farewell Pilgrimage. When women began to pass, the Prophet (peace be upon him) put his hand on Faḍl's face and turned it in the opposite direction. (See Abū Dā'ūd, *K. al-Manāsik*, 'Bāb al-Rajul Yaḥujj 'an Ghayrih' – Ed.) Another tradition states that during the same Farewell Pilgrimage a woman, belonging to the Khath'am tribe, stopped the Prophet (peace be upon him) and asked him to clarify a point about Pilgrimage while Faḍl ibn 'Abbās fixed his gaze on her. The Prophet (peace be upon him) thus held him by the face and turned it in the other direction. (Bukhārī, *K. al-Ḥajj*, 'Bāb Wujūb al-Ḥajj wa Faḍlih . . .' and Abū Dā'ūd, *K. al-Manāsik*, 'Bāb al-Rajul Yaḥujj 'an Ghayrih' – Ed.)

ii. This should not, however, give rise to the misunderstanding that the Qur'ānic command to lower one's gaze was prescribed at a time when women were allowed to move around with their faces uncovered. Some have argued, for example, that if the faces of women were already covered, the directive would be pointless. Such a view is both irrational and contrary to the actual facts. The assumption underlying this argument is not tenable because even in a society where women kept their faces covered, there were occasions when a man and a woman might quite accidentally come face to face. Moreover, even a woman who kept her face covered might uncover it for one reason or another. Furthermore, even if Muslim women covered their faces, non-Muslim women were likely to move around with uncovered faces. Hence, the injunction that people should lower their gaze does not warrant the conclusion that the injunction concerned could have been given only in a society in which women did not keep their faces covered.

> Our contention that such a presupposition is incorrect is established by the fact that the covering of their faces by women was a part of the lifestyle which came into vogue in Muslim society after the revelation of the injunctions about *ḥijāb* in *Sūrah al-Aḥzāb*. Moreover, sufficient historical evidence is available to show that women covering their faces was practised by Muslim women in the time of the Prophet (peace be upon him). This point is borne out by an authentic tradition narrated by 'Ā'ishah in connection with the slander incident. This tradition has also been reported by chains of reliable narrators. 'Ā'ishah says that after her return from the open space, away from the camp, where she had gone to answer the call of nature, she discovered that she had been left behind and the caravan had moved ahead. She sat down and was so overcome with fatigue that she lay down and slept. Ṣafwān passed that way in the morning and spotted someone lying on the ground as he drew closer. As soon as he saw her he recognized her, for he had seen her before the [revelation of the injunction regarding] *ḥijāb*. When he recognized her and exclaimed *innā lillāh wa innā ilayhi rāji'ūn* she woke up and covered her face with her jilbab. (See Bukhārī, *K. al-Maghāzī*, 'Bāb Ḥadīth al-Ifk' – Ed.) (The Arabic text quoted here does not mention *innā lillāh* – Ed.)

According to another tradition, the son of Umm Khallād had attained martyrdom in a battle. To enquire about him, she went to the Prophet (peace be upon him) with a veil covering her face. This amazed some Companions who said to her in astonishment: 'Even in this state your face is covered?' What they meant was that the calamity with which she had been afflicted usually makes a woman oblivious to such things as dressing herself properly. To this she replied: 'I have lost my son, not my modesty.' (See Abū Dā'ūd, *Kitāb al-Jihād*, 'Bāb Faḍl Qitāl al-Rūm 'alā Ghayrihim min al-Umam' – Ed.) There is yet another tradition narrated by 'Ā'ishah that someone presented a paper to the Prophet (peace be upon him) from behind a curtain. The Prophet asked whether that hand was of a man or of a woman. On being told that it was the hand of a woman, the Prophet (peace be upon him) said: 'If she is a woman, she should have dyed her nails with henna.' (See Abū Dā'ūd, *K. al-Tarajjul*, 'Bāb fī al-Khiḍāb li al-Nisā' – Ed.)

As for the two incidents during the Farewell Pilgrimage they cannot be cited as proof that veiling of the face was not observed in the days of the Prophet (peace be upon him). For in the state of *iḥrām*, it is forbidden to use *niqāb* to cover the face. In fact some women who are sensitive about veiling do not uncover their faces before unrelated males even during the state of *iḥrām*. 'Ā'ishah narrates that during the Farewell Pilgrimage while they were on their way to Makka in the state of *iḥrām*, they covered their faces when other pilgrims passed by but once they had gone they uncovered their faces. (See Abū Dā'ūd, *K. al-Manāsik*, 'Bāb fī al-Maḥramah tughaṭṭī Wajhahā' – Ed.)

iii. The only exceptions to this rule are those circumstances in which there is a genuine need to see a woman, e.g. seeing a woman whom one intends to marry. In this case, it is not only permissible to see her; it is in fact desirable that one should do so. Mughīrah ibn Shu'bah narrates: 'I proposed to someone. The Prophet (peace be upon him) asked me whether I had seen my prospective bride. When I replied in the negative, he said: "You better see her, for it might prompt a better understanding between the two of you." ' (See Tirmidhī, *K. al-Nikāḥ*, 'Bāb mā jā' fī al-Naẓar ilā al-Makhṭūbah' – Ed.)

   Abū Hurayrah narrates that someone proposed to a woman. The Prophet (peace be upon him) said: 'You better see her because the *Anṣār* women [usually] have some defect in their eyes.' (See Muslim, *K. al-Nikāḥ*, 'Bāb Nudb al-Naẓar ilā Wajh al-Mar'ah wa Kaffayhā li man yurīd Tazawwajahā' – Ed.) Jābir ibn 'Abd Allāh narrates that the Prophet (peace be upon him) said: 'When any of you makes engagement with a woman, he should see whether she has something that would prompt him to marry her.' (See Abū Dā'ūd, *K. al-Nikāḥ*, 'Bāb fī al-Rajul yanẓur ilā al-Mar'ah wa huwa yurīd Tazwījahā' – Ed.) A tradition on the authority of Abū Ḥumaydah states that the Prophet (peace be upon him) was asked whether one could see his prospective bride. According to Abū Ḥumaydah the Prophet (peace be upon him) replied that there was no harm in it. He also allowed that a person may even see her without her knowledge. (See Aḥmad ibn Ḥanbal, *Musnad*, vol. 5, p. 424 – Ed.) Accordingly, jurists have inferred that it is permissible for a person to see a woman whenever there is any need to do so, for example, to see a suspect woman during interrogation. Likewise, a judge may see a female witness at the time she gives evidence, or a doctor may examine a female patient.

iv. The purpose of this command, to look away, also implies that no one should look at the *satr* (the parts of the body which ought to remain covered) of a male or female. The Prophet (peace be upon him) said: 'No male should look at the *satr* of another male or a female at the *satr* of another female.' (See Muslim, *K. al-Ḥayā*, 'Bāb Taḥrīm al-Naẓar ilā al-'Awrāt' and Tirmidhī, *K. al-Ādāb*, 'Bāb fī Karāhiyat Mubāsharat al-Rijāl al-Rijāl wa al-Mar'ah al-Mar'ah' – Ed.) 'Alī said that the Prophet (peace be upon him) said to him: 'Do not look at the thigh of a person, be he alive or dead.' (Abū Dā'ūd, *K. al-Ḥammām*, 'Bāb al-Nahy 'an al-Ta'arrī' – Ed.)

guard their private parts.[31] That is purer for them. Surely Allah is well aware of all what they do.	وَيَحْفَظُوا فُرُوجَهُمْ ذَٰلِكَ أَزْكَىٰ لَهُمْ إِنَّ ٱللَّهَ خَبِيرٌۢ بِمَا يَصْنَعُونَ ﴿٣٠﴾
(31) And enjoin believing women to cast down their looks[32] ▶	وَقُل لِّلْمُؤْمِنَٰتِ يَغْضُضْنَ مِنْ أَبْصَٰرِهِنَّ

31. The directive 'to guard one's private parts' does not simply aim at dissuading people from engaging in unlawful satisfaction of their sexual passions. It also seeks to prevent people exposing their *satr* before others. For men, the *satr* denotes the entire part of the body from the naval to the knee. (See Aḥmad ibn Ḥanbal, *Musnad*, vol. 2, p. 187 – Ed.) It is forbidden to deliberately expose one's *satr* before anyone other than one's wife. Jarhad al-Aslamī reports that once his thigh became exposed while he was sitting in the Prophet's company. The Prophet (peace be upon him) said to him: 'Do you not know that the thigh should be covered?' (See Abū Dā'ūd, *K. al-Ḥammām*, 'Bāb al-Nahy 'an al-Ta'arrī' – Ed.) 'Alī reports that the Prophet (peace be upon him) said: 'Never expose your thigh [before others than your wife].' (See *loc. cit.*) It is prohibited to be naked even when one is alone, let alone in the presence of others. The Prophet (peace be upon him) said: 'Beware! Do not remain nude. For there are angels of goodness and mercy who never part your company except when you go to answer the call of nature or when you approach your wives. Be shy of them [i.e. those angels] and hold them in respect.' (See Tirmidhī, *K. al-Ādāb*, 'Bāb fī al-Istitār 'ind al-Jimā'' – Ed.) According to another tradition, the Prophet (peace be upon him) said: 'Guard your *satr* except when you are in the company of your wife or slave-girl.' Someone asked the Prophet (peace be upon him) what should one do when one is all alone? The Prophet (peace be upon him) replied: 'God has greater rights over His servants that they should be shy of Him.' (See Abū Dā'ūd, *K. al-Ḥammām*, 'Bāb mā jā' fī al-Ta'arrī' and Tirmidhī, *K. al-Ādāb*, 'Bāb mā jā' fī Ḥifz al-'Awrah' – Ed.)

32. On the whole, the rules pertaining to restraining one's looks are to be followed by men as well as by women. So similarly, if women accidentally happen to see a male, they should look away. Like men, they should also refrain from looking at the *satr* of others.

There is, however, a slight difference in the detailed ruling about women looking at men as compared with men looking at women. For in one *ḥadīth* we come across an incident whereby Umm Salamah and

Maymūnah are sitting with the Prophet (peace be upon him). Ibn Umm Maktūm also arrived there. The Prophet (peace be upon him) asked both of his wives to observe *ḥijāb* from him. The wives said: 'O Messenger of God, is he not blind? He will neither see nor recognize us.' The Prophet replied: 'Are you also blind? Do you not see him?' Umm Salamah clarifies that this incident happened after the Qur'ānic command about *ḥijāb* was revealed. (See Tirmidhī, *K. al-Ādāb*, 'Bāb mā jā' fī Iḥtijāb al-Nisā' min al-Rajul' – Ed.) This point is further reinforced by a tradition in *Muwaṭṭa'* whereby when a blind person visited 'Ā'ishah, she observed *ḥijāb*. It was pointed out to her that there was no need to do so since he could not see her. To this she replied: 'But I see him.'

On the other hand, there is a tradition also narrated by 'Ā'ishah. In 7 A.H. a delegation of Negroes visited Madina and presented a show in the precincts of the Prophet's Mosque. On this occasion the Prophet (peace be upon him) asked 'Ā'ishah to join him and see the show. (See Bukhārī, *K. al-Ṣalāh*, 'Bāb Aṣḥāb al-Ḥurūb fī al-Masjid' and Muslim, *K. al-Ṣalāt al-'Īdayan*, 'Bāb al-Rukhṣah fī al-La'b al-ladhī lā Ma'ṣiyah fīh fī Ayyām al-'Īd' – Ed.) Moreover, when the husband of Fāṭimah bint Qays divorced her three times, she was faced with the problem of where to spend the period of her *'iddah*. The Prophet (peace be upon him) first told her to stay with Umm Sharīk of the *Anṣār*. Later on he said to her: 'Many of my Companions visit her. [Since Umm Sharīk was a very rich and generous lady, she received many guests and played host to them.] You should therefore stay with Ibn Umm Maktūm instead. He is a blind person and you can stay there without any difficulty.' (See Muslim, *K. al-Ṭalāq*, 'Bāb Muṭallaqah Thalāthatan lā Nafqata lahā' – Ed.)

When we bring all these traditions together, they suggest that the rules regarding women looking at men are not as strict as those regarding men looking at women. For example, women are not allowed to look at men in close proximity, say sitting in an assembly, but they can look at men from a distance, or look at men who are taking part in a lawful play or show. Additionally, if there is genuine necessity, they may look at men even if they are in the same house. Almost the same view has been derived from the relevant traditions by Ghazālī and Ibn Ḥajar al-'Asqalānī. Ibn Ḥajar says: 'The permission [for women to look at men] is supported by the fact that it was always held permissible for women to go out. The women who went to mosques or market places or on journeys covered their faces with *niqāb* so that men may not see them. But men were never commanded to cover their faces so that women could not see them. This shows that the rules with regard to the two vary.' (Shawkānī, *Nayl al-Awṭār*, vol. 6, p. 101.) Having said this, it must also be pointed out that women are not allowed to freely gaze at men, satisfying the thirst of their eyes with men's attractiveness.

and guard their private parts[33] ▶	وَيَحْفَظْنَ فُرُوجَهُنَّ

33. Believing women are asked to shun any unlawful gratification of their sexual urges and to refrain from exposing their *satr* before others. These directives are applicable to both men and women, though the parts of the body that constitute *satr* for men are different from the parts of the body that constitute *satr* for women. Likewise, the parts of a woman's body which may not be exposed before men differ from the parts of a man's body which may not be exposed before women.

A woman may not expose any part of her body other than her hands and face before men. No other part of her body should be exposed before anyone other than her husband, and this prohibition applies even to her father and brother. Nor should a woman wear such transparent or tight clothes that expose her body or reveal its shape. According to 'Ā'ishah, when her sister Asmā' visited the Prophet (peace be upon him) she was wearing a semi-transparent dress. As soon as the Prophet saw her, he turned his face away, saying: 'O Asmā'! When a girl attains puberty, it is not appropriate that any part of the body other than this and this should be visible.' So saying he pointed to his face and cuffs. (See Abū Dā'ūd, *K. al-Libās*, 'Bāb fī mā tubdi'u al-Mar'ah 'an Zīnatihā' – Ed.) A similar tradition is narrated by Ibn Jarīr al-Ṭabarī on the authority of 'Ā'ishah. The daughter of 'Ā'ishah's uterine brother, 'Abd Allāh ibn al-Ṭufayl had come to visit her. When the Prophet (peace be upon him) came home and saw her, he turned his face away. 'Ā'ishah introduced her, saying that she was her niece. The Prophet (peace be upon him) said: 'When a girl attains puberty, it is not permissible for her to reveal any part of her body except her face and except what is less than this.' Then he clasped his forearm, leaving between the spot he had clasped the measure of another clasp. Thus, he identified the exact position of the forearm which might remain uncovered.

Some relaxation on this count may be made by a woman with those of her close relatives with whom for her marriage is forbidden (such as her father and brother). For example, she is permitted not to cover those parts of her body whose use is required in connection with domestic chores. She may thus expose her arms for kneading bread, or she may fold up her clothes a little above the usual position while washing the floor [which would also expose a part of her legs].

As for the *satr* of women in the presence of other women, this is the same as the *satr* of men in the presence of other men. This consists of the whole part of the body between the navel and the knee. This does not, however, mean that a woman may remain semi-naked in the company of other women. Rather, the point is that while it is obligatory to cover the whole body from the navel to the knee, it is not obligatory to cover other parts of the body.

and[34] not reveal their adornment[35] except that which is revealed of itself,[36] ▶	وَلَا يُبْدِينَ زِينَتَهُنَّ إِلَّا مَا ظَهَرَ مِنْهَا ۖ

34. It is worth noting that the requirement of the *Sharī'ah* with regard to women is different to what it requires of men. The *Sharī'ah* requires men to keep their looks away from the opposite sex and to guard their chastity. Women, however, are required to abide by some additional rules as well. This makes it quite clear that in this particular regard the sexes are not alike.

35. We have translated the word *zīnah* in this verse to mean 'adornment'. This essentially consists of those means used by women to make themselves look attractive: (i) good dress; (ii) ornaments, and (iii) other cosmetics used by women the world over to beautify their heads, faces, hands and feet. As for the question as to before whom can a woman display or not display these adornments, we shall discuss this later. (See nn. 37 ff. below.)

36. Even though this verse is quite clear in its meaning, its true import has become somewhat ambiguous because of the numerous interpretations to which it has been subjected by Qur'ānic commentators. Women are asked in the present verse not to reveal their adornments. This is followed by giving expression to exceptions in the words *illā mā ẓahara minhā* ('that which is revealed of itself').

Obviously, the intent of the verse is that women themselves should not intentionally display their charms and beauty. However, it is possible that certain attractive objects about them might nevertheless be revealed: for example, the outer garment might be blown up by the wind causing some of a woman's adornments to be exposed. When such things happen, the women concerned are not to be blamed. This meaning of the Qur'ānic verse is ascribed to 'Abd Allāh ibn Mas'ūd, Ḥasan al-Baṣrī, Muḥammad ibn Sīrīn and Ibrāhīm al-Nakha'ī.

On the other hand, some commentators tend to interpret the latter part of the verse to mean permission to uncover that which it is customary to keep uncovered. They include the face and hands along with all that is used to beautify them. According to them, it is perfectly permissible for a woman to wear make-up on her face and hands and adorn them with ornaments and display them publicly. 'Abd Allāh ibn 'Abbās and his disciples are credited with this opinion which is also shared by the majority of Ḥanafī jurists. (See al-Jaṣṣāṣ, *Aḥkām al-Qur'ān*, *Sūrah al-Nūr*, comments on verse 31 – Ed.)

It is, however, totally beyond us as to how the Qur'ānic expression mentioned above can be stretched to justify such an interpretation. Were one to accept this interpretation, one would be considering the words

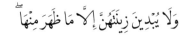

and to draw their veils over their bosoms,[37] ▶	وَلْيَضْرِبْنَ بِخُمُرِهِنَّ عَلَىٰ جُيُوبِهِنَّ

mā ẓahara as equivalent with *mā yuẓhiru*. There is a world of difference between revealing something and something being revealed of itself. The Qur'ān, no doubt, makes allowance for something which is revealed of itself. To interpret the verse to signify granting women permission to go about deliberately displaying their adornments which are attractive to men runs counter to the intent of the Qur'ān. Such a view is also discordant with the authentic traditions which indicate that after the Qur'ānic commands pertaining to *ḥijāb* were revealed, women did not appear in public with their faces uncovered. The *ḥijāb* injunction included the requirement to cover the face, and the veil thus assumed the position of an indispensable part of the female attire except in the state of *iḥrām*.

What is more intriguing is the argument put forward in support of the view that the face and hands do not constitute the prohibited parts (*satr*) of the female body. For the injunctions regarding *satr* and *ḥijāb* are two entirely different things. As for the injunction to keep one's *satr* covered, this applies even in the case of those men with whom marriage is forbidden. On the other hand, *ḥijāb* is an additional requirement laid down for women in respect of unrelated men. It should be emphasized that the point under discussion in this verse is *ḥijāb* rather than *satr*.

37. In the days of *Jāhilīyah* women had their hair tied with a kind of head-band which was fastened by a knot at the rear of the head. The front slit in their shirt remained partly open, thus revealing their neck and the upper part of their bosom. They wore nothing except this shirt to cover their breasts. Their hair was worn in two or three plaits which dangled freely behind. (See Zamakhsharī, *al-Kashshāf*, vol. 2, p. 990 and Ibn Kathīr, vol. 3, pp. 283–4.) Consequent upon the revelation of this verse, the practice of wearing a veil came into vogue among Muslim women. This veil was not used then in the manner Muslim women have begun to use it in our own time – as if it were a garland of cloth adorning their necks. Instead, it fully covered their head, waist and breasts.

No sooner had this verse been revealed than Muslim women hastened to change their dress sense. Praising believing women in this regard, 'Ā'ishah said: 'When *Sūrah al-Nūr* was revealed and the Prophet's Companions returned to their homes and recited its verses to their wives, daughters and sisters, there was not a single woman among the *Anṣār* who was not moved by the words ". . . let them draw their veils over their bosoms" (verse 31). Immediately everyone of them made veils out of whatever they had: a waist-band or a sheet of cloth. The next day, all Muslim women were present in the Prophet's Mosque for *Fajr* Prayers with their veils.' Another

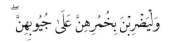

and not to reveal their adornment save[38] to their husbands, or their fathers, or the fathers of their husbands,[39] ▶	وَلَا يُبْدِينَ زِينَتَهُنَّ إِلَّا لِبُعُولَتِهِنَّ أَوْ ءَابَآئِهِنَّ أَوْ ءَابَآءِ بُعُولَتِهِنَّ

tradition from 'Ā'ishah contains the additional information that Muslim women cast away their transparent and semi-transparent clothes and especially selected thick material for their veil. (Ibn Kathīr and Abū Dā'ūd, *Kitab al-Libās*, 'Bāb Qawl Allāh ta'ālā: yudnīn 'alayhinna min Jalābībihinna' and 'wa la-yaḍribna bi Khumrihinna 'alā Juyūbihinna' – Ed.)

That the veil should not be of thin material is something which conforms with the spirit of these injunctions, and no one had any difficulty in arriving at that conclusion. The *Anṣār* women understood full well what kind of cloth should be used for the veil. Nonetheless, the Prophet (peace be upon him) did not leave this matter to the understanding of the people. Rather, he made it clear in quite unmistakable terms. Once the Prophet (peace be upon him) was presented with a thick material made in Egypt. He divided it into two and presented it to one of his Companions, saying: 'One is for your shirt, and the other is for your wife's veil. You should direct her to use an additional material inside so that the features of the body are not revealed.' (See Abū Dā'ūd, *Kitāb al-Libās*, 'Bāb mā jā' fī Libs al-Qabāṭī li-al-Nisā' – Ed.)

38. The relatives mentioned here form the social circle of close relatives among whom a woman is perfectly free to go about adorned with make-up and cosmetics. However, she is not allowed to display her beauty in front of anyone other than those here mentioned regardless of whether they are related to her or not. The Qur'ān commanded women '. . . not to reveal their adornment except that which is revealed of itself . . .' (verse 31). Here that very injunction is elaborated upon. This consists of emphasizing that a woman should not display her adornment, either deliberately or out of negligence, before anyone outside this well-defined circle of very close relatives. Nonetheless, if any lapses occur, despite a woman's efforts not to display her attractions and without her intent, or because it was not possible for her to keep herself covered despite her wanting to do so, God extends His assurance to such believing women that He will pardon them.

39. The word *ābā'* used in this verse covers one's father, both maternal and paternal, as also grandfathers and great-grandfathers. A woman may, therefore, appear before these elders of either her own family or of her husband's family in the same manner as she may appear before both her father and father-in-law.

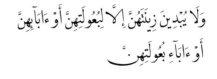

or of their own sons, or the sons of their husbands,[40] or their brothers,[41] or the sons of their brothers,[42] or the sons of their sisters,[43] ▶

أَوْ أَبْنَآئِهِنَّ أَوْ أَبْنَآءِ بُعُولَتِهِنَّ أَوْ إِخْوَٰنِهِنَّ
أَوْ بَنِىٓ إِخْوَٰنِهِنَّ أَوْ بَنِىٓ أَخَوَٰتِهِنَّ

40. The *abnā'ihinna* ('their sons') covers, apart from their own sons, their grandsons and great grandsons, i.e. those born both of one's sons and daughters. Furthermore, no distinction is made between one's own sons and one's step-sons. A woman may appear freely before the children of her step-sons as she may appear before her own children and grandchildren.

41. 'Brothers' here covers both real and step-brothers.

42. This refers to a woman's nieces and nephews, whether they are born of her brother or sister, and whether those brothers and sisters are real or are step-brothers and step-sisters.

43. Here the discussion about relatives is concluded. What follows is a discussion on how a woman is to appear before non-relatives. It seems necessary at this stage to fully comprehend three things, for without this confusion is bound to arise.

The first and foremost point is that some people consider that a woman is free to appear before only those relatives who are specified in this verse. They believe that a woman is obliged to observe full *ḥijāb* with all others including even her own uncles, both maternal and paternal. They cite the present Qur'ānic verse in support of this view, saying that in the verse no other relatives are mentioned.

This is not, however, the correct position. The Prophet (peace be upon him) did not let 'Ā'ishah observe *ḥijāb* with her foster uncles, let alone her own uncles. In the six most authentic works of *Ḥadīth* and in the *Musnad* of Aḥmad ibn Ḥanbal we find a tradition from 'Ā'ishah herself that Aflaḥ, Abū al-Qu'ays's brother, visited her and sought permission to enter the house. Since the Qur'ānic command about *ḥijāb* had already been revealed, 'Ā'ishah did not grant him such permission. Aflaḥ sent word to her that she was his niece, being the foster daughter of his brother's wife. 'Ā'ishah was unsure about whether such a relative belonged to that category specified in the Qur'ān with whom it was not necessary to observe *ḥijāb*. Meanwhile the Prophet (peace be upon him) arrived and told 'Ā'ishah that Aflaḥ may visit her. (See Bukhārī, *K. al-Tafsīr*, 'Bāb Tafsīr Tanzīl al-Sajdah', 'Bāb Qawlih: in-tubdū Shay'an aw tukhfūh fa inna Allāh kāna bi-kull Shay'in 'Alīmā' and Muslim, *K. al-Riḍā'*, 'Bāb Taḥrīm min mā' al-Faḥl' – Ed.)

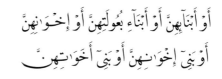

One, thus, learns that the Prophet (peace be upon him) did not interpret this verse to mean that a woman was required to observe *ḥijāb* with all her relatives except those mentioned in the present verse. He rather derived from this verse the general rule that a woman need not observe *ḥijāb* with all those relatives with whom for her marriage is forbidden. This category of relatives includes her uncles, both maternal and paternal, her sons-in-law and foster relatives. Among the Successors, Ḥasan al-Baṣrī held the same opinion, one which Jaṣṣāṣ supported in his work. (See *Aḥkām al-Qur'ān*, *Tafsīr Sūrah al-Nūr* (verse 31), 'Bāb mā yajibu min Ghaḍḍ al-Baṣar 'an al-Muḥarramāt' – Ed.)

The second point that might cause some confusion pertains to those relatives with whom neither marriage is permanently forbidden (which would make it permissible for a woman to freely appear before them) nor whom are total strangers so that it would be required to observe strict *ḥijāb*. The position with regard to such people has not been specifically laid down by the *Sharī'ah*. Therefore, a categorical ruling about them cannot be given. For such a ruling is contingent upon many considerations such as the nature of their kinship, their age, the age of the woman concerned, the nature of the relations between the two families, and the living conditions of the persons concerned (such as sharing a house or living separately, etc.). Since these circumstances vary from case to case, the ruling will also differ from one case to another. Furthermore, this is the guidance that we receive from the Prophet's own conduct. We learn from many *aḥādīth* that Asmā' bint Abī Bakr, 'Ā'ishah's sister, used to appear before the Prophet (peace be upon him) and even in the very last days of his life she did not cover her face and hands in his presence. We have also found a tradition to this effect which pertains to the time of the Prophet's Farewell Pilgrimage, i.e. only a few months before he passed away. This shows that the practice mentioned above also obtained till the very last days of the Prophet's life. (See Abū Dā'ūd, *Kitāb al-Ḥajj*, 'Bāb al-Maḥram Yu'addibu Ghulāmah'.) Likewise, Umm Hānī, the Prophet's cousin and Abū Ṭālib's daughter, appeared before the Prophet (peace be upon him) and she covered neither her face nor her hands in his presence. She narrates an incident that took place at the time of the conquest of Makka which substantiates this. (See Abū Dā'ūd, *Kitāb al-Ṣawm*, 'Bāb fī al-Nīyah fī al-Ṣiyām wa al-Rukhṣah fīh' – Ed.)

There is also a tradition to the effect that 'Abbās sent his son Faḍl and Rabī'ah ibn Hārith ibn 'Abd al-Muṭṭalib (the Prophet's cousin) to the Prophet. He directed them to ask the Prophet (peace be upon him) for employment, this because they were new adults and so should work in order to render themselves suitable for marriage. Both of them called on the Prophet at Zaynab's house. Zaynab, one of the Prophet's wives, was the maternal cousin of Faḍl. She thus had the same relationship with Rabī'ah as she had with Faḍl, and yet she did not appear before them, and in the Prophet's presence she talked to them from behind a curtain. (See Abū Dā'ūd, *Kitāb al-Kharāj, wa al-Imārah wa al-Fay'*, 'Bāb fī Bayān Mawāḍi'

or the women with whom they associate,[44] ▶	أَوْ نِسَآئِهِنَّ

Qasm al-Khums wa Sahm dhī al-Qurbā' – Ed.) When we consider the two types of traditions mentioned above, it seems that the correct position is that which we have just documented.

Third, whenever there is any doubt regarding the kinship between a woman and any of her relatives, it is preferable for her to observe *ḥijāb*, even if the man happens to be among those with whom marriage is forbidden. We learn that Sawdah, one of the wives of the Prophet (peace be upon him), had a step-brother (being the son of his father from a slave-girl). Sa'd ibn Abī Waqqāṣ's brother, 'Utbah, left a will addressed to Sa'd wherein he urged him to patronize this boy, considering him his own nephew because he was 'Utbah's son. The case was presented before the Prophet (peace be upon him), but he rejected Sa'd's claim saying: 'The child belongs to the one on whose bed it was born, and he who committed adultery will be lapidated.' At the same time, the Prophet (peace be upon him) told Sawdah to observe *ḥijāb* since there was doubt about whether he was her brother or not.

44. The words used are *nisā'ihinna* which translate as 'the women with whom they associate'. We shall consider a little later on who these women are.

The first point which merits attention here is that the word *al-nisā'*, which has a highly general connotation, has not been employed in this verse. For had it been used it would have been permissible for a Muslim woman to appear and display her attractions before all kinds of women. Instead, the words *nisā'ihinna* are used which has a relatively restricted connotation implying some restrictions, regardless of what they are, on a Muslim's freedom to associate with other women.

So who are the women to whom the words *nisā'ihinna* apply? Commentators on the Qur'ān and jurists hold different opinions on this matter. According to some, the expression signifies only Muslim women. A Muslim woman is required to observe *ḥijāb* with non-Muslim women, whether they are *dhimmīs* or otherwise, in the manner she is required to observe *ḥijāb* with men. They support this opinion by reference to 'Abd Allāh ibn 'Abbās, Mujāhid and Ibn Jurayj whose views are the same. They also cite the incident that 'Umar documented in writing to Abū 'Ubaydah ibn al-Jarrāḥ: 'I have come to know that some Muslim women have been visiting public baths along with non-Muslim women, this although it is not lawful for any woman who believes in God and the Last Day to allow those belonging to some other faith to see her body.' When Abū 'Ubaydah received this letter he was greatly upset and exclaimed: 'By God, a Muslim woman who visits the public bath merely to develop a fair complexion

or those that are in their bondage,[45] or the male attendants in their service ▶	أَوْ مَا مَلَكَتْ أَيْمَـٰنُهُنَّ أَوِ ٱلتَّـٰبِعِينَ

will have her face blackened on the Last Day.' (Ibn Jarīr al-Ṭabarī, Bayhaqī and Ibn Kathīr.)

Other jurists are of the opinion that the expression, *nisā'ihinna*, embraces all women. This is the view of Fakhr al-Dīn al-Rāzī. It is, however, hard to appreciate this since had all women been meant, why was the restrictive expression *nisā'ihinna* used? If that had been the case, it would have been appropriate to use *al-nisā'*.

There is a third opinion which seems both reasonable and in consonance with the spirit of the Qur'ān whereby the expression signifies all those women with whom a Muslim woman enjoys acquaintanceship or friendship, all those women who share with her the burden of domestic chores, whether they are Muslim or non-Muslim.

It seems that the purpose of this Qur'ānic verse is to exclude unrestricted association with those women who are total strangers or whose character and conduct are either not known or who are of doubtful character, making them unworthy of trust. This view seems to be corroborated by those authentic traditions which mention that non-Muslim women used to visit the wives of the Prophet (peace be upon him). In such matters the main consideration should be the character of the women concerned rather than their formal affiliation with one religious community or another. Muslim women may mix freely with all women of good character, with all women who are modest, good-mannered, and belong to families that are well known and are considered trustworthy regardless of whether they are Muslim or non-Muslim. On the other hand, no decent woman should mix freely with women who are devoid of modesty and a sense of honour and are, on the whole, women of low character, even if they are 'Muslims'. This because to mix with women of this type would be no different than a woman freely mixing with men. In our view, a Muslim woman should treat women whose character and conduct are not known to her in the manner she would treat her non-*maḥram* relatives. That is, a Muslim woman may appear before them without covering her face and hands, although all other parts of her body should be fully covered. (See also n. 42 above – Ed.)

45. Jurists have a variety of opinions regarding the import of this injunction. Some consider *mā malakat aymānuhunna* ('those that are in bondage') to signify only those slave-girls whom a woman owns. According to these jurists, a Muslim woman may display her adornments before her slave-girls regardless of whether they are polytheists or followers of the Scriptures. However, with male slaves, a woman should observe the same

restrictions as apply to free men who are not related to her. This opinion is held by 'Abd Allāh ibn Mas'ūd, Mujāhid, Ḥasan al-Baṣrī, Muḥammad ibn Sīrīn, Sa'īd ibn al-Musayyab, Ṭā'ūs and Abū Ḥanīfah. A statement to this effect has also been reported on the authority of Shāfi'ī. These scholars argue that a male slave cannot be considered the *maḥram* of the woman who owns him. If the slave becomes free, he may marry the woman who previously owned him.

It may be asked why the words *mā malakat aymānuhunna*, which are of general significance denoting slaves of both the sexes, are interpreted restrictively to mean only slave-girls to the exclusion of male slaves? In response, scholars point out that even though the words used here are of general significance, it is the context that makes them specific to slave-girls only. For, it is evident from the words *nisā'ihinna* used in the verse that a woman may freely mix with those women who have either kinship with her or with whom she is acquainted. This could have led to the misunderstanding that a woman's slave-girls were excluded from the category of those women with whom she may freely mix. All grounds for any such misunderstanding were removed by employing the words *mā malakat aymānuhunna*, suggesting thereby that a Muslim woman may freely mix with her slave-girls without having to conceal her adornments from them, in the way that she may do with free women.

According to another group of scholars, both female and male slaves are included in the category of persons before whom a Muslim woman is not required to conceal her adornments. This opinion is attributed to 'Ā'ishah, Umm Salamah and some leading jurists among the descendants of the Prophet (peace be upon him). It is also generally considered to be the opinion of Shāfi'ī. These scholars support their opinion by reiterating that the expression *mā malakat aymānuhunna* is of general significance. Additionally, they argue, on the basis of the *Sunnah* of the Prophet (peace be upon him), that reference is made to a visit the Prophet (peace be upon him) made to his daughter Fāṭimah along with a male slave, 'Abd Allāh. At that time she was wearing a sheet of cloth which was not long enough. If she had covered her head with it this would have left her feet uncovered and vice versa. On observing Fāṭimah's embarrassment the Prophet (peace be upon him) said: 'There is no blame on you. It is only your father and your slave who are here.' (See Abū Dā'ūd, *K. al-Libās*, 'Bāb fī al-'Abd yanẓur ilā sha'r Mawlātih' – Ed.) In his *Ta'rīkh Dimashq*, Ibn 'Asākir states that the Prophet (peace be upon him) had presented this slave to Fāṭimah who first brought him up and then set him free. (Curiously enough, this slave repaid Fāṭimah for the good she had done him in a strange way. He became 'Alī's worst enemy and a staunch supporter of Mu'āwiyah during the Battle of Ṣiffīn!) These jurists also cite the following saying of the Prophet (peace be upon him) in support of this opinion: 'When any of you women enter into *mukātabah* with your slave and he is in a position to repay the amount stipulated in that regard, it is required of such a woman that she observe

free of sexual interest,[46] or boys that are yet unaware ▶	غَيْرِ أُوْلِى ٱلْإِرْبَةِ مِنَ ٱلرِّجَالِ أَوِ ٱلطِّفْلِ ٱلَّذِينَ

ḥijāb with that slave.' (See Abū Dā'ūd, *K. al-'Itq*, 'Bāb fī al-Mukātib yuwaddī Ba'ḍ Kitābatih fa ya'jiz wa yamūt' and Tirmidhī, *K. al-Buyū'*, 'Bāb Ba'ḍ mā jā' fī al-Mukātib idhā kān 'induh mā yuwaddī' – Ed.)

46. The expression: التابعين غير أولي الإربة من الرجال means 'the male attendants in their service who are free of sexual interest'. These words indicate that a Muslim woman may display her adornments to any males other than her *maḥram* (i.e. those with whom for her marriage is permanently forbidden), only when two conditions are fulfilled. First, that such a person should be in a state of subservience and subordination to her, and second, that he should be free of sexual desire either owing to his advanced age, physical infirmity, imbecility, utter destitution, or owing to his subordinate status which renders him unable even to think of any sexual relations with the wife, daughter, sister or mother of the master of the household. Anyone who studies this injunction with the intent of following the commands of God, rather than simply finding loopholes that provide him with a pretext to violate the purpose of the Law, will readily observe that cooks, bearers, chauffeurs, and other youthful male servants with whom women in our time tend not to observe any restrictions of *ḥijāb* cannot be considered a part of this definition.

Let us now see how different scholars have interpreted these words:

i. 'Abd Allāh ibn 'Abbās regards these words to signify imbeciles who have no interest in women.
ii. Qatādah considers these words to mean a destitute who remains inalienably attached to someone because of his need for daily bread.
iii. Mujāhid considers these words to denote an idiot who is concerned with bread rather than women.
iv. Sha'bī believes these words to mean a person who is subordinate to and dependent on the head of a family, and who lacks the courage even to look at women.
v. According to Ibn Zayd, these words denote a person who persists with a family, in which he has been brought up, to such an extent as though he has become a member of the family. He does not cast amorous glances at the women of the family and even lacks the courage to do so. He persists with the family for the sake of his daily bread.
vi. Ṭā'ūs and Zuhrī believe that these words signify a stupid person who neither has any desire for women, nor the courage to seek

of illicit matters pertaining to women.[47] Nor should they stamp their feet on the ground ▶	لَمْ يَظْهَرُوا۟ عَلَىٰ عَوْرَٰتِ ٱلنِّسَآءِ ۖ وَلَا يَضْرِبْنَ بِأَرْجُلِهِنَّ

them. (Ibn Jarīr al-Ṭabarī, vol. 18, pp. 95–6 and Ibn Kathīr, vol. 3, p. 285.)

Much more illuminating than all this is the following incident which took place in the time of the Prophet (peace be upon him). This has been narrated on the authority of 'Ā'ishah and Umm Salamah. There was a eunuch in Madina who was considered to belong to the category of *ghayr ūlī al-irbah min al-rijāl* (i.e. men free of sexual interest) by the Prophet's wives and other women and who, therefore, had free access to their houses. Once while the Prophet (peace be upon him) was visiting his wife Umm Salamah he overheard the eunuch talking to 'Abd Allāh ibn Abī Umayyah, Umm Salamah's brother. He was telling 'Abd Allāh that if Ṭā'if was conquered he should make a point of getting hold of Bādiyah, the daughter of Ghaylān al-Thaqafī. He then started to praise her beauty vividly and describe her bodily attractions. He even graphically described the beauty of those parts of the body which are not normally visible. When the Prophet (peace be upon him) heard him saying all this, he interrupted him: 'O enemy of God! You have watched her so closely.' Then he ordered all women to observe *ḥijāb* with the eunuch and also forbade him to enter peoples' houses. Additionally, he banished him from Madina, and also forbade other eunuchs from entering the inner apartments. He did so because women, under the impression that they were eunuchs, and hence free of sexual desire, tended to relax their attitudes towards them. This enabled many eunuchs to observe the women of the household very closely and to inform others about their charms. (See Bukhārī, *K. al-Maghāzī*, 'Bāb Ghazwat al-Ṭā'if fī Shawwāl Sanat Thamān' and Muslim, *K. al-Salām*, 'Bāb Man' al-Mukhannath min al-Dukhūl 'alā al-Nisā' al-Ajānib' – Ed.)

We thus learn that in order for someone to be considered as belonging to the category of *ghayr ūlī al-irbah min al-rijāl* it is not enough for him to be physically incapable of the sexual act. What needs to be fully ensured is that such a person is altogether free of sexual desire, of every vestige of the same, and that he is truly not at all interested in women. For if there is even an iota of sexual desire in him, he is liable to cause much mischief.

47. That is those whose sexual urges have not yet been awakened. Included in this category are boys between 10 and 12 years of age. Although older boys may not have reached adolescence in a strictly technical sense, nevertheless they do have sexual desires.

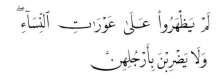

in such manner that their hidden ornament becomes revealed.[48] ▶	لِيُعْلَمَ مَا يُخْفِينَ مِن زِينَتِهِنَّ

48. The Prophet (peace be upon him) did not restrict this injunction stopping women from stamping their feet and so revealing their hidden ornaments just on the basis of that action. Instead, he derived from this injunction the general principle that any act which arouses the sexual passion of men, whether through hearing, sight or any other sense, comes into conflict with the purpose underlying God's directive to women that they may not reveal their adornments before men. Hence, the Prophet (peace be upon him) asked women not to go out wearing perfume. Abū Hurayrah narrates that the Prophet (peace be upon him) said: 'Do not prevent God's bondswomen from entering the mosque. But they should not go out in perfume.' (See Abū Dā'ūd, *K. al-Ṣalāh*, 'Bāb mā jā' fī Khurūj al-Nisā' ilā al-Masjid' – Ed.) The same point is made in another tradition: A woman was going out of the mosque when Abū Hurayrah passed her. He noted that she was wearing perfume. Stopping her he asked: 'O servant of God, are you coming from the mosque?' When she replied in the affirmative, Abū Hurayrah told her: 'I heard my beloved Abū al-Qāsim [Muḥammad] say: "The Prayer of a woman who wears perfume in a mosque is not accepted until she takes the bath of ritual purification at home." ' (See Abū Dā'ūd, *K. al-Tarajjul*, 'Bāb mā jā' fī al-Mar'ah tataṭayyib li al-Khurūj' – Ed.) According to Abū Mūsā al-Ash'arī, the Prophet (peace be upon him) said: 'If a women goes out after wearing perfume so that the men by whom she passes may enjoy the fragrance of the perfume she is a so and so', and here he used a very harsh word for such a woman. (See *loc. cit.* – Ed.) The Prophet (peace be upon him) directed women that if they were to wear perfume, they should wear one whose colour is bright. (See *loc. cit.* – Ed.)

In like manner, the Prophet (peace be upon him) disapproved of women unnecessarily making men hear their voice. The Qur'ān itself allows women to talk to men when it is necessary. (This seems to be the implication of *al-Aḥzāb* 33: 32 – Ed.) It is also known that the Prophet's wives themselves explained religious matters to people. But when no religious or moral benefit is expected to ensue from women talking to men, it is not considered desirable that they provide men with an opportunity to be gratified by the charm of the female voice. Islam's attitude in this respect seems to be indicated by the following legal ruling: Whenever the *imām* (leader) of the Prayer forgets something men are required to say *Subḥān Allāh* in order to draw his attention to that lapse, whereas women are required to clap mildly for the same purpose. (See Bukhārī, *K. al-'Amal fī al-Ṣalāh*, 'Bāb al-Taṣfīq li al-Nisā' ' and Muslim, *K. al-Ṣalāh*, 'Bāb tusabbiḥ al-Rajul wa tuṣaffiq al-Mar'ah idhā nabahumā Shay' fī al-Ṣalāh' – Ed.)

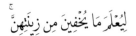

Believers, turn together, all of you, to Allah in repentance[49] that you may attain true success.[50]	وَتُوبُوٓا۟ إِلَى ٱللَّهِ جَمِيعًا أَيُّهَ ٱلْمُؤْمِنُونَ لَعَلَّكُمْ تُفْلِحُونَ ﴿٣١﴾

49. Believers are asked to repent for their lapses on this particular count. They are further directed to mend their ways and mould their conduct in accordance with the directives of God and His Messenger.

50. It seems pertinent to state briefly some other reforms that were introduced into Muslim society by the Prophet (peace be upon him) which are in keeping with the spirit of the above Qur'ānic injunctions:

i. The Prophet (peace be upon him), forbade people, even a woman's male relatives, from meeting her alone, i.e. in the absence of any of her *maḥram* relatives. Jābir ibn 'Abd Allāh narrates that the Prophet (peace be upon him) said: 'Do not visit women whose husbands are away, for Satan circulates in each of you like blood.' (See Tirmidhī, *K. al-Riḍā'*, 'Bāb mā jā' fī Karāhiyat al-Dukhūl 'alā al-Mughībāt' – Ed.) According to another tradition narrated by Jābir ibn 'Abd Allāh, the Prophet (peace be upon him) said: 'Anyone who believes in God and the Last Day should never meet a woman in privacy unless she is accompanied by a *maḥram* [i.e. a male with whom for her marriage is permanently forbidden]. For [if a man and a woman are alone] Satan becomes the third of the two.' (See Aḥmad ibn Ḥanbal, *Musnad*, vol. 3, p. 339 – Ed.) There is a similar tradition in the *Musnad* of Aḥmad ibn Ḥanbal on the authority of 'Āmir ibn Rabī'ah. The Prophet (peace be upon him) was so particular in this regard that once while he was going with his wife Ṣafīyah to her house at night, two Companions passed by the way. He stopped one of them and said that it was his wife Ṣafīyah who was accompanying him. They submitted: 'Glory be to God! O Messenger of God, who can think ill of you?' The Prophet (peace be upon him) replied: 'Satan is circulating in each man like blood. So I considered it better to clarify lest some evil thought might cross your mind.' (See Abū Dā'ūd, *K. al-Ṣawm*, 'Bāb al-Mu'takif yadkhul al-Bayt li Ḥājatihi' – Ed.)

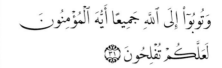

ii. The Prophet (peace be upon him) did not allow a non-*maḥram* male to touch the body of a woman. This is evident from the following practice of the Prophet (peace be upon him): when he took the oath of allegiance (*bay'ah*) from men, he had them place their palm in his. But he did not do so while taking the oath of allegiance from women. In their case, the Prophet considered it enough for them to express their allegiance verbally. Once they took that oath he told them that they might go back for their oath was now complete. (See Abū Dā'ūd, *K. al-Kharāj*, 'Bāb mā jā' fī al-Bay'ah' – Ed.)

iii. The Prophet (peace be upon him) strictly forbade women from travelling without any *maḥram*, or travelling with any non-*maḥram*. There is a tradition from 'Abd Allāh ibn 'Abbās that the Prophet (peace be upon him) once said in his sermon: 'No man should meet a woman in privacy unless she is accompanied by any of her *maḥram*, and no woman should travel unless she is accompanied by her *maḥram*.' Thereupon someone got up and said: 'My wife is going on *Ḥajj* while I am among those proceeding on a military expedition.' (Bukhārī, *K. al-Jihād*, 'Bāb man iktatataba fī Jaysh fa kharajat Imara'tuh Ḥājjatan . . .' – Ed.) The Prophet (peace be upon him) said to him: 'Go and perform *Ḥajj* with your wife.' (See Aḥmad ibn Ḥanbal, *Musnad*, vol. 1, p. 222 and Bukhārī, *K. al-Nikāḥ*, 'Bāb lā yakhluwann al-Rajul bi imra'tin illā Dhū Maḥram wa al-Dukhūl 'alā al-Mughībah' – Ed.)

Several traditions of similar import are found in authentic works of *Ḥadīth* on the authority of 'Abd Allāh ibn 'Umar, Abū Sa'īd al-Khudrī and Abū Hurayrah. The only variation in these traditions relates to the duration or distance of the journey. There is, however, agreement that a woman who truly believes in God and the Last Day may not travel without a *maḥram*. Some *aḥādīth* state that the maximum distance which a woman may travel without a *maḥram* is twelve miles or somewhat longer. In some traditions the time limit is one day, in others a day and a night, in others it is two days, and in some it is three days. This variation, however, does not impair the trustworthiness of these *aḥādīth*. As far as the apparent discrepancy about the duration of a journey is concerned, one plausible explanation is that the Prophet (peace be upon him) would have issued the directives as and when situations arose. For example, if a woman was proceeding on a journey for three days, he forbade her from doing so unless any of her *maḥram* accompanied her. It is also possible that a woman might have been proceeding on a journey for one whole day without a *maḥram* and he might have forbidden her from so doing. The Prophet's directives on this count were in response to the different circumstances of different people and are, thus, of little consequence. What really matters is the ruling which, in the words of 'Abd Allāh ibn 'Abbās, is that a woman should not travel without a *maḥram*.

iv. The Prophet (peace be upon him) discouraged intermingling between men and women both by precept and practice.

> It is well known that God made the Friday Prayer, which is offered in congregation, obligatory for all Muslims. As regards the importance of this congregational Prayer, we have the Prophet's statement to the effect that if someone performs this Prayer at home without any genuine reason for joining the Prayer in congregation, then his Prayer will not be accepted. (Abū Dā'ūd, Ibn Mājah, Dāraquṭnī and Ḥākim on the authority of 'Abd Allāh ibn 'Abbās.) Nevertheless, the Prophet (peace be upon him) exempted Muslim women from joining compulsory congregational Friday Prayers. (See Abū Dā'ūd, *K. al-Ṣalāh*, 'Bāb mā jā' fī Khurūj al-Nisā' ilā al-Masājid' – Ed.)

While women are not obliged to join congregational Prayers they are nonetheless not precluded from so doing if they want to. However, this permission is followed by the statement that their praying at home is more meritorious than their praying in the mosque. According to 'Abd Allāh ibn 'Umar and Abū Hurayrah the Prophet (peace be upon him) said: 'Do not prevent God's bondswomen from entering the mosques of God.' (Abū Dā'ūd.) Other traditions narrated by 'Abd Allāh ibn 'Umar make almost the same point: 'Let women visit the mosques at night.' (See Bukhārī, *K. al-Adhān*, 'Bāb Khurūj al-Nisā' ilā al-Masājid bi al-Layl li al-Ghalas' – Ed.) There is yet another tradition: 'Do not stop your womenfolk from visiting the mosques though their homes are better for them for Prayers.' (See Aḥmad ibn Ḥanbal, *Musnad*, vol. 2, pp. 76–7 – Ed.) Umm Ḥumayd al-Sa'dīyah says that she told the Prophet (peace be upon him) that she was very keen on saying Prayers under his leadership. He told her: 'It is better for you to Pray in your own room than in the courtyard; and it is better for you to Pray at home than in the mosque of your locality; and it is better for you to Pray in the mosque of your own locality than in the large mosque.' (*Ibid.*, vol. 6, p. 371 – Ed.) A tradition to the same effect is narrated by 'Abd Allāh ibn Mas'ūd (see Abū Dā'ūd). According to Umm Salamah, the Prophet (peace be upon him) said: 'The best mosques for women are the inner apartment of their own houses.' (*Ibid.*, vol. 6, p. 297 – Ed.) On observing the social conditions prevalent during the Umayyad period, 'Ā'ishah remarked: 'Had the Prophet (peace be upon him) seen the present conduct of women, he would have forbidden their entry into mosques as it was done earlier in the case of Israeli women.' (Bukhārī, Muslim and Abū Dā'ūd.)

> The Prophet (peace be upon him) earmarked a special door for women to enter his mosque. During 'Umar's reign, he strictly barred men from using that door either for entering or going out of the mosque. (Abū Dā'ūd, 'Bāb I'tizāl al-Nisā' fī al-Masājid' and 'Bāb mā jā' fī Khurūj al-Nisā' ilā al-Masājid'.) In congregational Prayers women

prayed in the rows behind those of the men and at the conclusion of the Prayer the Prophet (peace be upon him) would pause a little so that the women might leave the mosque before the men did. (Aḥmad ibn Ḥanbal and Bukhārī on the authority of Umm Salamah.) In the Prophet's words, the best row for men was the first and the worst the last row [i.e. the one next to that of the women]; and the best row for women was the last and the worst the first [i.e. the one next to that of the men]. (Muslim, Abū Dā'ūd, Tirmidhī, Nasā'ī and Aḥmad ibn Ḥanbal.)

Women used to join *'Īd* Prayers although they occupied a place separate from men. After delivering the sermon, the Prophet (peace be upon him) would go to the ladies' section and address them separately. (Abū Dā'ūd on the authority of Jābir ibn 'Abd Allāh, Bukhārī and Muslim on the authority of 'Abd Allāh ibn 'Abbās.) On one occasion the Prophet (peace be upon him) noticed that once men and women left the mosque they became intermingled. Seeing this he told the women that they should walk on the sides of the road rather than in the centre. No sooner had the Muslim women heard this, than they began to walk on the sides, alongside the walls of the houses. (Abū Dā'ūd.)

These injunctions make it clear how incongruent a mixed society is wherein men and women are ordinarily seated together. Given that a religion does not allow free mingling between the sexes in mosques even on the occasion of Prayer, how could it allow the same in colleges, offices, clubs and other meeting places?

v. Islam does not only allow women to adorn themselves but at times it even urges them to do so. At the same time, it has attempted to prevent their going to excess in this matter. There were a number of means by which women in the time of the Prophet adorned and beautified themselves. The Prophet (peace be upon him) decried some of these and branded them as a curse, as the cause of the destruction of several nations in the past. He particularly denounced the following: adding the hair of another to one's own with a view to making one's own appear longer and thicker; tattooing and other artificial marks on the body; plucking the hair from one's eyebrows so as to give them a special shape; plucking the hair from one's face; rubbing one's teeth in order to sharpen them or making artificial holes in them; applying saffron or other comestic materials on one's face so as to give an artificial complexion. Traditions to this effect are found in authentic works of *Ḥadīth* on the authority of 'Ā'ishah, Asmā' bint Abī Bakr, 'Abd Allāh ibn Mas'ūd, 'Abd Allāh ibn 'Umar, 'Abd Allāh ibn 'Abbās, and Mu'āwiyah.

In view of these explicit directives from God and His Messenger, a believer is left with only two options: to purge his own life,

(32) Marry those of you that are single,[51] (whether men or women), and those of your male and female slaves that are righteous.[52] ▶	وَأَنكِحُوا۟ ٱلْأَيَـٰمَىٰ مِنكُمْ وَٱلصَّـٰلِحِينَ مِنْ عِبَادِكُمْ وَإِمَآئِكُمْ

that of his family and that of society of the moral evils which are mentioned so exhaustively in the Qur'ān and the *Ḥadīth*. If he is not able to do this, he should at least admit that he is committing a sin by not following these directives. A Muslim who violates God's commands out of weakness should at least refrain from justifying his action. There are, however, people who openly flout the social norms set out by the Qur'ān and the *Sunnah* and adopt the ways in vogue in Western society. Such people go about trumpeting that in Islam there is no injunction at all about *ḥijāb*. Such people not only violate Islamic injunctions, what is even worse, they try to legitimize all that as perfectly Islamic. The stand of such people cannot be appreciated by any decent person as far as this world is concerned. Nor can they expect any good in the Hereafter. It is deplorable that in Muslim society we find people who are a few steps ahead of even the hypocrites, people who hold God's and the Prophet's directives to be faulty, and who consider the ways which they have taken over from non-Muslims as perfectly good. If such people are to be regarded as Muslims, then the words Islam and *kufr* become entirely meaningless.

Had such people changed their names and publicly disowned Islam, one could at least have commended them for their moral courage. What is more regrettable is that notwithstanding their espousal of opinions which are antithetical to Islam, they still profess to be Muslim. No category of people is more contemptible than these. One cannot rule out any fraud, deception, trickery or perfidy from people possessed of this kind of character.

51. The word *ayāmā* is generally used to denote widows. However, it covers both men and women who are without a spouse. *Ayāmā* is plural of *ayyim*, which applies to every man who has no wife and to every woman who does not have a husband. This sense is reflected in our translation of the verse.

52. This refers to those slaves, both male and female, who are possessed of good character and who are likely to prove good marriage partners. If a slave's attitude to his/her partner is not appropriate and his/her temperament does not justify the expectation that he/she will prove to be

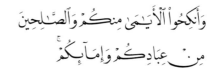

If they are poor,[53] Allah will enrich them out of His Bounty.[54] Allah is Immensely Resourceful, All-Knowing. ▶	إِن يَكُونُواْ فُقَرَآءَ يُغْنِهِمُ ٱللَّهُ مِن فَضْلِهِۦ ۗ وَٱللَّهُ وَٰسِعٌ عَلِيمٌ ﴿٣٢﴾

a good spouse, then it is not required of his/her master to arrange for his/her marriage. This is understandable because to facilitate the marriage of such a person would make one responsible for ruining the life of his/her spouse. This principle is not applicable, however, in the case of free men and women. For the role of anyone who strives to make a match between a free man and a free woman is, at the most, that of advising, assisting and introducing one party to the other. The marriage partners are themselves responsible for marrying if they so consent to do. In the case of a slave, however, the responsibility of the marriage falls on the master/mistress. If he/she wilfully assists someone to marry a person of ill temperament and bad character he/she will bear responsibility for the misery and suffering that ensues.

53. Since this injunction is couched in the imperative form, some scholars have inferred that arranging for the marriage of slaves, whether male or female, is an obligation placed on the master. In view of the nature of the matter, i.e. marriage, it is clear, however, that this cannot be an obligation in the strict sense of the term. If it were obligatory, one might well ask to whom is one obliged to marry one's slaves? Moreover, in such a case, what would be the role of the slave whom his master marries? Would that slave have no other option but to marry the person proposed by his master? This would mean negating a person's consent in the contract of his own marriage. If we affirm, however, that the proposed marriage partners have the right to refuse the suggestions made by others regarding their marriage, then how are those persons able to acquit themselves of their obligation to marry their slaves?

Consequently, jurists have rightly inferred that this Qur'ānic injunction is of a recommendatory rather than obligatory nature. In other words, Muslims should be concerned that the members of their society do not remain unmarried. Members of the family, friends and neighbours should take a keen interest in the marriage of those who do not have anyone to look after them. The state, too, should help people get married.

54. This obviously does not mean that God necessarily confers affluence on everyone who marries. Instead, the point that is being emphasized here is that when it comes to considering marriage, people should not be fussy about their financial situation.

(33) Let those who cannot afford to marry keep themselves chaste until Allah enriches them out of His Bounty.[55] And write out a deed of manumission for such ▶	وَلْيَسْتَعْفِفِ ٱلَّذِينَ لَا يَجِدُونَ نِكَاحًا حَتَّىٰ يُغْنِيَهُمُ ٱللَّهُ مِن فَضْلِهِۦ ۗ وَٱلَّذِينَ يَبْتَغُونَ ٱلْكِتَـٰبَ

The verse also offers useful guidance to the guardians of unmarried girls. They are virtually being told that if they receive any proposal from a good-charactered person, they should not turn it down simply because he is presently not too well off. Likewise, the relatives of the prospective bridegroom are advised not to delay marriage on the grounds that he is not earning much. The youth are also being told not to delay their marriage simply because of financial considerations. Even if they have little income they should still marry, reposing their trust in God's munificence. Quite often one's marriage changes one's circumstances for the better. With the help of one's wife one is able to manage one's expenses more prudently. Moreover, faced with the added responsibility placed upon one's shoulders after marriage, one tends to work harder. One's wife may also provide a helping hand in one's pursuit of a livelihood. Above all, no one can foresee the future. Adversity can suddenly change into prosperity and vice versa. Hence one should not be excessively calculating while considering the question of one's marriage.

55. The best explanation of these verses is found in those *aḥādīth* which have come down on this subject from the Prophet (peace be upon him). According to 'Abd Allāh ibn Mas'ūd, the Prophet (peace be upon him) said: 'O young people, those of you who can afford to marry should do so, for it will help you to keep your gaze away and will enable you to preserve your chastity. And whoever cannot afford to marry then he should fast, for fasting blunts sexual passion.' (See Bukhārī, *K. al-Nikāḥ*, 'Bāb man lam yastaṭī' al-Bā'ah fa al-yaṣum' and Muslim, *K. al-Nikāḥ*, 'Bāb Istiḥbāb al-Nikāḥ li man tāqat ilayah . . .' – Ed.) Abū Hurayrah narrates that the Prophet (peace be upon him) said: 'There are three types of Muslims whom God is bound to help: he who marries to preserve his chastity; he who enters into the contract of manumission and sincerely intends to pay that amount; and he who goes out in the way of God for *jihād*.' (See Tirmidhī, *K. Faḍā'il al-Jihād*, 'Bāb mā jā' fī al-Mujāhid wa al-Nākiḥ . . .' and Nasā'ī, *K. al-Nikāḥ*, 'Bāb Ma'ūnat Allāh al-ladhī yurīd al-'Afāf.' For further details see *Towards Understanding the Qur'ān*, vol. II, *al-Nisā'* 4: 25, p. 28 – Ed.)

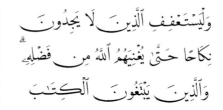

of your slaves that desire their freedom in lieu of payment[56] – execute such a deed with them[57] – ▶	مِمَّا مَلَكَتْ أَيْمَـٰنُكُمْ فَكَاتِبُوهُمْ

56. Literally, the word *mukātabah* denotes mutual writing, i.e. between two parties. As a legal term, however, it signifies the agreement between a slave and his/her master to the effect that the former pledges to pay an amount to the latter in order to obtain his/her freedom. It is one of the forms laid down in Islam for the emancipation of slaves. The payment which the slave is required to make to obtain his/her freedom is not necessarily a monetary payment. Some specified service rendered to the master might also serve the purpose of this payment, provided both parties agree to it.

Once such an agreement has been made, the master does not have the right to place undue obstruction in the way of the slave's freedom. Instead, the master is required to provide him/her with the opportunity to earn the money needed to make the payment. Once the slave pays the amount within the stipulated period of time or performs the service mutually agreed to by the parties, the master is bound to free the slave. In the days of 'Umar ibn al-Khaṭṭāb, a slave entered into a manumission agreement with his master. The slave, however, brought the agreed amount to the latter before the stipulated time. The master refused to accept the payment and insisted on taking it in instalments over a period of time. The slave reported the matter to 'Umar who asked him to deposit the amount in the Public Treasury after which he would be deemed to be free. 'Umar then informed the master about the money that had been deposited in the Public Treasury and that he could have it either in a lump sum or in instalments over a period of time. (Dāraquṭnī on the authority of Abū Sa'īd al-Khudrī.)

57. A group of jurists interprets this verse to mean that when a slave, whether male or female, asks his/her master to enter into a manumission agreement accession is binding on the latter. This view is held by 'Aṭā', 'Amr ibn Dīnār, Muḥammad ibn Sīrīn, Masrūq, Ḍaḥḥāk, 'Ikrimah, the Ẓāhirī jurists and Ibn Jarīr al-Ṭabarī. Initially, Shāfi'ī also subscribed to this view.

According to another group of jurists, it is not binding on the master to accept the agreement but it is nonetheless recommended that he do so. To this group belong the following leading jurists: Sha'bī, Muqātil ibn Ḥayyān, Ḥasan al-Baṣrī, 'Abd al-Raḥmān ibn Zayd, Sufyān al-Thawrī, Abū Ḥanīfah and Anas ibn Mālik. In the later part of his life Shāfi'ī also adopted this view.

The two arguments which follow are put forward in support of the former group's opinion. First, the imperative form in which the injunction is

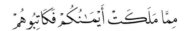

if you see any good in them[58] and give them out of the wealth ▶	إِنْ عَلِمْتُمْ فِيهِمْ خَيْرًا ۖ وَءَاتُوهُم مِّن مَّالِ

couched indicates that it is a command from God. Second, it is established by authentic traditions that when Sīrīn, the father of Muḥammad ibn Sīrīn, a leading scholar of *Ḥadīth* and jurisprudence, asked his master Anas to make a manumission agreement with him, Anas turned it down. Thereafter, Sīrīn presented his case to 'Umar. On learning of this, 'Umar whipped Anas, saying: 'It is God's command to enter into a manumission agreement.' (Bukhārī.)

It may be legitimately inferred from the above incident that the opinion expressed by 'Umar was not his personal opinion. He punished Anas in the presence of several Companions and no one objected to it. Hence, this opinion constitutes the correct interpretation of this Qur'ānic verse.

As for the latter group of jurists, they point out that the verse does not order the master to enter into a manumission agreement in absolute terms. Rather, the verse orders the master to enter into such an agreement '. . . if you see any good in them'. Now, whether there is goodness in the slave or not depends very much on the master's judgement. There is no definite criterion for determining that goodness that enables the courts to so determine it. Obviously, this is not how legal constructs are expressed. Hence, this injunction cannot be deemed to be of a binding character. It is meant, instead, to provide moral guidance. As for Sīrīn's case, there were thousands of slaves in the days of the Prophet (peace be upon him) and the four Rightly-Guided Caliphs, and innumerable slaves entered into manumission agreements. No incident other than that of Sīrīn's, however, is on record to show that the master of any slave was forced by law to enter into a manumission agreement.

It seems that 'Umar's action in this particular case should not be considered a legal verdict or a court order. It is quite obvious that 'Umar did not always act merely as a judge. His concern for the people was often that of a father for his children. He, therefore, often went beyond his legal and juridical jurisdiction and intervened in many a matter as a father would do in the affairs of his children.

58. 'Goodness' here embraces the following three points: first, that the slave should have the ability to pay the amount required for his manumission by his earnings, or by rendering certain services as the case might be. This is evident from the following *mursal* tradition according to which the Prophet (peace be upon him) said: 'Enter into an agreement of manumission with them if you know that they are versed in some skill. But do not let them go about begging from people.' (Ibn Kathīr on the

that Allah has given you.[59] And do not compel your slave-girls to prostitution for the sake of the benefits of worldly life ▶	ٱللَّهِ ٱلَّذِىٓ ءَاتَىٰكُمْ ۚ وَلَا تُكْرِهُوا۟ فَتَيَـٰتِكُمْ عَلَى ٱلْبِغَآءِ

authority of Abū Dā'ūd.) Second, that the slave should be known for his honesty and trustworthiness so that an agreement might be made with him. He should not be the kind of person who simply obtains release from his master by dint of the agreement or one who squanders away all that he earns and then remains in no position to honour his commitment to pay his master. Third, the slave should be known not to have immoral tendencies or strong feelings of hostility towards Islam and Muslims such that his manumission might threaten Muslim society. In other words, he should be such that one might duly expect him to grow into a good free citizen, rather than an active enemy of Muslim society. Manumission agreements also pertained to prisoners of war. Hence, such precautionary measures seemed very much in order.

59. This is a general directive which is addressed to the masters of slaves, to Muslims in general and to the Islamic State.

As for the masters, they are directed to remit at least a part of the amount which the slaves are required to pay according to the manumission agreement. A number of traditions corroborate that the Companions used to forego a considerable part of the amount which had been agreed upon as payment for manumission. 'Alī, for instance, always waived one-fourth of that amount and also exhorted others to do the same. (Ibn Jarīr al-Ṭabarī.)

Muslims in general are also directed that they should generously help those who ask them for money which is required for the manumission of slaves. As we know, one of the categories on which *Zakāh* may be spent is to secure the freedom of those in bondage (*al-Tawbah* 9: 60). This, according to another Qur'ānic verse, is an act of great religious merit (*al-Balad* 90: 13). According to a *ḥadīth*, a bedouin once asked the Prophet (peace be upon him) to tell him something that would ensure his entry into Paradise. The Prophet replied: 'In a few words you have asked a big question: free slaves; assist them in securing their freedom; when you give anyone a cattle make sure that it is one that yields ample milk; and do good even to those of your relatives who wrong you. If you cannot do that, feed the hungry; provide water to the thirsty; enjoin good and forbid evil. If you cannot do even that, restrain your tongue. Use your tongue only for good or else keep it shut.' (Bayhaqī.)

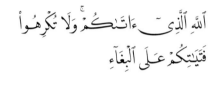

As for the Islamic State, the present verse provides the guidance for a part of the *Zakāh* in the Public Treasury to be spent on assisting slaves who have entered into manumission agreements so that they might become free.

At this stage, it is pertinent to point out that there were three kinds of slaves in times gone by: (i) prisoners of war; (ii) free persons who were enslaved and sold into the slave market; and (iii) those who had been slaves for so long that it was not known when their ancestors were enslaved and to which of the above-mentioned categories they originally belonged.

At the time of the advent of Islam, there were large numbers of all such categories of slaves, both within and outside Arabia. Moreover, the economic and social structure of the time depended more heavily on these slaves than on general labourers and servants.

Islam was faced with two major questions in this regard. First, what should be done with those who had been slaves for a long time? Second, what should be done in the future to solve the problem of slavery?

As regards long-term slaves, Islam did not take the drastic step of declaring that their masters instantly ceased to have rights over them, rights which they had enjoyed for centuries. Had that been done the whole social and economic fabric would have been paralyzed. The entire Arabian Peninsula would presumably have been engulfed in a terrible civil war, one which would not have solved the problem. For as we know, when the American Civil War ended, the problem of Negro slaves remained unresolved.

Avoiding such an unwise course of action, the Islamic State initiated a moral campaign for the 're-release of necks' [to wit, the emancipation of slaves]. Relying on exhortation and admonition, on religious injunctions and statutory laws, Islam tried to solve the problem of slavery. Appeals were made to people to voluntarily emancipate slaves in order to attain salvation in the Hereafter. People were also told either to gratuitously set slaves free as expiation for their sins, or to free them in lieu of reasonable compensation. As a part of this movement, the Prophet (peace be upon him) freed a total of 63 slaves. Of his wives, 'Ā'ishah alone freed 67 slaves. In like manner, 'Abbās, the Prophet's uncle, set free 70 slaves. Ḥakīm ibn Ḥizām set 100 free as did 'Abd Allāh ibn 'Umar. Somewhat incredibly, Dhū al-Kilā' al-Ḥimyarī freed slaves numbering some 8,000 and 'Abd al-Raḥmān ibn 'Awf 30,000. There are similar reports about other Companions, especially about Abū Bakr and 'Uthmān. There was much passion among the Companions to please God by freeing their own slaves and buying the slaves of others and then setting them free. Thus, as far as slaves of long-standing are concerned, almost all were freed by the end of the period of the four Rightly-Guided Caliphs.

As for the future, Islam explicitly forbade the practice of capturing free people, enslaving them and to buy and sell them. Islam did, however, allow – yes, allow rather than order – that prisoners of war may be enslaved under certain conditions. They may be enslaved if the respective states to which the prisoners of war belonged did not exchange them with

إِنْ أَرَدْنَ تَحَصُّنًا لِّتَبْتَغُوا۟ عَرَضَ ٱلْحَيَوٰةِ
ٱلدُّنْيَا ۚ وَمَن يُكْرِههُّنَّ فَإِنَّ ٱللَّهَ مِنۢ بَعْدِ
إِكْرَٰهِهِنَّ غَفُورٌ رَّحِيمٌ ﴿٣٣﴾

the while they desire to remain chaste.[60] And if anyone compels them to prostitution, Allah will be Most Pardoning, Much Merciful (to them) after their subjection to such compulsion.

Muslim captives of war, or if those captives did not pay their own ransom. Nonetheless, those who were taken as prisoners of war could obtain their freedom by entering into a manumission agreement. Furthermore, Islam issued several directives that slaves – and these were as much applicable to slaves who were initially war captives as they were to slaves who had been in bondage for a long time – be set free as expiation for their sins, and to please God. It was also prescribed that a person might will that his slaves gain their freedom after his death. Additionally, if the master of a slave-girl had sexual relations with her resulting in the birth of a child, she would automatically attain freedom upon her master's death, whether he had made a will to that effect or not.

These are some of the main Islamic solutions to the problem of slavery. Yet a number of ignorant and ill-informed people, who neither know nor try to aquaint themselves of the relevant facts, direct their vituperation against Islam on this account. On the other hand, those who are given to apologizing, go about claiming that Islam did not retain any form of slavery whatsoever.

60. Quite obviously this does not imply that if slave-girls do not wish to remain chaste, they will be forced into prostitution. What is meant, is that if a slave-girl indulges in prostitution of her own accord, she will herself be responsible for her actions. The law will take its course and she will be brought to book. However, if her master compels her into prostitution, it is the master who will be held accountable.

It is obvious that the element of compulsion enters into the picture only when a person is unwilling. As far as the words 'for the sake of the benefits of worldly life' are concerned, the injunction stated here is not contingent upon these words and obviously does not mean that a person will not be held guilty if he compels a woman into prostitution even though he does not seek to avail himself of her earnings. What is meant is that the earning itself is unlawful, that it is an earning which has been obtained unlawfully by compelling someone to engage in immorality.

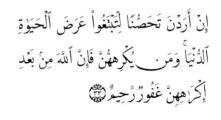

This injunction cannot, however, be fully grasped simply with the help of the words used in the verse and the context in which it occurs. For a better understanding, it is imperative to take note of the conditions pertaining at the time this injunction was revealed. In the Arabia of those days, there were two kinds of prostitution: domestic prostitution and professional prostitution carried on through fully-fledged brothels.

Most domestic prostitutes were either freed slave-girls who had no guardians, or free women who did not enjoy the protection of a family or tribe. These prostitutes usually lived in someone's house but had loose agreements with several men to the effect that the latter were entitled to use them for the gratification of their sexual needs. In return for this favour they paid their own living expenses. Should a child be conceived in this manner, they could ascribe its parentage to any one of the clients and that parentage was accordingly recognized. In other words, this practice was a well-established social institution which was considered by pre-Islamic Arabs to be a form of marriage. Islam, however, legitimized only that form of marriage contract according to which a woman could have no more than one husband, and the sexual relations of that woman with any other man were regarded as *zinā*, and hence a criminal offence. (See Abū Dā'ūd, *K. al-Nikāḥ*, 'Bāb fī Wujūh al-Nikāḥ' – Ed.)

As for open, professional prostitution, this was carried on by slave-girls. There were two main forms of such organized prostitution. First, that the masters of these slave-girls would fix a huge amount upon their slave-girls which they were required to pay each month. Obviously, these helpless girls could raise such a large amount only by pandering to men's sexual desires as prostitutes for they had no other source of income. Nor were their masters under any illusion about how they had earned their money. Quite obviously, they found nothing wrong with the prostitution of women for had they so objected, they would not have imposed the huge amounts they did upon these girls. Amounts that were many times higher than the ordinary wages that these young women could otherwise earn.

The other form of professional prostitution then in vogue was that masters would put their own slave-girls, who happened to be beautiful, into the brothels. Flags were hoisted above these brothels so that people driven by sexual passion would know even from afar the places they could frequent. These women were known as *qulayqiyāt* and their brothels were called *mawākhir*. These brothels were run by the wealthy notables of Arab society. 'Abd Allāh ibn Ubayy, the leader of the Madinan hypocrites, was among those who earned his income in this way, having placed six of his most beautiful slave-girls into a brothel. Additionally, he even used them to entertain his guests who visited him from all parts of Arabia. Furthermore, the illegitimate children born of these prostitutes gave him a whole retinue of servants. ('Abd Allāh ibn Ubayy is the same person whom the people of Madina [then called Yathrib] had decided to crown as their ruler before the Prophet's arrival there. He also played a leading role in spreading slanderous stories about 'Ā'ishah.) Mu'ādhah, one of these slave-girls, embraced Islam and wanted to repent and change her way of life. On learning of this 'Abd Allāh ibn Ubayy tortured her. She, therefore, reported the matter to Abū Bakr who passed it on to the Prophet (peace be upon him). The Prophet (peace be upon him) ordered that the slave-girl be freed from 'Abd Allāh ibn Ubayy's clutches. (See Ibn Kathīr, *Tafsīr*, comments on *Sūrah al-Nūr* 24: 33, Ibn Jarīr al-Ṭabarī, *Tafsīr*, vol. 18, pp. 55–8 and 103–4, Ibn 'Abd al-Barr, *al-Istī'āb*, vol. 2, p. 762 and Ibn Kathīr, *Tafsīr*, vol. 3, pp. 288–9 – Ed.)

It was during this period that the verse under discussion was revealed. If we examine the verse in this context it is quite clear that its true purpose was not merely to prevent the coercion of slave-girls into prostitution. Rather, its true purpose was to outlaw the whole business of prostitution in the Islamic realm. This was done alongside a declaration of clemency for those women who had earlier been forced into this trade.

After revelation of this injunction, the Prophet (peace be upon him) proclaimed: 'There is no room for prostitution in Islam.' (Abū Dā'ūd on the authority of 'Abd Allāh ibn 'Abbās in 'Abwāb Tafrī' al-Ṭalāq', 'Bāb fī Iddi'ā' Walad al-Zinā' – Ed.)

The Prophet's second directive was such that earnings acquired through illegal sex were unlawful, unclean and altogether forbidden. We learn from a tradition narrated by Rāfi' ibn Khadīj that money earned through illicit sex is unclean and the worst kind of earning. (See Abū Dā'ūd, *K. al-Buyū'*, 'Bāb fī Kasb al-Ḥarām' and Tirmidhī, *K. al-Buyū'*, 'Bāb mā jā' fī Thaman al-Kalb' – Ed.) Abū Juḥayfah narrates that the Prophet (peace be upon him) declared that income obtained through prostitution was absolutely forbidden. (See Bukhārī, *K. al-Ṭalāq*, 'Bāb Mahr al-Baghy wa al-Nikāḥ al-Fāsid' and Muslim, *K. al-Musāqah*, 'Bāb Taḥrīm Thaman al-Kalb' – Ed.) According to Abū Mas'ūd 'Uqbah ibn 'Amr, the Prophet (peace be upon him) prohibited both the giving and taking of money for prostitution. (Bukhārī, *K. al-Ṭalāq*, 'Bāb Mahr al-Baghy wa al-Nikāḥ al-Fāsid' – Ed.) He also declared that one may employ a slave-girl to carry out physical errands, but a master may not exact any money from her whose source he was unsure of. Rāfi' ibn Khadīj narrates that the Prophet (peace be upon him) forbade any income from a slave-girl unless he knew its source. (See Abū Dā'ūd, *Kitāb al-Ijārah*, 'Bāb fī Kasb al-Imā' – Ed.) A *ḥadīth* narrated by Rāfi' ibn Rif'ah al-Anṣārī contains a more explicit command. 'The Prophet (peace be upon him) forbade us from taking any earning made by slave-girls other than what she earned lawfully, and the Prophet used his fingers to point at wages acquired from making bread, spinning, cleaning, and combing wool and cotton.' (Aḥmad ibn Ḥanbal.) There is another tradition of similar import which is narrated on the authority of Abū Hurayrah which outlaws the income from slave-girls and prostitution. (See Abū Dā'ūd and Aḥmad ibn Ḥanbal.) It is clear from Muā'dhah's case, 'Abd Allāh ibn Ubayy's slave-girl, that if a slave-girl is

(34) Verily We have sent down for you revelations which clearly expound true guidance, and examples of those who passed away before you, and an admonition for those who fear (Allah).[61]

(35) Allah[62] is the Light of the heavens ▶

وَلَقَدْ أَنزَلْنَآ إِلَيْكُمْ ءَايَٰتٍ مُّبَيِّنَٰتٍ وَمَثَلًا
مِّنَ ٱلَّذِينَ خَلَوْا۟ مِن قَبْلِكُمْ وَمَوْعِظَةً
لِّلْمُتَّقِينَ ﴿٣٤﴾ ۞ ٱللَّهُ نُورُ ٱلسَّمَٰوَٰتِ

---

compelled into prostitution by her master, he forfeits the right to own her. This tradition is found in Ibn Kathīr's *Tafsīr* on the authority of Zuhrī. (See Ibn Kathīr, *Tafsīr*, comments on *Sūrah al-Nūr* 24: 33 – Ed.)

61. This verse not only relates to the earlier one but is in fact a part of the discourse which commences with the beginning of the *sūrah* through this point. 'Revelations which clearly expound true guidance' refer to those verses in which the laws pertaining to *zinā*, *qadhf* and *li'ān* were laid down, in which believers were directed to abstain from marrying immoral men and women, and slandering good-charactered people was forbidden. The same verses urged both men and women to restrain their eyes and guard their chastity, and laid down injunctions regarding the *ḥijāb* of women, expressed a disapproval of celibacy, provided for the institution of a *kitābah* for the liberation of slaves, and called for the extirpation of all forms of prostitution.

After laying down these laws, the people are told that the teaching needed by the God-fearing so that they can act righteously has been provided for them. If they violate these teachings, it clearly means that they are willing to court the same fate which befell those misguided nations of the past. Nations whose detailed accounts are provided in the Qur'ān. Perhaps no warning could have been more stern than the present one to conclude the exposition of this set of legal injunctions. Yet there were still to be found those people who said they believed, who recited the whole set of injunctions prescribed by God, who were also fully aware of the stern warning contained within these verses and yet who still violated these injunctions with absolute impunity.

62. Once again attention is being directed to the hypocrites who had all along been engaged in fomenting one mischief after another in Islamic society and who were as active as ever in causing harm to Islam, the Islamic movement and the Islamic community from within as were

and the earth.[63] His Light (in the Universe) may be likened to a niche wherein is a lamp, and the lamp is in the crystal which shines in star-like brilliance.▶	وَٱلۡأَرۡضِۚ مَثَلُ نُورِهِۦ كَمِشۡكَوٰةٖ فِيهَا مِصۡبَاحٌۖ ٱلۡمِصۡبَاحُ فِي زُجَاجَةٍۖ ٱلزُّجَاجَةُ كَأَنَّهَا كَوۡكَبٞ دُرِّيّٞ

the unbelievers who strived to cause harm from without as they openly declared themselves to be enemies of Islam.

These hypocrites claimed to be Muslims, were apparently a part of the Muslim community, and enjoyed ties of kinship with the Muslims, especially with the *Anṣār*. It is precisely for these reasons that they were in a better position to cause mischief. Because of their formal identification with Islam, even sincere Muslims fell prey to their designs either as a result of their gullibility or weakness and by acting as their agents or protectors.

These hypocrites had become totally myopic because of their excessive worldliness. Despite their profession of faith they were totally devoid of the light which, thanks to the Qur'ān and the Prophet (peace be upon him), had begun to radiate all around.

Without directly addressing the hypocrites, a few observations are made about them here. This is done with a three-fold purpose. First, to admonish them. For it is the foremost requirement of God's mercy and lordship that if a person falls into error, every effort should be made to make him see the truth and mend his ways. This effort should be made notwithstanding the evils and mischievous deeds of men. Second, to lay bare the distinction between faith and hypocrisy in unambiguous terms so that even an average person knows a believer from a hypocrite. If someone continues his allegiance to the hypocrites or supports them when they are fully aware of their traits then they are to be held responsible for their actions. Third, to clearly warn the hypocrites that God's promises are meant only for those believers who are sincere in their faith and fulfil its requirements. These promises are not meant for nominal believers, for those whose identification with Islam is no more than their registration as Muslims in official records. Hypocrites and those who wilfully transgress the commands of God should not expect that God's promise be fulfilled for them.

63. In Qur'ānic usage, the expression 'the heavens and the earth' are generally employed as an equivalent for the universe. An alternative rendering of the verse, therefore, could be that 'Allah is the Light of the whole universe'.

Light is that which causes other things to become visible. Light, thus, appears of itself and also causes other objects to become apparent. This is

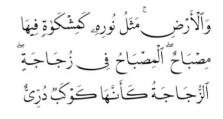

It is lit from (the oil) of a blessed olive tree[64] that is neither eastern ▶	يُوقَدُ مِن شَجَرَةٍ مُّبَـٰرَكَةٍ زَيْتُونَةٍ لَّا شَرْقِيَّةٍ

the general perception of light. Correspondingly, lack of light is branded by man as darkness. When one is able to see things properly and everything is clear, man says that there is light.

The word 'light' is used with respect to God in this very sense. It is not to be taken literally to mean that God is some ray of light which travels at the speed of 186,000 miles per second and reaches the retina of our eyes and ultimately affects the centre of vision in the brain. This particular attribute is not a part of the essential meaning for which man has invented this word.

The statement that God is the Light of the heavens and the earth is to be taken in its basic sense rather than in the material connotations of the word. Let us illustrate this by giving some examples. The Qur'ān speaks of God as the All-Seeing. Now this does not necessarily mean that God is possessed of a physical organ, an eye, in the manner of animals and human beings, and that He sees with the help of that organ. Likewise, we say that God is All-Hearing. This does not necessarily mean that God is possessed of a physical organ, an ear, and that He hears with the help of that organ. Likewise, we are told that God seizes. Again, this statement does not necessarily mean that God seizes in the manner that men and animals seize, namely with the help of our hands.

All such statements have an absolute meaning. Hence, it is people of very limited understanding who believe that there can be no other form of seeing, hearing and seizing except in the specific limited form with which we are familiar through our own experience. By the same token, it amounts to sheer narrow-mindedness if one interprets light in the sense of a ray which emanates from a thing and then strikes the retina. God is light in the absolute rather than the limited sense in which we ordinarily use the word. What is meant by this statement is that God alone is the main cause of all that is, while all else is mere darkness. Everything that emits any light does so because God has invested it with light, or otherwise there is nothing which is innately capable of emitting any light.

The word 'light' is also used to mean 'knowledge', whereas its antonym – ignorance – is characterized by 'darkness'. In this sense, once again, God is the light of the universe for one can gain knowledge of reality and the right way man should tread only from God. Unless one turns to God for light one is doomed to the darkness of ignorance and consequently to sheer error.

64. The olive tree is blessed in the sense that it carries numerous uses and benefits.

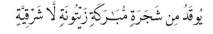

nor western.[65] Its oil well nigh glows forth (of itself) though no fire touched it: Light upon Light.[66] ▶	وَلَا غَرْبِيَّةٍ يَكَادُ زَيْتُهَا يُضِيٓءُ وَلَوْ لَمْ تَمْسَسْهُ نَارٌ ۚ نُّورٌ عَلَىٰ نُورٍ ۗ

65. That is, the tree is situated on an open site or at a height so that it is constantly exposed to the sun. It is not behind anything for had it been so located it would have received sunlight either only in the forenoon or only in the afternoon. Now an olive tree which is constantly exposed to the sun produces an oil which is very thin. Also, the olive oil produced by such a tree is used in a lamp and the light that it emits is very bright. By contrast, trees located eastward or westward produce a darker and thicker variety of oil. Hence when that oil is used in a lamp, the light it emits is not as bright.

66. In this parable, God is likened to a lamp, whereas the glass signifies the curtain by which He has concealed Himself from His creatures. The purpose behind this curtain is not concealment, it is rather because of the pressure to break out into the open. Thus, the inability of creatures to observe God is not because of the opaqueness of the curtain or its being covered with darkness. Rather our failure to observe God is because of the fact that the light passing through this transparent curtain is so intense and all-encompassing that those with limited faculties of vision fail to perceive it. Creatures possessed of limited vision can perceive only that limited light which vacillates, which appears at one moment and disappears the next moment. It is in contrast to darkness that such light becomes manifest. However, God's Light is absolute and has no peer; one that never vanishes. Thanks to the constancy and all-encompassing nature of this light, it cannot be fully grasped by the limited vision of humans.

The statement that this lamp is lit from the oil of an olive tree, 'neither eastern nor western', provides an impressive image of the perfection and intensity of the light of the lamp. In the past, light was mostly obtained from lamps lit by olive oil, and the brightest lamp was one which was lit from the oil of the olive tree situated in an open and elevated place.

The purpose of this parable is not to convey the idea that since God is akin to a lamp, He derives energy from some external source as a lamp does. Rather, the point that is being emphasized is that the lamp in question is not an ordinary lamp, but the brightest lamp that can be imagined, one that illuminates everything. So does God illuminate the whole universe.

Similarly, the statement that 'its oil well nigh glows forth (of itself) though no fire touches it', again reinforces the effect of the intense brightness of the lamp. The parable seeks to emphasize the brightness

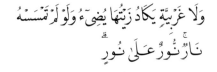

Allah guides to His Light whom He wills.[67] Allah sets forth parables to make people understand. ▶	يَهْدِى ٱللَّهُ لِنُورِهِۦ مَن يَشَآءُ ۚ وَيَضْرِبُ ٱللَّهُ ٱلْأَمْثَـٰلَ لِلنَّاسِ ۗ

of the image of an intensely luminous lamp which is lit from a fine and incandescent oil. All three components of the parable, namely the olive tree, its being neither of the east nor of the west, and its oil burning without fire, are dependent elements of the parable. Each idea complements the others so as to reinforce the uniqueness of the lamp. The essential components of the parable are lamp, niche, and crystal.

Since the verse draws attention to the similitude between God's Light and the light of the lamp, it removes any misunderstanding which might have arisen regarding the statement that 'Allah is the Light of the heavens and the earth'. It clearly indicates that in likening God to light, the intention is not to conceive God's essence to be nothing but light. Rather, God is possessed of perfection in all respects. This is true about His being possessed of knowledge, power, and wisdom alongside His being possessed of light. The Qur'ānic statement that 'Allah is the Light of the heavens and the earth' signifies that God personifies light. The purpose of such a statement is to stress this aspect of God. In other words, what is being said is that God is both the embodiment and source of light. This is a literary device meant to underscore something. In literature we occasionally come across use of this technique. For example, sometimes we say about a person in whom we find generosity at its best that he is generosity itself. Or we say about someone whose beauty is extraordinary that he (or she) is beauty personified.

67. Although God's Light illuminates the whole universe, not everyone perceives it. The ability to perceive this reality and to draw benefit from it are granted only to those whom God wills. Otherwise, as in the case of the blind man who cannot differentiate between day and night, anyone who is devoid of proper vision can readily observe the light radiated by electricity, by the sun, by the moon and the stars, but he fails to appreciate the Light that comes from God. On this particular count anyone who is devoid of proper vision finds darkness all around him. A physically blind person cannot see even what lies next to him, and realizes that there is something only when he stumbles against it, and it is this stumbling alone which makes him feel its presence. In the same manner, a man without proper vision fails to grasp the very realities which are quite near to him and are radiant with the Light of God. Failing to see these realities, he

Allah knows everything.[68] (36) (Those who are directed to this Light are found) in houses which Allah has allowed to be raised and wherein His name is to be remembered:[69] in them people glorify Him in the morning and in the evening, ▶

وَٱللَّهُ بِكُلِّ شَىْءٍ عَلِيمٌ ﴿٣٥﴾ فِى بُيُوتٍ أَذِنَ
ٱللَّهُ أَن تُرْفَعَ وَيُذْكَرَ فِيهَا ٱسْمُهُۥ يُسَبِّحُ
لَهُۥ فِيهَا بِٱلْغُدُوِّ وَٱلْآصَالِ ﴿٣٦﴾

---

realizes their existence only when he stumbles against them, thereby incurring his utter destruction.

68. This statement can be understood in two ways. First, it may mean that God knows very well how to bring home a point with reference to a particular parable. Second, it may be interpreted in the sense that God knows best who deserves this blessing. Anyone who does not search for God's Light and who wholly pursues worldly interests, material comforts and mundane benefits does not need to be forcibly shown God's Light. It is only those who, in God's knowledge, are for sure sincere seekers of God's Light who are endowed with it.

69. Some commentators of the Qur'ān interpret the word 'houses' used in this verse to mean mosques. Accordingly, they interpret the words 'enjoined to be raised' to mean constructing mosques and holding them in high esteem. Other commentators of the Qur'ān, however, consider these words to mean the houses of believers. As for the expression 'to be raised', this suggests that these houses are morally elevated.

The other part of the verse, where it says 'Allah has enjoined to be raised [houses] and wherein His names are remembered', fits in well with the interpretation of 'houses' as mosques. However, with a little reflection one realizes that this part of the verse supports the second interpretation as well. For the *Sharī'ah* does not restrict God's worship only to those places designated for it where we may perform ritual worship only with the aid of the clergy. In Islam the ordinary house is also a place of worship like the mosque, and everyone may function within it as his own priest. Since this *sūrah* is full of directives aimed at elevating one's family and social life, the latter interpretation seems more plausible. This does not, however, rule out the former interpretation altogether. It seems appropriate, therefore, to consider the word 'houses' to signify both mosques and the houses of believers.

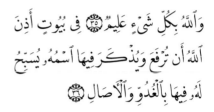

(37) people whom neither commerce nor striving after profit diverts them from remembering Allah, from establishing Prayer, and from paying *Zakāh*; people who dread the Day on which all hearts will be overturned and eyes will be petrified; (38) (people who do all this so) that Allah may reward them in accordance with the best that they did; indeed He will bestow upon them more out of His Bounty, for Allah grants whomsoever He wills beyond all measure.[70] (39) But for those who deny the Truth,[71] ▶

رِجَالٌ لَّا تُلْهِيهِمْ تِجَـٰرَةٌ وَلَا بَيْعٌ عَن ذِكْرِ
ٱللَّهِ وَإِقَامِ ٱلصَّلَوٰةِ وَإِيتَآءِ ٱلزَّكَوٰةِ ۙ يَخَافُونَ
يَوْمًا تَتَقَلَّبُ فِيهِ ٱلْقُلُوبُ وَٱلْأَبْصَـٰرُ ٣٧
لِيَجْزِيَهُمُ ٱللَّهُ أَحْسَنَ مَا عَمِلُوا۟ وَيَزِيدَهُم
مِّن فَضْلِهِۦ ۗ وَٱللَّهُ يَرْزُقُ مَن يَشَآءُ
بِغَيْرِ حِسَابٍ ٣٨ وَٱلَّذِينَ كَفَرُوٓا۟

70. This sets forth the prerequisites for perceiving God's Light and benefiting from it. God's distribution of His bounties is not arbitrary. He bestows His Bounty, i.e. truth, in consideration of a person's worthiness, depending on whether he loves Him, holds Him in proper awe, has the desire to earn His reward, and is motivated by an urge to avoid His Wrath. Such persons are those who have not totally immersed themselves in worldly pursuits. Despite all their preoccupations, their hearts pulsate with remembrance of Him. Far from content with self-indulgence and moral degradation, such people strive to reach the heights which God directs them to. They do not aspire only to the benefits of this ephemeral world. Their eyes are rather set on the abiding rewards of the Hereafter. It is in consideration of these that God decides upon whom He bestows the ability to benefit from His Light. But once He decides this, His Munificence knows no bounds.

71. That is, they deliberately decided against accepting the Message which they had received through God's Messengers, a Message which at that particular time was being delivered to them by the Prophet Muḥammad (peace be upon him). The preceding verses characterized those who partake of God's Light, and these are true, sincere believers.

their deeds are like a mirage
in the desert, which the
thirsty supposes to be water
until he comes to it only to
find that it was nothing; he
found instead that Allah
was with him and He paid
his account in full. Allah is
swift in settling the account.[72]
(40) Or its similitude is that
of depths of darkness upon
an abysmal sea, covered by
a billow, above which is a
billow, above which is cloud,
creating darkness piled
one upon another; when
he puts forth his hand,▶

أَعْمَٰلُهُمْ كَسَرَابٍۭ بِقِيعَةٍ يَحْسَبُهُ ٱلظَّمْـَٔانُ
مَآءً حَتَّىٰٓ إِذَا جَآءَهُۥ لَمْ يَجِدْهُ شَيْـًٔا وَوَجَدَ
ٱللَّهَ عِندَهُۥ فَوَفَّىٰهُ حِسَابَهُۥ ۗ وَٱللَّهُ سَرِيعُ
ٱلْحِسَابِ ﴿٣٩﴾ أَوْ كَظُلُمَٰتٍ فِى بَحْرٍ لُّجِّىٍّ
يَغْشَىٰهُ مَوْجٌ مِّن فَوْقِهِۦ مَوْجٌ مِّن فَوْقِهِۦ سَحَابٌ
ظُلُمَٰتٌۢ بَعْضُهَا فَوْقَ بَعْضٍ إِذَآ أَخْرَجَ يَدَهُۥ

By contrast, the verses that follow are an account of those who deliberately refuse to draw on God's Light. Those who do not believe in and follow the Messenger of God, do not follow God, for God's Messengers are the only true source of His Light. It is immaterial whether they are rejectionists in their hearts whilst verbally professing to believe, or whether they reject both verbally and in their hearts.

72. This parable relates to those who, despite their disbelief and hypocrisy, do some apparently good deeds and appear to believe in the Hereafter. At the same time these people mistakenly think that even without their sincerely believing, without cultivating the attributes of true believers, and without obeying and following the Messenger of God, their good deeds will benefit them in the Hereafter. Here, they are being told that such an expectation is no more than a mirage. A thirsty person traversing a desert is taken in by the mirage and mistakenly believes it to be a spring, and frantically pursues it so as to quench his thirst. However, on reaching the spot he discovers that the place has no water. In the same manner, when these hypocrites die and find themselves in the Next World, they will realize that none of their deeds will benefit them. On the contrary, God will take full account of their unbelief, their hypocrisy, and their misdeeds which just happened to be accompanied by a few good deeds.

he would scarcely see it.[73] He to whom Allah assigns no light, he will have no light.[74]

(41) Do you not see[75] that all that is in the heavens and the earth, even the birds that go about spreading their wings in flight, extol His glory? Each knows the way of its prayer and of its extolling Allah's glory. ▶

لَمْ يَكَدْ يَرَىٰهَا ۗ وَمَن لَّمْ يَجْعَلِ ٱللَّهُ لَهُۥ نُورًا
فَمَا لَهُۥ مِن نُّورٍ ۝ أَلَمْ تَرَ أَنَّ ٱللَّهَ يُسَبِّحُ لَهُۥ
مَن فِى ٱلسَّمَٰوَٰتِ وَٱلْأَرْضِ وَٱلطَّيْرُ
صَٰٓفَّٰتٍ ۖ كُلٌّ قَدْ عَلِمَ صَلَاتَهُۥ وَتَسْبِيحَهُۥ ۗ

73. This parable portrays the state of all unbelievers and hypocrites including those who do good deeds primarily for show and ostentation. What is common to them is that they spend their whole life in total ignorance even though they may have been regarded as the most outstanding scholars and specialists in their fields. They are like a person who is entrapped in a place and overwhelmed with darkness, a place devoid of even a single ray of light. Such a person tends to entertain the illusion that knowledge consists in manufacturing atomic and hydrogen bombs, making supersonic aeroplanes and vehicles for inter-stellar travel. He may also believe that knowledge consists in acquiring mastery in economics, finance, law or philosophy. But true knowledge is something quite different, something of which they have no idea. If the true concept of knowledge is remembered and used as a yardstick, then these so-called experts will have to be reckoned as ignoramuses. On the other hand, if an unlettered villager knows the truth he will be deemed as truly knowledgeable.

74. Here the main purpose of the discourse which commenced with the introductory statement: 'Allah is the Light of the heavens and the earth' is brought out. The thrust of the discourse is that since there is no light in the whole universe save the Light of God, and everything becomes visible by God's Light alone, anyone who remains deprived of this light will have no light whatsoever. Such a person is doomed to remain in darkness. Since there is no other light save God's such a person will not have access even to a single ray of light.

75. It has been pointed out earlier (see n. 70 above) that although God is the Light of the whole universe, only those who truly believe and act righteously will benefit from this light. As for all others, even though light

Allah is well aware of whatever they do. (42) Allah's is the dominion of the heavens and the earth and to Him are all destined to return.

(43) Do you not see that it is Allah Who gently drives the clouds, then He joins them together and then turns them into a thick mass and thereafter you see rain-drops fall down from its midst? And then He sends down hail from the heaven – thanks to the mountains[76] – and causes it to smite whom He wills and averts it from whom He wills. The flash of His lightning almost takes away the sight. (44) It is Allah Who alternates the night and the day. Surely there is a lesson in it for those that have sight. ▶

وَٱللَّهُ عَلِيمٌۢ بِمَا يَفْعَلُونَ ﴿٤١﴾ وَلِلَّهِ مُلْكُ
ٱلسَّمَـٰوَٰتِ وَٱلْأَرْضِ ۖ وَإِلَى ٱللَّهِ ٱلْمَصِيرُ
﴿٤٢﴾ أَلَمْ تَرَ أَنَّ ٱللَّهَ يُزْجِى سَحَابًا ثُمَّ يُؤَلِّفُ
بَيْنَهُۥ ثُمَّ يَجْعَلُهُۥ رُكَامًا فَتَرَى ٱلْوَدْقَ يَخْرُجُ
مِنْ خِلَـٰلِهِۦ وَيُنَزِّلُ مِنَ ٱلسَّمَآءِ مِن جِبَالٍ
فِيهَا مِنۢ بَرَدٍ فَيُصِيبُ بِهِۦ مَن يَشَآءُ وَيَصْرِفُهُۥ
عَن مَّن يَشَآءُ ۖ يَكَادُ سَنَا بَرْقِهِۦ يَذْهَبُ
بِٱلْأَبْصَـٰرِ ﴿٤٣﴾ يُقَلِّبُ ٱللَّهُ ٱلَّيْلَ وَٱلنَّهَارَ ۚ
إِنَّ فِى ذَٰلِكَ لَعِبْرَةً لِّأُو۟لِى ٱلْأَبْصَـٰرِ ﴿٤٤﴾

---

abounds around them, they will continue to stumble in darkness. There are many signs that point to this light. Anyone who looks at these signs with his heart's eye will perceive God at work all around him. But those whose hearts are blind, no matter how much they strain their eyes, their perception will not go beyond biology, zoology and other such ologies, and they will utterly fail to see God's hand operating in the universe.

76. This statement may refer to snow-laden clouds which have figuratively been called the mountains of heaven. It could, however, also mean in quite literal terms the mountains of the earth which rise high in the sky. As a result, the winds there occasionally become so cold that they freeze the clouds. This, in turn, leads to hailstorms.

(45) Allah has created every animal from water. Of them some move on their bellies, some move on two legs and some on four. Allah creates whatever He wills. Surely Allah has power over everything.

(46) Verily We have sent down revelations that clearly explain the Truth. Allah guides whomsoever He wills to a Straight Way.

(47) They say: "We believe in Allah and the Messenger, and we obey," but thereafter a faction of them turns away (from obedience). These indeed are not believers.[77] (48) When they are called to Allah and His Messenger that he (that is, the Messenger) may judge (the disputes) among them,[78] ▶

وَٱللَّهُ خَلَقَ كُلَّ دَآبَّةٍ مِّن مَّآءٍ فَمِنْهُم
مَّن يَمْشِى عَلَىٰ بَطْنِهِۦ وَمِنْهُم مَّن يَمْشِى
عَلَىٰ رِجْلَيْنِ وَمِنْهُم مَّن يَمْشِى عَلَىٰٓ أَرْبَعٍ
يَخْلُقُ ٱللَّهُ مَا يَشَآءُ إِنَّ ٱللَّهَ عَلَىٰ كُلِّ شَىْءٍ
قَدِيرٌ ﴿٤٥﴾ لَّقَدْ أَنزَلْنَآ ءَايَٰتٍ مُّبَيِّنَٰتٍ وَٱللَّهُ
يَهْدِى مَن يَشَآءُ إِلَىٰ صِرَٰطٍ مُّسْتَقِيمٍ ﴿٤٦﴾
وَيَقُولُونَ ءَامَنَّا بِٱللَّهِ وَبِٱلرَّسُولِ وَأَطَعْنَا
ثُمَّ يَتَوَلَّىٰ فَرِيقٌ مِّنْهُم مِّنۢ بَعْدِ ذَٰلِكَ
وَمَآ أُو۟لَٰٓئِكَ بِٱلْمُؤْمِنِينَ ﴿٤٧﴾ وَإِذَا
دُعُوٓا۟ إِلَى ٱللَّهِ وَرَسُولِهِۦ لِيَحْكُمَ بَيْنَهُمْ

---

77. Their disobedience contradicts their profession of faith. Their action fully reveals that they lied when they claimed to believe.

78. These words clearly establish that the Messenger's verdict is the same as God's and the Messenger's command is the same as God's. Likewise, when someone is called to the Messenger (peace be upon him), this call is not merely to the Messenger. In fact it amounts to calling him to both God and the Messenger.

The present verse, in combination with the preceding one, makes it clear beyond any shadow of a doubt that it is meaningless for anyone to claim that he believes unless his claim is supported by obedience to God and to His Messenger. Likewise, a person's claim that he obeys God and His Messenger is devoid of meaning unless he follows, both in his

إِذَا فَرِيقٌ مِّنْهُم مُّعْرِضُونَ ﴿٤٨﴾ وَإِن
يَكُن لَّهُمُ ٱلْحَقُّ يَأْتُوٓا۟ إِلَيْهِ مُذْعِنِينَ
﴿٤٩﴾ أَفِى قُلُوبِهِم مَّرَضٌ أَمِ ٱرْتَابُوٓا۟

a faction of them turns away.[79] (49) However if the right is on their side they come to him (professing) their submissiveness.[80] (50) Do their hearts suffer from the disease (of hypocrisy)? Or have they fallen prey to doubts? ▶

---

individual and collective spheres of life, the laws expounded by God and His Messenger. If anyone is found deficient in this respect, his claim to faith betrays his sheer hypocrisy. (Cf. *Towards Understanding the Qur'ān*, vol. II, *al-Nisā'* 4, verses 59–61, nn. 89–92, pp. 50–4.)

79. Here people are urged to willingly accept the judgements made in accordance with the Qur'ān and the *Sunnah*. It is quite obvious that this requirement is not restricted to the time of the Prophet (peace be upon him) alone. Instead, this is something that will always be required of Muslims, whether they lived in the time of the Prophet (peace be upon him) or in any subsequent period. Thus, whenever a judge, who decides cases according to the Qur'ān and the *Sunnah*, sends a summons to someone, it will be deemed to be the summons of the court of God and of His Messenger. The person who declines to respond to this summons and who turns away from it, does not simply turn away from the judge who sent the summons; in reality he turns away from God and His Messenger. This point is made abundantly clear by the following *mursal* tradition narrated by Ḥasan al-Baṣrī: 'He who is summoned by a Muslim *ḥākim* (magistrate), and then fails to turn up is a wrong-doer who is devoid of all rights.' (See Jaṣṣāṣ, *Aḥkām al-Qur'ān*, vol. 3, p. 229, comments on *Sūrah al-Nūr* 24: 48 – Ed.) Such a person deserves to be punished for not responding to the summons. Additionally, he will be presumed to be in the wrong and an *ex parte* judgement may be awarded against him.

80. This verse characterizes those who follow the rulings of the *Sharī'ah* which suit them but turn away from those which run counter to their interests and desires. As a result, such people turn to man-made laws in those matters where the rulings of the *Sharī'ah* appear to be inconvenient and irksome. Such people are not sincere believers; they are hypocrites. Their claim to faith is false for they do not truly believe in God and His Messenger; they rather believe in their own interests and desires. With such conduct even if they were to follow a part of the *Sharī'ah*, it would carry no weight with God.

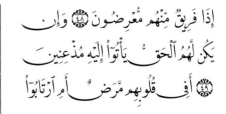

Or do they fear that Allah and His Messenger will wrong them? Nay, the truth is that they themselves are wrong-doers.[81] (51) When those that believe are called to Allah and His Messenger in order that he (that is, the Messenger) may judge their disputes among them, nothing becomes them but to say: "We hear and we obey." Such shall attain true success. (52) Those who obey Allah and His Messenger and fear Him and avoid disobeying Him: such, indeed, shall triumph.

أَمْ يَخَافُونَ أَن يَحِيفَ ٱللَّهُ عَلَيْهِمْ وَرَسُولُهُۥ ۚ
بَلْ أُو۟لَـٰٓئِكَ هُمُ ٱلظَّـٰلِمُونَ ﴿٥٠﴾ إِنَّمَا كَانَ
قَوْلَ ٱلْمُؤْمِنِينَ إِذَا دُعُوٓا۟ إِلَى ٱللَّهِ وَرَسُولِهِۦ
لِيَحْكُمَ بَيْنَهُمْ أَن يَقُولُوا۟ سَمِعْنَا وَأَطَعْنَا ۚ
وَأُو۟لَـٰٓئِكَ هُمُ ٱلْمُفْلِحُونَ ﴿٥١﴾ وَمَن يُطِعِ
ٱللَّهَ وَرَسُولَهُۥ وَيَخْشَ ٱللَّهَ وَيَتَّقْهِ فَأُو۟لَـٰٓئِكَ
هُمُ ٱلْفَآئِزُونَ ﴿٥٢﴾

---

81. There can only be three possible reasons for such conduct. First, that the person concerned does not truly believe, but only hypocritically pretends to be a Muslim so as to deceive others and draw benefits as a member of the Muslim society. Second, that even after becoming a Muslim he is still in doubt about whether the Messenger has truly been designated by God, whether the Hereafter is a reality (rather than a fantasy) which will inevitably come to pass. In fact, he might even be in doubt whether God truly exists or has been invented to achieve some beneficial purpose. Third, that even when he believes in God and is convinced that the Prophet (peace be upon him) is indeed His Messenger, he entertains the fear that he might be treated unjustly, or he thinks that certain injunctions of the Qur'ān or certain directives of God's Messenger are harmful for him.

Regardless of the category to which such a person belongs, he is undoubtedly steeped in error. Anyone who holds these views and still claims to be a believer and a member of the Muslim society and who seeks to derive benefits from this association is indeed a cheat, a betrayer of trust, a fake and perfidious person. He also wrongs himself because his constant deception and cheating make him the embodiment of the worst moral traits. He also wrongs his fellow-Muslims who take him at his word, consider him to be a part of the Muslim society, and establish a myriad of social, cultural and political relations with him.

(53) (The hypocrites) solemnly swear by Allah: "If you order us, we shall surely go forth (and fight in the cause of Allah)." Tell them: "Do not swear. The state of your obedience is known.[82] Allah is well aware of all that you do."[83] (54) Say: "Obey Allah and obey the Messenger. But if you turn away, then (know well) that the Messenger is responsible for what he has been charged with and you are responsible for what you have been charged with. But if you obey him, you will be guided to the Right Way. The Messenger has no other responsibility but to clearly convey (the command)."

(55) Allah has promised those of you who believe and do righteous deeds that He will surely bestow power on them in the land ▸

۞ وَأَقْسَمُوا بِاللَّهِ جَهْدَ أَيْمَٰنِهِمْ لَئِنْ أَمَرْتَهُمْ
لَيَخْرُجُنَّ قُل لَّا تُقْسِمُوا طَاعَةٌ مَّعْرُوفَةٌ إِنَّ
اللَّهَ خَبِيرٌ بِمَا تَعْمَلُونَ ﴿٥٣﴾ قُلْ أَطِيعُوا اللَّهَ
وَأَطِيعُوا الرَّسُولَ فَإِن تَوَلَّوْا فَإِنَّمَا عَلَيْهِ
مَا حُمِّلَ وَعَلَيْكُم مَّا حُمِّلْتُمْ وَإِن تُطِيعُوهُ
تَهْتَدُوا وَمَا عَلَى الرَّسُولِ إِلَّا الْبَلَٰغُ الْمُبِينُ
﴿٥٤﴾ وَعَدَ اللَّهُ الَّذِينَ ءَامَنُوا مِنكُمْ وَعَمِلُوا
الصَّٰلِحَٰتِ لَيَسْتَخْلِفَنَّهُمْ فِي الْأَرْضِ

82. Alternatively, it might mean that the obedience and surrender to God required of believers is of a well-known quality. Those who are truly obedient to God stand apart from others, their distinctiveness can be perceived by everyone. Their conduct leaves no room whatsoever for any doubt that might prompt them to swear so as to convince others about the sincerity of their faith.

83. Such fraudulent measures might possibly enable people to deceive their fellow-men. But as far as God is concerned, such things cannot deceive Him for He is fully aware of everything, whether it is open or secret. His knowledge extends even to the innermost thoughts of human beings.

even as He bestowed power on those that preceded them, and that He will firmly establish their religion which He has been pleased to choose for them, and He will replace with security the state of fear that they are in. Let them serve Me and associate none with Me in My Divinity.[84] ▶

كَمَا ٱسْتَخْلَفَ ٱلَّذِينَ مِن قَبْلِهِمْ
وَلَيُمَكِّنَنَّ لَهُمْ دِينَهُمُ ٱلَّذِى ٱرْتَضَىٰ
لَهُمْ وَلَيُبَدِّلَنَّهُم مِّنۢ بَعْدِ خَوْفِهِمْ أَمْنًا ۚ
يَعْبُدُونَنِى لَا يُشْرِكُونَ بِى شَيْـًٔا ۚ

84. As we have indicated at the outset of this discourse, the present statement aims at warning the hypocrites that God's promise to bestow His vicegerency on Muslims does not apply to those who only have Muslim names or who were registered as Muslims on the occasion of a census or at the time of their birth. That promise was in fact meant for true Muslims who are firm in their belief, who are righteous and God-fearing in their character and conduct, and who faithfully follow the religion of God, who are committed to purge themselves of every taint of polytheism and who worship with full devotion the One True God and none else. Those who are devoid of these qualities and only claim with their tongues that they are believers do not deserve to receive this favour, nor was the promise of this favour meant for them.

Some people tend to interpret vicegerency in the narrow sense of mere power, of dominance and hegemony. With this false assumption, they infer that whoever is in power is *ipso facto* a true believer, is righteous, is on the way of God, and that *ipso facto* he worships God and shuns polytheism. What is even more deplorable is that in order to justify their inference they misinterpret several key terms of the Qur'ān such as faith, righteousness, religion, worship of God, and polytheism. Such people tend to distort whatever they find, i.e. find it discordant with their preconceived notions. This is the worst misinterpretation of the teachings of the Qur'ān, even worse than the distortion of the Scriptures by the Jews and Christians. For this interpretation ascribes a meaning to this Qur'ānic verse which distorts the teachings of the Qur'ān in its entirety and disturbs the whole Islamic scheme of things. If one understands God's vicegerency in the above sense, the promise to bestow God's vicegerency is applicable to all those who have been dominant in the world either in the past, or are so in the present. This applies to all holders of power, even to those who have rejected God, revelation, Prophethood, the Hereafter, and all the other articles of faith. It also applies to all those who are steeped in what the Qur'ān brands as major sins such as dealing in interest, having unlawful sexual relations, and drinking and gambling. If all such people are true believers and are elevated to God's vicegerency owing to this twisted understanding of the verse, then faith is bound to be perceived as no more than following the laws of nature, and righteousness as no more than efficiently exploiting and harnessing those laws to serve one's own purpose. If these assumptions are accepted, then true religion would mean nothing else but gaining perfect mastery in natural sciences and thereby making the utmost progress in trade, industry, business and in other walks of life. By the same token, serving God would mean strictly following the laws which, insofar as they are natural laws, are essential for the success of every human endeavour, both individual and collective. Likewise, if these assumptions are correct, then polytheism can only mean that a person or a people adheres, along with following these natural laws which are useful in pragmatic terms, to ways that are conducive to harm.

Now, can anyone who has studied the Qur'ān with an open mind, ever subscribe such meaning to the key concepts of the Qur'ān, namely faith, righteousness, true religion, worship of God, the Oneness of God, and polytheism? The interpretations to which those concepts have been subjected can only be entertained by those who have either never studied the Qur'ān, or who are guilty of picking up Qur'ānic verses at random and adapting them to their preconceived ideas. Alternatively such an attitude may be adopted by those who have the audacity to go about dismissing as meaningless and faulty all those verses of the Qur'ān which describe God as the One True Lord and the only true object of worship, service and obedience, revelation from God as the only true source of guidance, and the Messengers of God as those who ought to be followed faithfully. Or such notions may be entertained by those who contemptuously disregard those Qur'ānic verses which not only ask people to believe that another life will follow the present one, and that those who set their minds to worldly success alone, either because they deny or are heedless of their accountability in the Next World, can never achieve true success. These major themes recur so often and in such a variety of ways in the Qur'ān and are expressed in such categorical and unmistakable terms that it is hard for us to believe that any student of the Qur'ān can genuinely misunderstand the verse, which promises that power on the land will be bestowed upon those who believe and do righteous deeds, to mean what has been described above. As a matter of fact, the interpretation of the terms *khilāfah* and *istikhlāf* on which this whole structure of false ideas has been raised, is too patently absurd to be accepted by any student of the Qur'ān.

To look at the matter more carefully, the Qur'ān employs the term *khilāfah* (vicegerency) and the verbal form *istikhlāf* (bestowing power on the land) which is derived from it in three different ways. In each case it is the context which determines the meaning in which these terms are used.

One of the meanings of the term *khilāfah* is to possess the powers granted by God. In this sense all the descendants of Adam are vicegerents of God on earth. The second meaning of the word *khilāfah* is to possess and exercise the powers of vicegerency within the parameters of God's sovereignty and in accordance with God's Will (that is, God's revealed Will or command rather than the will which underlies the cosmic order and consists of natural laws). Taken in this sense, only a believer who acts righteously can be considered to have assumed the vicegerency that conforms to this description. On the contrary, an unbeliever or a wicked person cannot be God's vicegerent in this sense; instead, he is a rebel because he abuses the powers that have been granted to him by His Lord in His realm.

In its third usage, the word *khilāfah* means one community's succession by another community; its replacing the dominant community in the sense of wresting power from it.

Whereas in the earlier-mentioned usage of the term, *khilāfah* denotes vicegerency, in its latter usage it is closely related to the idea of succession to power. Both these meanings of the term *khilāfah* are well known in Arabic lexicon.

Anyone who reads the present verse on *khilāfah* and remembers the context in which it occurs, can never have any illusion as to the sense in which the expression *khilāfah* has been employed here. In this particular instance, *khilāfah* denotes a government which fulfils all the obligations of vicegerency according to God's revealed command (rather than simply according to natural laws).

It is significant that even the hypocrites who claimed to be Muslims, let alone those who were declared unbelievers, were excluded from God's promise that *khilāfah* would be bestowed upon them. The intent of the Qur'ān is unmistakable: it proclaims that only those characterized with the virtues of faith and righteousness deserve to be invested with the vicegerency of God. In the same vein, it is being made clear that the fruit of such vicegerency is Islam, and that this way of life prescribed by God, will be pervasive. Accordingly, the condition for obtaining this favour from God is that believers should serve and worship the One True God to the exclusion of all else and shun every iota of polytheism.

To contend that this promise of God applies to the dominant powers of our own time such as the USA or the former USSR is tantamount to gross ignorance. If these superpowers, by the sheer dint of their redoubtable material power are considered to be the holders of the office of *khilāfah*, one is left wondering why God should have cursed Pharaoh and Nimrod. (For further elaboration see *Towards Understanding the Qur'ān*, vol. V, *al-Anbiyā'* 21, n. 99, pp. 299–304.)

Another point seems noteworthy, namely that while this promise of God pertains indirectly to Muslims of a later date, it was in the first instance directly addressed to the Prophet's Companions. Moreover, this promise was made at a time when Muslims lived in a state of dire insecurity because Islam had by then not put down any strong roots even in the Hijaz. However, after only a few years this state of insecurity was replaced by a state of peace and security as Islam spread from Arabia to dominate major parts of Asia and Africa. Not only was Islam established in the region from which it had arisen, but also in many other parts of the world. That God did make His promise come true is corroborated by the events which unfolded during the Caliphate of Abū Bakr, 'Umar and 'Uthmān. God's promise was fulfilled in such a resounding manner that a fair-minded person can hardly have any doubt about the validity of the Caliphate of these three since the Qur'ān itself testifies to it, and God Himself confirmed them to be true believers. If anyone has any doubt regarding this, he would be well-advised to read 'Alī ibn Abī Ṭālib's speech in *Nahj al-Balāghah* which he delivered in order to dissuade 'Umar from personally joining the battle against the Persians. He said:

That this cause should gain strength or be weakened is not contingent upon the numbers [of the believers who take part in the fighting]. It is the religion of God which He Himself has promoted; and it is God's army which He Himself has strengthened and supported until it has reached its present stage. God Himself promised us: 'Allah has promised those of you who believe and do righteous deeds that He will surely bestow power on them in the land . . .' (*al-Nūr* 24: 55). God will fulfil His promise and certainly help His army to victory. The position of leader (*qayyim*) in Islam is that of the cohesive thread in a necklace of pearls. If that cohesive thread is broken, the pearls will be scattered. Once things become disorderly, it becomes that much harder to reorder them. The Arabs are no doubt small in number, yet Islam has made them large in number, and their cohesion has made them strong. You should better remain here as the axis and keep the handmill of Arabs revolving around yourself and keep directing the war from here. Once you move away, the cohesion of the Arabs will start to shatter and things might reach a point when you will be more concerned with threats from the rear than from the enemy in the front. On the other hand, the Persians have focused their eyes upon you. They believe that you are the very root of the Arabs. They believe that once this root is amputated, they will enjoy smooth sailing. Therefore, they are concentrating all their strength upon destroying you. You say that the Persians have amassed in large numbers [and hence you should personally go and fight]. To this I say that we have also been confronting them in the past, but not by dint of our numbers. It is God's help and support which has led us to victory uptil now.

Anyone who reads this can readily understand what 'Alī understood by the use of the term *istikhlāf* in the present verse.

Whoso thereafter engages in unbelief,[85] such indeed are the ungodly. (56) Establish Prayer and pay *Zakāh* and obey the Messenger so that mercy may be shown to you. (57) Do not even imagine that those who disbelieve can render Allah powerless in the land. Their abode is the Fire; what an evil abode!

(58) Believers![86] At three times let those whom your right hands possess[87] ▶

وَمَن كَفَرَ بَعْدَ ذَٰلِكَ فَأُولَٰٓئِكَ هُمُ
ٱلْفَٰسِقُونَ ﴿٥٥﴾ وَأَقِيمُوا۟ ٱلصَّلَوٰةَ وَءَاتُوا۟
ٱلزَّكَوٰةَ وَأَطِيعُوا۟ ٱلرَّسُولَ لَعَلَّكُمْ
تُرْحَمُونَ ﴿٥٦﴾ لَا تَحْسَبَنَّ ٱلَّذِينَ كَفَرُوا۟
مُعْجِزِينَ فِى ٱلْأَرْضِ ۚ وَمَأْوَىٰهُمُ ٱلنَّارُ ۖ
وَلَبِئْسَ ٱلْمَصِيرُ ﴿٥٧﴾ يَٰٓأَيُّهَا ٱلَّذِينَ ءَامَنُوا۟
لِيَسْتَـْٔذِنكُمُ ٱلَّذِينَ مَلَكَتْ أَيْمَٰنُكُمْ

85. The word *kufr*, [which is translated here as 'unbelief'], can variously mean ingratitude or rejection of the truth. Taken in the former sense, the statement means that although God favoured them with vicegerency, they nonetheless drifted away from the Right Path. Taken in the latter sense, it applies to those who persist in their hypocrisy despite their knowledge of God's promise.

86. Beginning with the present verse, the enunciation of injunctions pertaining to social life is resumed. It is not improbable that this part of the *sūrah* might have been revealed some time after the revelation of the discourse above.

87. In the opinion of the majority of Qur'ānic commentators and jurists, the expression *al-ladhīna malakat aymānukum* stands for one's slaves, regardless of whether they are male or female. However, 'Abd Allāh ibn 'Umar and Mujāhid interpret the expression to mean male slaves thereby excluding female slaves. In view of the Qur'ānic injunction that follows there is no ground whatsoever to exclude slave-girls. The point that is being brought home here is that in the same way that it is improper for one's minor children to invade one's privacy, it is also improper for one's slaves to do so.

Jurists are, however, agreed that the injunction pertains to both adult and minor slaves.

and those of your children who have not yet reached puberty[88] ask leave of you before entering your quarters: before the Morning Prayer and when you take off your clothes at noon, and after the Night Prayer. These are the three times of privacy for you.[89] If they come to you at other times then there is no sin for them nor for you,[90] ▶

وَٱلَّذِينَ لَمۡ يَبۡلُغُواْ ٱلۡحُلُمَ مِنكُمۡ ثَلَٰثَ
مَرَّٰتٍۚ مِّن قَبۡلِ صَلَوٰةِ ٱلۡفَجۡرِ وَحِينَ
تَضَعُونَ ثِيَابَكُم مِّنَ ٱلظَّهِيرَةِ وَمِنۢ بَعۡدِ
صَلَوٰةِ ٱلۡعِشَآءِۚ ثَلَٰثُ عَوۡرَٰتٍ لَّكُمۡۚ
لَيۡسَ عَلَيۡكُمۡ وَلَا عَلَيۡهِمۡ جُنَاحُۢ بَعۡدَهُنَّۚ

88. Alternatively, it might be translated as 'those who have reached the age to dream that which adults dream'. Jurists, therefore, are of the opinion that the criterion to establish the puberty of a boy is whether he has had wet dreams or not. Although this is an undisputed view, the translation preferred by us is one that is based on the assumption that the injunction applies to both boys and girls. If one interprets the word *ḥulm* to strictly mean wet dream, the above injunction would only pertain to boys. For the criterion of a girl's puberty is her menstruation. In our opinion, the intent of the injunction is that until the children of the household reach puberty, they should follow this command. Once they become adults, they should abide by the injunctions which follow in the next verse.

89. The verse says that there are 'three times of *'awrāt* for you'. In Arabic, *'awrah* (pl. *'awrāt*) means the place that is vulnerable or insecure. The word also means an object whose exposure is embarrassing or disagreeable. The word also denotes something that is unprotected. All these nuances are interrelated and are variously intended in the verse to one extent or another.

The purpose of the statement is to emphasize that even minor children and slaves should not enter the private chambers of their parents/masters for there are certain times when people are either all alone or are with their spouses. It is inappropriate even for children or servants to enter someone's private chambers unannounced because they might observe them in an embarrassing state. Hence, it was laid down that at the three times of privacy mentioned in the verse even children and servants should seek permission before entering.

90. Except for these times of privacy, minor children and slaves may freely enter the private chambers of both men and women without seeking

for you have to visit one another frequently.[91] Thus does Allah clearly explain His directives to you. Allah is All-Knowing, All-Wise. (59) And when your children attain puberty[92] let them ask leave to come to you like their elders used to ask leave. Thus does Allah clearly explain to you His Signs. He is All-Knowing, All-Wise.

طَوَّٰفُونَ عَلَيْكُم بَعْضُكُمْ عَلَىٰ بَعْضٍ ۚ
كَذَٰلِكَ يُبَيِّنُ ٱللَّهُ لَكُمُ ٱلْءَايَٰتِ ۗ وَٱللَّهُ
عَلِيمٌ حَكِيمٌ ﴿٥٨﴾ وَإِذَا بَلَغَ ٱلْأَطْفَٰلُ مِنكُمُ
ٱلْحُلُمَ فَلْيَسْتَـْٔذِنُوا۟ كَمَا ٱسْتَـْٔذَنَ ٱلَّذِينَ مِن
قَبْلِهِمْ ۚ كَذَٰلِكَ يُبَيِّنُ ٱللَّهُ لَكُمْ ءَايَٰتِهِۦ ۗ
وَٱللَّهُ عَلِيمٌ حَكِيمٌ ﴿٥٩﴾

---

their prior permission. But if they enter their rooms during hours other than those mentioned above and find them improperly dressed, it is not fair to rebuke them. For in such a case the fault lies with the person who is not properly dressed. If anyone intrudes during the hours that are mentioned, it is he who is responsible, provided the person concerned properly instructed them. If they had failed to instruct their children and slaves on how to behave, this should be reckoned a serious failure on their part, a failure which amounts to a sin.

91. This explains the reason behind granting permission to the children and slaves of the family to enter freely at all other times than the ones declared as 'times of privacy'. It also brings into sharp relief the point that there is some rationale underlying every injunction of the *Sharī'ah* regardless of whether it is clearly indicated in the relevant texts or not.

92. That is, when they become adults. As stated earlier (see n. 87 above) having wet dreams and menstruation signify the puberty of boys and girls respectively. There is some disagreement among jurists, however, with regard to the question of how we determine the puberty of those boys and girls who, for one reason or another do not go through these biological changes. Shāfi'ī, Abū Yūsuf, Mālik and Aḥmad ibn Ḥanbal are of the opinion that a 15-year-old boy and girl will be regarded as having attained puberty. There is also a statement from Abū Ḥanīfah in support of this opinion. The more popular ruling of Abū Ḥanīfah, however, is that in such a case a boy and a girl will be assumed to have attained puberty at the age of 18 and 17 years respectively.

It is pertinent to point out that these opinions do not have any definite textual basis. They, rather, represent jurists' opinions based on their *ijtihād*.

It is, therefore, not binding on Muslims the world over to accept a 17-year-old girl and an 18-year-old boy as adults when they do not show any physical signs of adulthood. As things stand physical growth has varied in different regions and at different times.

In our opinion, what can be done to solve the problem is to consider, in a given space-time context, the average age when boys start having wet dreams and girls begin menstruating. The puberty of those boys and girls who do not experience these physical changes, should be determined in light of the average age at which boys and girls in a particular country do do so. Hence, if boys in a country show physical signs of puberty between 12 and 15, the average age will be 13 and a half. As for boys who have late growth, they may be assumed to have reached puberty at 16 and a half. The same formula can be used by legal experts in different countries, taking local conditions into account.

A *ḥadīth* is cited in support of the opinion that 15 years of age may be considered the age of puberty. The tradition, narrated by 'Abd Allāh ibn 'Umar, is as follows: 'When I was 14 years old, I presented myself before the Prophet (peace be upon him) so that I might obtain permission to take part in the Battle of Uḥud. However, the Prophet (peace be upon him) refused to grant me such permission. Then at the time of the Battle of Khandaq when I was 15 years old, I was presented before the Prophet once again and he granted me permission to take part.' (See Bukhārī, *K. al-Maghāzī*, 'Bāb Ghazwat al-Khandaq wa huwa al-Aḥzāb' – Ed.)

This tradition is not, however, a decisive argument in support of the opinion, and this on two counts. First, the Battle of Uḥud took place in Shawwāl 3 A.H. and the Battle of Khandaq, as reported by Muḥammad ibn Isḥāq, was fought in Shawwāl 5 A.H., and according to Ibn Sa'd, in Dhū al-Qa'dah 5 A.H. In other words, there is a time lapse of two years or a little more between the two battles. Thus, had 'Abd Allāh ibn 'Umar been 14 years old at the time of the Battle of Uḥud, he would not have been 15 at the time of the Battle of Khandaq. Perhaps 'Abd Allāh ibn 'Umar rounded off the figure.

Moreover, to be eligible to take part in a battle and to be considered adult in the legal sense, i.e. with regard to social matters, are two entirely different matters. There is no correspondence whatsoever between the two. Hence, this particular tradition does not establish the legal point for which it was adduced. The more plausible opinion seems to be that fixing of the age of 15 years for a boy, who otherwise does not show any signs of puberty, is, at best, an opinion based on *qiyās* (analogy) and *ijtihād* (juristic opinion) rather than an injunction rooted in clear religious text.

(60) The women who are past their youth[93] (and can no longer bear children) and do not look forward to marriage will incur no sin if they cast off their outer garments[94] without displaying their adornment.[95] But if they remain modest, that is still better for them. Allah is All-Hearing, All-Knowing.

(61) There is no blame on the blind nor any blame on the lame nor any blame on the sick nor on yourselves that you eat in your own houses, or your fathers' houses, or your mothers' houses, ▶

وَٱلْقَوَٰعِدُ مِنَ ٱلنِّسَآءِ ٱلَّٰتِى لَا يَرْجُونَ
نِكَاحًا فَلَيْسَ عَلَيْهِنَّ جُنَاحٌ أَن يَضَعْنَ
ثِيَابَهُنَّ غَيْرَ مُتَبَرِّجَٰتٍۭ بِزِينَةٍ ۖ وَأَن
يَسْتَعْفِفْنَ خَيْرٌ لَّهُنَّ ۗ وَٱللَّهُ سَمِيعٌ عَلِيمٌ ﴿٦٠﴾
لَّيْسَ عَلَى ٱلْأَعْمَىٰ حَرَجٌ وَلَا عَلَى ٱلْأَعْرَجِ
حَرَجٌ وَلَا عَلَى ٱلْمَرِيضِ حَرَجٌ وَلَا عَلَىٰٓ
أَنفُسِكُمْ أَن تَأْكُلُوا۟ مِنۢ بُيُوتِكُمْ
أَوْ بُيُوتِ ءَابَآئِكُمْ أَوْ بُيُوتِ أُمَّهَٰتِكُمْ

---

93. The words that are used are *qawā'id min al-nisā'* (literally 'women who have taken to sitting'). These words signify women who have passed the age of child-bearing; women who have themselves become bereft of desire and do not arouse any sexual passion in men. This significance is borne out by the statement that follows.

94. If one translates the words *yaḍa'na thiyābahunna* literally to mean women 'who cast off their garments', this would be incorrect. Hence, jurists and commentators on the Qur'ān are agreed that what is meant by *thiyāb* is that they cast off their outer garments which were required to be worn in observance of *ḥijāb*. (See, for this, *al-Aḥzāb* 33: 59.)

95. The actual words are *ghayra mutabarrijāt bi zīnatin* ('those who do not display their adornment'). The word *bārij* denotes a boat or ship without a roof. When this word is used with regard to a woman, it means a woman who makes full display of her beauty before men. The import of the verse, therefore, is that the permission to cast off outer garments is granted to older women who are no longer interested in displaying their beauty or whose sexual passions have subsided. If it is felt, however, that if some spark of sexual passion continues to smoulder in a woman despite her age, it is inappropriate for her to avail herself of this permission.

or your brothers' houses, or the houses of your sisters, or the houses of your fathers' brothers or the houses of your fathers' sisters, or in the houses of your mothers' brothers, or in the houses of your mothers' sisters or in the houses whose keys you possess, or the house of a friend.[96] There is no blame if you eat together ▶

أَوْ بُيُوتِ إِخْوَٰنِكُمْ أَوْ بُيُوتِ أَخَوَٰتِكُمْ
أَوْ بُيُوتِ أَعْمَٰمِكُمْ أَوْ بُيُوتِ عَمَّٰتِكُمْ
أَوْ بُيُوتِ أَخْوَٰلِكُمْ أَوْ بُيُوتِ خَٰلَٰتِكُمْ
أَوْ مَا مَلَكْتُم مَّفَاتِحَهُۥٓ أَوْ صَدِيقِكُمْ ۚ
لَيْسَ عَلَيْكُمْ جُنَاحٌ أَن تَأْكُلُوا۟ جَمِيعًا

---

96. For a better appreciation of this verse one should grasp three points. First, that it is composed of two parts. The first part applies to the sick, the lame, the blind and other handicapped persons, while the other part pertains to normal people. Second, that as a result of the revelation of verse 29 of *Sūrah al-Nisā'* prohibiting the eating of someone's property unlawfully, the Muslims had become quite sensitive about this matter. As narrated by 'Abd Allāh ibn 'Abbās, when God directed that Muslims may not eat one another's property, they began to exercise utmost caution in eating at one another's place. Unless the host of the house granted permission in very clear and explicit terms, Muslims thought that it was unlawful for them to partake of food even in the houses of their relatives and friends. (See Ibn Kathīr, *Tafsīr*, comments on *Sūrah al-Nūr* 24: 61 – Ed.) Third, that the present verse not only grants permission, it even emphasizes that taking food at the houses of one's relatives and friends is as good as having it at one's own place. Furthermore, it is quite obvious that one does not need permission to take food in one's own home.

Once we have grasped these three points it is easier to understand the verse, for insofar as a physically handicapped person is concerned, he may take food anywhere. The physical disability of such people entitles them to enjoy this right in society. Therefore, it is perfectly lawful for them to have food wherever they happen to get it. As for others, i.e. those who are normal, their homes and those of their relatives and friends are equal and they may eat wherever they wish. No preconditions are required for taking food at the homes of friends. Nor is it required that they have to seek prior permission from their friends and relatives to eat at their places, or that if they fail to do so this amounts to dishonesty or a breach of trust. If one visits someone and food is being served by members of the family, even if the head of the family is not present, one may freely partake of it.

or separately.[97] But when you enter such houses, greet each other with a salutation appointed by Allah, a salutation that is blessed and good. Thus, does Allah expound His signs to you in order that you will act with understanding.

(62) The true believers[98] are only those who sincerely believe in Allah and in His Messenger and who, whenever they are with him on some common matter of concern, they do not go away until they have asked leave of him.[99] Verily those who ask leave of you, ▶

أَوْ أَشْتَاتًا ۚ فَإِذَا دَخَلْتُم بُيُوتًا فَسَلِّمُوا۟ عَلَىٰٓ
أَنفُسِكُمْ تَحِيَّةً مِّنْ عِندِ ٱللَّهِ مُبَـٰرَكَةً
طَيِّبَةً ۚ كَذَٰلِكَ يُبَيِّنُ ٱللَّهُ لَكُمُ
ٱلْـَٔايَـٰتِ لَعَلَّكُمْ تَعْقِلُونَ ﴿٦١﴾ إِنَّمَا
ٱلْمُؤْمِنُونَ ٱلَّذِينَ ءَامَنُوا۟ بِٱللَّهِ وَرَسُولِهِۦ
وَإِذَا كَانُوا۟ مَعَهُۥ عَلَىٰٓ أَمْرٍ جَامِعٍ لَّمْ يَذْهَبُوا۟
حَتَّىٰ يَسْتَـْٔذِنُوهُ ۚ إِنَّ ٱلَّذِينَ يَسْتَـْٔذِنُونَكَ

Although mention is made of relatives, no reference is made to one's own children. This because the home of one's children is no different from one's own. As for friends, the verse refers to those very close friends who, far from feeling upset, are in fact happy to find that their friends feel free to eat at their homes.

97. For some time some Arab tribes had followed the practice of eating separately. They did not approve of eating together, even as some Hindus do in our own time. By contrast, there were certain tribes which disapproved of so eating separately. They would rather starve than eat alone. The present verse does away with all such undue restrictions.

98. These final directives are intended to ensure the reinforcement of the inner cohesion and unity of the Muslim community.

99. This command is equally applicable to the Successors of the Prophet (peace be upon him) and to the rulers of the Islamic State. Whenever Muslims are summoned to a collective cause, whether it be in times of peace or war, they should not fail to respond to it and they should not disperse without the permission of the ruler.

it is they who truly believe in Allah and His Messenger. So if they ask your leave in connection with some of their affairs,[100] give leave to those whom you will,[101] and ask Allah for forgiveness on their behalf.[102] Surely Allah is Much Forgiving, Ever Merciful.

(63) (Muslims!) Do not make the calling of the Messenger among you as your calling one another.[103] ▶

أُوْلَـٰٓئِكَ ٱلَّذِينَ يُؤۡمِنُونَ بِٱللَّهِ وَرَسُولِهِۦۚ
فَإِذَا ٱسۡتَـٔۡذَنُوكَ لِبَعۡضِ شَأۡنِهِمۡ فَأۡذَن
لِّمَن شِئۡتَ مِنۡهُمۡ وَٱسۡتَغۡفِرۡ لَهُمُ ٱللَّهَۚ إِنَّ
ٱللَّهَ غَفُورٞ رَّحِيمٞ ﴿٦٢﴾ لَّا تَجۡعَلُواْ دُعَآءَ
ٱلرَّسُولِ بَيۡنَكُمۡ كَدُعَآءِ بَعۡضِكُم بَعۡضٗاۚ

100. This is to warn the Muslims that seeking permission to withdraw from the Prophet's company without any genuine reason is altogether unlawful. Only when someone has a genuine need should he seek permission to leave.

101. Whether someone should be exempt from taking part in collective duties and be allowed to stay at home after having asked for it was at the discretion of the Prophet (peace be upon him), and after him, it continues to be at the discretion of the heads of the Muslim community. If it is believed that the larger interests will suffer by granting such permission, the leader is fully entitled to refuse such permission. In this case a sincere believer should accept the decision ungrudgingly.

102. This constitutes another warning. If one resorts to false pretexts in order to obtain permission to leave, or if personal interests are accorded priority over collective interests, this amounts to a sin. Hence, when the Messenger (peace be upon him) and his Successors granted people the leave they asked for, they added the following words to the permission: 'May God forgive you.'

103. The word used here is *du'ā'* which denotes 'to call' as well as 'to pray'. In view of these different meanings, *du'ā' al-Rasūl* might signify two things: (i) the Messenger's own act of calling or praying; and (ii) other people's act of calling the Messenger. This gives rise to three possible meanings of the verse, each of which is equally valid. First, one should not treat the Messenger's summons as an ordinary summons. If the Prophet (peace be upon him) summons someone, it is a matter of extraordinary

Allah knows well those of you who surreptitiously steal away, taking shelter behind one another.[104] Let those who go against the order (of the Messenger) beware lest a trial or severe punishment afflict them.[105] (64) Lo! Whatsoever is in the heavens and the earth belongs to Allah. He is well aware of your ways. And the Day when they will be returned to Him, He will tell them all what they did. Allah knows everything.

قَدْ يَعْلَمُ ٱللَّهُ ٱلَّذِينَ يَتَسَلَّلُونَ مِنكُمْ لِوَاذًا ۚ
فَلْيَحْذَرِ ٱلَّذِينَ يُخَالِفُونَ عَنْ أَمْرِهِۦٓ أَن
تُصِيبَهُمْ فِتْنَةٌ أَوْ يُصِيبَهُمْ عَذَابٌ أَلِيمٌ ﴿٦٣﴾
أَلَآ إِنَّ لِلَّهِ مَا فِى ٱلسَّمَٰوَٰتِ وَٱلْأَرْضِ ۖ
قَدْ يَعْلَمُ مَآ أَنتُمْ عَلَيْهِ وَيَوْمَ يُرْجَعُونَ إِلَيْهِ
فَيُنَبِّئُهُم بِمَا عَمِلُوا۟ ۗ وَٱللَّهُ بِكُلِّ شَىْءٍ عَلِيمٌۢ ﴿٦٤﴾

---

importance. One may not honour anyone else's summons but in the case of the Messenger, if a person does not respond to his summons or is constricted by it, then this amounts to risking one's faith.

Second, one should not regard the Prophet's Prayer as ordinary Prayer. If he prays for someone while he is pleased with him, nothing can match this great favour and privilege. Conversely, if the Prophet (peace be upon him) curses someone because he is displeased with him, this represents the very height of that person's misfortune.

Third, a person's calling the Messenger (peace be upon him) should not be equated with the calling of any other person. One may call others by using their names in a loud voice. This should, however, not be done in the case of the Messenger (peace be upon him). It is imperative that the utmost respect be shown him. For any impropriety in this regard might see the person liable be taken to task by God.

Although all three meanings are valid and are borne out by the words of the Qur'ān, the first seems to be closer and more consistent with the spirit of the verse that follows.

104. This indicates another attribute of the hypocrites. When they are summoned in connection with any collective cause, they somehow respond to it for they want to be reckoned as Muslims. However, they deeply resent such a summons and seize the earliest opportunity to sneak away.

105. The word *fitnah* used in this verse has been interpreted by Ja'far al-Ṣādiq to mean the 'dominance of wrong-doers'. If Muslims disobey the

commands of the Messenger (peace be upon him) they will be subjected to the yoke of unjust and oppressive rulers. While this is one of the forms of fitnah, it is by no means the only form. For fitnah might manifest itself in countless other ways such as mutual dissension and feuding, moral degeneration, the dissipation of collective cohesion, the spread of internal disorder and chaos, the breakdown of the material power of a people and its subjugation by others.

Glossary of Terms

'Ahd (covenant) in 2: 27, for instance, refers to the command of God to His servants. This *'ahd* consists of God's eternal command that His creatures are obligated to render their service, obedience and worship to Him alone. In other usages in the Qur'ān, the word denotes commitment, contract or obligation of a person with respect to others (see, for instance, 2: 177, 8: 56, 9: 4, etc.)

Ahl al-Ḥadīth refers to the group of scholars in Islam who pay relatively greater importance to 'traditions' than to other sources of Islamic doctrine such as *qiyās*, and tend to interpret the traditions more literally and rigorously. The term has also come to be used lately for a group of Muslims in the Indo-Pakistan subcontinent who are close to the Ḥanbalī school in theology, and claim to follow no single school on legal matters.

Ākhirah (After-Life, Hereafter, Next World). The term embraces the following ideas:

1. That man is answerable to God.
2. That the present order of existence will some day come to an end.
3. That when that happens, God will bring another order into being in which He will resurrect all human beings, gather them together and examine their conduct, and reward them with justice and mercy.
4. That those who are reckoned good will be sent to Paradise whereas the evil-doers will be consigned to Hell.
5. That the real measure of success or failure of a person is not the extent of his prosperity in the present life, but his success in the Next.

Amānah (trusts) encompass all types of trust which either God or society or an individual places in someone's charge.

'Awrāt, singular *'awrah*, means the places that are vulnerable or insecure. The word also denotes things that are unprotected. It also signifies the objects whose exposure is embarrassing or disagreeable. As a technical term in Islam the word *'awrah* signifies the parts of the body which one keeps covered from others out of one's innate sense of modesty. In *Sūrah al-Nūr* 24: 58, the word *'awrāt* has been used to denote the three times when even children and slaves should not enter the private chambers of their parents/masters for at these times they are habitually alone with their spouses, and thus in a state that might be embarrassing if seen by others. In another instance (24: 31), the word has been used figuratively. The verse here mentions the children who are not aware of the *'awrāt* of women, meaning thereby the children whose sexual urge has not yet been awakened.

Barzakh is an Arabicized form of the Persian word *pardah* (signifying a barrier). According to the Qur'ān, there is presently a barrier between those who are dead and the present world. This barrier prevents the dead from returning to life and so they will stay where they are till the Day of Judgement. In technical Islamic usage it signifies the stage since one's death until one's resurrection for God's final judgement.

Biya' (singular *Bī'ah*) denotes the place consecrated for Christian worship.

Dhikr means remembrance. In the Islamic context, it is used in the sense of 'remembrance of God'. In verse 2: 199, *dhikr* refers to remembering God on a specific occasion, namely during the Pilgrimage at Minā. As used in 23: 71, *dhikr* has three possible meanings: (1) human nature; (2) admonition and good counsel; and (3) honour. Each of the above meanings seems to be correct in the context of the verses mentioned.

Falāḥ means success and prosperity. It is used as an antonym of *khusrān* which signifies loss and failure. To say that someone has acquired *falāḥ*, therefore, amounts to saying that he has achieved his objective, that he has attained prosperity and well-being, that his efforts have borne fruit.

Firdaws, the most commonly used word for Paradise in the Qur'ān, signifies a large, enclosed garden adjoining one's residence, a garden that abounds in fruits, especially grapes.

Ḥajj (Major Pilgrimage) is one of the five pillars of Islam, a duty one must perform during one's life-time if one has the financial resources for it. It resembles *'Umrah* (q.v.) in some respects, but differs from it insofar as it can be performed only during certain specified dates of Dhū al-Ḥijjah. In addition to *ṭawāf* and *sa'y* (which are also required for *'Umrah*), there are a few other requirements but especially one's 'standing' (i.e. stay) in 'Arafāt during the day-time on 9th of Dhū al-Ḥijjah. For details of the rules of *Ḥajj*, see the books of *Fiqh*.

Hijrah signifies migration from a land where a Muslim is unable to live according to the precepts of his faith to a land where it is possible to do so. The *Hijrah par excellence* for Muslims is the *Hijrah* of the Prophet (peace be upon him) which not only provided him and his followers refuge from persecution, but also an opportunity to build a society and state according to the ideals of Islam.

Iblīs literally means 'thoroughly disappointed; one in utter despair'. In Islamic terminology it denotes the *jinn*, who refused the command of God to prostrate before Adam out of vanity. He also asked God to allow him a term when he might mislead and tempt mankind into error. This term was granted to him by God whereafter he became the chief promoter of evil and prompted Adam and Eve to disobey God's order. He is also called *al-Shayṭān* (Satan). He is possessed of a specific personality and is not just an abstract force.

'Iddah denotes the waiting period that a woman is required to observe as a consequence of the nullification of her marriage with her husband or because of the husband's death.

Iḥrām refers to the state in which the pilgrim is considered to be from the time he performs certain prescribed rituals making his entry into the state of *iḥrām* (literally 'prohibiting'). *Iḥrām* is so called in view of the numerous prohibitions that ought to be observed (e.g. abstention from all sexual acts, from the use of perfume, from hunting or killing animals, trimming the beard or shaving the head, cutting the nails, plucking blades of grass or cutting green trees).

Iḥṣān literally means to make inaccessible, to fortify, to protect, to entrench. In view of this, there are three different meanings in which the word has been used in the Qur'ān: (1) Islam, since that protects one from *kufr* (infidelity); (2) marriage, since that enables one to protect oneself from indecent behaviour; and (3) freedom, since that protects one from slavery.

Īlā' denotes a husband's vow to abstain from sexual relations with his wife. The maximum permissible limit for abstaining from sexual relations in wedlock under such a vow is four months, after which *īlā'* would automatically mean repudiation of the marriage.

Jāhilīyah denotes all those world-views and ways of life which are based on rejection or disregard of heavenly guidance communicated to mankind through the Prophets and Messengers of God; the attitude of treating human life – either wholly or partly – as independent of the directives of God.

Jihād means 'to strive, to exert to the utmost'. The words *jihād* and *mujāhid* imply the existence of forces of resistance against whom it is necessary to wage a struggle. Moreover, the usual stipulation in the Qur'ān that *jihād* should be *fī sabīl Allāh* (in the way of God) makes it clear that there are forces of resistance which obstruct people from serving God and pursuing His good pleasure, and that it is necessary to engage in strife and struggle to overcome those forces. The term, however, embraces all kinds of striving aimed at making the Word of God supreme in human life and is not confined only to fighting and warfare. The Prophet (peace be upon him) even declared the striving to subdue one's self to the will of God as one of the forms of 'greater *jihād*'.

Khul' signifies a woman's securing the annulment of her marriage through the payment of some compensation to her husband.

Khushū' means to lower oneself before someone, to be submissive, to display humility. The state called *khushū'* is related both to the heart and to the outward condition of one's bodily organs. The *khushū'* of the heart consists in man's feeling overwhelmed by someone's awe, grandeur, and majesty. As for *khushū'* of bodily organs, that is manifest in a number of ways: one's head is lowered, one's gaze is downcast, and one speaks in a subdued voice.

Al-Lāt was the chief idol of the Thaqīf tribe in al-Ṭā'if, and among the most famous idols in pre-Islamic Arabia.

Li'ān is the legal procedure laid down in the Qur'ān for the person who accuses his wife of indulging in unlawful sexual intercourse without producing the required evidence provided in that the wife denies the charge. In such a case, the husband will be spared the punishment of *qadhf* only if he takes the oath four times that his charge was true and follows it by invoking God's curse on himself if he was lying. The accused wife, on the other hand, if she wishes to be spared the punishment for *zinā*, would be required to back up her denial of the charge by taking four oaths and then invoking God's wrath on herself if the husband was true in his accusation.

Magians (*Majūs*), were a religious entity known for their dualist doctrine evident from their belief in the two gods of light and darkness. They were fire-worshippers and claimed to be the followers of Zoroaster.

Maḥram refers to those relatives whom it is prohibited to marry.

Al-Manāt was the chief idol worshipped by the Khuzā'ah and Hudhayl tribes.

Muḥṣanāt means 'protected women'. It has been used in the Qur'ān in two different meanings. First, it has been used in the sense of 'married women', that is, those who enjoy the protection of their husbands. Second, it has been used in the sense of those who enjoy the protection of families as opposed to slave-girls.

Mursal in *Ḥadīth* terminology is a tradition from the Prophet (peace be upon him) which does not specifically mention any Companion (*Ṣaḥābī*) as the initial transmitter of that tradition, even though the tradition was narrated by a Successor (*Tābi'ī*) who mentions a specific saying or act of the Prophet.

Mut'ah was a form of marriage-contract in pre-Islamic Arabia, signifying a marriage contract according to which the male partner takes a woman in marriage for a fixed period of time and undertakes to pay *mahr*. At the expiry of the stipulated period, the marriage tie is automatically dissolved without specifically requiring its repudiation. Islam, however, prohibits this practice.

Nabī, a word for which we have used the word Prophet as an equivalent, refers to a person chosen by God to whom He entrusts the task to warn people against that which would lead to their perdition and to direct them to the way that would lead to their felicity. Prophets are enabled to perform this task because of the special knowledge that is providentially made available only to them, because of the special power that is bestowed upon them by God (which is evident from the miracles they are enabled to perform), and because of the special ability to live a life of absolute probity. The function of a *nabī* is close to, but not necessarily identical with, that of a *rasūl* (q.v. '*rasūl*').

Qadhf literally means to throw stones from afar. Metaphorically it means to abuse. As an Islamic legal term, it means to accuse someone of *zinā* (unlawful sexual intercourse). In case one accuses someone of *zinā* and fails to support it by the required number of witnesses, the punishment laid down in Islamic Law is eighty lashes.

Rasūl (plural *rusul*), literally meaning 'message-bearer', has been used in the Qur'ān with reference both to the angels who bear God's Message to the Prophets, and with reference to the Prophets who are entrusted with communicating God's Message to His creatures. In its technical sense, the word *rasūl* is used in Islamic parlance in the latter sense. There is some disagreement among Muslim scholars as to whether the terms *nabī* (Prophet) and *rasūl* (Messenger) are equivalents, and which of the two – *nabī* or *rasūl* – has a higher status. The majority of scholars are of the opinion that while every *rasūl* (Messenger) is a *nabī* (Prophet), every *nabī* is not a *rasūl*; and that the Messengers (*rusul*), therefore, have a higher status and are entrusted with a greater mission than the Prophets.

Ṣalawāt is the name of the place of worship of the Jews. It is a derivative of *ṣalawta* which is originally an Aramaic word.

Ṣawāmi', singular *ṣawmi'ah*, are the places of retreat of monks and ascetics.

Sha'ā'ir Allāh refer to all those rites which, in opposition to polytheism and outright disbelief and atheism, are the characteristic symbols of exclusive devotion to God.

Ṭawāf is a rite which is part of both *Ḥajj* and *'Umrah* and consists of circumambulating the Ka'bah seven times.

Ṭawāf al-Ifāḍah is one of the rituals of *Ḥajj* and consists of making seven circuits around the Ka'bah which is required to be performed during the days earmarked for ritual sacrifice. It is an obligatory requirement of *Ḥajj*.

'Umrah (Minor Pilgrimage) is an Islamic rite and consists of Pilgrimage to the Ka'bah. It consists essentially of *iḥrām* (q.v.), *ṭawāf* (i.e. circumambulation) around the Ka'bah (seven times), and *sa'y* (i.e. running) between Ṣafā and Marwah (seven times). It is called minor *Ḥajj* since it need not be performed at a particular time of the year and its performance requires fewer ceremonies than the *Ḥajj* proper.

Al-'Uzzā has been identified with Venus, but it was worshipped under the form of an acacia tree, and was the deity of the Ghaṭfān tribe.

Ẓihār was one of the recognized forms of divorce in pre-Islamic Arabia. It consisted of a person's statement in which he declared his wife to be like his mother, daughter or sister. Islam abolished this form of divorce and if a person makes such a statement he would be committing a sin for which he is required to expiate.

Ẓuln literally means placing a thing where it does not belong. Technically, it refers to exceeding the right and hence committing wrong or injustice. *Ẓuln*, however, does not signify one specific act; it rather embraces all acts that are inconsistent with righteousness and justice, and which share the attribute of 'wrong-doing'.

Biographical Notes

'Abd Allāh ibn 'Abbās, see Biographical Notes, vols. I and II.

'Abd Allāh ibn 'Āmir, d. 59 A.H./679 C.E., was a military commander, who is credited with a number of outstanding conquests.

'Abd Allāh ibn 'Amr ibn al-'Āṣ, d. 65 A.H./694 C.E., was a Companion and son of 'Amr ibn al-'Āṣ, the conqueror of Egypt, who embraced Islam before his father. He was noted for his religious devotion and learning. He is credited with one of the first collections of *Ḥadīth*.

'Abd Allāh ibn Mas'ūd, see Biographical Notes, vol. I.

'Abd Allāh ibn Mubārak, d. 181 A.H./797 C.E., was a noted scholar of *Ḥadīth*, *Fiqh* and Arabic language.

'Abd Allāh ibn 'Ubayy ibn Salūl, see Biographical Notes, vol. I.

'Abd Allāh ibn 'Umar, see Biographical Notes, vol. I.

Abū Bakr, 'Abd Allāh ibn 'Uthmān ibn Abī Quḥāfaḥ see Biographical Notes, vols. I and II.

Abū Dā'ūd, Sulaymān ibn al-Ash'ath, see Biographical Notes, vol. I.

Abū Ḥanīfah, see Biographical Notes, vol. II.

Abū Ḥanīfah, al-Nu'mān ibn Thābit, see Biographical Notes, vol. II.

Abū Hurayrah, see Biographical Notes, vol. II.

Abū Jahl, see Biographical Notes, vol. I.

Abū Mūsā al-Ash'arī, see Biographical Notes, vol. I.

Abū Yūsuf, Ya'qūb ibn Ibrāhīm, see Biographical Notes, vol. II.

Aḥmad ibn Ḥanbal, see Biographical Notes, vols. I and II.

'Ā'ishah, see Biographical Notes, vols. I and II.

'Alī ibn Abī Ṭālib, see Biographical Notes, vols. I and II.

'Alqamah ibn Qays al-Nakha'ī, d. 62 A.H./681 C.E., of Kūfah, belonged to the generation following the Companions, and was among the most outstanding jurists of Iraq in his time.

Al-Ālūsī, Maḥmūd ibn 'Abd Allāh al-Ḥusaynī, see Biographical Notes, vol. I.

'Ammār ibn Yāsir, see Biographical Notes, vol. II.

'Amr ibn al-'Āṣ, see Biographical Notes, vol. V.

Anas ibn Mālik, see Biographical Notes, vol. I.

Asmā' bint Abī Bakr, d. 73 A.H./692 C.E., was the sister of 'Ā'ishah, and wife of the famous Companion al-Zubayr ibn al-'Awwām (q.v.) and mother of 'Abd Allāh ibn al-Zubayr who is known for the valiant resistance he put up against the Umayyads.

Al-'Asqalānī, Shihāb al-Dīn Aḥmad ibn 'Alī ibn Ḥajar, d. 852 A.H./1494 C.E., was a major scholar of *Ḥadīth*, who specialized in the branch known as *Rijāl* (i.e. the science dealing with the transmitters of Tradition).

'Aṭā' ibn Abī Rabāḥ, see Biographical Notes, vols. I and II.

'Ayyāsh ibn Abī Rabī'ah, see Biographical Notes, vol. V.

Al-Bayhaqī, Aḥmad ibn al-Ḥusayn, d. 458 A.H./1066 C.E., was an authority on *Ḥadīth*. He left a vast treasure of scholarly works of which the following deserve special mention: *al-Sunan al-Kubrā*, *al-Sunan al-Ṣughrā*, *Dalā'il al-Nubūwah* and *Manāqib al-Imām al-Shāfi'ī*.

Al-Bazzār, Aḥmad ibn 'Amr ibn 'Abd al-Khāliq Abī Bakr, d. 292 A.H./905 C.E., was a distinguished scholar of *Ḥadīth* from Baṣrah. He has two famous works to his credit in the *musnad* genre of *Ḥadīth*.

Buraydah ibn al-Ḥusayb al-Aslamī, see Biographical Notes, vol. V.

Dāḥḥāk, Abu 'Āṣim al-Nabīl ibn Makhlad ibn Ḍaḥḥāk ibn Muslim al-Shaybānī, d. 212 A.H./828 C.E., was an outstanding scholar of *Ḥadīth*. He was born in Makka, but subsequently settled in Baṣrah.

Al-Dāḥḥāk ibn Sufyān ibn 'Awf al-Kilābī, d. 11 A.H./632 C.E., was a heroic Companion whom the Prophet appointed, in Najd, to look after the affairs of those of his people who had embraced Islam. He was a great warrior who was said to be the equal of a hundred soldiers.

Dā'ūd ibn 'Alī al-Ẓāhirī, d. 270 A.H./884 C.E., was an outstanding jurist who became the founder of a school of law in Islam called the Ẓāhirī school. Dā'ūd's legal theory was based entirely on the Qur'ān and the *Sunnah* and he disregarded such other sources as *qiyās* and *ra'y*.

Al-Dawsī 'Abd Allāh ibn al-Ṭufayl, d. 13 A.H./634 C.E., was a highly respected Companion of the Prophet (peace be upon him). He embraced Islam quite early. He was also among those who migrated to Abyssinia and took part in the expeditions of conquest during the Caliphate of Abū Bakr.

Al-Fazārī, 'Abd Allāh ibn Mis'adah, d. 65 A.H./685 C.E., was one of the distinguished commanders of the Umayyad period. He was entrusted with command of the expeditions against the Byzantines during the Caliphate of Mu'āwiyah.

Hammād ibn Salamah ibn Dīnār al-Baṣrī, d. 167 A.H./784 C.E., was *muftī* of Baṣrah and a scholar of *Ḥadīth* and Grammar.

Ḥasan al-Baṣrī, see Biographical Notes, vols. I and II.

Ḥasan ibn Ṣāliḥ al-Zaydī, d. 168 A.H./784 C.E., was a jurist and theologian. His works include *Kitāb al-Tawḥīd* and *al-Jāmi' fī al-Fiqh*.

Ḥassān ibn Thābit al-Khazrajī al-Anṣārī, d. 54 A.H./674 C.E., was a Companion and an accomplished poet who devoted his poetic skill to defend Islam against the propaganda campaign of the enemies of Islam. Because of his distinguished service to the cause of Islam as a poet, he was known as the 'poet of the Prophet' (peace be upon him).

Hilāl ibn Umayyah, see Biographical Notes, vol. III.

Hūd, see Biographical Notes, vol. III.

Ḥudhayfah ibn al-Yamān, see Biographical Notes, vol. II.

Ibn Abī Hātim, 'Abd al-Raḥmān, d. 327 A.H./938 C.E., was a great scholar of *Ḥadīth*, especially of its branch called *Rijāl*. He also distinguished himself as a scholar of *Fiqh*, *Uṣūl al-Fiqh*, *Kalām* and *Tafsīr*.

Ibn al-'Arabī, Abū Bakr ibn Muḥammad ibn 'Abd Allāh, d. 543 A.H./1148 C.E., is one of the foremost commentators of the Qur'ān. He is the author of a *Tafsīr* work entitled *Aḥkām al-Qur'ān*. As the title indicates, it is oriented towards the legal aspects of the Qur'ān.

Ibn Ḥazm, 'Alī ibn Aḥmad, see Biographical Notes, vol. II.

Ibn Isḥāq, see Biographical Notes, vol. IV.

Ibn Kathīr, Ismā'īl ibn 'Umar, see Biographical Notes, vols. I and II.

Ibn Mājah, Muḥammad ibn Yazīd, see Biographical Notes, vol. I.

Ibn Qayyim al-Jawzīyah, Muḥammad ibn Abī Bakr, d. 757 A.H./1350 C.E., was a distinguished, all-round scholar of Islam who contributed to *Uṣūl al-Fiqh*, *Tafsīr*, *Kalām* and *Naḥw*. He was a disciple of Ibn Taymīyah and is considered among the best representatives of his school of thought.

Ibn Sa'd, Muḥammad, see Biographical Notes, vol. I.

Ibn Sīrīn, Muḥammad, see Biographical Notes, vol. I.

Ibrāhīm al-Nakha'ī, see Biographical Notes, vols. I and II.

'Ikrimah ibn Abī Jahl, see Biographical Notes, vol. II.

Isḥāq ibn Rāhawayh, see Biographical Notes, vol. V.

Jābir ibn 'Abd Allāh [al-Anṣārī], see Biographical Notes, vol. I.

Ja'far al-Ṣādiq, ibn Muḥammad al-Bāqir, see Biographical Notes, vol. V.

Al-Jaṣṣāṣ, Aḥmad ibn 'Alī, see Biographical Notes, vol. I.

Khālid ibn al-Walīd, see Biographical Notes, vol. I.

Layth ibn Sa'd, see Biographical Notes, vol. II.

Makḥūl ibn Abī Muslim, see Biographical Notes, vol. I.

Mālik ibn Anas, see Biographical Notes, vols. I and II.

Maymūnah bint al-Ḥārith, d. 51 A.H./671 C.E., was the last woman whom the Prophet (peace be upon him) married. Maymūnah embraced Islam in Makka before *Hijrah*. She was the source of 76 Traditions.

Miqdād ibn 'Amr [ibn al-Aswad], see Biographical Notes, vol. III.

Mu'āwiyah ibn Abī Sufyān, see Biographical Notes, vol. II.

Mughīrah ibn Shu'bah, see Biographical Notes, vol. V.

Muḥammad ibn al-Bāqir ibn 'Alī Zayn al-'Ābidīn ibn al-Ḥusayn, see Biographical Notes, vol. V.

Muḥammad ibn al-Ḥasan al-Shaybānī, see Biographical Notes, vol. II.

Mujāhid ibn Jabr, see Biographical Notes, vol. II.

Mūsā ibn 'Uqbah, ibn 'Abī 'Ayyāsh al-Asadī, d. 141 A.H./758 C.E., was a great scholar of *Sīrah* who also concerned himself with *Ḥadīth*. His *Kitāb al-Maghāzī* is one of the earliest works in that genre.

Qāḍī 'Iyāḍ ibn Mūsā, d. 544 A.H./1149 C.E., was a noted Andalusian scholar. He was *qāḍī* of Ceuta, his home town, and later of Granada. His works include *Tartīb al-Madārik wa Taqrīb al-Masālik*, *Sharḥ Saḥīḥ Muslim* and *Mashāriq al-Anwār*.

Qatādah ibn Di'āmah, see Biographical Notes, vol. II.

Qurṭubī, Muḥammad ibn Aḥmad, see Biographical Notes, vol. I.

Al-Rāzī, Muḥammad ibn 'Umar Fakhr al-Dīn, see Biographical Notes, vol. III.

Sa'd ibn 'Ubādah al-Khazrajī al-Anṣārī, d. 14 A.H./635 C.E., was the chief of the Khazraj tribe of Madina. He took part in several battles including those of Uḥud and Khandaq.

Ṣafīyah, see Biographical Notes, vol. I.

Sahl ibn Sa'd al-Khazrajī al-Anṣārī, d. 91 A.H./710 C.E., was a famous Companion who lived for about a hundred years. The traditions which have come down from him number 188.

Sa'īd ibn Jubayr, see Biographical Notes, vol. II.

Sa'īd ibn al-Musayyab, see Biographical Notes, vol. I.

Ṣāliḥ, see Biographical Notes, vol. III.

Sālim, the *mawlā* of Abū Ḥudhayfah, see Biographical Notes, vol. I.

Al-Suddī, Ismā'īl ibn 'Abd al-Raḥmān, d. 128 A.H./745 C.E., was one of the early scholars of *Tafsīr* who left a work in that field.

Al-Sha'bī, 'Āmir ibn Shuraḥbīl, see Biographical Notes, vol. II.

Al-Shāfi'ī, Muḥammad ibn Idrīs, see Biographical Notes, vol. I.

Al-Shawkānī, Muḥammad ibn 'Alī, d. 1250 A.H./1834 C.E., was a distinguished Islamic scholar of Yemen. He contributed richly to virtually all branches of Islamic learning – *Tafsīr*, *Ḥadīth*, *Fiqh*, *Uṣūl al-Fiqh*, History, etc.

Shu'ayb, an Arabian Prophet of Madyan, see Biographical Notes, vol. III.

Shurayḥ ibn al-Ḥārith al-Kindī, see Biographical Notes, vol. II.

Ṣuhayb ibn Sinān, see Biographical Notes, vol. II.

Suhayl ibn 'Amr, see Biographical Notes, vols. II and III.

Al-Ṭabarānī, Sulaymān ibn Aḥmad ibn Ayyūb, d. 360 A.H./971 C.E., specialized in *Ḥadīth*. His works cover the fields of *Ḥadīth*, *Tafsīr* and Theology.

Al-Ṭabarī, Muḥammad ibn Jarīr, see Biographical Notes, vols. I and II.

Ṭā'ūs ibn Kaysān, see Biographical Notes, vol. I.

Al-Thawrī, Sufyān ibn Sa'īd ibn Masrūq, d. 161 A.H./778 C.E., was considered an authority in different branches of Islamic learning, especially *Ḥadīth*. His works include *al-Jāmi' al-Kabīr* and *al-Jāmi' al-Ṣaghīr*, both of which are included in *Ḥadīth*.

Al-Tirmidhī, Muḥammad ibn 'Īsā, see Biographical Notes, vols. I and II.

'Umar ibn 'Abd al-'Azīz, see Biographical Notes, vol. I.

'Umar ibn al-Khaṭṭāb, see Biographical Notes, vols. I and II.

Umm Salamah, Hind bint Abī Umayyah, see Biographical Notes, vol. I.

'Uqbah ibn 'Āmir, see Biographical Notes, vol. I.

'Urwah ibn al-Zubayr, see Biographical Notes, vol. II.

Usāmah ibn Zayd ibn Ḥārithah, d. 54 A.H./674 C.E., was the son of Zayd whom the Prophet (peace be upon him) had adopted as his son. The Prophet greatly loved both the father and the son. The Prophet entrusted the command of an expedition to Usāmah while he was still at a very tender age.

'Uthmān ibn 'Affān, see Biographical Notes, vol. I.

Al-Wāḥidī, 'Alī ibn Aḥmad, d. 468 A.H./1076 C.E., contributed to *Tafsīr*, *Fiqh*, *Maghāzī* (a branch of *Sīrah*), and Grammar and Philology.

Al-Zamakhsharī, Maḥmūd ibn Muḥammad ibn Aḥmad, see Biographical Notes, vol. IV.

Zayd ibn 'Alī ibn al-Ḥusayn ibn 'Alī, d. 122 A.H./740 C.E., rose in revolt against the Umayyads. He was known for his religious devotion and learning. The following books are credited to him: *al-Majmū' fī al-Fiqh* and *Tafsīr Gharīb al-Qur'ān*.

Zayd ibn Aslam al-'Adawī al-'Umarī was a noted Madinan jurist, an exegete of the Qur'ān and a scholar of *Ḥadīth*. He is credited with a work on *Tafsīr*.

Zayd ibn Ḥārithah ibn Sharaḥbīl (or Shuraḥbīl al-Kalbī, d. 8 A.H./29 C.E.), was a Companion of the Prophet (peace be upon him). He was a slave whom the Prophet (peace be upon him) set free and adopted as his son. Whenever the Prophet (peace be upon him) sent Zayd on an expedition, the command of the army was always entrusted to him.

Zayd ibn Khālid al-Juhanī (d. 67 A.H./697 C.E.), was a Companion of the Prophet (peace be upon him) who carried the flag of his tribe at the time of the conquest of Makka. He is the source of a large number of traditions.

Zaynab bint Jaḥsh al-Asadīyah, d. 20 A.H./641 C.E., was a cousin of the Prophet (peace be upon him) who was first married to Zayd ibn Ḥārithah. But the marriage broke up whereafter the Prophet (peace be upon him) married Zaynab.

Al-Zubayr ibn al-'Awwām, see Biographical Notes, vol. III.

Zufar ibn al-Hudhayl, see Biographical Notes, vol. II.

Al-Zuhrī, Muḥammad ibn Muslim ibn Shihāb, see Biographical Notes, vols. I and II.

Bibliography

Abū Dā'ūd, Sulaymān ibn al-Ash'ath al-Sijistānī, *al-Sunan.*

Āzād, Abū al-Kalām, *Tarjumān al-Qur'ān*, New Delhi, 1970.

Al-Azharī, *Tahdhīb al-Lughah*, Cairo, 1967.

Al-Bukhārī, Abū 'Abd Allāh Muḥammad ibn Ismā'īl, *al-Jāmi' al-Ṣaḥīḥ.*

Al-Dāraquṭnī, 'Alī ibn 'Umar, *al-Sunan*, 4 vols., Beirut. 'Ālam al-Kutub, n.d.

Al-Dārimī, Abū Muḥammad 'Abd Allāh ibn 'Abd al-Raḥmān, *al-Sunan*, 2 vols., Cairo, Dār al-Fikr, 1978.

Al-Firūzābādī, *al-Qāmūs al-Muḥīṭ*, second edition, Cairo, al-Ḥalabī, 1952.

Hershon, Paul Isaac, *Talmudic Miscellany*, London, 1880.

The Holy Bible, Revised Standard Edition, New York, 1952.

Ibn al-'Arabī, Abū Bakr, *Aḥkām al-Qur'ān.*

Ibn Baṭṭūṭah, *Muhadhdhab Riḥlat Ibn Baṭṭūṭah*, ed. Aḥmad al-'Awāmir Muḥammad Jād al-Mawlā, Cairo, al-Amīrīyah, 1934.

Ibn Hishām, Abū Muḥammad 'Abd al-Malik, *Sīrah*, eds. Muṣṭafā al-Saqqā et al., second edition, Cairo, 1955.

Ibn Isḥāq, *The Life of Muḥammad*, tr. and notes by A. Guillaume, Karachi, Oxford University Press, 1955.

Ibn Kathīr, *Mukhtaṣar Tafsīr Ibn Kathīr*, ed. Muḥammad 'Alī al-Ṣābūnī, seventh edition, 3 vols., Beirut, 1402/1981.

Ibn Mājah, Abū 'Abd Allāh Muḥammad ibn Yazīd al-Qazwīnī, *al-Sunan.*

Ibn Manẓūr, *Lisān al-'Arab*, Beirut, Dār Ṣādir, n.d.

Ibn Rushd, *Bidāyat al-Mujtahid*, 2 vols., Cairo, n.d.

Ibn Sa'd, Abū 'Abd Allāh Muḥammad, *Al-Ṭabaqāt al-Kubrā*, 8 vols., Beirut, 1957–60.

Ibn Taymīyah, Taqī al-Dīn, *Majmū' al-Fatāwā Ibn Taymīyah*, ed. Muḥammad ibn 'Abd al-Raḥmān ibn Qāsim, 37 vols., Riyadh. 1398.

Al-Jaṣṣāṣ, Abū Bakr, *Aḥkām al-Qur'ān*, 3 vols., Cairo, 1347 A.H.

Al-Jazīrī, 'Abd al-Raḥmān, *al-Fiqh 'alā al-Madhāhib al-Arba'ah*, 5 vols., Beirut, Dār Iḥyā' al-Turāth, 1980.

Mālik ibn Anas, *al-Muwaṭṭa'*, ed. Muḥammad Fu'ād 'Abd al-Bāqī, 2 vols., Cairo, 1951.

Mawdūdī, Abūl A'lā, *Rasā'il wa Masā'il* (Urdu), Lahore, 1957.

Muslim ibn al-Ḥajjāj, *al-Ṣaḥīḥ*.

Al-Nasā'ī, Abū 'Abd al-Raḥmān Aḥmad ibn Shu'ayb, *al-Sunan*.

Polano, H., *The Talmud Selections*, London, Frederick Warne & Co.

Al-Qurṭubī, *al-Jāmi' li Aḥkām al-Qur'ān*, 8 vols., Cairo, Dār al-Sha'b, n.d.

Al-Ṣābūnī, Muḥammad 'Alī, *Ṣafwat al-Tafāsīr*, 3 vols., fourth edition, Beirut, 1402/1981.

Al-Ṣāliḥ, Ṣubḥī, *Mabāḥith fī 'Ulūm al-Qur'ān*, Beirut, 1977.

Al-Ṭabarī, Muḥammad ibn Jarīr, *Tafsīr*.

Thānawī, Muḥammad ibn A'lā, *Kashshāf Iṣṭilāḥāt al-Funūn*, Calcutta, 1863.

Al-Tirmidhī, Abū 'Īsā Muḥammad ibn 'Īsā, *al-Jāmi' al-Ṣaḥīḥ*.

Al-Wāqidī, Muḥammad ibn 'Umar, *al-Maghāzī*, ed. M. Jones, 3 vols., Cairo, 1966.

Wensinck, A. J., *Concordance et indices de la tradition musulmane*, 7 vols., Leiden, 1939–69.

Subject Index

Abraham (peace be upon him):
- His story, 49
- Inaugurates *Ḥajj*, 4
- Builds the Ka'bah, 4, 21–2
- Prescribes, by Allah's leave, *Ḥajj* rituals, 21
- His central position in Islam, 75

'Ād:
- Their story, 49, 101

Al-Ākirah (see Hereafter).

Angels:
- Have no share in divinity, 71
- As God's Messengers, 71

Animal Sacrifice:
- Prescribed by all the *Sharī'ah*, 37–8
- Its general command, 39–44
- Its religious aspects, 37–42
- God reckons the piety underlying it, 42
- Commands for it at the time of *Ḥajj*, 37–40
- How to sacrifice the camel, 40

Associating Others with God in His Divinity (*Shirk*):
- Its exposition, 13–14, 113
- Its instances, 113
- Taking someone other than God as the knower of the Unseen, 128–9
- Its variety as practised by the Arab polytheists, 125–6
- The polytheists fail to appreciate God, 71
- It is a filthy practice, 33
- It is against truth, 66
- It is a mighty lie, 33–4
- It is a wrong-doing, 69–70
- It cannot be substantiated, 69–70
- The Qur'ānic arguments against it, 13–14, 70, 125–9

Hypocrites:
- Their conduct, 89, 257–8, 269–70, 279–82, 295
- Their mischief in Madina, 142, 148, 219–20

Iblīs (See also Satan):
- Its literal meaning, 123

Idolatry:
- It is forbidden, 33

Ifk (the Incident of):
- 'Alī's role in this incident, 147, 221–2
- Allah exonerates 'Ā'ishah, 217–25
- Its account, 143–9, 217–19
- Those behind this slander campaign, 219–20
- The good emerging out of it, 219–21
- The main issue behind it, 220–1, 225
- The Prophet (peace be upon him) did not suspect 'Ā'ishah, 148, 223–4
- Who initiated it, 221

Illicit Sex:
- Being an evil in all times and places, 156–7
- Its social and moral consequences, 156–7
- Its definition, 157–9
- Islamic Law on it, 161–2
- Islamic programme for eradicating it, 161–2, 266–9
- Eradication of prostitution, 266–9
- Gradual development of relevant Islamic Laws about it, 162–3
- It is forbidden, 160–1
- Its punishment, 163–5
- Why such a stringent punishment for it, 160–5
- Distinction between a married and unmarried person who is guilty of it, 165–6
- Its punishment, as borne out by *Sunnah*, for a married person, 170
- Its account in the Torah, 158–9
- A fallacy regarding its punishment, 165–6
- Can a *Dhimmī* be stoned to death? 169–70
- What constitutes it, 166–7
- Command about foreplay, 166–7
- Cases in which one is to be punished for it, 166–8
- The victim is not to be punished, 170–2, 266–9
- Islamic State alone can enforce its punishment, 170–3
- Are non-Muslims to be punished alike? 172–3
- Confession not mandatory, 173
- Reporting it to authorities is not binding on one, 173, 192
- Once reported this crime cannot be condoned, 173
- Not to be mutually settled, 173
- Not to be settled by paying monetary compensation, 173

- Has to return to God, 278
- Will be recompensed for his deeds, 276

Martyr:
- His immense rewards, 64

Maryam (Mary), 106

Messengership:
- All Messengers were human beings, 97, 102–3, 105
- The ignorant people have always disregarded the humanness of the Messengers, 97, 102, 105
- Messengers have no share in divinity, 71
- Messengers do not force people into believing, 282
- How it is tested, 118–19, 121
- Messengers as witnesses for their community, 76
- Defended by God, 52
- Its call, 105
- Its place in the faith system, 164–6
- Obedience to Messengers is essential, 293–4
- No faith without belief in it, 279–82
- No guidance without obedience to the Messengers, 282
- Those rejecting it suffer, 295–6
- All Messengers being identical with different *Sharī'ahs*, 69, 75–6, 107, 109
- Features of those who reject it, 102
- The unbelievers always accuse Messengers of a quest for power, 97–8, 102–3
- Ultimate end of those who reject it, 49–50, 102–3

Migration (*Hijrah*):
- Immense reward for it, 64

Migration to Madina:
- Its circumstantial background, 46–7

Miracle:
- Granted by God to the Messengers, 105
- After witnessing it a community cannot escape punishment for its rejection, 106
- Prophet Jesus' birth, 106

Monasticism:
- Islam does not admit it, 108

Monotheism (*Tawḥīd*):
- It is the truth whereas polytheism is false, 66
- Arguments for it, 9–11, 18–19, 92–6, 108, 109, 124–8
- Requisites for professing it, 37–8, 108, 109

Morals and Moral Teachings, 4, 12–13, 33–4, 65, 81–91, 108, 110–15, 130, 151–3, 222–8, 260, 263–4

– His appearance at Pharaoh's court, 105
– Granted the Scripture and *Sharī'ah*, 105

Prophet Muḥammad (peace be upon him):
– As warner and bearer of glad tidings, 51
– Revelation was sent down to him, 77–8
– His *Sharī'ah* represents the truth, 69
– He is wholly on the Straight Way, 69
– He invited everyone to the Straight Way, 122
– As leader and ruler, 164–5
– Did not possess the knowledge of the Unseen, 217–19, 221–2
– Warned people, 51–2
– Arguments for his messengership, 90–1, 117–18, 121
– The conduct of his Companions as a proof of his messengership, 81, 90–1, 113
– His call, 69
– His call being identical with that of earlier Messengers, 75–6, 78–80
– His excellent morals and manners, 219–21
– Reasons for his victory, 140–2, 149, 219–21
– The Quraysh's moves to defeat his mission and the causes of their failure, 47
– His enemies' plots in Madina, 140–3
– Objections against him and its refutation, 118–19

Prophet Noah (peace be upon him):
– His story, 49, 96–100

Prosperity (*Falāḥ*):
– Its Qur'ānic definition, 81, 90–1, 110–12
– How one can attain it, 72–4, 258–9
– Who will attain it, 78, 81, 281
– Who cannot achieve it, 112–15

Prostration:
– During the recital of the Qur'ān, 18, 127–9

Punishment:
– Its law, 50, 54–5
– Who will incur it, 5, 7, 11, 64, 217, 224, 225, 228–9, 295–6
– Its intense forms, 75
– It cannot be averted, 63
– It is to be feared, 129–30, 135

Qadhf (Accusing One's Wife of Infidelity), 193–205

The Qur'ān:
– Sent down by God, 154, 269
– Its account of Prophet Muḥammad's status, 51, 220–1
– Arguments for this being the 'Word of God', 269
– Some of its *Sūrahs* are both Makkan and Madinan, 1
– Style of its Makkan *Sūrahs*, 77

- Simple to follow, 117
- Spells out the truth openly and clearly, 16
- Its message is compatible with human nature, 120
- Its message, 37–8
- Its message is identical with that of earlier Scriptures, 117–18
- Proper way to interpret it, 21, 61–3
- Improper way to interpret it, 61–3, 86–7, 107, 164–6, 283–6
- Its unique style, 3, 50–1, 65, 66–7, 92–3, 107, 109–10, 270–1
- Its line of argumentation, 21, 78, 90–1, 124
- Appeals to human reason, 50–1, 117, 124, 135, 278
- Asks man to eschew conjectures and whims, 7, 12, 119–20
- Invokes man's reason and observation, 19, 124, 278
- On the working and creation of the universe, 65–7, 90–1
- On history, 46, 47–8, 49–50, 51, 78–80, 90–2, 100–1
- On morals, 109–12, 191–2, 229–30
- On psychology, 229–30
- Purpose of its stories, 78–80

Qur'ānic Laws:
- Muslim community life, 293
- Saluting, 293
- Food and drink, 33, 41–2
- Lying, 33–4
- Oath, 227–8
- Masturbation, 87
- Partaking food at the house of friends and relatives, 292–3
- The disabled and handicapped are free to eat anywhere, 292

Qur'ānic Parables:
- Allah being the Light of the Universe, 272–3
- Unbelievers being deprived of the light of guidance, 276–7

Qur'ānic Stories:
- Story of Prophet Noah, 96, 98–100
- Story of Prophet Hud, 101–4
- Story of Prophet Moses, 105
- Story of Prophet Jesus, 106

Qur'ānic Supplications:
- Seeking refuge against Satan's promptings, 129–30
- Of the righteous servants of God, 133, 136

Quraysh:
- Their efforts to obliterate Islam in the Makkan phase and the causes of their failure, 47
- Barred Muslims from performing *Ḥajj*, 3–4, 21, 32–3

Record of One's Deeds, 115

Repentance:
- Its moral, ethical and spiritual consequences, 187–8, 199–201
- Its link with sin, 199–201
- It does not cancel the punishment in this life, as prescribed by the *Sharī'ah*, 200–1

Repudiating the Child, 205–12

Revelation:
- Prophet Noah constructed the Ark under divine guidance, 99
- Its similarity with rainwater, 66–7

The Rightly-Guided Caliphs:
- The Qur'ān endorses their position, 285–6

Sabaeans, 16, 65, 75

Sacred Mosque, 2, 3, 4, 22, 23, 24, 25, 26, 33, 37, 148

Satan:
- Enjoins evil and indecency, 226
- Obedience to him ruins man, 226
- His efforts to thwart the Messengers' mission, 52
- His presence as a touchstone to distinguish between good and evil, 53–4
- Terrible end of those who obey him, 7

Seeking Permission to Enter:
- Commands related to it, 231–6
- Commands related to children and servants, 289–90

Segregation of the Sexes:
- Commands related to it, 137–9, 149–51
- Its essential nature, 151–2
- Why it is so, 161–2
- The Qur'ānic norms about it, 236–59, 291
- Veiling the face by females, 238–40, 245–6
- It was customary in the days of the Prophet (peace be upon him) and Companions for females to cover the face, 146
- Parts of the body to be covered by males and females, 236–43
- Nudity is forbidden, 238–43
- Meaning of safeguarding the private parts, 241–3
- It is forbidden to look at females, 236–40
- When can one look at females?, 238
- Commands related to females regarding men, 241–2
- Free mixing of men and women is forbidden, 255–7
- Dress norms for females, 243
- What is meant by make-up, 244–5
- Meaning of 24: 31, 244–5
- Females not to display publicly their beauty, 244–5

General Index

Decrees, 7, 15, 16, 38; Displeasure, 7, 79; Divinity, 3, 7, 17, 18, 33, 34, 41, 113, 126, 127, 135, 170, 283; Favour, 79, 112, 283, 285, 287; Forgiveness, 52, 114, 171, 187, 230, 294; Guidance, 11, 41, 42, 60, 76, 91, 154, 206, 269, 284; Knowledge, 227, 274; Law(s), 13, 37, 159, 161, 189; Messenger(s), 3, 54, 103, 121, 275, 276, 281; Pleasure, 79; Power(s), 7, 10, 14, 66; Punishment, 51, 55, 129, 131, 207; Scourge, 49, 54, 55, 64, 130; Signs, 55, 113; Symbols of, 35, 36, 39; Unity, 3; Way prescribed by, 2, 46; Will, 9, 18, 19, 285; Wisdom, 10, 11, 53; Word of, 4, 38, 52; Wrath, 5, 50, 110, 111, 112, 205, 275

Greece, 157, 158

Ḥadd, 25, 167, 168, 171, 172, 173, 174, 181, 182, 184, 186, 188, 189, 195, 196, 197, 198, 199, 200, 201, 204, 205, 211, 213, 214, 216
Ḥadīth, 2, 5, 22, 23, 26, 34, 42, 43, 57, 58, 59, 62, 73, 82, 108, 114, 142, 146n, 167, 170, 173, 175, 177, 179, 181, 182, 183, 189, 206, 207, 213, 218, 219, 228, 233, 241, 247, 256, 258, 259, 263, 264, 268, 290
Ḥajj, 1, 2, 4, 21, 22, 23, 24, 25, 26, 28, 29, 32, 33, 35, 39, 40, 43, 44, 45, 46, 60, 61, 73, 91, 188, 238, 248, 256
Ḥajjāj ibn Yūsuf al-Thaqafī, 73
Ḥākim, 78, 114, 257, 265, 280
Ḥammād ibn Salamah, 58
Ḥamnah bint Jaḥsh, 147, 219, 220
Ḥanafī(s), 26, 30, 65, 82, 87, 166, 172, 184, 185, 186, 195, 199, 200, 204, 211, 213, 233, 244
Ḥarrān, 16
Ḥasan al-Baṣrī, 30, 31, 73, 114, 177, 201, 244, 248, 251, 262, 280
Ḥasan ibn Ṣāliḥ, 171, 177, 181, 197, 201, 213
Ḥasan ibn Ziyād, 216
Ḥassān ibn Thābit, 147, 219, 220, 221
Hazzāl ibn Nu'aym, 173, 177
Hell, 20, 130, 132, 189
Hereafter, 3, 7, 13, 14, 15, 18, 78, 79, 80, 81, 91, 102, 109, 116, 122, 134, 136, 150, 161, 169, 170, 203, 207, 224, 225, 226, 228, 259, 265, 275, 276, 281, 283
Herod, 107
Ḥijāb, 137, 138, 139, 146, 239, 242, 245, 247, 248, 249, 252, 253, 259, 269
Hijaz, 286
Hijrah, 1, 2, 44, 46, 88, 122
Hilāl ibn Umayyah, 206, 207
Hindu(s), 157, 158, 293
Hishām ibn 'Abd al-Mālik, 221
Holy Mosque, 2, 3, 4, 22, 23, 28, 33, 37
Hour of Judgement, 5, 9
Hubal, 75
Hūd, 103, 117
Ḥudayfah, 229
Ḥudūd, 173, 175
Huzayl ibn Shuraḥbīl, 233

'Ibādah, 105
Iblīs, 123
Ibn 'Abd al-Barr, 148n, 268
Ibn Abī Ḥātim, 5, 57
Ibn Abī Laylā, 177, 181, 185, 198, 205
Ibn Abī Nujayḥ, 201
Ibn al-'Arabī, 57, 58, 177
Ibn 'Asākir, 251
Ibn Ḥabīb, 210
Ibn Ḥajar, 58, 148n, 242
Ibn Ḥazm, 139
Ibn Hishām, 2, 47, 138, 139, 148n
Ibn Jarīr al-Ṭabarī, 5, 31, 114, 201, 234, 243, 250, 253, 262, 264, 268
Ibn Jurayj, 249
Ibn Kathīr, 2, 5, 6, 15, 21, 22, 23, 24, 25, 26, 30, 34, 36, 40, 57, 221, 234, 245, 246, 250, 253, 263, 268, 269, 292
Ibn Khuzaymah, 57
Ibn Lahī'ah, 73
Ibn Mājah, 42, 43, 73, 114, 174, 175, 182, 189, 207, 257
Ibn Mardūwayh, 57, 73
Ibn al-Mundhir, 57
Ibn al-Qāsim, 210
Ibn al-Qayyim, 139, 186
Ibn Sa'd, 57, 59, 138, 143, 290
Ibn Shihāb al-Zuhrī, 58
Ibn Shubrumah, 197
Ibn Umm Maktūm, 242
Ibn Zayd, 252
Ibrāhīm al-Nakha'ī, 23, 24, 30, 31, 44, 73, 201, 216, 244
'Īd al-Aḍḥā, 43, 44
'Iddah, 88, 207, 216, 242